Two Thousand Years of Economic Statistics: World Population, GDP and PPP

Two Thousand Years of Economic Statistics: World Population, GDP and PPP

Alexander V. Avakov

Algora Publishing
New York

Library of Congress Cataloging-in-Publication Data

Avakov, Aleksandr V. (Aleksandr Vladimirovich), 1954-
    Two thousand years of economic statistics : world population, GDP, and PPP /
Alexander V. Avakov.
        p. cm.
    Includes bibliographical references.
    ISBN 978-0-87586-750-2 (soft cover : alk. paper) — ISBN 978-0-87586-751-9 (case
laminate : alk. paper) 1. Economic history—Statistics. 2. Economic indicators. I. Title. II.
Title: 2000 years of economic statistics.
    HC21.A97 2010
    339.3'1021—dc22

                        2009037757

Printed in the United States

TABLE OF CONTENTS

CHAPTER 2. GDP AT PURCHASING POWER PARITIES   72

CHAPTER 3. GROSS DOMESTIC PRODUCT   138

INTRODUCTION

Two Thousand Years of Economic Statistics presents historical statistics in six sections: (1) Population, (2) GDP Per Capita, (3) GDP, (4) Population Growth Rates, (5) GDP Per Capita Growth Rates, (6) GDP Growth Rates.

The advantage of this work is that it contains data generally not available elsewhere. It gives statistics for two groups of countries within their 2007 borders. First, since year 1950 (for 1950, 1960, 1970, 1980, 1990, 2000, and 2007), it provides statistical data for all countries of the world (232 countries). Second, since the first year AD (for 0001, 1000, 1500, 1600, 1700, 1820, 1870, 1880, 1890, 1900, 1913, 1920, 1929, and 1938), it provides data for a smaller group of countries (133 countries).

This book is based on the groundbreaking works of Angus Maddison but it differs from his books in that it gives data up to the most recent year and calculates GDP (gross and per capita) in the prices of the most recent year. For recent years I use the World Bank, CIA, and Encyclopedia Britannica as primary sources. But, despite my great debt to these sources, the preponderance of data in the book is not directly cited from them but rather are the result of original calculations. Among other computational techniques, I use a new logarithmic interpolation which takes into account cross-country statistical distortions when calculating in the prices of the most recent year. For every line of data (for every country each year) I provide a note of the technique used in obtaining my estimate (i.e., proxy, exponential interpolation, direct estimate with source citation, etc.).

The statistics provided in these pages are complementary to those in my annual, *Quality of Life, Balance of Powers, and Nuclear Weapons*. While the foregoing gives an updto-date snapshot of the world in statistics, the present work sets current population and GDP data in a historical perspective.

SOURCES

Where the source is the same for all the countries in a table, it is noted in a footnote. Otherwise, sources are shown in the form Year(Source) or Year(Source A/ Source B), where the Sources are one of the following:

WB	The World Bank (1)
E	Encyclopedia Britannica
CIA	Central Intelligence Agency
Madd	Maddison
EST	Estimate
POP*GPCPPP	Obtained by multiplying Population by GDP Per Capita at Purchasing Power Parities
PROXY(X(Source))	Approximation based on data for country or group of countries X from source Source
PROXY(X(Source A/Source B))	Approximation based on data for country or group of countries X from sources Source A and Source B
INTERPOL(X(Source))	Exponential interpolation based on data for country or group of countries X from source Source
INTERPOL(X(Source A/Source B))	Exponential interpolation based on data for country or group of countries X from sources Source A and Source B
YY(Source A)WEIGHT(Country X(Source B))	Data for year YY from Source A weighted to data for Country X from Source B
MIN(Source)	Minimum per capita GDP at purchasing power parities in 1990 international dollars (400 dollars) when it is greater than the per capita GDP calculated based on the source Source.
AVG(Region(Source))	Average for the Region based according to the Source.

REGIONS

9 European cs	9 small European countries: Andorra, Channel Islands, Faeroe Islands, Gibraltar, Greenland, Isle of Man, Liechtenstein, Monaco, and San Marino
7 Caribbean cs	7 small Caribbean countries: Antigua & Barbuda, Bermuda, Guadeloupe, Guiana (Fr.), Martinique, Neth. Antilles, and St. Kitts & Nevis
8 Caribbean cs	8 small Caribbean countries: Anguilla, Aruba, Cayman Islands, Montserrat, St. Pierre & Miquelon, Turks & Caicos Islands, Virgin Islands (U.S.), and British Virgin Islands
14 Pacific is	14 Pacific islands: American Samoa, French Polynesia, Guam, Kiribati, Marshall Islands, Micronesia, New Caledonia, Northern Mariana Islands, Palau, Solomon Islands, Tonga, Vanuatu, Wallis & Futuna, and (Western) Samoa
3 Afr. cs	3 small African countries: Mayotte, St. Helena, Western Sahara
E. Europe	Eastern Europe
Eur. Russia	European Russia
Eu. Rs./Sb.	European Russia & Siberia
Other W. offshoots	Other Western offshots: Canada, Australia, and New Zealand
26 E. Asian cs	26 East Asian countries: Afghanistan, Cambodia, Laos, Mongolia, North Korea, Vietnam, Bhutan, Brunei, Fiji, Macao, Maldives, Papua New Guinea, American Samoa, French Polynesia, Guam, Kiribati, Marshall Islands, Micronesia, New Caledonia, Northern Mariana Islands, Palau, Solomon Islands, Tonga, Vanuatu, Wallis & Futuna, and (Western) Samoa
Other E. Asia	East Asia other than Japan, China, and India
Pak./wh. India	Pakistan/whole India
Ban./wh. India	Bangladesh/whole India
Ind./wh. India	India/whole India
Other N. Africa	Other North Africa: Algeria, Tunisia, and Libya

Sahel & W. Africa	Sahel & Other West Africa
Sahel	Chad, Mauritania, Mali, and Niger
Other W. Africa	Other West Africa: Senegal, Gambia, Guinea-Bissau, Guinea, Sierra Leone, Liberia, Burkina Faso, Ivory Coast, Ghana, Togo, Benin, Nigeria, Cape Verde, and Western Sahara
Other E. Africa	Other East Africa: Burundi, Djibouti, Kenya, Rwanda, Tanzania, and Uganda
Rest of Africa	Africa other than North Africa, Sahel, and West Africa
Mal., Zam., Zim.	Malawi, Zambia, and Zimbabwe
S. Afr., Sw., Ls.	South Africa, Swaziland, and Lesotho
Ethiopia & Eritr.	Ethiopia & Eritrea
Namibia & Botsw.	Namibia & Botswana
Indian Ocean	Comoros, Mauritius, Mayotte, Reunion, and Seychelles
Gulf Coast	Bahrain, Kuwait, Qatar, and United Arab Emirates
Arabia	Bahrain, Kuwait, Oman, Qatar, Saudi Arabia, United Arab Emirates, and Yemen
W. Asia	West Asia
Other W. Asia	Other West Asia: West Asia other than Arabia, Iran, Iraq, and Turkey
Other L. Am.	Other Latin America: Latin America other than Mexico
8 L. American cs	8 Latin American countries: Argentina, Brazil, Chile, Colombia, Mexico, Peru, Uruguay, and Venezuela
15 L. American cs	15 Latin American countries: Bolivia, Costa Rica, Cuba, Dominican Rep, Ecuador, El Salvador, Guatemala, Haiti, Honduras, Jamaica, Nicaragua, Panama, Paraguay, Puerto Rico, and Trinidad and Tobago
Caribbean cs.	30 Caribbean countries: Cuba, Dominican Rep, Haiti, Jamaica, Puerto Rico, Trinidad and Tobago, Bahamas, Barbados, Belize, Dominica, Grenada, Guyana, St. Lucia, St. Vincent, Suriname, Antigua & Barbuda, Bermuda, Guadeloupe, Guiana (Fr.), Martinique, Neth. Antilles, St. Kitts & Nevis, Anguilla, Aruba, Cayman Islands, Montserrat, St. Pierre & Miquelon, Turks & Caicos Islands, Virgin Islands (U.S.), and British Virgin Islands
Other Sp. Am.	15 Other Spanish America (ex. Caribbean): Argentina, Chile, Colombia, Peru, Uruguay, Venezuela, Bolivia, Costa Rica, Ecuador, El Salvador, Guatemala, Honduras, Nicaragua, Panama, and Paraguay

ABBREVIATIONS

OBS	Number of Countries Observed
GPCPPP	Gross Domestic Product at Purchasing Power Parities Per Capita
POP	Population
GDPPPP	Gross Domestic Product at Purchasing Power Parities
GPCxxxx	Gross National Income Per Capita at Market Exchange Rates, Year xxxx
GPCPPPxxxx	Gross Domestic Product Per Capita at Purchasing Power Parities, Year xxxx
GRPCPPP	Growth Rates of GDP Per Capita at Purchasing Power Parities
GRPOP	Population Growth Rates
GRRL	GDP Real Growth Rates
GRPCRL	GDP Per Capita Real Growth Rates

CHAPTER 1. WORLD POPULATION

\multicolumn{4}{c}{TABLE 1.1 - POPULATION IN THOUSANDS, YEAR 0001}

OBS	COUNTRY	POP	SOURCE
1	India	62,924	PROXY(Undivided India(Maddison))
2	China	59,600	0001(Maddison)
3	Italy	8,000	0001(Maddison)
4	Bangladesh	7,177	PROXY(Undivided India(Maddison))
5	Turkey	6,866	PROXY(W. Asia(Maddison))
6	France	5,000	0001(Maddison)
7	Pakistan	4,899	PROXY(Undivided India(Maddison))
8	Iran	4,360	PROXY(W. Asia(Maddison))
9	Egypt	4,000	0001(Maddison)
10	Spain	3,750	0001(Maddison)
11	Indonesia	3,244	PROXY(Other E. Asia)
12	Germany	3,000	0001(Maddison)
13	Japan	3,000	0001(Maddison)
14	Yemen	2,445	PROXY(W. Asia(Maddison))
15	Mexico	2,200	0001(Maddison)
16	Algeria	2,000	0001(Maddison)
17	Greece	2,000	0001(Maddison)
18	Sudan	2,000	0001(Maddison)
19	Saudi Arabia	1,971	PROXY(W. Asia(Maddison))
20	Korea, South	1,658	PROXY(Other E. Asia(Maddison))
21	Russia	1,409	PROXY(40(E)/Eu. Rs./Sb.(Maddison))
22	Syria	1,314	PROXY(W. Asia(Maddison))
23	Vietnam	1,163	PROXY(Other E. Asia(Maddison))
24	Iraq	1,090	PROXY(W. Asia(Maddison))
25	Morocco	1,000	0001(Maddison)
26	Romania	800	0001(Maddison)
27	Tunisia	800	0001(Maddison)
28	Korea, North	767	PROXY(Other E. Asia(Maddison))
29	UK	747	PROXY(UK & Irealnd(Maddison))
30	Czechia	720	PROXY(Czechoslovakia(Maddison))
31	Nepal	689	PROXY(Other E. Asia(Maddison))
32	US	680	0001(Maddison)
33	Burma	622	PROXY(Other E. Asia(Maddison))
34	Thailand	606	PROXY(Other E. Asia(Maddison))
35	Afghanistan	582	PROXY(Other E. Asia(Maddison))
36	Serbia	540	PROXY(Yugoslavia(Maddison))
37	Ukraine	527	PROXY(40(E)/Eur. Russia(Maddison))
38	Peru	503	PROXY(Other L. Am.(Maddison))
39	Austria	500	0001(Maddison)
40	Bulgaria	500	0001(Maddison)
41	Uzbekistan	494	PROXY(40(E)/Turkestan(Maddison))
42	Ethiopia	468	PROXY(Ethiopia & Eritr.(Maddison))
43	Kazakhstan	464	PROXY(40(E)/Turkestan(Maddison))
44	Colombia	460	PROXY(Other L. Am.(Maddison))
45	Poland	450	0001(Maddison)
46	Bolivia	420	PROXY(Other L. Am.(Maddison))
47	Libya	400	0001(Maddison)
48	Portugal	400	0001(Maddison)
49	Cambodia	371	PROXY(Other E. Asia(Maddison))

OBS	COUNTRY	POP	SOURCE
	**TABLE 1.1 - POPULATION IN THOUSANDS, YEAR 0001**

OBS	COUNTRY	POP	SOURCE
50	Croatia	353	PROXY(Yugoslavia(Maddison))
51	Brazil	340	PROXY(Other L. Am.(Maddison))
52	Lebanon	326	PROXY(W. Asia(Maddison))
53	Sri Lanka	303	PROXY(Other E. Asia(Maddison))
54	Belgium	300	0001(Maddison)
55	Hungary	300	0001(Maddison)
56	Switzerland	300	0001(Maddison)
57	Oman	300	PROXY(W. Asia(Maddison))
58	Chile	291	PROXY(Other L. Am.(Maddison))
59	Slovakia	280	PROXY(Czechoslovakia(Maddison))
60	Venezuela	274	PROXY(Other L. Am.(Maddison))
61	Australia	248	PROXY(Other W. offshots(Maddison))
62	Bosnia	245	PROXY(Yugoslavia(Maddison))
63	Guatemala	227	PROXY(Other L. Am.(Maddison))
64	Jordan	213	PROXY(W. Asia(Maddison))
65	Argentina	204	PROXY(Other L. Am.(Maddison))
66	Albania	200	0001(Maddison)
67	Cyprus	200	0001(Maddison)
68	Netherlands	200	0001(Maddison)
69	Somalia	200	0001(Maddison)
70	Sweden	200	0001(Maddison)
71	Ghana	198	PROXY(Other W. Africa(Maddison))
72	Ecuador	191	PROXY(Other L. Am.(Maddison))
73	Israel	180	PROXY(W. Asia(Maddison))
74	Denmark	180	0001(Maddison)
75	Philippines	152	PROXY(Other E. Asia(Maddison))
76	Slovenia	135	PROXY(Yugoslavia(Maddison))
77	Guinea	135	PROXY(Other W. Africa(Maddison))
78	Ireland	116	PROXY(UK(Maddison))
79	Belarus	115	PROXY(40(E)/Eur. Russia(Maddison))
80	Kyrgyzstan	115	PROXY(40(E)/Turkestan(Maddison))
81	Tajikistan	115	PROXY(40(E)/Turkestan(Maddison))
82	Macedonia	113	PROXY(Yugoslavia(Maddison))
83	Mongolia	110	PROXY(Other E. Asia(Maddison))
84	Georgia	108	PROXY(40(E)/Caucasus(Maddison))
85	Sierra Leone	100	PROXY(Other W. Africa(Maddison))
86	Norway	100	0001(Maddison)
87	Turkmenistan	98	PROXY(40(E)/Turkestan(Maddison))
88	Azerbaijan	98	PROXY(40(E)/Caucasus(Maddison))
89	El Salvador	95	PROXY(Other L. Am.(Maddison))
90	South Africa	93	PROXY(S. Afr., Sw., Ls.(Maddison))
91	Laos	83	PROXY(Other E. Asia(Maddison))
92	Canada	80	0001(Maddison)
93	Kuwait	78	PROXY(W. Asia(Maddison))
94	Kosovo	77	PROXY(Yugoslavia(Maddison))
95	Nicaragua	71	PROXY(Other L. Am.(Maddison))
96	Taiwan	61	PROXY(Other E. Asia(Maddison))
97	Bahrain	59	PROXY(W. Asia(Maddison))
98	New Zealand	55	PROXY(Other W. offshots(Maddison))
99	Paraguay	55	PROXY(Other L. Am.(Maddison))
100	Honduras	52	PROXY(Other L. Am.(Maddison))

TABLE 1.1 - POPULATION IN THOUSANDS, YEAR 0001

OBS	COUNTRY	POP	SOURCE
101	Malaysia	51	PROXY(Other E. Asia(Maddison))
102	Mozambique	50	0001(Maddison)
103	Haiti	42	PROXY(Other L. Am.(Maddison))
104	Namibia	40	PROXY(Namibia & Botsw.(Maddison))
105	Armenia	39	PROXY(40(E)/Caucasus(Maddison))
106	UAE	39	PROXY(W. Asia(Maddison))
107	Lithuania	37	PROXY(40(E)/Eur. Russia(Maddison))
108	Montenegro	37	PROXY(Yugoslavia(Maddison))
109	Panama	36	PROXY(Other L. Am.(Maddison))
110	Cuba	35	PROXY(Other L. Am.(Maddison))
111	Botswana	35	PROXY(Namibia & Botsw.(Maddison))
112	Eritrea	32	PROXY(Ethiopia & Eritr.(Maddison))
113	Moldova	31	PROXY(40(E)/Eur. Russia(Maddison))
114	Guinea-Bissau	30	PROXY(Other W. Africa(Maddison))
115	Burundi	29	PROXY(Other E. Africa(Maddison))
116	Zimbabwe	26	PROXY(Mal., Zam., Zim.(Maddison))
117	Malawi	26	PROXY(Mal., Zam., Zim.(Maddison))
118	Costa Rica	24	PROXY(Other L. Am.(Maddison))
119	Latvia	24	PROXY(40(E)/Eur. Russia(Maddison))
120	Jamaica	23	PROXY(Other L. Am.(Maddison))
121	Zambia	23	PROXY(Mal., Zam., Zim.(Maddison))
122	Uruguay	21	PROXY(Other L. Am.(Maddison))
123	Finland	20	0001(Maddison)
124	Puerto Rico	14	PROXY(Other L. Am.(Maddison))
125	Estonia	13	PROXY(40(E)/Eur. Russia(Maddison))
126	Qatar	13	PROXY(W. Asia(Maddison))
127	Dominican Rep	5	PROXY(Other L. Am.(Maddison))
128	Lesotho	5	PROXY(S. Afr., Sw., Ls.(Maddison))
129	Trinidad/Tobago	3	PROXY(Other L. Am.(Maddison))
130	Hong Kong	3	PROXY(China(Maddison))
131	Swaziland	2	PROXY(S. Afr., Sw., Ls.(Maddison))
132	Madagascar	1	0001(EST)
133	Singapore	1	PROXY(Other E. Asia(Maddison))

TABLE 1.2 - POPULATION IN THOUSANDS, YEAR 1000

OBS	COUNTRY	POP	SOURCE
1	India	62,924	PROXY(Undivided India(Maddison))
2	China	59,000	1000(Maddison)
3	Japan	7,500	1000(Maddison)
4	Bangladesh	7,177	PROXY(Undivided India(Maddison))
5	Turkey	7,079	PROXY(W. Asia(Maddison))
6	France	6,500	1000(Maddison)
7	Indonesia	6,005	PROXY(Other E. Asia)
8	Egypt	5,000	1000(Maddison)
9	Italy	5,000	1000(Maddison)
10	Pakistan	4,899	PROXY(Undivided India(Maddison))
11	Mexico	4,500	1000(Maddison)
12	Iran	4,494	PROXY(W. Asia(Maddison))

OBS	COUNTRY	POP	SOURCE
	TABLE 1.2 - POPULATION IN THOUSANDS, YEAR 1000		
13	Spain	4,000	1000(Maddison)
14	Germany	3,500	1000(Maddison)
15	Korea, South	3,070	PROXY(Other E. Asia(Maddison))
16	Sudan	3,000	1000(Maddison)
17	Russia	2,750	PROXY(40(E)/Eu. Rs./Sb.(Maddison))
18	Yemen	2,520	PROXY(W. Asia(Maddison))
19	Vietnam	2,152	PROXY(Other E. Asia(Maddison))
20	Saudi Arabia	2,032	PROXY(W. Asia(Maddison))
21	Algeria	2,000	1000(Maddison)
22	Morocco	2,000	1000(Maddison)
23	UK	1,867	PROXY(UK & Ireland(Maddison))
24	Korea, North	1,420	PROXY(Other E. Asia(Maddison))
25	Syria	1,355	PROXY(W. Asia(Maddison))
26	US	1,300	1000(Maddison)
27	Nepal	1,275	PROXY(Other E. Asia(Maddison))
28	Poland	1,200	1000(Maddison)
29	Burma	1,152	PROXY(Other E. Asia(Maddison))
30	Iraq	1,124	PROXY(W. Asia(Maddison))
31	Thailand	1,122	PROXY(Other E. Asia(Maddison))
32	Greece	1,100	1000(Maddison)
33	Afghanistan	1,078	PROXY(Other E. Asia(Maddison))
34	Ukraine	1,053	PROXY(40(E)/Eur. Russia(Maddison))
35	Peru	1,020	PROXY(Other L. Am.(Maddison))
36	Tunisia	1,000	1000(Maddison)
37	Ethiopia	935	PROXY(Ethiopia & Eritr.(Maddison))
38	Colombia	934	PROXY(Other L. Am.(Maddison))
39	Czechia	900	PROXY(Czechoslovakia(Maddison))
40	Bolivia	852	PROXY(Other L. Am.(Maddison))
41	Uzbekistan	823	PROXY(40(E)/Turkestan(Maddison))
42	Bulgaria	800	1000(Maddison)
43	Romania	800	1000(Maddison)
44	Kazakhstan	773	PROXY(40(E)/Turkestan(Maddison))
45	Austria	700	1000(Maddison)
46	Brazil	690	PROXY(Other L. Am.(Maddison))
47	Cambodia	687	PROXY(Other E. Asia(Maddison))
48	Serbia	630	PROXY(Yugoslavia(Maddison))
49	Portugal	600	1000(Maddison)
50	Chile	591	PROXY(Other L. Am.(Maddison))
51	Sri Lanka	561	PROXY(Other E. Asia(Maddison))
52	Venezuela	556	PROXY(Other L. Am.(Maddison))
53	Hungary	500	1000(Maddison)
54	Libya	500	1000(Maddison)
55	Ghana	463	PROXY(Other W. Africa(Maddison))
56	Guatemala	461	PROXY(Other L. Am.(Maddison))
57	Argentina	414	PROXY(Other L. Am.(Maddison))
58	Croatia	412	PROXY(Yugoslavia(Maddison))
59	Belgium	400	1000(Maddison)
60	Somalia	400	1000(Maddison)
61	Sweden	400	1000(Maddison)
62	Ecuador	387	PROXY(Other L. Am.(Maddison))
63	Denmark	360	1000(Maddison)

TABLE 1.2 - POPULATION IN THOUSANDS, YEAR 1000

OBS	COUNTRY	POP	SOURCE
64	Slovakia	349	PROXY(Czechoslovakia(Maddison))
65	Lebanon	336	PROXY(W. Asia(Maddison))
66	Australia	321	PROXY(Other W. offshots(Maddison))
67	Guinea	315	PROXY(Other W. Africa(Maddison))
68	Oman	309	PROXY(W. Asia(Maddison))
69	Mozambique	300	1000(Maddison)
70	Netherlands	300	1000(Maddison)
71	Switzerland	300	1000(Maddison)
72	Burundi	293	PROXY(Other E. Africa(Maddison))
73	Ireland	289	PROXY(UK(Maddison))
74	Bosnia	286	PROXY(Yugoslavia(Maddison))
75	Philippines	281	PROXY(Other E. Asia(Maddison))
76	South Africa	279	PROXY(S. Afr., Sw., Ls.(Maddison))
77	Sierra Leone	234	PROXY(Other W. Africa(Maddison))
78	Belarus	230	PROXY(40(E)/Eur. Russia(Maddison))
79	Jordan	220	PROXY(W. Asia(Maddison))
80	Mongolia	203	PROXY(Other E. Asia(Maddison))
81	Albania	200	1000(Maddison)
82	Madagascar	200	1000(Maddison)
83	Norway	200	1000(Maddison)
84	El Salvador	192	PROXY(Other L. Am.(Maddison))
85	Kyrgyzstan	192	PROXY(40(E)/Turkestan(Maddison))
86	Tajikistan	192	PROXY(40(E)/Turkestan(Maddison))
87	Israel	186	PROXY(W. Asia(Maddison))
88	Georgia	180	PROXY(40(E)/Caucasus(Maddison))
89	Zimbabwe	173	PROXY(Mal., Zam., Zim.(Maddison))
90	Malawi	171	PROXY(Mal., Zam., Zim.(Maddison))
91	Turkmenistan	164	PROXY(40(E)/Turkestan(Maddison))
92	Azerbaijan	163	PROXY(40(E)/Caucasus(Maddison))
93	Canada	160	1000(Maddison)
94	Slovenia	158	PROXY(Yugoslavia(Maddison))
95	Zambia	155	PROXY(Mal., Zam., Zim.(Maddison))
96	Laos	154	PROXY(Other E. Asia(Maddison))
97	Cyprus	150	1000(Maddison)
98	Nicaragua	144	PROXY(Other L. Am.(Maddison))
99	Macedonia	132	PROXY(Yugoslavia(Maddison))
100	Taiwan	112	PROXY(Other E. Asia(Maddison))
101	Paraguay	111	PROXY(Other L. Am.(Maddison))
102	Honduras	105	PROXY(Other L. Am.(Maddison))
103	Malaysia	94	PROXY(Other E. Asia(Maddison))
104	Haiti	85	PROXY(Other L. Am.(Maddison))
105	Kosovo	82	PROXY(Yugoslavia(Maddison))
106	Kuwait	80	PROXY(W. Asia(Maddison))
107	Lithuania	75	PROXY(40(E)/Eur. Russia(Maddison))
108	Panama	73	PROXY(Other L. Am.(Maddison))
109	Cuba	71	PROXY(Other L. Am.(Maddison))
110	New Zealand	71	PROXY(Other W. offshots(Maddison))
111	Guinea-Bissau	69	PROXY(Other W. Africa(Maddison))
112	Armenia	66	PROXY(40(E)/Caucasus(Maddison))
113	Eritrea	65	PROXY(Ethiopia & Eritr.(Maddison))
114	Moldova	63	PROXY(40(E)/Eur. Russia(Maddison))

TABLE 1.2 - POPULATION IN THOUSANDS, YEAR 1000

OBS	COUNTRY	POP	SOURCE
115	Bahrain	61	PROXY(W. Asia(Maddison))
116	Namibia	54	PROXY(Namibia & Botsw.(Maddison))
117	Costa Rica	49	PROXY(Other L. Am.(Maddison))
118	Latvia	48	PROXY(40(E)/Eur. Russia(Maddison))
119	Jamaica	47	PROXY(Other L. Am.(Maddison))
120	Botswana	46	PROXY(Namibia & Botsw.(Maddison))
121	Montenegro	43	PROXY(Yugoslavia(Maddison))
122	Uruguay	43	PROXY(Other L. Am.(Maddison))
123	Finland	40	1000(Maddison)
124	UAE	40	PROXY(W. Asia(Maddison))
125	Puerto Rico	29	PROXY(Other L. Am.(Maddison))
126	Estonia	27	PROXY(40(E)/Eur. Russia(Maddison))
127	Lesotho	15	PROXY(S. Afr., Sw., Ls.(Maddison))
128	Qatar	14	PROXY(W. Asia(Maddison))
129	Dominican Rep	10	PROXY(Other L. Am.(Maddison))
130	Trinidad/Tobago	7	PROXY(Other L. Am.(Maddison))
131	Swaziland	6	PROXY(S. Afr., Sw., Ls.(Maddison))
132	Hong Kong	3	PROXY(China(Maddison))
133	Singapore	2	PROXY(Other E. Asia(Maddison))

TABLE 1.3 - POPULATION THOUSANDS, YEAR 1500

OBS	COUNTRY	POP	SOURCE
1	China	103,000	1500(Maddison)
2	India	92,289	PROXY(Undivided India(Maddison))
3	Japan	15,400	1500(Maddison)
4	France	15,000	1500(Maddison)
5	Germany	12,000	1500(Maddison)
6	Indonesia	10,700	1500(Maddison)
7	Bangladesh	10,526	PROXY(Undivided India(Maddison))
8	Italy	10,500	1500(Maddison)
9	Russia	8,183	PROXY(40(E)/Eu. Rs./Sb.(Maddison))
10	Mexico	7,500	1500(Maddison)
11	Pakistan	7,185	PROXY(Undivided India(Maddison))
12	Spain	6,800	1500(Maddison)
13	Turkey	6,300	1500(Maddison)
14	Korea, South	5,470	1500(Maddison)
15	Egypt	4,000	1500(Maddison)
16	Iran	4,000	1500(Maddison)
17	Poland	4,000	1500(Maddison)
18	Sudan	4,000	1500(Maddison)
19	Vietnam	3,835	PROXY(Other E. Asia(Maddison))
20	UK	3,681	PROXY(UK & Ireland(Maddison))
21	Ukraine	3,160	PROXY(40(E)/Eur. Russia(Maddison))
22	Korea, North	2,530	1500(Maddison)
23	Nepal	2,272	PROXY(Other E. Asia(Maddison))
24	Yemen	2,243	PROXY(Arabia(Maddison))
25	Czechia	2,161	PROXY(Czechoslovakia(Maddison))
26	Burma	2,052	PROXY(Other E. Asia(Maddison))
27	Austria	2,000	1500(Maddison)

	TABLE 1.3 - POPULATION THOUSANDS, YEAR 1500		
OBS	COUNTRY	POP	SOURCE
28	Romania	2,000	1500(Maddison)
29	Thailand	2,000	1500(Maddison)
30	US	2,000	1500(Maddison)
31	Afghanistan	1,920	PROXY(Other E. Asia(Maddison))
32	Ethiopia	1,870	PROXY(Ethiopia & Eritr.(Maddison))
33	Saudi Arabia	1,809	PROXY(Arabia(Maddison))
34	Algeria	1,500	1500(Maddison)
35	Morocco	1,500	1500(Maddison)
36	Peru	1,479	PROXY(Other Sp. Am.(Maddison))
37	Belgium	1,400	1500(Maddison)
38	Colombia	1,354	PROXY(Other Sp. Am.(Maddison))
39	Hungary	1,250	1500(Maddison)
40	Bolivia	1,235	PROXY(Other Sp. Am.(Maddison))
41	Cambodia	1,224	PROXY(Other E. Asia(Maddison))
42	Syria	1,206	PROXY(Other W. Asia(Maddison))
43	Uzbekistan	1,153	PROXY(40(E)/Turkestan(Maddison))
44	Kazakhstan	1,082	PROXY(40(E)/Turkestan(Maddison))
45	Brazil	1,000	1500(Maddison)
46	Greece	1,000	1500(Maddison)
47	Iraq	1,000	1500(Maddison)
48	Mozambique	1,000	1500(Maddison)
49	Portugal	1,000	1500(Maddison)
50	Sri Lanka	1,000	1500(Maddison)
51	Netherlands	950	1500(Maddison)
52	Chile	857	PROXY(Other Sp. Am.(Maddison))
53	Slovakia	839	PROXY(Czechoslovakia(Maddison))
54	Serbia	810	PROXY(Yugoslavia(Maddison))
55	Venezuela	806	PROXY(Other Sp. Am.(Maddison))
56	Bulgaria	800	1500(Maddison)
57	Somalia	800	1500(Maddison)
58	Tunisia	800	1500(Maddison)
59	Ghana	727	PROXY(Other W. Africa(Maddison))
60	Madagascar	700	1500(Maddison)
61	Belarus	691	PROXY(40(E)/Eur. Russia(Maddison))
62	Guatemala	668	PROXY(Other Sp. Am.(Maddison))
63	Switzerland	650	1500(Maddison)
64	Denmark	600	1500(Maddison)
65	Argentina	600	PROXY(Other Sp. Am.(Maddison))
66	Burundi	587	PROXY(Other E. Africa(Maddison))
67	Ireland	569	PROXY(whole Ireland(Maddison))
68	Ecuador	561	PROXY(Other Sp. Am.(Maddison))
69	South Africa	559	PROXY(S. Afr., Sw., Ls.(Maddison))
70	Sweden	550	1500(Maddison)
71	Croatia	530	PROXY(Yugoslavia(Maddison))
72	Libya	500	1500(Maddison)
73	Philippines	500	1500(Maddison)
74	Guinea	495	PROXY(Other W. Africa(Maddison))
75	Australia	450	1500(Maddison)
76	Georgia	450	PROXY(40(E)/Caucasus(Maddison))
77	Azerbaijan	408	PROXY(40(E)/Caucasus(Maddison))
78	Sierra Leone	367	PROXY(Other W. Africa(Maddison))
79	Bosnia	367	PROXY(Yugoslavia(Maddison))

TABLE 1.3 - POPULATION THOUSANDS, YEAR 1500

OBS	COUNTRY	POP	SOURCE
80	Mongolia	362	PROXY(Other E. Asia(Maddison))
81	Zimbabwe	347	PROXY(Mal., Zam., Zim.(Maddison))
82	Malawi	343	PROXY(Mal., Zam., Zim.(Maddison))
83	Zambia	310	PROXY(Mal., Zam., Zim.(Maddison))
84	Finland	300	1500(Maddison)
85	Norway	300	1500(Maddison)
86	Lebanon	299	PROXY(Other W. Asia(Maddison))
87	El Salvador	278	PROXY(Other Sp. Am.(Maddison))
88	Laos	275	PROXY(Other E. Asia(Maddison))
89	Oman	275	PROXY(Arabia(Maddison))
90	Kyrgyzstan	269	PROXY(40(E)/Turkestan(Maddison))
91	Tajikistan	268	PROXY(40(E)/Turkestan(Maddison))
92	Canada	250	1500(Maddison)
93	Turkmenistan	229	PROXY(40(E)/Turkestan(Maddison))
94	Lithuania	224	PROXY(40(E)/Eur. Russia(Maddison))
95	Nicaragua	209	PROXY(Other Sp. Am.(Maddison))
96	Slovenia	203	PROXY(Yugoslavia(Maddison))
97	Albania	200	1500(Maddison)
98	Taiwan	200	1500(Maddison)
99	Jordan	196	PROXY(Other W. Asia(Maddison))
100	Moldova	189	PROXY(40(E)/Eur. Russia(Maddison))
101	Macedonia	170	PROXY(Yugoslavia(Maddison))
102	Malaysia	168	PROXY(Other E. Asia(Maddison))
103	Israel	166	PROXY(Other W. Asia(Maddison))
104	Armenia	164	PROXY(40(E)/Caucasus(Maddison))
105	Paraguay	161	PROXY(Other Sp. Am.(Maddison))
106	Honduras	152	PROXY(Other Sp. Am.(Maddison))
107	Latvia	144	PROXY(40(E)/Eur. Russia(Maddison))
108	Eritrea	130	PROXY(Ethiopia & Eritr.(Maddison))
109	Haiti	124	PROXY(Caribbean cs(Maddison))
110	Guinea-Bissau	108	PROXY(Other W. Africa(Maddison))
111	Namibia	108	PROXY(Namibia & Botsw.(Maddison))
112	Panama	106	PROXY(Other Sp. Am.(Maddison))
113	Kosovo	105	PROXY(Yugoslavia(Maddison))
114	Cuba	103	PROXY(Caribbean cs(Maddison))
115	New Zealand	100	1500(Maddison)
116	Botswana	92	PROXY(Namibia & Botsw.(Maddison))
117	Estonia	81	PROXY(40(E)/Eur. Russia(Maddison))
118	Kuwait	71	PROXY(Arabia(Maddison))
119	Costa Rica	71	PROXY(Other Sp. Am.(Maddison))
120	Jamaica	69	PROXY(Caribbean cs(Maddison))
121	Cyprus	65	PROXY(Greece(Maddison))
122	Uruguay	62	PROXY(Other Sp. Am.(Maddison))
123	Montenegro	55	PROXY(Yugoslavia(Maddison))
124	Bahrain	54	PROXY(Arabia(Maddison))
125	Puerto Rico	42	PROXY(Caribbean cs(Maddison))
126	UAE	35	PROXY(Arabia(Maddison))
127	Lesotho	30	PROXY(S. Afr., Sw., Ls.(Maddison))
128	Dominican Rep	15	PROXY(Caribbean cs(Maddison))
129	Qatar	12	PROXY(Arabia(Maddison))
130	Swaziland	11	PROXY(S. Afr., Sw., Ls.(Maddison))

TABLE 1.3 - POPULATION THOUSANDS, YEAR 1500

OBS	COUNTRY	POP	SOURCE
131	Trinidad/Tobago	10	PROXY(Caribbean cs(Maddison))
132	Hong Kong	5	PROXY(China(Maddison))
133	Singapore	3	PROXY(Other E. Asia(Maddison))

TABLE 1.4 - POPULATION IN THOUSANDS, YEAR 1600

OBS	COUNTRY	POP	SOURCE
1	China	160,000	1600(Maddison)
2	India	113,264	PROXY(Undivided India(Maddison))
3	France	18,500	1600(Maddison)
4	Japan	18,500	1600(Maddison)
5	Germany	16,000	1600(Maddison)
6	Italy	13,100	1600(Maddison)
7	Bangladesh	12,919	PROXY(Undivided India(Maddison))
8	Indonesia	11,839	INTERPOL(Maddison)
9	Russia	10,195	PROXY(40(E)/Eu. Rs./Sb.(Maddison))
10	Pakistan	8,818	PROXY(Undivided India(Maddison))
11	Spain	8,240	1600(Maddison)
12	Turkey	7,275	INTERPOL(Maddison)
13	Korea, South	6,755	INTERPOL(Maddison)
14	UK	5,761	PROXY(UK & Ireland(Maddison))
15	Egypt	5,000	1600(Maddison)
16	Poland	5,000	1600(Maddison)
17	Iran	4,472	INTERPOL(Maddison)
18	Vietnam	4,447	PROXY(Other E. Asia(Maddison))
19	Sudan	4,200	1600(Maddison)
20	Ukraine	3,950	PROXY(40(E)/Eur. Russia(Maddison))
21	Czechia	3,242	PROXY(Czechoslovakia(Maddison))
22	Korea, North	3,124	INTERPOL(Maddison)
23	Nepal	2,635	PROXY(Other E. Asia(Maddison))
24	Austria	2,500	1600(Maddison)
25	Mexico	2,500	1600(Maddison)
26	Burma	2,380	PROXY(Other E. Asia(Maddison))
27	Algeria	2,250	1600(Maddison)
28	Morocco	2,250	1600(Maddison)
29	Yemen	2,243	INTERPOL(Maddison)
30	Thailand	2,236	INTERPOL(Maddison)
31	Afghanistan	2,227	PROXY(Other E. Asia(Maddison))
32	Ethiopia	2,104	PROXY(Ethiopia & Eritr.(Maddison))
33	Romania	2,000	1600(Maddison)
34	Saudi Arabia	1,809	INTERPOL(Maddison)
35	Belgium	1,600	1600(Maddison)
36	Greece	1,500	1600(Maddison)
37	Netherlands	1,500	1600(Maddison)
38	US	1,500	1600(Maddison)
39	Cambodia	1,419	PROXY(Other E. Asia(Maddison))
40	Uzbekistan	1,318	PROXY(40(E)/Turkestan(Maddison))
41	Slovakia	1,258	PROXY(Czechoslovakia(Maddison))
42	Bulgaria	1,250	1600(Maddison)

OBS	COUNTRY	POP	SOURCE
\multicolumn{4}{c}{TABLE 1.4 - POPULATION IN THOUSANDS, YEAR 1600}			
43	Hungary	1,250	1600(Maddison)
44	Mozambique	1,250	1600(Maddison)
45	Kazakhstan	1,236	PROXY(40(E)/Turkestan(Maddison))
46	Syria	1,175	INTERPOL(Maddison)
47	Portugal	1,100	1600(Maddison)
48	Sri Lanka	1,095	INTERPOL(Maddison)
49	Iraq	1,000	INTERPOL(Maddison)
50	Switzerland	1,000	1600(Maddison)
51	Tunisia	1,000	1600(Maddison)
52	Serbia	990	PROXY(Yugoslavia(Maddison))
53	Ghana	926	PROXY(Other W. Africa(Maddison))
54	Peru	887	PROXY(Other Sp. Am.(Maddison))
55	Belarus	864	PROXY(40(E)/Eur. Russia(Maddison))
56	Colombia	812	PROXY(Other Sp. Am.(Maddison))
57	Brazil	800	1600(Maddison)
58	Madagascar	800	1600(Maddison)
59	Somalia	800	1600(Maddison)
60	Philippines	791	INTERPOL(Maddison)
61	Sweden	760	1600(Maddison)
62	Bolivia	741	PROXY(Other Sp. Am.(Maddison))
63	Ireland	712	PROXY(whole Ireland(Maddison))
64	Burundi	685	PROXY(Other E. Africa(Maddison))
65	South Africa	652	PROXY(S. Afr., Sw., Ls.(Maddison))
66	Denmark	650	1600(Maddison)
67	Croatia	647	PROXY(Yugoslavia(Maddison))
68	Guinea	630	PROXY(Other W. Africa(Maddison))
69	Georgia	540	PROXY(40(E)/Caucasus(Maddison))
70	Chile	519	PROXY(Other Sp. Am.(Maddison))
71	Libya	500	1600(Maddison)
72	Azerbaijan	498	PROXY(40(E)/Caucasus(Maddison))
73	Venezuela	484	PROXY(Other Sp. Am.(Maddison))
74	Sierra Leone	468	PROXY(Other W. Africa(Maddison))
75	Australia	450	1600(Maddison)
76	Bosnia	449	PROXY(Yugoslavia(Maddison))
77	Taiwan	447	INTERPOL(Maddison)
78	Mongolia	420	PROXY(Other E. Asia(Maddison))
79	Guatemala	401	PROXY(Other Sp. Am.(Maddison))
80	Finland	400	1600(Maddison)
81	Norway	400	1600(Maddison)
82	Zimbabwe	382	PROXY(Mal., Zam., Zim.(Maddison))
83	Malawi	377	PROXY(Mal., Zam., Zim.(Maddison))
84	Argentina	360	PROXY(Other Sp. Am.(Maddison))
85	Zambia	342	PROXY(Mal., Zam., Zim.(Maddison))
86	Ecuador	337	PROXY(Other Sp. Am.(Maddison))
87	Laos	319	PROXY(Other E. Asia(Maddison))
88	Kyrgyzstan	307	PROXY(40(E)/Turkestan(Maddison))
89	Tajikistan	307	PROXY(40(E)/Turkestan(Maddison))
90	Lebanon	292	INTERPOL(Maddison)
91	Lithuania	279	PROXY(40(E)/Eur. Russia(Maddison))
92	Oman	275	INTERPOL(Maddison)
93	Turkmenistan	262	PROXY(40(E)/Turkestan(Maddison))

OBS	COUNTRY	POP	SOURCE
\multicolumn{4}{c}{TABLE 1.4 - POPULATION IN THOUSANDS, YEAR 1600}			
94	Canada	250	1600(Maddison)
95	Slovenia	248	PROXY(Yugoslavia(Maddison))
96	Moldova	236	PROXY(40(E)/Eur. Russia(Maddison))
97	Macedonia	208	PROXY(Yugoslavia(Maddison))
98	Albania	200	1600(Maddison)
99	Armenia	197	PROXY(40(E)/Caucasus(Maddison))
100	Malaysia	195	PROXY(Other E. Asia(Maddison))
101	Jordan	191	INTERPOL(Maddison)
102	Latvia	180	PROXY(40(E)/Eur. Russia(Maddison))
103	El Salvador	167	PROXY(Other Sp. Am.(Maddison))
104	Israel	161	INTERPOL(Maddison)
105	Eritrea	146	PROXY(Ethiopia & Eritr.(Maddison))
106	Guinea-Bissau	138	PROXY(Other W. Africa(Maddison))
107	Kosovo	129	PROXY(Yugoslavia(Maddison))
108	Nicaragua	125	PROXY(Other Sp. Am.(Maddison))
109	Namibia	108	PROXY(Namibia & Botsw. (Maddison))
110	Estonia	101	PROXY(40(E)/Eur. Russia(Maddison))
111	New Zealand	100	1600(Maddison)
112	Cyprus	98	PROXY(Greece(Maddison))
113	Paraguay	96	PROXY(Other Sp. Am.(Maddison))
114	Botswana	92	PROXY(Namibia & Botsw. (Maddison))
115	Honduras	91	PROXY(Other Sp. Am.(Maddison))
116	Kuwait	71	INTERPOL(Maddison)
117	Montenegro	67	PROXY(Yugoslavia(Maddison))
118	Panama	64	PROXY(Other Sp. Am.(Maddison))
119	Bahrain	54	INTERPOL(Maddison)
120	Haiti	49	PROXY(Caribbean cs(Maddison))
121	Costa Rica	42	PROXY(Other Sp. Am.(Maddison))
122	Cuba	41	PROXY(Caribbean cs(Maddison))
123	Uruguay	37	PROXY(Other Sp. Am.(Maddison))
124	UAE	35	INTERPOL(Maddison)
125	Lesotho	35	PROXY(S. Afr., Sw., Ls.(Maddison))
126	Jamaica	27	PROXY(Caribbean cs(Maddison))
127	Puerto Rico	17	PROXY(Caribbean cs(Maddison))
128	Swaziland	13	PROXY(S. Afr., Sw., Ls.(Maddison))
129	Qatar	12	INTERPOL(Maddison)
130	Hong Kong	8	PROXY(China(Maddison))
131	Dominican Rep	6	PROXY(Caribbean cs(Maddison))
132	Trinidad/Tobago	4	PROXY(Caribbean cs(Maddison))
133	Singapore	3	PROXY(Other E. Asia(Maddison))

OBS	COUNTRY	POP	SOURCE
\multicolumn{4}{c}{TABLE 1.5 - POPULATION THOUSANDS, YEAR 1700}			
1	India	138,433	PROXY(Undivided India(Maddison))
2	China	138,000	1700(Maddison)

OBS	COUNTRY	POP	SOURCE
	TABLE 1.5 - POPULATION THOUSANDS, YEAR 1700		
3	Japan	27,000	1700(Maddison)
4	France	21,471	1700(Maddison)
5	Bangladesh	15,789	PROXY(Undivided India(Maddison))
6	Germany	15,000	1700(Maddison)
7	Russia	13,616	PROXY(40(E)/Eu. Rs./Sb.(Maddison))
8	Italy	13,300	1700(Maddison)
9	Indonesia	13,100	1700(Maddison)
10	Pakistan	10,777	PROXY(Undivided India(Maddison))
11	Spain	8,770	1700(Maddison)
12	Turkey	8,400	1700(Maddison)
13	Korea, South	8,342	1700(Maddison)
14	UK	7,997	PROXY(UK & Ireland(Maddison))
15	Poland	6,000	1700(Maddison)
16	Ukraine	5,267	PROXY(40(E)/Eur. Russia(Maddison))
17	Vietnam	5,171	PROXY(Other E. Asia(Maddison))
18	Iran	5,000	1700(Maddison)
19	Egypt	4,500	1700(Maddison)
20	Mexico	4,500	1700(Maddison)
21	Sudan	4,400	1700(Maddison)
22	Korea, North	3,858	1700(Maddison)
23	Czechia	3,242	PROXY(Czechoslovakia(Maddison))
24	Nepal	3,064	PROXY(Other E. Asia(Maddison))
25	Burma	2,768	PROXY(Other E. Asia(Maddison))
26	Afghanistan	2,589	PROXY(Other E. Asia(Maddison))
27	Austria	2,500	1700(Maddison)
28	Romania	2,500	1700(Maddison)
29	Thailand	2,500	1700(Maddison)
30	Ethiopia	2,338	PROXY(Ethiopia & Eritr.(Maddison))
31	Yemen	2,243	PROXY(Arabia(Maddison))
32	Belgium	2,000	1700(Maddison)
33	Portugal	2,000	1700(Maddison)
34	Netherlands	1,900	1700(Maddison)
35	Saudi Arabia	1,809	PROXY(Arabia(Maddison))
36	Algeria	1,750	1700(Maddison)
37	Morocco	1,750	1700(Maddison)
38	Cambodia	1,650	PROXY(Other E. Asia(Maddison))
39	Greece	1,500	1700(Maddison)
40	Hungary	1,500	1700(Maddison)
41	Mozambique	1,500	1700(Maddison)
42	Uzbekistan	1,482	PROXY(40(E)/Turkestan(Maddison))
43	Kazakhstan	1,391	PROXY(40(E)/Turkestan(Maddison))
44	Ireland	1,370	PROXY(whole Ireland(Maddison))
45	Sweden	1,260	1700(Maddison)
46	Slovakia	1,258	PROXY(Czechoslovakia(Maddison))
47	Brazil	1,250	1700(Maddison)
48	Bulgaria	1,250	1700(Maddison)
49	Philippines	1,250	1700(Maddison)
50	Sri Lanka	1,200	1700(Maddison)
51	Switzerland	1,200	1700(Maddison)
52	Ghana	1,190	PROXY(Other W. Africa(Maddison))
53	Belarus	1,152	PROXY(40(E)/Eur. Russia(Maddison))
54	Syria	1,145	PROXY(Other W. Asia(Maddison))

TABLE 1.5 - POPULATION THOUSANDS, YEAR 1700

OBS	COUNTRY	POP	SOURCE
55	Peru	1,009	PROXY(Other Sp. Am.(Maddison))
56	Iraq	1,000	1700(Maddison)
57	Madagascar	1,000	1700(Maddison)
58	Taiwan	1,000	1700(Maddison)
59	US	1,000	1700(Maddison)
60	Serbia	990	PROXY(Yugoslavia(Maddison))
61	Somalia	950	1700(Maddison)
62	South Africa	931	PROXY(S. Afr., Sw., Ls.(Maddison))
63	Colombia	924	PROXY(Other Sp. Am.(Maddison))
64	Bolivia	843	PROXY(Other Sp. Am.(Maddison))
65	Guinea	810	PROXY(Other W. Africa(Maddison))
66	Tunisia	800	1700(Maddison)
67	Burundi	782	PROXY(Other E. Africa(Maddison))
68	Denmark	700	1700(Maddison)
69	Croatia	647	PROXY(Yugoslavia(Maddison))
70	Georgia	630	PROXY(40(E)/Caucasus(Maddison))
71	Sierra Leone	601	PROXY(Other W. Africa(Maddison))
72	Chile	591	PROXY(Other Sp. Am.(Maddison))
73	Azerbaijan	571	PROXY(40(E)/Caucasus(Maddison))
74	Venezuela	550	PROXY(Other Sp. Am.(Maddison))
75	Libya	500	1700(Maddison)
76	Norway	500	1700(Maddison)
77	Mongolia	489	PROXY(Other E. Asia(Maddison))
78	Guatemala	456	PROXY(Other Sp. Am.(Maddison))
79	Australia	450	1700(Maddison)
80	Bosnia	449	PROXY(YUgoslavia(Maddison))
81	Zimbabwe	416	PROXY(Mal., Zam., Zim.(Maddison))
82	Malawi	411	PROXY(Mal., Zam., Zim.(Maddison))
83	Argentina	409	PROXY(Other Sp. Am.(Maddison))
84	Finland	400	1700(Maddison)
85	Ecuador	383	PROXY(Other Sp. Am.(Maddison))
86	Lithuania	373	PROXY(40(E)/Eur. Russia(Maddison))
87	Zambia	373	PROXY(Mal., Zam., Zim.(Maddison))
88	Laos	371	PROXY(Other E. Asia(Maddison))
89	Kyrgyzstan	346	PROXY(40(E)/Turkestan(Maddison))
90	Tajikistan	345	PROXY(40(E)/Turkestan(Maddison))
91	Moldova	314	PROXY(40(E)/Eur. Russia(Maddison))
92	Albania	300	1700(Maddison)
93	Turkmenistan	295	PROXY(40(E)/Turkestan(Maddison))
94	Lebanon	284	PROXY(Other W. Asia(Maddison))
95	Oman	275	PROXY(Arabia(Maddison))
96	Slovenia	248	PROXY(Yugoslavia(Maddison))
97	Latvia	240	PROXY(40(E)/Eur. Russia(Maddison))
98	Armenia	230	PROXY(40(E)/Caucasus(Maddison))
99	Malaysia	227	PROXY(Other E. Asia(Maddison))
100	Macedonia	208	PROXY(Yugoslavia(Maddison))
101	Canada	200	1700(Maddison)
102	El Salvador	190	PROXY(Other Sp. Am.(Maddison))
103	Jordan	186	PROXY(Other W. Asia(Maddison))
104	Guinea-Bissau	177	PROXY(Other W. Africa(Maddison))
105	Eritrea	162	PROXY(Ethiopia & Eritr.(Maddison))
106	Israel	157	PROXY(Other W. Asia(Maddison))

TABLE 1.5 - POPULATION THOUSANDS, YEAR 1700

OBS	COUNTRY	POP	SOURCE
107	Nicaragua	142	PROXY(Other Sp. Am.(Maddison))
108	Estonia	134	PROXY(40(E)/Eur. Russia(Maddison))
109	Kosovo	129	PROXY(Yugoslavia(Maddison))
110	Haiti	124	PROXY(Caribbean cs(Maddison))
111	Paraguay	110	PROXY(Other Sp. Am.(Maddison))
112	Namibia	108	PROXY(Namibia & Botsw.(Maddison))
113	Honduras	103	PROXY(Other Sp. Am.(Maddison))
114	Cuba	103	PROXY(Caribbean cs(Maddison))
115	New Zealand	100	1700(Maddison)
116	Cyprus	98	PROXY(Greece(Maddison))
117	Botswana	92	PROXY(Namibia & Botsw.(Maddison))
118	Panama	72	PROXY(Other Sp. Am.(Maddison))
119	Kuwait	71	PROXY(Arabia(Maddison))
120	Jamaica	69	PROXY(Caribbean cs(Maddison))
121	Montenegro	67	PROXY(Yugoslavia(Maddison))
122	Bahrain	54	PROXY(Arabia(Maddison))
123	Lesotho	50	PROXY(S. Afr., Sw., Ls.(Maddison))
124	Costa Rica	48	PROXY(Other Sp. Am.(Maddison))
125	Puerto Rico	42	PROXY(Caribbean cs(Maddison))
126	Uruguay	42	PROXY(Other Sp. Am.(Maddison))
127	UAE	35	PROXY(Arabia(Maddison))
128	Swaziland	19	PROXY(S. Afr., Sw., Ls.(Maddison))
129	Dominican Rep	15	PROXY(Caribbean cs(Maddison))
130	Qatar	12	PROXY(Arabia(Maddison))
131	Trinidad/Tobago	10	PROXY(Caribbean cs(Maddison))
132	Hong Kong	7	PROXY(China(Maddison))
133	Singapore	4	PROXY(Other E. Asia(Maddison))

TABLE 1.6 - POPULATION THOUSANDS YEAR 1820

OBS	COUNTRY	POP	SOURCE
1	China	381,000	1820(Maddison)
2	India	175,349	1820(Maddison)
3	France	31,250	1820(Maddison)
4	Japan	31,000	1820(Maddison)
5	Russia	30,588	PROXY(40(E)/Eu. Rs./Sb.(Maddison))
6	Germany	24,905	1820(Maddison)
7	Italy	20,176	1820(Maddison)
8	Bangladesh	20,000	1820(Maddison)
9	UK	19,831	PROXY(UK & Ireland(Maddison))
10	Indonesia	17,927	1820(Maddison)
11	Pakistan	13,651	1820(Maddison)
12	Spain	12,203	1820(Maddison)
13	Ukraine	11,629	PROXY(40(E)/Eur. Russia(Maddison))
14	Poland	10,426	1820(Maddison)
15	Turkey	10,074	1820(Maddison)
16	US	9,981	1820(Maddison)
17	Korea, South	9,395	1820(Maddison)
18	Mexico	6,587	1820(Maddison)
19	Iran	6,560	1820(Maddison)
20	Vietnam	6,551	1820(Maddison)

TABLE 1.6 - POPULATION THOUSANDS YEAR 1820

OBS	COUNTRY	POP	SOURCE
21	Romania	6,389	1820(Maddison)
22	Czechia	5,516	PROXY(Czechoslovakia(Maddison))
23	Sudan	5,156	1820(Maddison)
24	Ireland	5,053	PROXY(whole Ireland(Maddison))
25	Thailand	4,665	1820(Maddison)
26	Brazil	4,507	1820(Maddison)
27	Egypt	4,394	1820(Mitchell)
28	Korea, North	4,345	1820(Maddison)
29	Hungary	4,146	1820(Maddison)
30	Nepal	3,881	1820(Maddison)
31	Burma	3,506	1820(Maddison)
32	Belgium	3,434	1820(Maddison)
33	Austria	3,369	1820(Maddison)
34	Portugal	3,297	1820(Maddison)
35	Afghanistan	3,280	1820(Maddison)
36	Ethiopia	2,949	PROXY(Ethiopia & Eritr.(Maddison))
37	Algeria	2,689	1820(Maddison)
38	Morocco	2,689	1820(Maddison)
39	Yemen	2,593	1820(Maddison)
40	Sweden	2,585	1820(Maddison)
41	Belarus	2,545	PROXY(40(E)/Eur. Russia(Maddison))
42	Netherlands	2,333	1820(Maddison)
43	Greece	2,312	1820(Maddison)
44	Uzbekistan	2,217	PROXY(40(E)/Turkestan(Maddison))
45	Bulgaria	2,187	1820(Maddison)
46	Philippines	2,176	1820(Maddison)
47	Slovakia	2,140	PROXY(Czechoslovakia(Maddison))
48	Mozambique	2,096	1820(Maddison)
49	Saudi Arabia	2,091	1820(Maddison)
50	Cambodia	2,090	1820(Maddison)
51	Kazakhstan	2,081	PROXY(40(E)/Turkestan(Maddison))
52	Taiwan	2,000	1820(Maddison)
53	Switzerland	1,986	1820(Maddison)
54	Serbia	1,878	PROXY(Yugoslavia(Maddison))
55	Madagascar	1,683	1820(Maddison)
56	South Africa	1,444	PROXY(S. Afr., Sw., Ls.(Maddison))
57	Ghana	1,374	1820(Maddison)
58	Syria	1,337	1820(Maddison)
59	Peru	1,317	1820(Maddison)
60	Croatia	1,228	PROXY(Yugoslavia(Maddison))
61	Sri Lanka	1,213	1820(Maddison)
62	Colombia	1,206	1820(Maddison)
63	Finland	1,169	1820(Maddison)
64	Denmark	1,155	1820(Maddison)
65	Bolivia	1,100	1820(Maddison)
66	Iraq	1,093	1820(Maddison)
67	Burundi	1,016	PROXY(Other E. Africa(Maddison))
68	Somalia	1,000	1820(Maddison)
69	Norway	970	1820(Maddison)
70	Guinea	935	PROXY(Other W. Africa(Maddison))
71	Tunisia	875	1820(Maddison)
72	Georgia	874	PROXY(40(E)/Caucasus(Maddison))

TABLE 1.6 - POPULATION THOUSANDS YEAR 1820

OBS	COUNTRY	POP	SOURCE
73	Bosnia	851	PROXY(Yugoslavia(Maddison))
74	Lithuania	823	PROXY(40(E)/Eur. Russia(Maddison))
75	Canada	816	1820(Maddison)
76	Azerbaijan	792	PROXY(40(E)/Caucasus(Maddison))
77	Chile	771	1820(Maddison)
78	Haiti	723	1820(Maddison)
79	Venezuela	718	1820(Maddison)
80	Moldova	694	PROXY(40(E)/Eur. Russia(Maddison))
81	Sierra Leone	694	PROXY(Other W. Africa(Maddison))
82	Mongolia	619	1820(Maddison)
83	Cuba	605	1820(Maddison)
84	Guatemala	595	1820(Maddison)
85	Libya	538	1820(Maddison)
86	Argentina	534	1820(Maddison)
87	Latvia	531	PROXY(40(E)/Eur. Russia(Maddison))
88	Kyrgyzstan	517	PROXY(40(E)/Turkestan(Maddison))
89	Tajikistan	516	PROXY(40(E)/Turkestan(Maddison))
90	Ecuador	500	1820(Maddison)
91	Laos	470	1820(Maddison)
92	Slovenia	469	PROXY(Yugoslavia(Maddison))
93	Zimbabwe	467	PROXY(Mal., Zam., Zim.(Maddison))
94	Malawi	461	PROXY(Mal., Zam., Zim.(Maddison))
95	Turkmenistan	441	PROXY(40(E)/Turkestan(Maddison))
96	Albania	437	1820(Maddison)
97	Zambia	418	PROXY(Mal., Zam., Zim.(Maddison))
98	Jamaica	401	1820(Maddison)
99	Macedonia	394	PROXY(Yugoslavia(Maddison))
100	Australia	334	1820(Maddison)
101	Lebanon	332	1820(Maddison)
102	Armenia	319	PROXY(40(E)/Caucasus(Maddison))
103	Oman	318	1820(Maddison)
104	Estonia	296	PROXY(40(E)/Eur. Russia(Maddison))
105	Malaysia	287	1820(Maddison)
106	El Salvador	248	1820(Maddison)
107	Puerto Rico	248	1820(Maddison)
108	Kosovo	244	PROXY(Yugoslavia(Maddison))
109	Jordan	217	1820(Maddison)
110	Eritrea	205	PROXY(Ethiopia & Eritr.(Maddison))
111	Guinea-Bissau	205	PROXY(Other W. Africa(Maddison))
112	Nicaragua	186	1820(Maddison)
113	Israel	184	PROXY(Palestine(Maddison))
114	Cyprus	151	PROXY(Greece(Maddison))
115	Paraguay	143	1820(Maddison)
116	Honduras	135	1820(Maddison)
117	Montenegro	127	PROXY(Yugoslavia(Maddison))
118	Namibia	118	PROXY(Namibia & Botsw.(Maddison))
119	Botswana	101	PROXY(Namibia & Botsw.(Maddison))
120	New Zealand	100	1820(Maddison)
121	Panama	94	PROXY(15 L. American cs(Maddison))
122	Dominican Rep	89	1820(Maddison)
123	Kuwait	82	PROXY(Gulf Coast(Maddison))
124	Lesotho	77	PROXY(S. Afr., Sw., Ls.(Maddison))

TABLE 1.6 - POPULATION THOUSANDS YEAR 1820

OBS	COUNTRY	POP	SOURCE
125	Costa Rica	63	1820(Maddison)
126	Bahrain	63	PROXY(Gulf Coast(Maddison))
127	Trinidad/Tobago	60	1820(Maddison)
128	Uruguay	55	1820(Maddison)
129	UAE	41	PROXY(Gulf Coast(Maddison))
130	Swaziland	29	PROXY(S. Afr., Sw., Ls.(Maddison))
131	Hong Kong	20	1820(Maddison)
132	Qatar	14	PROXY(Gulf Coast(Maddison))
133	Singapore	5	1820(Maddison)

TABLE 1.7 POPULATION IN THOUSANDS, YEAR 1870

OBS	COUNTRY	POP	SOURCE
1	China	358,000	1870(Maddison)
2	India	212,189	1870(Maddison)
3	Russia	50,303	PROXY(40(E)/USSR(Maddison))
4	US	40,241	1870(Maddison)
5	Germany	39,231	1870(Maddison)
6	France	38,440	1870(Maddison)
7	Japan	34,437	1870(Maddison)
8	UK	29,319	PROXY(UK & Ireland(Maddison))
9	Indonesia	28,922	1870(Maddison)
10	Italy	27,888	1870(Maddison)
11	Bangladesh	24,721	1870(Maddison)
12	Ukraine	18,888	PROXY(40(E)/USSR(Maddison))
13	Poland	16,865	1870(Maddison)
14	Spain	16,201	1870(Maddison)
15	Pakistan	16,090	1870(Maddison)
16	Turkey	11,793	1870(Maddison)
17	Vietnam	10,528	1870(Maddison)
18	Brazil	9,797	1870(Maddison)
19	Korea, South	9,753	1870(Maddison)
20	Mexico	9,219	1870(Maddison)
21	Romania	9,179	1870(Maddison)
22	Iran	8,415	1870(Maddison)
23	Czechia	7,316	PROXY(Czechoslovakia(Maddison))
24	Egypt	6,394	1870(MItchell)
25	Ethiopia	6,179	INTERPOL(Maddison)
26	Sudan	6,120	INTERPOL(Maddison)
27	Hungary	5,917	1870(Maddison)
28	Thailand	5,775	1870(Maddison)
29	Belgium	5,096	1870(Maddison)
30	Philippines	5,063	1870(Maddison)
31	Nepal	4,698	1870(Maddison)
32	Austria	4,520	1870(Maddison)
33	Korea, North	4,511	1870(Maddison)
34	Portugal	4,327	1870(Maddison)
35	Burma	4,245	1870(Maddison)
36	Afghanistan	4,207	1870(Maddison)
37	Sweden	4,169	1870(Maddison)
38	Belarus	4,133	PROXY(40(E)/USSR(Maddison))

OBS	COUNTRY	POP	SOURCE
	TABLE 1.7 POPULATION IN THOUSANDS, YEAR 1870		
39	Ireland	3,856	PROXY(whole Ireland(Maddison))
40	Canada	3,781	1870(Maddison)
41	Algeria	3,776	1870(Maddison)
42	Morocco	3,776	1870(Maddison)
43	Greece	3,657	1870(Maddison)
44	Netherlands	3,610	1870(Maddison)
45	Mozambique	3,191	INTERPOL(Maddison)
46	Uzbekistan	2,993	PROXY(40(E)/USSR(Maddison))
47	Serbia	2,972	PROXY(Yugoslavia(Maddison))
48	Yemen	2,840	1870(Maddison)
49	Slovakia	2,839	PROXY(Czechoslovakia(Maddison))
50	Kazakhstan	2,809	PROXY(40(E)/USSR(Maddison))
51	Sri Lanka	2,786	1870(Maddison)
52	Switzerland	2,655	1870(Maddison)
53	Peru	2,606	1870(Maddison)
54	Bulgaria	2,586	1870(Maddison)
55	South Africa	2,547	1870(Maddison)
56	Madagascar	2,400	INTERPOL(Maddison)
57	Colombia	2,392	1870(Maddison)
58	Taiwan	2,345	1870(Maddison)
59	Cambodia	2,340	1870(Maddison)
60	Saudi Arabia	2,338	1870(Maddison)
61	Chile	1,945	1870(Maddison)
62	Croatia	1,943	PROXY(Yugoslavia(Maddison))
63	Denmark	1,888	1870(Maddison)
64	Argentina	1,796	1870(Maddison)
65	Australia	1,775	1870(Maddison)
66	Finland	1,754	1870(Maddison)
67	Norway	1,735	1870(Maddison)
68	Venezuela	1,653	1870(Maddison)
69	Georgia	1,650	PROXY(40(E)/USSR(Maddison))
70	Syria	1,582	1870(Maddison)
71	Iraq	1,580	1870(Maddison)
72	Ghana	1,500	1870(Maddison)
73	Azerbaijan	1,496	PROXY(40(E)/USSR(Maddison))
74	Bolivia	1,495	1870(Maddison)
75	Burundi	1,406	INTERPOL(Maddison)
76	Guinea	1,389	INTERPOL(Maddison)
77	Somalia	1,369	INTERPOL(Maddison)
78	Bosnia	1,347	PROXY(Yugoslavia(Maddison))
79	Lithuania	1,336	PROXY(40(E)/USSR(Maddison))
80	Cuba	1,331	1870(Maddison)
81	Tunisia	1,176	1870(Maddison)
82	Haiti	1,150	1870(Maddison)
83	Moldova	1,128	PROXY(40(E)/USSR(Maddison))
84	Guatemala	1,080	1870(Maddison)
85	Sierra Leone	1,031	INTERPOL(Maddison)
86	Ecuador	1,013	1870(Maddison)
87	Zimbabwe	936	INTERPOL(Maddison)
88	Malawi	924	INTERPOL(Maddison)
89	Latvia	862	PROXY(40(E)/USSR(Maddison))
90	Zambia	838	INTERPOL(Maddison)

TABLE 1.7 POPULATION IN THOUSANDS, YEAR 1870

OBS	COUNTRY	POP	SOURCE
91	Malaysia	800	1870(Maddison)
92	Laos	755	1870(Maddison)
93	Slovenia	743	PROXY(Yugoslavia(Maddison))
94	Kyrgyzstan	698	PROXY(40(E)/USSR(Maddison))
95	Tajikistan	697	PROXY(40(E)/USSR(Maddison))
96	Mongolia	668	1870(Maddison)
97	Libya	660	INTERPOL(Madd/Mitchell)
98	Puerto Rico	645	1870(Maddison)
99	Macedonia	623	PROXY(Yugoslavia(Maddison))
100	Armenia	603	PROXY(40(E)/USSR(Maddison))
101	Albania	603	1870(Maddison)
102	Turkmenistan	595	PROXY(40(E)/USSR(Maddison))
103	Jamaica	499	1870(Maddison)
104	El Salvador	492	1870(Maddison)
105	Estonia	482	PROXY(40(E)/USSR(Maddison))
106	Lebanon	476	1870(Maddison)
107	Eritrea	429	INTERPOL(Maddison)
108	Honduras	404	1870(Maddison)
109	Kosovo	387	PROXY(Yugoslavia(Maddison))
110	Paraguay	384	1870(Maddison)
111	Oman	367	1870(Maddison)
112	Uruguay	343	1870(Maddison)
113	Nicaragua	337	1870(Maddison)
114	Guinea-Bissau	304	INTERPOL(Maddison)
115	New Zealand	291	1870(Maddison)
116	Jordan	266	1870(Maddison)
117	Dominican Rep	242	1870(Maddison)
118	Cyprus	239	PROXY(Greece(Maddison))
119	Israel	238	PROXY(Palestine(Maddison))
120	Namibia	203	INTERPOL(Maddison)
121	Montenegro	201	PROXY(Yugoslavia(Maddison))
122	Lesotho	184	INTERPOL(Maddison)
123	Panama	176	1870(Maddison)
124	Botswana	174	INTERPOL(Maddison)
125	Costa Rica	137	1870(Maddison)
126	Trinidad/Tobago	124	1870(Maddison)
127	Hong Kong	123	1870(Maddison)
128	Singapore	84	1870(Maddison)
129	Kuwait	82	PROXY(Gulf Coast(Maddison))
130	Swaziland	68	INTERPOL(Maddison)
131	Bahrain	63	PROXY(Gulf Coast(Maddison))
132	UAE	41	PROXY(Gulf Coast(Maddison))
133	Qatar	14	PROXY(Gulf Coast(Maddison))

TABLE 1.8 - POPULATION IN THOUSANDS, YEAR 1880

OBS	COUNTRY	POP	SOURCE
1	China	368,000	1880(Maddison)
2	India	215,157	INTERPOL(Ind./wh. India(Maddison))
3	Russia	56,196	40(E)/INTERPOL(Maddison)

TABLE 1.8 - POPULATION IN THOUSANDS, YEAR 1880

OBS	COUNTRY	POP	SOURCE
4	US	50,458	1880(Maddison)
5	Germany	43,500	1880(Maddison)
6	France	39,045	1880(Maddison)
7	Japan	36,807	1880(Maddison)
8	Indonesia	32,876	1880(Maddison)
9	UK	32,328	PROXY(UK & Ireland(Maddison))
10	Italy	29,534	1880(Maddison)
11	Bangladesh	25,536	INTERPOL(Ban./wh. India(Maddison))
12	Ukraine	21,101	40(E)/INTERPOL(Maddison)
13	Poland	19,632	INTERPOL(Maddison)
14	Spain	16,859	1880(Maddison)
15	Pakistan	16,492	INTERPOL(Pak./wh. India(Maddison))
16	Turkey	12,472	INTERPOL(Maddison)
17	Vietnam	12,127	INTERPOL(Maddison)
18	Brazil	11,794	1880(Maddison)
19	Mexico	10,399	1880(Maddison)
20	Korea, South	9,800	INTERPOL(Maddison)
21	Romania	9,758	INTERPOL(Maddison)
22	Iran	8,955	INTERPOL(Maddison)
23	Czechia	7,701	INTERPOL(Maddison)
24	Egypt	7,578	1880(Mitchell)
25	Ethiopia	7,164	INTERPOL(Maddison)
26	Sudan	6,333	INTERPOL(Maddison)
27	Hungary	6,260	INTERPOL(Maddison)
28	Thailand	6,206	INTERPOL(Maddison)
29	Philippines	5,726	INTERPOL(Maddison)
30	Burma	5,638	INTERPOL(Maddison)
31	Belgium	5,541	1880(Maddison)
32	Austria	4,941	1880(Maddison)
33	Nepal	4,939	INTERPOL(Maddison)
34	Belarus	4,617	40(E)/INTERPOL(Maddison)
35	Portugal	4,610	1880(Maddison)
36	Korea, North	4,598	INTERPOL(Maddison)
37	Sweden	4,572	1880(Maddison)
38	Afghanistan	4,520	INTERPOL(Maddison)
39	Canada	4,384	1880(Maddison)
40	Algeria	4,183	1880(Maddison)
41	Morocco	4,051	INTERPOL(Maddison)
42	Greece	4,049	1880(Maddison)
43	Netherlands	4,043	1880(Maddison)
44	Ireland	3,702	PROXY(whole Ireland(Maddison))
45	Mozambique	3,470	INTERPOL(Maddison)
46	Uzbekistan	3,344	40(E)/INTERPOL(Maddison)
47	Serbia	3,220	INTERPOL(Maddison)
48	Kazakhstan	3,138	40(E)/INTERPOL(Maddison)
49	South Africa	3,127	INTERPOL(Maddison)
50	Sri Lanka	3,021	1880(Maddison)
51	Slovakia	2,988	INTERPOL(Maddison)
52	Bulgaria	2,985	INTERPOL(Maddison)
53	Peru	2,953	INTERPOL(Maddison)
54	Yemen	2,938	INTERPOL(Maddison)
55	Switzerland	2,839	1880(Maddison)

OBS	COUNTRY	POP	SOURCE
\multicolumn{4}{c}{TABLE 1.8 - POPULATION IN THOUSANDS, YEAR 1880}			
56	Colombia	2,839	INTERPOL(Maddison)
57	Madagascar	2,576	INTERPOL(Maddison)
58	Cambodia	2,493	INTERPOL(Maddison)
59	Argentina	2,462	INTERPOL(Maddison)
60	Taiwan	2,421	INTERPOL(Maddison)
61	Saudi Arabia	2,413	INTERPOL(Maddison)
62	Chile	2,271	INTERPOL(Maddison)
63	Australia	2,197	1880(Maddison)
64	Croatia	2,105	INTERPOL(Maddison)
65	Denmark	2,081	1880(Maddison)
66	Finland	2,047	1880(Maddison)
67	Venezuela	1,952	1880(Maddison)
68	Norway	1,919	1880(Maddison)
69	Georgia	1,844	40(E)/INTERPOL(Maddison)
70	Iraq	1,776	INTERPOL(Maddison)
71	Azerbaijan	1,671	40(E)/INTERPOL(Maddison)
72	Syria	1,669	INTERPOL(Maddison)
73	Ghana	1,570	INTERPOL(Maddison)
74	Bolivia	1,559	INTERPOL(Maddison)
75	Guinea	1,504	INTERPOL(Maddison)
76	Burundi	1,500	INTERPOL(Maddison)
77	Lithuania	1,493	40(E)/INTERPOL(Maddison)
78	Bosnia	1,460	INTERPOL(Maddison)
79	Somalia	1,458	INTERPOL(Maddison)
80	Cuba	1,432	INTERPOL(Maddison)
81	Tunisia	1,310	INTERPOL(Maddison)
82	Haiti	1,273	INTERPOL(Maddison)
83	Moldova	1,260	40(E)/INTERPOL(Maddison)
84	Guatemala	1,149	INTERPOL(Maddison)
85	Ecuador	1,128	INTERPOL(Maddison)
86	Malaysia	1,126	INTERPOL(Maddison)
87	Sierra Leone	1,116	INTERPOL(Maddison)
88	Zimbabwe	1,076	INTERPOL(Maddison)
89	Malawi	1,063	INTERPOL(Maddison)
90	Zambia	963	INTERPOL(Maddison)
91	Latvia	963	40(E)/INTERPOL(Maddison)
92	Laos	870	INTERPOL(Maddison)
93	Slovenia	805	INTERPOL(Maddison)
94	Kyrgyzstan	780	40(E)/INTERPOL(Maddison)
95	Tajikistan	778	40(E)/INTERPOL(Maddison)
96	Puerto Rico	736	INTERPOL(Maddison)
97	Libya	688	INTERPOL(Madd/Mitchell)
98	Mongolia	681	INTERPOL(Maddison)
99	Macedonia	675	INTERPOL(Maddison)
100	Armenia	674	40(E)/INTERPOL(Maddison)
101	Turkmenistan	665	40(E)/INTERPOL(Maddison)
102	Albania	662	INTERPOL(Maddison)
103	El Salvador	570	INTERPOL(Maddison)
104	Jamaica	564	INTERPOL(Maddison)
105	Estonia	538	40(E)/INTERPOL(Maddison)
106	New Zealand	520	1880(Maddison)
107	Lebanon	512	INTERPOL(Maddison)

TABLE 1.8 - POPULATION IN THOUSANDS, YEAR 1880

OBS	COUNTRY	POP	SOURCE
108	Eritrea	498	INTERPOL(Maddison)
109	Uruguay	464	1880(Maddison)
110	Honduras	434	INTERPOL(Maddison)
111	Kosovo	419	INTERPOL(Maddison)
112	Paraguay	402	INTERPOL(Maddison)
113	Oman	384	INTERPOL(Maddison)
114	Nicaragua	379	INTERPOL(Maddison)
115	Guinea-Bissau	329	INTERPOL(Maddison)
116	Dominican Rep	311	INTERPOL(Maddison)
117	Jordan	283	INTERPOL(Maddison)
118	Israel	266	INTERPOL(Maddison)
119	Cyprus	264	PROXY(Greece(Maddison))
120	Namibia	226	INTERPOL(Maddison)
121	Lesotho	219	INTERPOL(Maddison)
122	Montenegro	218	INTERPOL(Maddison)
123	Panama	201	INTERPOL(Maddison)
124	Botswana	194	INTERPOL(Maddison)
125	Costa Rica	177	INTERPOL(Maddison)
126	Hong Kong	162	INTERPOL(Maddison)
127	Trinidad/ Tobago	160	INTERPOL(Maddison)
128	Singapore	115	INTERPOL(Maddison)
129	Kuwait	87	INTERPOL(Maddison)
130	Swaziland	81	INTERPOL(Maddison)
131	Bahrain	66	INTERPOL(Maddison)
132	UAE	43	INTERPOL(Maddison)
133	Qatar	15	INTERPOL(Maddison)

TABLE 1.9 - POPULATION IN THOUSANDS, YEAR 1890

OBS	COUNTRY	POP	SOURCE
1	China	380,000	1890(Maddison)
2	India	233,315	INTERPOL(Ind./wh. India(Maddison))
3	US	63,302	1890(Maddison)
4	Russia	62,779	PROXY(40(E)/USSR(Maddison))
5	Germany	47,607	1890(Maddison)
6	Japan	40,077	1890(Maddison)
7	France	40,014	1890(Maddison)
8	Indonesia	37,579	1890(Maddison)
9	UK	35,001	PROXY(UK & Ireland(Maddison))
10	Italy	31,702	1890(Maddison)
11	Bangladesh	28,210	INTERPOL(Ban./wh. India(Maddison))
12	Ukraine	23,572	PROXY(40(E)/USSR(Maddison))
13	Poland	22,854	1890(Maddison)
14	Pakistan	18,078	INTERPOL(Pak./wh. India(Maddison))
15	Spain	17,757	1890(Maddison)
16	Brazil	14,199	1890(Maddison)
17	Vietnam	13,969	INTERPOL(Maddison)
18	Turkey	13,189	INTERPOL(Maddison)
19	Mexico	11,729	1890(Maddison)

OBS	COUNTRY	POP	SOURCE
20	Romania	10,373	1890(Maddison)
21	Korea, South	9,848	1890(Maddison)
22	Iran	9,529	INTERPOL(Maddison)
23	Egypt	8,777	1890(Mitchell)
24	Ethiopia	8,306	INTERPOL(Maddison)
25	Czechia	8,107	PROXY(Czechoslovakia(Maddison))
26	Burma	7,489	1890(Maddison)
27	Thailand	6,670	1890(Maddison)
28	Hungary	6,622	1890(Maddison)
29	Sudan	6,554	INTERPOL(Maddison)
30	Philippines	6,476	1890(Maddison)
31	Belgium	6,096	1890(Maddison)
32	Austria	5,394	1890(Maddison)
33	Nepal	5,192	1890(Maddison)
34	Belarus	5,158	PROXY(40(E)/USSR(Maddison))
35	Portugal	5,028	1890(Maddison)
36	Canada	4,918	1890(Maddison)
37	Afghanistan	4,857	INTERPOL(Maddison)
38	Sweden	4,780	1890(Maddison)
39	Korea, North	4,697	INTERPOL(Maddison)
40	Algeria	4,548	INTERPOL(Maddison)
41	Netherlands	4,535	1890(Maddison)
42	Greece	4,482	1890(Maddison)
43	Morocco	4,347	INTERPOL(Maddison)
44	South Africa	3,839	INTERPOL(Maddison)
45	Mozambique	3,775	INTERPOL(Maddison)
46	Uzbekistan	3,735	PROXY(40(E)/USSR(Maddison))
47	Kazakhstan	3,506	PROXY(40(E)/USSR(Maddison))
48	Serbia	3,489	PROXY(Yugoslavia(Maddison))
49	Bulgaria	3,445	1890(Maddison)
50	Argentina	3,376	1890(Maddison)
51	Colombia	3,369	1890(Maddison)
52	Ireland	3,357	PROXY(whole Ireland(Maddison))
53	Peru	3,346	1890(Maddison)
54	Sri Lanka	3,343	1890(Maddison)
55	Slovakia	3,145	PROXY(Czechoslovakia(Maddison))
56	Australia	3,107	1890(Maddison)
57	Yemen	3,039	INTERPOL(Maddison)
58	Switzerland	2,951	1890(Maddison)
59	Madagascar	2,766	INTERPOL(Maddison)
60	Cambodia	2,655	INTERPOL(Maddison)
61	Chile	2,651	1890(Maddison)
62	Taiwan	2,500	1890(Maddison)
63	Saudi Arabia	2,490	INTERPOL(Maddison)
64	Finland	2,364	1890(Maddison)
65	Denmark	2,294	1890(Maddison)
66	Croatia	2,281	PROXY(Yugoslavia(Maddison))
67	Venezuela	2,224	1890(Maddison)
68	Georgia	2,060	PROXY(40(E)/USSR(Maddison))
69	Norway	1,997	1890(Maddison)
70	Iraq	1,997	INTERPOL(Maddison)
71	Azerbaijan	1,867	PROXY(40(E)/USSR(Maddison))

TABLE 1.9 - POPULATION IN THOUSANDS, YEAR 1890

TABLE 1.9 - POPULATION IN THOUSANDS, YEAR 1890

OBS	COUNTRY	POP	SOURCE
72	Syria	1,762	INTERPOL(Maddison)
73	Lithuania	1,668	PROXY(40(E)/USSR(Maddison))
74	Ghana	1,643	INTERPOL(Maddison)
75	Guinea	1,628	INTERPOL(Maddison)
76	Bolivia	1,626	INTERPOL(Maddison)
77	Burundi	1,601	INTERPOL(Maddison)
78	Malaysia	1,585	1890(Maddison)
79	Bosnia	1,582	PROXY(Yugoslavia(Maddison))
80	Somalia	1,553	INTERPOL(Maddison)
81	Cuba	1,541	INTERPOL(Maddison)
82	Tunisia	1,459	INTERPOL(Maddison)
83	Haiti	1,409	INTERPOL(Maddison)
84	Moldova	1,407	PROXY(40(E)/USSR(Maddison))
85	Ecuador	1,257	INTERPOL(Maddison)
86	Zimbabwe	1,237	INTERPOL(Maddison)
87	Guatemala	1,222	INTERPOL(Maddison)
88	Malawi	1,221	INTERPOL(Maddison)
89	Sierra Leone	1,208	INTERPOL(Maddison)
90	Zambia	1,107	INTERPOL(Maddison)
91	Latvia	1,075	PROXY(40(E)/USSR(Maddison))
92	Laos	1,002	INTERPOL(Maddison)
93	Slovenia	872	PROXY(Yugoslavia(Maddison))
94	Kyrgyzstan	871	PROXY(40(E)/USSR(Maddison))
95	Tajikistan	870	PROXY(40(E)/USSR(Maddison))
96	Puerto Rico	840	INTERPOL(Maddison)
97	Armenia	753	PROXY(40(E)/USSR(Maddison))
98	Turkmenistan	742	PROXY(40(E)/USSR(Maddison))
99	Macedonia	731	PROXY(Yugoslavia(Maddison))
100	Albania	726	1890(Maddison)
101	Libya	717	INTERPOL(Madd/Mitchell)
102	Mongolia	694	INTERPOL(Maddison)
103	Uruguay	686	1890(Maddison)
104	New Zealand	665	1890(Maddison)
105	El Salvador	661	INTERPOL(Maddison)
106	Jamaica	637	INTERPOL(Maddison)
107	Estonia	601	PROXY(40(E)/USSR(Maddison))
108	Eritrea	577	INTERPOL(Maddison)
109	Lebanon	550	INTERPOL(Maddison)
110	Honduras	466	INTERPOL(Maddison)
111	Kosovo	454	PROXY(Yugoslavia(Maddison))
112	Nicaragua	425	INTERPOL(Maddison)
113	Paraguay	420	INTERPOL(Maddison)
114	Oman	401	INTERPOL(Maddison)
115	Dominican Rep	400	INTERPOL(Maddison)
116	Guinea-Bissau	356	INTERPOL(Maddison)
117	Jordan	301	INTERPOL(Maddison)
118	Israel	298	INTERPOL(Maddison)
119	Cyprus	293	PROXY(Greece(Maddison))
120	Lesotho	260	INTERPOL(Maddison)
121	Namibia	252	INTERPOL(Maddison)
122	Montenegro	236	PROXY(Yugoslavia(Maddison))
123	Panama	230	INTERPOL(Maddison)

| OBS	COUNTRY	POP	SOURCE
| 124	Costa Rica	229	INTERPOL(Maddison)
| 125	Botswana	217	INTERPOL(Maddison)
| 126	Hong Kong	214	1890(Maddison)
| 127	Trinidad/ Tobago	207	INTERPOL(Maddison)
| 128	Singapore	157	1890(Maddison)
| 129	Swaziland	97	INTERPOL(Maddison)
| 130	Kuwait	92	INTERPOL(Maddison)
| 131	Bahrain	70	INTERPOL(Maddison)
| 132	UAE	46	INTERPOL(Maddison)
| 133	Qatar	16	INTERPOL(Maddison)

TABLE 1.9 - POPULATION IN THOUSANDS, YEAR 1890

TABLE 1.10 - POPULATION IN THOUSANDS, YEAR 1900

OBS	COUNTRY	POP	SOURCE
1	China	400,000	1900(Maddison)
2	India	236,772	INTERPOL(Ind./wh. India(Maddison))
3	US	76,391	1900(Maddison)
4	Russia	70,628	PROXY(40(E)/USSR(Maddison))
5	Germany	54,388	1900(Maddison)
6	Japan	44,103	1900(Maddison)
7	Indonesia	42,746	1900(Maddison)
8	France	40,598	1900(Maddison)
9	UK	38,428	PROXY(UK & Ireland(Maddison))
10	Italy	33,672	1900(Maddison)
11	Bangladesh	29,164	INTERPOL(Ban./wh. India(Maddison))
12	Ukraine	26,520	PROXY(40(E)/USSR(Maddison))
13	Poland	24,750	1900(Maddison)
14	Spain	18,566	1900(Maddison)
15	Pakistan	18,544	INTERPOL(Pak./wh. India(Maddison))
16	Brazil	17,984	1900(Maddison)
17	Vietnam	16,091	INTERPOL(Maddison)
18	Turkey	13,948	INTERPOL(Maddison)
19	Mexico	13,607	1900(Maddison)
20	Romania	11,000	1900(Maddison)
21	Egypt	10,186	1900(Mitchell)
22	Burma	10,174	1900(Maddison)
23	Iran	10,140	INTERPOL(Maddison)
24	Korea, South	9,896	1900(Maddison)
25	Ethiopia	9,630	INTERPOL(Maddison)
26	Czechia	8,747	PROXY(Czechoslovakia(Maddison))
27	Philippines	7,324	1900(Maddison)
28	Thailand	7,320	1900(Maddison)
29	Hungary	7,127	1900(Maddison)
30	Sudan	6,783	INTERPOL(Maddison)
31	Belgium	6,719	1900(Maddison)
32	Austria	5,973	1900(Maddison)
33	Belarus	5,803	PROXY(40(E)/USSR(Maddison))
34	Canada	5,457	1900(Maddison)
35	Portugal	5,404	1900(Maddison)

TABLE 1.10 - POPULATION IN THOUSANDS, YEAR 1900

OBS	COUNTRY	POP	SOURCE
36	Nepal	5,283	1900(Maddison)
37	Afghanistan	5,219	INTERPOL(Maddison)
38	Netherlands	5,142	1900(Maddison)
39	Sweden	5,117	1900(Maddison)
40	Greece	4,962	1900(Maddison)
41	Algeria	4,946	INTERPOL(Maddison)
42	Korea, North	4,777	INTERPOL(Maddison)
43	South Africa	4,713	INTERPOL(Maddison)
44	Argentina	4,693	1900(Maddison)
45	Morocco	4,664	INTERPOL(Maddison)
46	Uzbekistan	4,202	PROXY(40(E)/USSR(Maddison))
47	Mozambique	4,106	INTERPOL(Maddison)
48	Serbia	4,024	PROXY(Yugoslavia(Maddison))
49	Bulgaria	4,000	1900(Maddison)
50	Colombia	3,998	1900(Maddison)
51	Kazakhstan	3,944	PROXY(40(E)/USSR(Maddison))
52	Sri Lanka	3,912	1900(Maddison)
53	Peru	3,791	1900(Maddison)
54	Australia	3,741	1900(Maddison)
55	Slovakia	3,394	PROXY(Czechoslovakia(Maddison))
56	Switzerland	3,300	1900(Maddison)
57	Ireland	3,180	PROXY(whole Ireland(Maddison))
58	Yemen	3,143	INTERPOL(Maddison)
59	Chile	2,974	1900(Maddison)
60	Madagascar	2,969	INTERPOL(Maddison)
61	Taiwan	2,864	1900(Maddison)
62	Cambodia	2,828	INTERPOL(Maddison)
63	Finland	2,646	1900(Maddison)
64	Croatia	2,631	PROXY(Yugoslavia(Maddison))
65	Saudi Arabia	2,569	INTERPOL(Maddison)
66	Denmark	2,561	1900(Maddison)
67	Venezuela	2,542	1900(Maddison)
68	Georgia	2,317	PROXY(40(E)/USSR(Maddison))
69	Iraq	2,244	INTERPOL(Maddison)
70	Malaysia	2,232	1900(Maddison)
71	Norway	2,230	1900(Maddison)
72	Azerbaijan	2,100	PROXY(40(E)/USSR(Maddison))
73	Lithuania	1,876	PROXY(40(E)/USSR(Maddison))
74	Syria	1,859	INTERPOL(Maddison)
75	Bosnia	1,824	PROXY(Yugoslavia(Maddison))
76	Ghana	1,784	INTERPOL(Maddison)
77	Guinea	1,762	INTERPOL(Maddison)
78	Burundi	1,708	INTERPOL(Maddison)
79	Bolivia	1,696	1900(Maddison)
80	Cuba	1,658	1900(Maddison)
81	Somalia	1,653	INTERPOL(Maddison)
82	Tunisia	1,625	INTERPOL(Maddison)
83	Moldova	1,583	PROXY(40(E)/USSR(Maddison))
84	Haiti	1,560	1900(Maddison)
85	Zimbabwe	1,422	INTERPOL(Maddison)
86	Malawi	1,404	INTERPOL(Maddison)
87	Ecuador	1,400	1900(Maddison)

TABLE 1.10 - POPULATION IN THOUSANDS, YEAR 1900

OBS	COUNTRY	POP	SOURCE
88	Sierra Leone	1,308	INTERPOL(Maddison)
89	Guatemala	1,300	1900(Maddison)
90	Zambia	1,272	INTERPOL(Maddison)
91	Latvia	1,210	PROXY(40(E)/USSR(Maddison))
92	Laos	1,154	INTERPOL(Maddison)
93	Slovenia	1,006	PROXY(Yugoslavia(Maddison))
94	Kyrgyzstan	980	PROXY(40(E)/USSR(Maddison))
95	Tajikistan	978	PROXY(40(E)/USSR(Maddison))
96	Puerto Rico	959	1900(Maddison)
97	Uruguay	915	1900(Maddison)
98	Armenia	847	PROXY(40(E)/USSR(Maddison))
99	Macedonia	843	PROXY(Yugoslavia(Maddison))
100	Turkmenistan	835	PROXY(40(E)/USSR(Maddison))
101	New Zealand	807	1900(Maddison)
102	Albania	800	1900(Maddison)
103	El Salvador	766	1900(Maddison)
104	Libya	747	INTERPOL(Madd/Mitchell)
105	Jamaica	720	1900(Maddison)
106	Mongolia	707	INTERPOL(Maddison)
107	Estonia	676	PROXY(40(E)/USSR(Maddison))
108	Eritrea	669	INTERPOL(Maddison)
109	Lebanon	591	INTERPOL(Maddison)
110	Kosovo	524	PROXY(Yugoslavia(Maddison))
111	Dominican Rep	515	1900(Maddison)
112	Honduras	500	1900(Maddison)
113	Nicaragua	478	1900(Maddison)
114	Paraguay	440	1900(Maddison)
115	Oman	419	INTERPOL(Maddison)
116	Guinea-Bissau	386	INTERPOL(Maddison)
117	Israel	334	INTERPOL(Maddison)
118	Cyprus	324	PROXY(Greece(Maddison))
119	Jordan	321	INTERPOL(Maddison)
120	Lesotho	309	INTERPOL(Maddison)
121	Hong Kong	306	1900(Maddison)
122	Costa Rica	297	1900(Maddison)
123	Namibia	282	INTERPOL(Maddison)
124	Montenegro	272	PROXY(Yugoslavia(Maddison))
125	Trinidad/ Tobago	268	1900(Maddison)
126	Panama	263	1900(Maddison)
127	Botswana	241	INTERPOL(Maddison)
128	Singapore	215	1900(Maddison)
129	Swaziland	115	INTERPOL(Maddison)
130	Kuwait	97	INTERPOL(Maddison)
131	Bahrain	74	INTERPOL(Maddison)
132	UAE	48	INTERPOL(Maddison)
133	Qatar	17	INTERPOL(Maddison)

TABLE 1.11 - POPULATION IN THOUSANDS, YEAR 1913

OBS	COUNTRY	POP	SOURCE
1	China	437,140	1913(Maddison)
2	India	251,906	1913(Maddison)
3	US	97,606	1913(Maddison)
4	Russia	88,606	PROXY(40(E)/USSR(Maddison))
5	Germany	65,058	1913(Maddison)
6	Japan	51,672	1913(Maddison)
7	Indonesia	49,934	1913(Maddison)
8	UK	42,624	PROXY(UK & Ireland(Maddison))
9	France	41,463	1913(Maddison)
10	Italy	37,248	1913(Maddison)
11	Ukraine	33,270	PROXY(40(E)/USSR(Maddison))
12	Bangladesh	31,786	1913(Maddison)
13	Poland	26,710	1913(Maddison)
14	Brazil	23,660	1913(Maddison)
15	Spain	20,263	1913(Maddison)
16	Pakistan	20,008	1913(Maddison)
17	Vietnam	19,339	1913(Maddison)
18	Turkey	15,000	1913(Maddison)
19	Mexico	14,970	1913(Maddison)
20	Romania	12,527	1913(Maddison)
21	Burma	12,326	1913(Maddison)
22	Egypt	12,186	1913(Mitchell)
23	Ethiopia	11,671	INTERPOL(Maddison)
24	Iran	10,994	1913(Maddison)
25	Korea, South	10,589	1913(Maddison)
26	Czechia	9,542	PROXY(Czechoslovakia(Maddison))
27	Philippines	9,384	1913(Maddison)
28	Thailand	8,689	1913(Maddison)
29	Canada	7,852	1913(Maddison)
30	Hungary	7,840	1913(Maddison)
31	Belgium	7,666	1913(Maddison)
32	Argentina	7,653	1913(Maddison)
33	Belarus	7,280	PROXY(40(E)/USSR(Maddison))
34	Sudan	7,092	INTERPOL(Maddison)
35	Austria	6,767	1913(Maddison)
36	Netherlands	6,164	1913(Maddison)
37	South Africa	6,153	1913(Maddison)
38	Portugal	5,972	1913(Maddison)
39	Afghanistan	5,730	1913(Maddison)
40	Nepal	5,639	1913(Maddison)
41	Sweden	5,621	1913(Maddison)
42	Algeria	5,497	1913(Maddison)
43	Greece	5,425	1913(Maddison)
44	Uzbekistan	5,272	PROXY(40(E)/USSR(Maddison))
45	Colombia	5,195	1913(Maddison)
46	Morocco	5,111	1913(Maddison)
47	Kazakhstan	4,948	PROXY(40(E)/USSR(Maddison))
48	Korea, North	4,897	1913(Maddison)
49	Serbia	4,894	PROXY(Yugoslavia(Maddison))
50	Australia	4,821	1913(Maddison)
51	Sri Lanka	4,811	1913(Maddison)
52	Bulgaria	4,720	1913(Maddison)

OBS	COUNTRY	POP	SOURCE

TABLE 1.11 - POPULATION IN THOUSANDS, YEAR 1913

OBS	COUNTRY	POP	SOURCE
53	Mozambique	4,580	INTERPOL(Maddison)
54	Peru	4,339	1913(Maddison)
55	Switzerland	3,864	1913(Maddison)
56	Slovakia	3,702	PROXY(Czechoslovakia(Maddison))
57	Taiwan	3,469	1913(Maddison)
58	Chile	3,431	1913(Maddison)
59	Yemen	3,284	1913(Maddison)
60	Madagascar	3,256	INTERPOL(Maddison)
61	Croatia	3,199	PROXY(Yugoslavia(Maddison))
62	Ireland	3,092	PROXY(whole Ireland(Maddison))
63	Malaysia	3,084	1913(Maddison)
64	Cambodia	3,070	1913(Maddison)
65	Finland	3,027	1913(Maddison)
66	Denmark	2,983	1913(Maddison)
67	Georgia	2,907	PROXY(40(E)/USSR(Maddison))
68	Venezuela	2,874	1913(Maddison)
69	Saudi Arabia	2,676	1913(Maddison)
70	Azerbaijan	2,635	PROXY(40(E)/USSR(Maddison))
71	Iraq	2,613	1913(Maddison)
72	Norway	2,447	1913(Maddison)
73	Cuba	2,431	1913(Maddison)
74	Lithuania	2,354	PROXY(40(E)/USSR(Maddison))
75	Bosnia	2,219	PROXY(Yugoslavia(Maddison))
76	Ghana	2,043	1913(Maddison)
77	Syria	1,994	1913(Maddison)
78	Moldova	1,986	PROXY(40(E)/USSR(Maddison))
79	Guinea	1,953	INTERPOL(Maddison)
80	Haiti	1,891	1913(Maddison)
81	Bolivia	1,881	1913(Maddison)
82	Tunisia	1,870	1913(Maddison)
83	Burundi	1,858	INTERPOL(Maddison)
84	Somalia	1,794	INTERPOL(Maddison)
85	Zimbabwe	1,704	INTERPOL(Maddison)
86	Ecuador	1,689	1913(Maddison)
87	Malawi	1,683	INTERPOL(Maddison)
88	Zambia	1,525	INTERPOL(Maddison)
89	Latvia	1,518	PROXY(40(E)/USSR(Maddison))
90	Guatemala	1,486	1913(Maddison)
91	Sierra Leone	1,450	INTERPOL(Maddison)
92	Laos	1,387	1913(Maddison)
93	Kyrgyzstan	1,230	PROXY(40(E)/USSR(Maddison))
94	Tajikistan	1,227	PROXY(40(E)/USSR(Maddison))
95	Slovenia	1,223	PROXY(Yugoslavia(Maddison))
96	Puerto Rico	1,181	1913(Maddison)
97	Uruguay	1,177	1913(Maddison)
98	New Zealand	1,122	1913(Maddison)
99	Armenia	1,062	PROXY(40(E)/USSR(Maddison))
100	Turkmenistan	1,048	PROXY(40(E)/USSR(Maddison))
101	Macedonia	1,026	PROXY(Yugoslavia(Maddison))
102	El Salvador	1,008	1913(Maddison)
103	Albania	898	1913(Maddison)
104	Estonia	848	PROXY(40(E)/USSR(Maddison))

TABLE 1.11 - POPULATION IN THOUSANDS, YEAR 1913

OBS	COUNTRY	POP	SOURCE
105	Jamaica	837	1913(Maddison)
106	Eritrea	811	INTERPOL(Maddison)
107	Libya	788	INTERPOL(Madd/Mitchell)
108	Dominican Rep	750	1913(Maddison)
109	Mongolia	725	1913(Maddison)
110	Honduras	660	1913(Maddison)
111	Lebanon	649	1913(Maddison)
112	Kosovo	637	PROXY(Yugoslavia(Maddison))
113	Paraguay	594	1913(Maddison)
114	Nicaragua	578	1913(Maddison)
115	Hong Kong	487	1913(Maddison)
116	Oman	444	1913(Maddison)
117	Guinea-Bissau	427	INTERPOL(Maddison)
118	Israel	387	PROXY(Palestine(Maddison))
119	Lesotho	387	INTERPOL(Maddison)
120	Costa Rica	372	1913(Maddison)
121	Cyprus	354	PROXY(Greece(Maddison))
122	Trinidad/ Tobago	352	1913(Maddison)
123	Jordan	348	1913(Maddison)
124	Panama	348	1913(Maddison)
125	Montenegro	331	PROXY(Yugoslavia(Maddison))
126	Namibia	324	INTERPOL(Maddison)
127	Singapore	323	1913(Maddison)
128	Botswana	278	INTERPOL(Maddison)
129	Swaziland	144	INTERPOL(Maddison)
130	Kuwait	105	PROXY(Gulf Coast(Maddison))
131	Bahrain	79	PROXY(Gulf Coast(Maddison))
132	UAE	52	PROXY(Gulf Coast(Maddison))
133	Qatar	18	PROXY(Gulf Coast(Maddison))

TABLE 1.12 - POPULATION IN THOUSANDS, YEAR 1920

OBS	COUNTRY	POP	SOURCE
1	China	472,000	1920(Maddison)
2	India	253,309	INTERPOL(Ind./wh. India(Maddison))
3	US	106,881	1920(Maddison)
4	Russia	87,707	PROXY(40(E)/USSR(Maddison))
5	Germany	60,894	1920(Maddison)
6	Japan	55,818	1920(Maddison)
7	Indonesia	53,723	1920(Maddison)
8	UK	43,718	1920(Maddison)
9	France	39,000	1920(Maddison)
10	Italy	37,398	1920(Maddison)
11	Ukraine	32,933	PROXY(40(E)/USSR(Maddison))
12	Bangladesh	32,161	INTERPOL(Ban./wh. India(Maddison))
13	Brazil	27,404	1920(Maddison)
14	Poland	23,968	1920(Maddison)
15	Spain	21,232	1920(Maddison)
16	Vietnam	20,652	INTERPOL(Maddison)

OBS	COUNTRY	POP	SOURCE
\multicolumn{4}{c}{TABLE 1.12 - POPULATION IN THOUSANDS, YEAR 1920}

OBS	COUNTRY	POP	SOURCE
17	Pakistan	20,477	INTERPOL(Pak./wh. India(Maddison))
18	Mexico	14,900	1920(Maddison)
19	Turkey	13,877	1923(Maddison)
20	Egypt	13,222	1920(Mitchell)
21	Burma	13,096	1920(Maddison)
22	Ethiopia	12,945	INTERPOL(Maddison)
23	Romania	12,340	1920(Maddison)
24	Iran	11,927	INTERPOL(Maddison)
25	Korea, South	11,804	1920(Maddison)
26	Philippines	10,725	1920(Maddison)
27	Thailand	9,802	1920(Maddison)
28	Czechia	9,350	PROXY(Czechoslovakia(Maddison))
29	Argentina	8,861	1920(Maddison)
30	Canada	8,798	1920(Maddison)
31	Hungary	7,950	1920(Maddison)
32	Belgium	7,552	1920(Maddison)
33	Sudan	7,264	INTERPOL(Maddison)
34	Belarus	7,206	PROXY(40(E)/USSR(Maddison))
35	South Africa	7,157	INTERPOL(Maddison)
36	Netherlands	6,848	1920(Maddison)
37	Austria	6,455	1920(Maddison)
38	Colombia	6,213	1920(Maddison)
39	Afghanistan	6,125	INTERPOL(Maddison)
40	Nepal	6,113	INTERPOL(Maddison)
41	Portugal	6,029	1920(Maddison)
42	Sweden	5,876	1920(Maddison)
43	Algeria	5,785	1920(Maddison)
44	Greece	5,700	1920(Maddison)
45	Morocco	5,683	INTERPOL(Maddison)
46	Korea, North	5,577	INTERPOL(Maddison)
47	Australia	5,358	1920(Maddison)
48	Sri Lanka	5,250	1920(Maddison)
49	Uzbekistan	5,219	PROXY(40(E)/USSR(Maddison))
50	Bulgaria	5,072	1920(Maddison)
51	Kazakhstan	4,898	PROXY(40(E)/USSR(Maddison))
52	Mozambique	4,857	INTERPOL(Maddison)
53	Peru	4,667	1920(Maddison)
54	Serbia	4,473	PROXY(Yugoslavia(Maddison))
55	Switzerland	3,877	1920(Maddison)
56	Chile	3,827	1920(Maddison)
57	Taiwan	3,736	1920(Maddison)
58	Slovakia	3,628	PROXY(Czechoslovakia(Maddison))
59	Malaysia	3,545	1920(Maddison)
60	Yemen	3,525	INTERPOL(Maddison)
61	Madagascar	3,422	INTERPOL(Maddison)
62	Cambodia	3,296	INTERPOL(Maddison)
63	Denmark	3,242	1920(Maddison)
64	Finland	3,133	1920(Maddison)
65	Ireland	3,103	1920(Maddison)
66	Cuba	2,997	1920(Maddison)
67	Venezuela	2,992	1920(Maddison)
68	Iraq	2,991	INTERPOL(Maddison)

TABLE 1.12 - POPULATION IN THOUSANDS, YEAR 1920

OBS	COUNTRY	POP	SOURCE
69	Croatia	2,924	PROXY(Yugoslavia(Maddison))
70	Georgia	2,877	PROXY(40(E)/USSR(Maddison))
71	Saudi Arabia	2,768	INTERPOL(Maddison)
72	Norway	2,625	1920(Maddison)
73	Azerbaijan	2,608	PROXY(40(E)/USSR(Maddison))
74	Ghana	2,447	INTERPOL(Maddison)
75	Lithuania	2,330	PROXY(40(E)/USSR(Maddison))
76	Syria	2,217	INTERPOL(Maddison)
77	Bolivia	2,136	1920(Maddison)
78	Haiti	2,124	1920(Maddison)
79	Tunisia	2,107	INTERPOL(Maddison)
80	Guinea	2,065	INTERPOL(Maddison)
81	Bosnia	2,028	PROXY(Yugoslavia(Maddison))
82	Moldova	1,966	PROXY(40(E)/USSR(Maddison))
83	Burundi	1,945	INTERPOL(Maddison)
84	Zimbabwe	1,879	INTERPOL(Maddison)
85	Somalia	1,875	INTERPOL(Maddison)
86	Malawi	1,855	INTERPOL(Maddison)
87	Ecuador	1,790	1920(Maddison)
88	Zambia	1,681	INTERPOL(Maddison)
89	Guatemala	1,597	1920(Maddison)
90	Sierra Leone	1,533	INTERPOL(Maddison)
91	Latvia	1,502	PROXY(40(E)/USSR(Maddison))
92	Laos	1,412	INTERPOL(Maddison)
93	Uruguay	1,371	1920(Maddison)
94	Puerto Rico	1,312	1920(Maddison)
95	New Zealand	1,241	1920(Maddison)
96	Kyrgyzstan	1,217	PROXY(40(E)/USSR(Maddison))
97	Tajikistan	1,215	PROXY(40(E)/USSR(Maddison))
98	El Salvador	1,170	1920(Maddison)
99	Slovenia	1,118	PROXY(Yugoslavia(Maddison))
100	Armenia	1,052	PROXY(40(E)/USSR(Maddison))
101	Turkmenistan	1,037	PROXY(40(E)/USSR(Maddison))
102	Macedonia	937	PROXY(Yugoslavia(Maddison))
103	Albania	932	1920(Maddison)
104	Eritrea	900	INTERPOL(Maddison)
105	Dominican Rep	879	1920(Maddison)
106	Jamaica	855	1920(Maddison)
107	Estonia	840	PROXY(40(E)/USSR(Maddison))
108	Libya	811	INTERPOL(Madd/Mitchell)
109	Lebanon	755	INTERPOL(Maddison)
110	Mongolia	729	INTERPOL(Maddison)
111	Honduras	720	1920(Maddison)
112	Paraguay	699	1920(Maddison)
113	Hong Kong	648	1920(Maddison)
114	Nicaragua	640	1920(Maddison)
115	Kosovo	582	PROXY(Yugoslavia(Maddison))
116	Panama	487	1920(Maddison)
117	Israel	486	INTERPOL(Maddison)
118	Guinea-Bissau	452	INTERPOL(Maddison)
119	Oman	446	INTERPOL(Maddison)
120	Lesotho	437	INTERPOL(Maddison)

TABLE 1.12 - POPULATION IN THOUSANDS, YEAR 1920

OBS	COUNTRY	POP	SOURCE
121	Costa Rica	420	1920(Maddison)
122	Singapore	391	1920(Maddison)
123	Trinidad/Tobago	389	1920(Maddison)
124	Cyprus	372	PROXY(Greece(Maddison))
125	Jordan	369	INTERPOL(Maddison)
126	Namibia	350	INTERPOL(Maddison)
127	Montenegro	303	PROXY(Yugoslavia(Maddison))
128	Botswana	300	INTERPOL(Maddison)
129	Swaziland	162	INTERPOL(Maddison)
130	Kuwait	111	INTERPOL(Maddison)
131	Bahrain	84	INTERPOL(Maddison)
132	UAE	55	INTERPOL(Maddison)
133	Qatar	19	INTERPOL(Maddison)

TABLE 1.13 - POPULATION IN THOUSANDS, YEAR 1929

OBS	COUNTRY	POP	SOURCE
1	China	487,273	1929(Maddison)
2	India	275,861	1929(Maddison)
3	US	122,245	1929(Maddison)
4	Russia	97,584	PROXY(40(E)/USSR(Maddison))
5	Germany	64,739	1929(Maddison)
6	Japan	63,244	1929(Maddison)
7	Indonesia	59,863	1929(Maddison)
8	UK	45,672	1929(Maddison)
9	France	41,230	1929(Maddison)
10	Italy	40,469	1929(Maddison)
11	Ukraine	36,641	PROXY(40(E)/USSR(Maddison))
12	Bangladesh	34,427	1929(Maddison)
13	Brazil	32,894	1929(Maddison)
14	Poland	27,856	1929(Maddison)
15	Spain	23,210	1929(Maddison)
16	Pakistan	22,812	1929(Maddison)
17	Vietnam	22,472	INTERPOL(Maddison)
18	Mexico	16,875	1929(Maddison)
19	Ethiopia	14,788	INTERPOL(Maddison)
20	Turkey	14,705	1929(Maddison)
21	Egypt	14,602	1929(Mitchell)
22	Burma	14,364	1929(Maddison)
23	Romania	13,952	1929(Maddison)
24	Korea, South	13,716	1929(Maddison)
25	Iran	13,245	INTERPOL(Maddison)
26	Philippines	12,890	1929(Maddison)
27	Thailand	12,058	1929(Maddison)
28	Argentina	11,592	1929(Maddison)
29	Canada	10,305	1929(Maddison)
30	Czechia	10,002	PROXY(Czechoslovakia(Maddison))
31	South Africa	8,693	INTERPOL(Maddison)
32	Hungary	8,583	1929(Maddison)

TABLE 1.13 - POPULATION IN THOUSANDS, YEAR 1929

OBS	COUNTRY	POP	SOURCE
33	Belgium	8,032	1929(Maddison)
34	Belarus	8,018	PROXY(40(E)/USSR(Maddison))
35	Colombia	7,821	1929(Maddison)
36	Netherlands	7,782	1929(Maddison)
37	Sudan	7,492	INTERPOL(Maddison)
38	Nepal	6,783	INTERPOL(Maddison)
39	Portugal	6,701	1929(Maddison)
40	Afghanistan	6,673	INTERPOL(Maddison)
41	Austria	6,664	1929(Maddison)
42	Korea, North	6,592	INTERPOL(Maddison)
43	Morocco	6,513	INTERPOL(Maddison)
44	Algeria	6,431	INTERPOL(Maddison)
45	Australia	6,396	1929(Maddison)
46	Greece	6,275	1929(Maddison)
47	Sweden	6,113	1929(Maddison)
48	Bulgaria	5,950	1929(Maddison)
49	Uzbekistan	5,806	PROXY(40(E)/USSR(Maddison))
50	Sri Lanka	5,669	1929(Maddison)
51	Kazakhstan	5,449	PROXY(40(E)/USSR(Maddison))
52	Peru	5,294	1929(Maddison)
53	Mozambique	5,239	INTERPOL(Maddison)
54	Serbia	5,111	PROXY(Yugoslavia(Maddison))
55	Taiwan	4,493	1929(Maddison)
56	Malaysia	4,316	1929(Maddison)
57	Chile	4,306	1929(Maddison)
58	Switzerland	4,022	1929(Maddison)
59	Slovakia	3,881	PROXY(Czechoslovakia(Maddison))
60	Yemen	3,862	INTERPOL(Maddison)
61	Cuba	3,742	1929(Maddison)
62	Madagascar	3,648	INTERPOL(Maddison)
63	Cambodia	3,612	INTERPOL(Maddison)
64	Iraq	3,559	INTERPOL(Maddison)
65	Denmark	3,518	1929(Maddison)
66	Finland	3,424	1929(Maddison)
67	Croatia	3,342	PROXY(Yugoslavia(Maddison))
68	Venezuela	3,259	1929(Maddison)
69	Georgia	3,201	PROXY(40(E)/USSR(Maddison))
70	Ghana	3,085	INTERPOL(Maddison)
71	Ireland	2,937	1929(Maddison)
72	Azerbaijan	2,902	PROXY(40(E)/USSR(Maddison))
73	Saudi Arabia	2,892	INTERPOL(Maddison)
74	Norway	2,795	1929(Maddison)
75	Lithuania	2,593	PROXY(40(E)/USSR(Maddison))
76	Syria	2,542	INTERPOL(Maddison)
77	Tunisia	2,457	INTERPOL(Maddison)
78	Haiti	2,390	1929(Maddison)
79	Bolivia	2,370	1929(Maddison)
80	Bosnia	2,317	PROXY(Yugoslavia(Maddison))
81	Guinea	2,217	INTERPOL(Maddison)
82	Moldova	2,187	PROXY(40(E)/USSR(Maddison))
83	Zimbabwe	2,130	INTERPOL(Maddison)
84	Malawi	2,103	INTERPOL(Maddison)

TABLE 1.13 - POPULATION IN THOUSANDS, YEAR 1929

OBS	COUNTRY	POP	SOURCE
85	Burundi	2,062	INTERPOL(Maddison)
86	Somalia	1,984	INTERPOL(Maddison)
87	Ecuador	1,928	1929(Maddison)
88	Zambia	1,906	INTERPOL(Maddison)
89	Guatemala	1,753	1929(Maddison)
90	Uruguay	1,685	1929(Maddison)
91	Latvia	1,672	PROXY(40(E)/USSR(Maddison))
92	Sierra Leone	1,646	INTERPOL(Maddison)
93	Puerto Rico	1,526	1929(Maddison)
94	New Zealand	1,471	1929(Maddison)
95	Laos	1,445	INTERPOL(Maddison)
96	El Salvador	1,410	1929(Maddison)
97	Kyrgyzstan	1,354	PROXY(40(E)/USSR(Maddison))
98	Tajikistan	1,352	PROXY(40(E)/USSR(Maddison))
99	Slovenia	1,278	PROXY(Yugoslavia(Maddison))
100	Dominican Rep	1,213	1929(Maddison)
101	Armenia	1,170	PROXY(40(E)/USSR(Maddison))
102	Turkmenistan	1,154	PROXY(40(E)/USSR(Maddison))
103	Macedonia	1,071	PROXY(Yugoslavia(Maddison))
104	Eritrea	1,028	INTERPOL(Maddison)
105	Jamaica	985	1929(Maddison)
106	Albania	977	1929(Maddison)
107	Estonia	934	PROXY(40(E)/USSR(Maddison))
108	Honduras	930	1929(Maddison)
109	Lebanon	917	INTERPOL(Maddison)
110	Paraguay	860	1929(Maddison)
111	Libya	841	INTERPOL(Madd/Mitchell)
112	Hong Kong	785	1929(Maddison)
113	Mongolia	734	INTERPOL(Maddison)
114	Nicaragua	680	1929(Maddison)
115	Kosovo	665	PROXY(Yugoslavia(Maddison))
116	Israel	650	INTERPOL(Maddison)
117	Singapore	575	1929(Maddison)
118	Lesotho	510	INTERPOL(Maddison)
119	Panama	506	1929(Maddison)
120	Costa Rica	490	1929(Maddison)
121	Guinea-Bissau	485	INTERPOL(Maddison)
122	Oman	449	INTERPOL(Maddison)
123	Cyprus	410	PROXY(Greece(Maddison))
124	Trinidad/Tobago	398	1929(Maddison)
125	Jordan	397	INTERPOL(Maddison)
126	Namibia	386	INTERPOL(Maddison)
127	Montenegro	346	PROXY(Yugoslavia(Maddison))
128	Botswana	331	INTERPOL(Maddison)
129	Swaziland	190	INTERPOL(Maddison)
130	Kuwait	120	INTERPOL(Maddison)
131	Bahrain	91	INTERPOL(Maddison)
132	UAE	60	INTERPOL(Maddison)
133	Qatar	21	INTERPOL(Maddison)

TABLE 1.14 - POPULATION IN THOUSANDS, YEAR 1938

OBS	COUNTRY	POP	SOURCE
1	China	513,336	1938(Maddison)
2	India	309,434	INTERPOL(Ind./wh. India(Maddison))
3	US	130,476	1938(Maddison)
4	Russia	106,933	PROXY(40(E)/USSR(Maddison))
5	Japan	71,879	1938(Maddison)
6	Germany	68,558	1938(Maddison)
7	Indonesia	68,131	1938(Maddison)
8	UK	47,494	1938(Maddison)
9	Italy	43,419	1938(Maddison)
10	France	41,960	1938(Maddison)
11	Ukraine	40,152	PROXY(40(E)/USSR(Maddison))
12	Bangladesh	39,934	INTERPOL(Ban./wh. India(Maddison))
13	Brazil	39,480	1938(Maddison)
14	Poland	31,062	1938(Maddison)
15	Pakistan	26,719	INTERPOL(Pak./wh. India(Maddison))
16	Spain	25,279	1938(Maddison)
17	Vietnam	24,452	INTERPOL(Maddison)
18	Mexico	19,705	1938(Maddison)
19	Turkey	17,016	1938(Maddison)
20	Ethiopia	16,894	INTERPOL(Maddison)
21	Egypt	16,295	1938(Mitchell)
22	Burma	16,145	1938(Maddison)
23	Philippines	15,934	1938(Maddison)
24	Romania	15,601	1938(Maddison)
25	Korea, South	15,381	1938(Maddison)
26	Thailand	14,980	1938(Maddison)
27	Iran	14,708	INTERPOL(Maddison)
28	Argentina	13,724	1938(Maddison)
29	Canada	11,452	1938(Maddison)
30	South Africa	10,559	INTERPOL(Maddison)
31	Czechia	10,520	PROXY(Czechoslovakia(Maddison))
32	Hungary	9,167	1938(Maddison)
33	Belarus	8,786	PROXY(40(E)/USSR(Maddison))
34	Colombia	8,702	1938(Maddison)
35	Netherlands	8,685	1938(Maddison)
36	Belgium	8,374	1938(Maddison)
37	Korea, North	7,791	INTERPOL(Maddison)
38	Sudan	7,727	INTERPOL(Maddison)
39	Nepal	7,525	INTERPOL(Maddison)
40	Portugal	7,488	1938(Maddison)
41	Morocco	7,465	INTERPOL(Maddison)
42	Algeria	7,326	INTERPOL(Maddison)
43	Afghanistan	7,271	INTERPOL(Maddison)
44	Greece	7,061	1938(Maddison)
45	Australia	6,904	1938(Maddison)
46	Austria	6,753	1938(Maddison)
47	Bulgaria	6,564	1938(Maddison)
48	Uzbekistan	6,363	PROXY(40(E)/USSR(Maddison))
49	Sweden	6,298	1938(Maddison)
50	Peru	6,093	1938(Maddison)
51	Sri Lanka	6,045	1938(Maddison)
52	Kazakhstan	5,971	PROXY(40(E)/USSR(Maddison))

TABLE 1.14 - POPULATION IN THOUSANDS, YEAR 1938

OBS	COUNTRY	POP	SOURCE
53	Serbia	5,792	PROXY(Yugoslavia(Maddison))
54	Taiwan	5,678	1938(Maddison)
55	Mozambique	5,650	INTERPOL(Maddison)
56	Malaysia	5,207	1938(Maddison)
57	Chile	4,915	1938(Maddison)
58	Cuba	4,428	1938(Maddison)
59	Iraq	4,235	INTERPOL(Maddison)
60	Yemen	4,230	INTERPOL(Maddison)
61	Switzerland	4,192	1938(Maddison)
62	Slovakia	4,082	PROXY(Czechoslovakia(Maddison))
63	Cambodia	3,958	INTERPOL(Maddison)
64	Ghana	3,889	INTERPOL(Maddison)
65	Madagascar	3,888	INTERPOL(Maddison)
66	Croatia	3,787	PROXY(Yugoslavia(Maddison))
67	Denmark	3,777	1938(Maddison)
68	Finland	3,656	1938(Maddison)
69	Venezuela	3,623	1938(Maddison)
70	Georgia	3,508	PROXY(40(E)/USSR(Maddison))
71	Azerbaijan	3,180	PROXY(40(E)/USSR(Maddison))
72	Saudi Arabia	3,020	INTERPOL(Maddison)
73	Ireland	2,937	1938(Maddison)
74	Norway	2,936	1938(Maddison)
75	Syria	2,913	INTERPOL(Maddison)
76	Tunisia	2,865	INTERPOL(Maddison)
77	Lithuania	2,841	PROXY(40(E)/USSR(Maddison))
78	Haiti	2,682	1938(Maddison)
79	Bolivia	2,629	1938(Maddison)
80	Bosnia	2,626	PROXY(Yugoslavia(Maddison))
81	Zimbabwe	2,414	INTERPOL(Maddison)
82	Moldova	2,397	PROXY(40(E)/USSR(Maddison))
83	Malawi	2,383	INTERPOL(Maddison)
84	Guinea	2,381	INTERPOL(Maddison)
85	Ecuador	2,355	1938(Maddison)
86	Burundi	2,186	INTERPOL(Maddison)
87	Zambia	2,160	INTERPOL(Maddison)
88	Guatemala	2,110	1938(Maddison)
89	Somalia	2,100	INTERPOL(Maddison)
90	Uruguay	1,952	1938(Maddison)
91	Latvia	1,832	PROXY(40(E)/USSR(Maddison))
92	Puerto Rico	1,810	1938(Maddison)
93	Sierra Leone	1,768	INTERPOL(Maddison)
94	New Zealand	1,604	1938(Maddison)
95	Dominican Rep	1,596	1938(Maddison)
96	El Salvador	1,590	1938(Maddison)
97	Kyrgyzstan	1,484	PROXY(40(E)/USSR(Maddison))
98	Tajikistan	1,481	PROXY(40(E)/USSR(Maddison))
99	Hong Kong	1,479	1938(Maddison)
100	Laos	1,478	INTERPOL(Maddison)
101	Slovenia	1,448	PROXY(Yugoslavia(Maddison))
102	Armenia	1,282	PROXY(40(E)/USSR(Maddison))
103	Turkmenistan	1,265	PROXY(40(E)/USSR(Maddison))
104	Macedonia	1,214	PROXY(Yugoslavia(Maddison))

TABLE 1.14 - POPULATION IN THOUSANDS, YEAR 1938

OBS	COUNTRY	POP	SOURCE
105	Eritrea	1,174	INTERPOL(Maddison)
106	Jamaica	1,163	1938(Maddison)
107	Lebanon	1,114	INTERPOL(Maddison)
108	Honduras	1,100	1938(Maddison)
109	Paraguay	1,061	1938(Maddison)
110	Albania	1,040	1938(Maddison)
111	Estonia	1,024	PROXY(40(E)/USSR(Maddison))
112	Libya	873	INTERPOL(Mitchell/E)
113	Israel	871	INTERPOL(Maddison)
114	Nicaragua	780	1938(Maddison)
115	Kosovo	754	PROXY(Yugoslavia(Maddison))
116	Mongolia	740	INTERPOL(Maddison)
117	Singapore	710	1938(Maddison)
118	Panama	640	1938(Maddison)
119	Lesotho	596	INTERPOL(Maddison)
120	Costa Rica	590	1938(Maddison)
121	Guinea-Bissau	521	INTERPOL(Maddison)
122	Cyprus	461	PROXY(Greece(Maddison))
123	Trinidad/Tobago	458	1938(Maddison)
124	Oman	452	INTERPOL(Maddison)
125	Jordan	428	INTERPOL(Maddison)
126	Namibia	426	INTERPOL(Maddison)
127	Montenegro	392	PROXY(Yugoslavia(Maddison))
128	Botswana	365	INTERPOL(Maddison)
129	Swaziland	222	INTERPOL(Maddison)
130	Kuwait	130	INTERPOL(Maddison)
131	Bahrain	99	INTERPOL(Maddison)
132	UAE	65	INTERPOL(Maddison)
133	Qatar	22	INTERPOL(Maddison)

TABLE 1.15 - POPULATION IN THOUSANDS, YEAR 1950

OBS	COUNTRY	POP	SOURCE
1	China	562,580	50(E)
2	India	369,880	50(E)
3	US	152,271	50(E)
4	Russia	101,937	50(E)
5	Japan	83,625	50(E)
6	Indonesia	79,538	50(E)
7	Germany	68,377	50(E)
8	Brazil	53,975	50(E)
9	UK	50,290	50(E)
10	Italy	47,104	50(E)
11	Bangladesh	45,646	50(E)
12	France	41,736	50(E)
13	Pakistan	39,448	50(E)
14	Ukraine	36,906	50(E)
15	Nigeria	33,960	50(E)
16	Spain	27,868	50(E)
17	Mexico	27,741	50(E)

OBS	COUNTRY	POP	SOURCE
	TABLE 1.15 - POPULATION IN THOUSANDS, YEAR 1950		
18	Vietnam	27,367	50(E)
19	Poland	24,824	50(E)
20	Turkey	21,122	50(E)
21	Thailand	20,607	50(E)
22	Egypt	20,461	50(E)
23	Ethiopia	20,175	50(E)
24	Philippines	19,996	50(E)
25	Burma	19,488	50(E)
26	Korea, South	18,859	50(E)
27	Argentina	17,150	50(E)
28	Iran	16,913	50(E)
29	Romania	16,311	50(E)
30	Canada	13,737	50(E)
31	South Africa	13,683	50(E)
32	Colombia	12,568	50(E)
33	Congo, Dem R	12,184	50(E)
34	Netherlands	10,090	50(E)
35	Korea, North	9,737	50(E)
36	Hungary	9,338	50(E)
37	Morocco	8,953	50(E)
38	Czechia	8,925	50(E)
39	Algeria	8,753	50(E)
40	Nepal	8,643	50(E)
41	Belgium	8,639	50(E)
42	Portugal	8,443	50(E)
43	Australia	8,219	50(E)
44	Afghanistan	8,151	50(E)
45	Sudan	8,051	50(E)
46	Tanzania	7,935	50(E)
47	Belarus	7,745	50(E)
48	Peru	7,632	50(E)
49	Taiwan	7,619	50(E)
50	Greece	7,566	50(E)
51	Sri Lanka	7,544	50(E)
52	Bulgaria	7,251	50(E)
53	Sweden	7,014	50(E)
54	Austria	6,935	50(E)
55	Kazakhstan	6,693	50(E)
56	Uzbekistan	6,314	50(E)
57	Mozambique	6,250	50(E)
58	Kenya	6,121	50(E)
59	Malaysia	6,110	50(E)
60	Chile	6,082	50(E)
61	Cuba	5,920	50(E)
62	Serbia	5,869	50(E)
63	Uganda	5,522	50(E)
64	Iraq	5,340	50(E)
65	Ghana	5,297	50(E)
66	Venezuela	5,009	50(E)
67	Cameroon	4,888	50(E)
68	Yemen	4,777	50(E)
69	Switzerland	4,694	50(E)

TABLE 1.15 - POPULATION IN THOUSANDS, YEAR 1950

OBS	COUNTRY	POP	SOURCE
70	Cambodia	4,471	50(E)
71	Burkina Faso	4,376	50(E)
72	Denmark	4,271	50(E)
73	Madagascar	4,234	50(E)
74	Angola	4,118	50(E)
75	Finland	4,009	50(E)
76	Croatia	3,837	50(E)
77	Mali	3,688	50(E)
78	Georgia	3,527	50(E)
79	Tunisia	3,517	50(E)
80	Syria	3,495	50(E)
81	Slovakia	3,463	50(E)
82	Ecuador	3,387	50(E)
83	Norway	3,265	50(E)
84	Haiti	3,221	50(E)
85	Saudi Arabia	3,201	50(E)
86	Guatemala	2,969	50(E)
87	Ireland	2,969	50(E)
88	Azerbaijan	2,885	50(E)
89	Zimbabwe	2,853	50(E)
90	Malawi	2,817	50(E)
91	Bolivia	2,714	50(E)
92	Bosnia	2,661	50(E)
93	Senegal	2,654	50(E)
94	Guinea	2,619	50(E)
95	Chad	2,608	50(E)
96	Lithuania	2,553	50(E)
97	Zambia	2,553	50(E)
98	Ivory Coast	2,505	50(E)
99	Burundi	2,363	50(E)
100	Dominican Rep	2,353	50(E)
101	Moldova	2,341	50(E)
102	Somalia	2,264	50(E)
103	Uruguay	2,239	50(E)
104	Hong Kong	2,237	50(E)
105	Puerto Rico	2,218	50(E)
106	Niger	2,208	50(E)
107	Rwanda	2,162	50(E)
108	El Salvador	1,951	50(E)
109	Latvia	1,949	50(E)
110	Sierra Leone	1,944	50(E)
111	New Zealand	1,909	50(E)
112	Papua New Gu	1,798	50(E)
113	Kyrgyzstan	1,740	50(E)
114	Benin	1,673	50(E)
115	Tajikistan	1,532	50(E)
116	Laos	1,524	50(E)
117	Paraguay	1,473	50(E)
118	Slovenia	1,467	50(E)
119	Lebanon	1,443	50(E)
120	Honduras	1,431	50(E)
121	Jamaica	1,403	50(E)

OBS	COUNTRY	POP	SOURCE
TABLE 1.15 - POPULATION IN THOUSANDS, YEAR 1950

OBS	COUNTRY	POP	SOURCE
122	Eritrea	1,402	50(E)
123	Armenia	1,354	50(E)
124	Togo	1,329	50(E)
125	Central African Rep.	1,314	50(E)
126	Nicaragua	1,295	50(E)
127	Israel	1,258	50(E)
128	Macedonia	1,230	50(E)
129	Albania	1,215	50(E)
130	Turkmenistan	1,204	50(E)
131	Estonia	1,096	50(E)
132	Libya	1,029	50(E)
133	Singapore	1,022	50(E)
134	Costa Rica	862	50(E)
135	Panama	860	50(E)
136	Liberia	824	50(E)
137	Congo, Rep	808	50(E)
138	West Bank	772	50(W Bank/Gaza(Maddison)- Gaza(E))
139	Kosovo	764	50(E)
140	Mongolia	747	50(E)
141	Lesotho	734	50(E)
142	Mauritania	692	50(E)
143	Trinidad/Tobago	668	50(E)
144	Guinea-Bissau	573	50(E)
145	Cyprus	494	50(E)
146	Namibia	485	50(E)
147	Mauritius	479	50(E)
148	Jordan	472	50(E)
149	Gabon	469	50(E)
150	Oman	456	50(E)
151	East Timor	433	50(E)
152	Guyana	423	50(E)
153	Botswana	416	50(E)
154	Montenegro	397	50(E)
155	Malta	312	50(E)
156	Luxembourg	296	50(E)
157	Gambia	294	50(E)
158	Fiji	289	50(E)
159	Swaziland	273	50(E)
160	Gaza Strip	245	50(E)
161	Reunion	244	50(E)
162	Equatorial G	226	50(E)
163	Martinique	222	50(E)
164	Suriname	215	50(E)
165	Barbados	211	50(E)
166	Guadeloupe	208	50(Maddison)
167	Macao	205	50(E)
168	Bhutan	168	50(E)
169	Comoros	148	50(E)
170	Cape Verde	146	50(E)
171	Kuwait	145	50(E)
172	Iceland	143	50(E)
173	Neth Antilles	112	50(E)

OBS	COUNTRY	POP	SOURCE

TABLE 1.15 - POPULATION IN THOUSANDS, YEAR 1950

OBS	COUNTRY	POP	SOURCE
174	Bahrain	110	50(E)
175	Solomon Is	90	50(E)
176	St Lucia	83	50(E)
177	Samoa, W	82	50(E)
178	Bahamas	79	50(E)
179	Maldives	79	50(E)
180	Grenada	76	50(E)
181	UAE	72	50(E)
182	Belize	68	50(E)
183	St Vincent	67	50(E)
184	New Caledonia	65	50(E)
185	Fr Polynesia	62	50(E)
186	Djibouti	60	50(E)
187	Guam	60	50(E)
188	San Tome & Principe	60	50(E)
189	Jersey	57	50(E)
190	Isle of Man	55	50(E)
191	Aruba	51	50(E)
192	Dominica	51	50(E)
193	Tonga	50	50(E)
194	St Kitts & Nevis	49	50(E)
195	Vanuatu	48	50(E)
196	Antigua & Barbuda	46	50(E)
197	Brunei	45	50(E)
198	Guernsey	44	50(E)
199	Bermuda	39	50(E)
200	Seychelles	34	50(E)
201	Kiribati	33	50(E)
202	Micronesia	32	50(E)
203	Faeroe Is	31	50(E)
204	Guiana, Fr	27	50(E)
205	Virgin I, US	27	50(E)
206	Qatar	25	50(E)
207	Gibraltar	23	50(E)
208	Greenland	23	50(E)
209	Samoa, Ameri	19	50(E)
210	Monaco	18	50(E)
211	Mayotte	17	50(E)
212	Liechtenstein	14	50(E)
213	W Sahara	14	50(E)
214	San Marino	13	50(E)
215	Marshall Is	11	50(E)
216	Palau	7	50(E)
217	St Helena	7	PROXY(Falkland Islands(E))
218	Cook Is	7	PROXY(14 Pacific is(Maddison))
219	Andorra	6	50(E)
220	Cayman Is	6	50(E)
221	N Mariana Is	6	50(E)
222	Montserrat	6	PROXY(8 Caribbean cs(Maddison))
223	Virgin Is, Brit.	6	PROXY(8 Caribbean cs(Maddison))
224	Wallis & Futuna	5	PROXY(14 Pacific is(Maddison))
225	Tuvalu	5	50(E)

	TABLE 1.15 - POPULATION IN THOUSANDS, YEAR 1950		
OBS	COUNTRY	POP	SOURCE
226	Turks & Caicos	5	PROXY(8 Caribbean cs(Maddison))
227	Anguilla	3	PROXY(8 Caribbean cs(Maddison))
228	Nauru	3	50(E)
229	St Pierre &	3	PROXY(8 Caribbean cs(Maddison))
230	Falkland Is	2	50(E)
231	Niue	1	PROXY(14 Pacific is(Maddison))
232	Tokelau	1	PROXY(14 Pacific is(Maddison))

	TABLE 1.16 - POPULATION IN THOUSANDS, YEAR 1960		
OBS	COUNTRY	POP	SOURCE
1	China	650,661	60(E)
2	India	445,393	60(E)
3	US	180,671	60(E)
4	Russia	119,632	60(E)
5	Indonesia	95,931	60(E)
6	Japan	94,096	60(E)
7	Brazil	72,742	60(E)
8	Germany	72,674	60(E)
9	Bangladesh	54,622	60(E)
10	UK	52,372	60(E)
11	Pakistan	50,387	60(E)
12	Italy	50,200	60(E)
13	France	45,684	60(E)
14	Ukraine	42,783	60(E)
15	Nigeria	42,356	60(E)
16	Mexico	37,877	60(E)
17	Vietnam	33,648	60(E)
18	Spain	30,303	60(E)
19	Poland	29,561	60(E)
20	Turkey	28,217	60(E)
21	Thailand	27,652	60(E)
22	Philippines	27,054	60(E)
23	Egypt	26,085	60(E)
24	Korea, South	25,012	60(E)
25	Ethiopia	24,169	60(E)
26	Burma	22,839	60(E)
27	Iran	21,704	60(E)
28	Argentina	20,616	60(E)
29	Romania	18,407	60(E)
30	Canada	17,909	60(E)
31	South Africa	17,396	60(E)
32	Colombia	16,841	60(E)
33	Congo, Dem R	15,451	60(E)
34	Morocco	11,626	60(E)
35	Netherlands	11,494	60(E)
36	Korea, North	10,946	60(E)
37	Algeria	10,800	60(E)
38	Taiwan	10,668	60(E)

39	Sudan	10,589	60(E)
40	Australia	10,315	60(E)
41	Tanzania	10,260	60(E)
42	Nepal	10,070	60(E)
43	Hungary	9,984	60(E)
44	Kazakhstan	9,982	60(E)
45	Peru	9,931	60(E)
46	Sri Lanka	9,896	60(E)
47	Afghanistan	9,616	60(E)
48	Czechia	9,539	60(E)
49	Belgium	9,153	60(E)
50	Portugal	9,037	60(E)
51	Uzbekistan	8,559	60(E)
52	Greece	8,327	60(E)
53	Belarus	8,190	60(E)
54	Kenya	8,157	60(E)
55	Malaysia	8,140	60(E)
56	Bulgaria	7,867	60(E)
57	Chile	7,643	60(E)
58	Venezuela	7,556	60(E)
59	Sweden	7,480	60(E)
60	Mozambique	7,472	60(E)
61	Iraq	7,332	60(E)
62	Uganda	7,262	60(E)
63	Cuba	7,141	60(E)
64	Austria	7,047	60(E)
65	Ghana	6,958	60(E)
66	Serbia	6,610	60(E)
67	Yemen	5,872	60(E)
68	Cambodia	5,761	60(E)
69	Cameroon	5,609	60(E)
70	Madagascar	5,371	60(E)
71	Switzerland	5,362	60(E)
72	Burkina Faso	4,866	60(E)
73	Angola	4,797	60(E)
74	Denmark	4,581	60(E)
75	Syria	4,533	60(E)
76	Mali	4,495	60(E)
77	Ecuador	4,439	60(E)
78	Finland	4,430	60(E)
79	Georgia	4,159	60(E)
80	Tunisia	4,149	60(E)
81	Slovakia	4,145	60(E)
82	Guatemala	4,100	60(E)
83	Saudi Arabia	4,075	60(E)
84	Croatia	4,036	60(E)
85	Zimbabwe	4,011	60(E)
86	Azerbaijan	3,882	60(E)
87	Haiti	3,869	60(E)
88	Norway	3,581	60(E)
89	Ivory Coast	3,557	60(E)
90	Malawi	3,450	60(E)
91	Bolivia	3,351	60(E)
92	Senegal	3,270	60(E)
93	Zambia	3,254	60(E)
94	Dominican Rep	3,231	60(E)

95	Bosnia	3,180	60(E)
96	Guinea	3,118	60(E)
97	Hong Kong	3,075	60(E)
98	Niger	3,053	60(E)
99	Chad	3,042	60(E)
100	Moldova	3,004	60(E)
101	Rwanda	2,887	60(E)
102	Ireland	2,834	60(E)
103	Somalia	2,819	60(E)
104	Burundi	2,815	60(E)
105	Lithuania	2,765	60(E)
106	El Salvador	2,578	60(E)
107	Uruguay	2,538	60(E)
108	New Zealand	2,377	60(E)
109	Puerto Rico	2,358	60(E)
110	Sierra Leone	2,256	60(E)
111	Kyrgyzstan	2,173	60(E)
112	Latvia	2,121	60(E)
113	Israel	2,114	60(E)
114	Tajikistan	2,082	60(E)
115	Papua New Gu	2,080	60(E)
116	Benin	2,055	60(E)
117	Laos	1,986	60(E)
118	Honduras	1,952	60(E)
119	Paraguay	1,907	60(E)
120	Lebanon	1,888	60(E)
121	Armenia	1,867	60(E)
122	Nicaragua	1,764	60(E)
123	Singapore	1,646	60(E)
124	Jamaica	1,629	60(E)
125	Eritrea	1,615	60(E)
126	Albania	1,611	60(E)
127	Turkmenistan	1,585	60(E)
128	Slovenia	1,580	60(E)
129	Togo	1,572	60(E)
130	Central African Rep.	1,530	60(E)
131	Macedonia	1,392	60(E)
132	Libya	1,349	60(E)
133	Costa Rica	1,236	60(E)
134	Estonia	1,211	60(E)
135	Panama	1,126	60(E)
136	Liberia	1,052	60(E)
137	Congo, Rep	1,003	60(E)
138	Kosovo	944	60(E)
139	Mongolia	931	60(E)
140	Jordan	896	60(E)
141	Mauritania	892	60(E)
142	Lesotho	851	60(E)
143	Trinidad/Tobago	828	60(E)
144	West Bank	805	60(W Bank/Gaza(Maddison) - Gaza(E))
145	Mauritius	662	60(E)
146	Guinea-Bissau	617	60(E)
147	Namibia	599	60(E)
148	Cyprus	573	60(E)
149	Guyana	569	60(E)
150	Oman	565	60(E)

151	Botswana	532	60(E)
152	East Timor	501	60(E)
153	Gabon	486	60(E)
154	Montenegro	467	60(E)
155	Fiji	394	60(E)
156	Gambia	360	60(E)
157	Swaziland	353	60(E)
158	Reunion	338	60(E)
159	Malta	329	60(E)
160	Luxembourg	314	60(E)
161	Gaza Strip	308	60(E)
162	Kuwait	292	60(E)
163	Suriname	290	60(E)
164	Martinique	282	60(E)
165	Guadeloupe	266	60(E)
166	Equatorial G	254	60(E)
167	Barbados	231	60(E)
168	Bhutan	224	60(E)
169	Cape Verde	196	60(E)
170	Macao	186	60(E)
171	Comoros	183	60(E)
172	Iceland	176	60(E)
173	Bahrain	149	60(E)
174	Neth Antilles	136	60(E)
175	Solomon Is	118	60(E)
176	Bahamas	110	60(E)
177	Samoa, W	110	60(E)
178	UAE	103	60(E)
179	Maldives	92	60(E)
180	Belize	90	60(E)
181	Grenada	90	60(E)
182	St Lucia	90	60(E)
183	Fr Polynesia	84	60(E)
184	Brunei	83	60(E)
185	St Vincent	81	60(E)
186	Djibouti	78	60(E)
187	New Caledonia	78	60(E)
188	Guam	67	60(E)
189	Tonga	65	60(E)
190	San Tome & Principe	64	60(E)
191	Vanuatu	64	60(E)
192	Jersey	63	60(E)
193	Dominica	60	60(E)
194	Aruba	57	60(E)
195	Antigua & Barbuda	55	60(E)
196	St Kitts & Nevis	51	60(E)
197	Isle of Man	49	60(E)
198	Guernsey	45	60(E)
199	Micronesia	45	60(E)
200	Qatar	45	60(E)
201	Bermuda	44	60(E)
202	Seychelles	42	60(E)
203	Kiribati	41	60(E)
204	Faeroe Is	35	60(E)
205	Guiana, Fr	33	60(E)
206	W Sahara	33	60(E)

207	Greenland	32	60(E)
208	Virgin I, US	32	60(E)
209	Mayotte	25	60(E)
210	Gibraltar	24	60(E)
211	Monaco	21	60(E)
212	Samoa, Ameri	20	60(E)
213	Liechtenstein	16	60(E)
214	Marshall Is	15	60(E)
215	San Marino	15	60(E)
216	N Mariana Is	9	60(E)
217	Palau	9	60(E)
218	Cook Is	9	INTERPOL(14 Pacific is(Maddison))
219	Andorra	8	60(E)
220	Cayman Is	8	60(E)
221	Montserrat	7	INTERPOL(8 Caribbean cs(Maddison))
222	Virgin Is, Brit.	7	INTERPOL(8 Caribbean cs(Maddison))
223	Wallis & Futuna	7	INTERPOL(14 Pacific is(Maddison))
224	St Helena	7	PROXY(Falkland Islands(E))
225	Turks & Caicos	6	INTERPOL(8 Caribbean cs(Maddison))
226	Tuvalu	5	60(E)
227	Anguilla	4	INTERPOL(8 Caribbean cs(Maddison))
228	Nauru	4	60(E)
229	St Pierre &	4	INTERPOL(8 Caribbean cs(Maddison))
230	Falkland Is	2	60(E)
231	Niue	1	INTERPOL(14 Pacific is(Maddison))
232	Tokelau	1	INTERPOL(14 Pacific is(Maddison))

TABLE 1.17 - POPULATION IN THOUSANDS, YEAR 1970

OBS	COUNTRY	POP	SOURCE
1	China	820,403	70(E)
2	India	553,889	70(E)
3	US	204,879	70(E)
4	Russia	130,245	70(E)
5	Indonesia	120,532	70(E)
6	Japan	104,331	70(E)
7	Brazil	95,989	70(E)
8	Germany	77,709	70(E)
9	Bangladesh	67,403	70(E)
10	Pakistan	65,706	70(E)
11	UK	55,632	70(E)
12	Italy	53,822	70(E)
13	Nigeria	53,764	70(E)
14	Mexico	52,028	70(E)
15	France	50,770	70(E)
16	Ukraine	47,317	70(E)
17	Vietnam	42,898	70(E)
18	Thailand	37,247	70(E)
19	Philippines	36,551	70(E)
20	Turkey	35,758	70(E)
21	Spain	33,779	70(E)
22	Egypt	33,329	70(E)
23	Poland	32,526	70(E)

24	Korea, South	32,241	70(E)
25	Ethiopia	29,469	70(E)
26	Iran	28,805	70(E)
27	Burma	27,393	70(E)
28	Argentina	23,962	70(E)
29	South Africa	22,657	70(E)
30	Colombia	22,500	70(E)
31	Canada	21,717	70(E)
32	Congo, Dem R	20,598	70(E)
33	Romania	20,253	70(E)
34	Morocco	15,310	70(E)
35	Taiwan	14,583	70(E)
36	Korea, North	14,247	70(E)
37	Tanzania	13,807	70(E)
38	Sudan	13,788	70(E)
39	Algeria	13,746	70(E)
40	Peru	13,193	70(E)
41	Kazakhstan	13,106	70(E)
42	Netherlands	13,020	70(E)
43	Australia	12,552	70(E)
44	Sri Lanka	12,514	70(E)
45	Nepal	12,155	70(E)
46	Uzbekistan	11,973	70(E)
47	Afghanistan	11,840	70(E)
48	Kenya	11,247	70(E)
49	Malaysia	10,853	70(E)
50	Venezuela	10,758	70(E)
51	Hungary	10,337	70(E)
52	Iraq	10,112	70(E)
53	Czechia	9,805	70(E)
54	Uganda	9,743	70(E)
55	Belgium	9,690	70(E)
56	Chile	9,570	70(E)
57	Mozambique	9,304	70(E)
58	Portugal	9,044	70(E)
59	Belarus	9,040	70(E)
60	Greece	8,793	70(E)
61	Ghana	8,789	70(E)
62	Cuba	8,710	70(E)
63	Bulgaria	8,490	70(E)
64	Sweden	8,042	70(E)
65	Austria	7,467	70(E)
66	Cambodia	7,395	70(E)
67	Serbia	7,153	70(E)
68	Yemen	7,098	70(E)
69	Madagascar	6,930	70(E)
70	Cameroon	6,727	70(E)
71	Syria	6,258	70(E)
72	Switzerland	6,187	70(E)
73	Ecuador	5,970	70(E)
74	Saudi Arabia	5,745	70(E)
75	Angola	5,606	70(E)
76	Mali	5,546	70(E)
77	Zimbabwe	5,515	70(E)
78	Ivory Coast	5,310	70(E)
79	Burkina Faso	5,304	70(E)

80	Guatemala	5,264	70(E)
81	Azerbaijan	5,169	70(E)
82	Tunisia	5,099	70(E)
83	Denmark	4,929	70(E)
84	Haiti	4,713	70(E)
85	Georgia	4,707	70(E)
86	Finland	4,606	70(E)
87	Slovakia	4,528	70(E)
88	Malawi	4,508	70(E)
89	Dominican Rep	4,423	70(E)
90	Senegal	4,318	70(E)
91	Zambia	4,252	70(E)
92	Niger	4,217	70(E)
93	Bolivia	4,212	70(E)
94	Croatia	4,205	70(E)
95	Hong Kong	3,959	70(E)
96	Norway	3,877	70(E)
97	Guinea	3,819	70(E)
98	Rwanda	3,776	70(E)
99	Chad	3,730	70(E)
100	Somalia	3,600	70(E)
101	El Salvador	3,598	70(E)
102	Moldova	3,595	70(E)
103	Bosnia	3,564	70(E)
104	Burundi	3,522	70(E)
105	Lithuania	3,138	70(E)
106	Kyrgyzstan	2,964	70(E)
107	Israel	2,958	70(E)
108	Ireland	2,954	70(E)
109	Tajikistan	2,942	70(E)
110	New Zealand	2,820	70(E)
111	Uruguay	2,808	70(E)
112	Honduras	2,761	70(E)
113	Puerto Rico	2,722	70(E)
114	Sierra Leone	2,697	70(E)
115	Benin	2,620	70(E)
116	Papua New Gu	2,554	70(E)
117	Laos	2,551	70(E)
118	Armenia	2,518	70(E)
119	Paraguay	2,484	70(E)
120	Lebanon	2,443	70(E)
121	Nicaragua	2,395	70(E)
122	Latvia	2,359	70(E)
123	Turkmenistan	2,181	70(E)
124	Eritrea	2,160	70(E)
125	Togo	2,138	70(E)
126	Albania	2,136	70(E)
127	Singapore	2,075	70(E)
128	Libya	1,994	70(E)
129	Central African Rep.	1,871	70(E)
130	Jamaica	1,869	70(E)
131	Costa Rica	1,758	70(E)
132	Slovenia	1,727	70(E)
133	Jordan	1,623	70(E)
134	Macedonia	1,568	70(E)
135	Panama	1,506	70(E)

136	Liberia	1,387	70(E)
137	Estonia	1,360	70(E)
138	Congo, Rep	1,323	70(E)
139	Mongolia	1,248	70(E)
140	Kosovo	1,220	70(E)
141	Mauritania	1,150	70(E)
142	Lesotho	1,033	70(E)
143	Trinidad/Tobago	941	70(E)
144	Mauritius	829	70(E)
145	Namibia	772	70(E)
146	Kuwait	748	70(E)
147	Oman	747	70(E)
148	Guyana	709	70(E)
149	Botswana	701	70(E)
150	Guinea-Bissau	620	70(E)
151	Cyprus	615	70(E)
152	West Bank	608	70(E)
153	East Timor	604	70(E)
154	Gabon	529	70(E)
155	Fiji	520	70(E)
156	Montenegro	520	70(E)
157	Gambia	482	70(E)
158	Swaziland	454	70(E)
159	Reunion	447	70(E)
160	Suriname	372	70(E)
161	Gaza Strip	370	70(E)
162	Luxembourg	339	70(E)
163	Malta	326	70(E)
164	Martinique	325	70(E)
165	Guadeloupe	310	70(E)
166	Bhutan	298	70(E)
167	Equatorial G	294	70(E)
168	Cape Verde	267	70(E)
169	Macao	261	70(E)
170	UAE	249	70(E)
171	Barbados	239	70(E)
172	Comoros	236	70(E)
173	Bahrain	210	70(E)
174	Iceland	204	70(E)
175	Bahamas	170	70(E)
176	Neth Antilles	163	70(E)
177	Solomon Is	161	70(E)
178	Djibouti	158	70(E)
179	Samoa, W	142	70(E)
180	Brunei	128	70(E)
181	Belize	120	70(E)
182	Fr Polynesia	117	70(E)
183	Maldives	115	70(E)
184	Qatar	111	70(E)
185	New Caledonia	105	70(E)
186	St Lucia	104	70(E)
187	Grenada	95	70(E)
188	St Vincent	90	70(E)
189	Vanuatu	86	70(E)
190	Guam	85	70(E)
191	Tonga	80	70(E)

192	W Sahara	77	70(E)
193	San Tome & Principe	74	70(E)
194	Jersey	71	70(E)
195	Dominica	70	70(E)
196	Antigua & Barbuda	66	70(E)
197	Virgin I, US	63	70(E)
198	Aruba	61	70(E)
199	Micronesia	61	70(E)
200	Seychelles	54	70(E)
201	Bermuda	53	70(E)
202	Isle of Man	52	70(E)
203	Guernsey	51	70(E)
204	Guiana, Fr	49	70(E)
205	Kiribati	49	70(E)
206	Greenland	46	70(E)
207	St Kitts & Nevis	46	70(E)
208	Faeroe Is	39	70(E)
209	Mayotte	35	70(E)
210	Samoa, Ameri	27	70(E)
211	Gibraltar	26	70(E)
212	Monaco	24	70(E)
213	Marshall Is	22	70(E)
214	Liechtenstein	21	70(E)
215	Andorra	20	70(E)
216	San Marino	19	70(E)
217	N Mariana Is	12	70(E)
218	Palau	12	70(E)
219	Cook Is	11	INTERPOL(14 Pacific is(Maddison))
220	Cayman Is	10	70(E)
221	Wallis & Futuna	9	INTERPOL(14 Pacific is(Maddison))
222	Montserrat	9	INTERPOL(8 Caribbean cs (Maddison)
223	Virgin Is, Brit.	9	INTERPOL(8 Caribbean cs (Maddison)
224	Turks & Caicos	7	INTERPOL(8 Caribbean cs(Maddison)
225	Nauru	7	70(E)
226	St Helena	7	PROXY(Falkland Islands(E))
227	Tuvalu	6	70(E)
228	Anguilla	5	INTERPOL(8 Caribbean cs(Maddison))
229	St Pierre &	5	INTERPOL(8 Caribbean cs (Maddison)
230	Falkland Is	2	70(E)
231	Niue	1	INTERPOL(14 Pacific is(Maddison))
232	Tokelau	1	INTERPOL(14 Pacific is(Maddison))

TABLE 1.18 - POPULATION IN THOUSANDS, YEAR 1980			
OBS	COUNTRY	POP	SOURCE
1	China	984,736	80(E)

2	India	684,888	80(E)
3	US	227,726	80(E)
4	Indonesia	151,108	80(E)
5	Russia	139,039	80(E)
6	Brazil	118,563	80(E)
7	Japan	116,807	80(E)
8	Bangladesh	88,077	80(E)
9	Pakistan	85,219	80(E)
10	Germany	78,275	80(E)
11	Nigeria	71,065	80(E)
12	Mexico	69,325	80(E)
13	Italy	56,434	80(E)
14	UK	56,330	80(E)
15	France	53,880	80(E)
16	Vietnam	53,005	80(E)
17	Ukraine	50,034	80(E)
18	Philippines	48,088	80(E)
19	Thailand	46,809	80(E)
20	Turkey	44,439	80(E)
21	Egypt	40,546	80(E)
22	Iran	39,330	80(E)
23	Korea, South	38,124	80(E)
24	Spain	37,636	80(E)
25	Ethiopia	36,036	80(E)
26	Poland	35,578	80(E)
27	Burma	33,061	80(E)
28	South Africa	29,140	80(E)
29	Colombia	28,356	80(E)
30	Argentina	28,094	80(E)
31	Congo, Dem R	28,071	80(E)
32	Canada	24,516	80(E)
33	Romania	22,201	80(E)
34	Morocco	19,567	80(E)
35	Sudan	19,064	80(E)
36	Algeria	18,811	80(E)
37	Tanzania	18,665	80(E)
38	Taiwan	17,642	80(E)
39	Peru	17,325	80(E)
40	Korea, North	17,239	80(E)
41	Kenya	16,331	80(E)
42	Uzbekistan	15,952	80(E)
43	Nepal	15,159	80(E)
44	Kazakhstan	14,967	80(E)
45	Venezuela	14,768	80(E)
46	Sri Lanka	14,747	80(E)
47	Australia	14,471	80(E)
48	Netherlands	14,150	80(E)
49	Iraq	14,093	80(E)
50	Afghanistan	13,946	80(E)
51	Malaysia	13,763	80(E)
52	Uganda	12,415	80(E)
53	Mozambique	12,103	80(E)
54	Chile	11,174	80(E)
55	Ghana	11,017	80(E)
56	Hungary	10,707	80(E)
57	Czechia	10,326	80(E)

58	Belgium	9,859	80(E)
59	Cuba	9,823	80(E)
60	Portugal	9,778	80(E)
61	Belarus	9,650	80(E)
62	Greece	9,643	80(E)
63	Saudi Arabia	9,320	80(E)
64	Yemen	9,133	80(E)
65	Madagascar	9,059	80(E)
66	Bulgaria	8,862	80(E)
67	Syria	8,774	80(E)
68	Cameroon	8,762	80(E)
69	Ivory Coast	8,344	80(E)
70	Sweden	8,310	80(E)
71	Ecuador	7,961	80(E)
72	Serbia	7,670	80(E)
73	Austria	7,549	80(E)
74	Zimbabwe	7,170	80(E)
75	Cambodia	6,869	80(E)
76	Mali	6,758	80(E)
77	Angola	6,743	80(E)
78	Guatemala	6,650	80(E)
79	Somalia	6,485	80(E)
80	Tunisia	6,443	80(E)
81	Switzerland	6,319	80(E)
82	Burkina Faso	6,315	80(E)
83	Malawi	6,259	80(E)
84	Azerbaijan	6,169	80(E)
85	Niger	5,784	80(E)
86	Senegal	5,776	80(E)
87	Zambia	5,700	80(E)
88	Dominican Rep	5,697	80(E)
89	Haiti	5,691	80(E)
90	Bolivia	5,355	80(E)
91	Rwanda	5,197	80(E)
92	Denmark	5,123	80(E)
93	Georgia	5,073	80(E)
94	Hong Kong	5,063	80(E)
95	Slovakia	4,976	80(E)
96	Finland	4,800	80(E)
97	El Salvador	4,586	80(E)
98	Guinea	4,575	80(E)
99	Chad	4,542	80(E)
100	Croatia	4,383	80(E)
101	Burundi	4,300	80(E)
102	Norway	4,086	80(E)
103	Moldova	4,010	80(E)
104	Tajikistan	3,953	80(E)
105	Bosnia	3,914	80(E)
106	Israel	3,862	80(E)
107	Kyrgyzstan	3,627	80(E)
108	Benin	3,444	80(E)
109	Lithuania	3,436	80(E)
110	Honduras	3,402	80(E)
111	Ireland	3,401	80(E)
112	Nicaragua	3,257	80(E)
113	Sierra Leone	3,236	80(E)

114	Puerto Rico	3,210	80(E)
115	Papua New Gu	3,199	80(E)
116	Paraguay	3,198	80(E)
117	New Zealand	3,144	80(E)
118	Laos	3,103	80(E)
119	Armenia	3,096	80(E)
120	Libya	3,063	80(E)
121	Uruguay	2,914	80(E)
122	Turkmenistan	2,875	80(E)
123	Lebanon	2,785	80(E)
124	Togo	2,784	80(E)
125	Albania	2,671	80(E)
126	Eritrea	2,569	80(E)
127	Latvia	2,512	80(E)
128	Singapore	2,414	80(E)
129	Central African Rep.	2,329	80(E)
130	Costa Rica	2,302	80(E)
131	Jordan	2,225	80(E)
132	Jamaica	2,133	80(E)
133	Panama	1,949	80(E)
134	Slovenia	1,901	80(E)
135	Liberia	1,868	80(E)
136	Congo, Rep	1,802	80(E)
137	Macedonia	1,795	80(E)
138	Mongolia	1,663	80(E)
139	Kosovo	1,555	80(E)
140	Mauritania	1,503	80(E)
141	Estonia	1,477	80(E)
142	Kuwait	1,358	80(E)
143	Lesotho	1,296	80(E)
144	Oman	1,187	80(E)
145	Trinidad/Tobago	1,082	80(E)
146	UAE	1,000	80(E)
147	Botswana	996	80(E)
148	Namibia	993	80(E)
149	Mauritius	966	80(E)
150	Guinea-Bissau	789	80(E)
151	Guyana	761	80(E)
152	West Bank	733	80(E)
153	Gabon	682	80(E)
154	Gambia	671	80(E)
155	Cyprus	658	80(E)
156	Fiji	634	80(E)
157	Swaziland	615	80(E)
158	East Timor	581	80(E)
159	Montenegro	579	80(E)
160	Reunion	507	80(E)
161	Gaza Strip	456	80(E)
162	Bhutan	423	80(E)
163	Luxembourg	364	80(E)
164	Malta	364	80(E)
165	Suriname	356	80(E)
166	Bahrain	334	80(E)
167	Comoros	334	80(E)
168	Martinique	326	80(E)
169	Guadeloupe	318	80(E)

170	Cape Verde	289	80(E)
171	Djibouti	279	80(E)
172	Macao	256	80(E)
173	Barbados	249	80(E)
174	Qatar	229	80(E)
175	Solomon Is	229	80(E)
176	Iceland	228	80(E)
177	Equatorial G	219	80(E)
178	Bahamas	210	80(E)
179	Brunei	185	80(E)
180	Neth Antilles	174	80(E)
181	Maldives	155	80(E)
182	Samoa, W	155	80(E)
183	Fr Polynesia	151	80(E)
184	W Sahara	150	80(E)
185	Belize	146	80(E)
186	New Caledonia	143	80(E)
187	St Lucia	118	80(E)
188	Vanuatu	117	80(E)
189	Guam	107	80(E)
190	St Vincent	100	80(E)
191	Virgin I, US	98	80(E)
192	San Tome & Principe	94	80(E)
193	Tonga	92	80(E)
194	Grenada	89	80(E)
195	Jersey	76	80(E)
196	Dominica	75	80(E)
197	Micronesia	73	80(E)
198	Antigua & Barbuda	69	80(E)
199	Guiana, Fr	68	80(E)
200	Isle of Man	64	80(E)
201	Seychelles	63	80(E)
202	Aruba	60	80(E)
203	Kiribati	58	80(E)
204	Bermuda	55	80(E)
205	Guernsey	53	80(E)
206	Mayotte	52	80(E)
207	Greenland	50	80(E)
208	St Kitts & Nevis	44	80(E)
209	Faeroe Is	43	80(E)
210	Andorra	34	80(E)
211	Samoa, Ameri	32	80(E)
212	Marshall Is	31	80(E)
213	Gibraltar	30	80(E)
214	Monaco	27	80(E)
215	Liechtenstein	26	80(E)
216	San Marino	21	80(E)
217	Cayman Is	17	80(E)
218	N Mariana Is	17	80(E)
219	Cook Is	14	INTERPOL(14 Pacific is(Maddison))
220	Palau	13	80(E)
221	Wallis & Futuna	12	INTERPOL(14 Pacific is(Maddison))
222	Montserrat	11	INTERPOL(8 Caribbean cs(Maddison)
223	Virgin Is, Brit.	11	INTERPOL(8 Caribbean cs (Maddison)
224	Turks & Caicos	8	INTERPOL(8 Caribbean cs (Maddison)
225	Nauru	8	80(E)

226	Tuvalu	8	80(E)
227	St Helena	7	PROXY(Falkland Islands(E))
228	Anguilla	6	INTERPOL(8 Caribbean cs(Maddison)
229	St Pierre &	6	INTERPOL(8 Caribbean cs(Maddison)
230	Falkland Is	2	80(E)
231	Niue	2	INTERPOL(14 Pacific is(Maddison))
232	Tokelau	1	INTERPOL(14 Pacific is(Maddison))

TABLE 1.19 - POPULATION IN THOUSANDS, YEAR 1990			
OBS	COUNTRY	POP	SOURCE
1	China	1,148,364	90(E)
2	India	838,159	90(E)
3	US	249,806	90(E)
4	Indonesia	182,847	90(E)
5	Russia	147,973	90(E)
6	Brazil	146,593	90(E)
7	Japan	123,537	90(E)
8	Bangladesh	109,897	90(E)
9	Pakistan	109,710	90(E)
10	Nigeria	94,454	90(E)
11	Mexico	84,002	90(E)
12	Germany	79,365	90(E)
13	Vietnam	66,173	90(E)
14	Philippines	61,226	90(E)
15	UK	57,237	90(E)
16	Italy	56,719	90(E)
17	France	56,699	90(E)
18	Turkey	56,098	90(E)
19	Thailand	54,291	90(E)
20	Iran	54,134	90(E)
21	Egypt	51,959	90(E)
22	Ukraine	51,892	90(E)
23	Ethiopia	48,197	90(E)
24	Korea, South	42,869	90(E)
25	Burma	39,243	90(E)
26	Spain	38,798	90(E)
27	Poland	38,031	90(E)
28	Congo, Dem R	37,942	90(E)
29	South Africa	37,450	90(E)
30	Colombia	34,875	90(E)
31	Argentina	32,581	90(E)
32	Canada	27,701	90(E)
33	Sudan	26,050	90(E)
34	Algeria	25,283	90(E)
35	Tanzania	25,214	90(E)
36	Morocco	24,808	90(E)
37	Kenya	23,354	90(E)
38	Romania	23,207	90(E)
39	Peru	21,762	90(E)
40	Uzbekistan	20,515	90(E)
41	Taiwan	20,279	90(E)
42	Korea, North	20,143	90(E)

43	Venezuela	19,325	90(E)
44	Nepal	19,114	90(E)
45	Iraq	18,515	90(E)
46	Malaysia	18,103	90(E)
47	Uganda	17,456	90(E)
48	Australia	17,065	90(E)
49	Kazakhstan	16,398	90(E)
50	Sri Lanka	16,267	90(E)
51	Ghana	15,414	90(E)
52	Saudi Arabia	15,187	90(E)
53	Netherlands	14,952	90(E)
54	Chile	13,179	90(E)
55	Ivory Coast	12,780	90(E)
56	Mozambique	12,667	90(E)
57	Afghanistan	12,659	90(E)
58	Syria	12,436	90(E)
59	Yemen	12,416	90(E)
60	Madagascar	12,033	90(E)
61	Cameroon	11,884	90(E)
62	Cuba	10,605	90(E)
63	Hungary	10,374	90(E)
64	Czechia	10,363	90(E)
65	Ecuador	10,272	90(E)
66	Belarus	10,186	90(E)
67	Greece	10,161	90(E)
68	Zimbabwe	10,153	90(E)
69	Belgium	9,967	90(E)
70	Portugal	9,923	90(E)
71	Malawi	9,536	90(E)
72	Cambodia	9,355	90(E)
73	Guatemala	8,966	90(E)
74	Bulgaria	8,718	90(E)
75	Sweden	8,559	90(E)
76	Burkina Faso	8,336	90(E)
77	Angola	8,297	90(E)
78	Tunisia	8,154	90(E)
79	Mali	8,085	90(E)
80	Zambia	7,978	90(E)
81	Senegal	7,846	90(E)
82	Serbia	7,834	90(E)
83	Niger	7,822	90(E)
84	Austria	7,678	90(E)
85	Rwanda	7,294	90(E)
86	Azerbaijan	7,200	90(E)
87	Haiti	7,110	90(E)
88	Dominican Rep	7,083	90(E)
89	Switzerland	6,834	90(E)
90	Somalia	6,717	90(E)
91	Bolivia	6,669	90(E)
92	Guinea	6,033	90(E)
93	Chad	6,023	90(E)
94	Hong Kong	5,688	90(E)
95	Burundi	5,505	90(E)
96	Georgia	5,439	90(E)
97	Tajikistan	5,303	90(E)
98	Slovakia	5,256	90(E)

99	Denmark	5,140	90(E)
100	El Salvador	5,110	90(E)
101	Finland	4,986	90(E)
102	Honduras	4,792	90(E)
103	Benin	4,676	90(E)
104	Israel	4,613	90(E)
105	Croatia	4,508	90(E)
106	Kyrgyzstan	4,395	90(E)
107	Moldova	4,389	90(E)
108	Libya	4,364	90(E)
109	Bosnia	4,308	90(E)
110	Paraguay	4,248	90(E)
111	Norway	4,241	90(E)
112	Nicaragua	4,141	90(E)
113	Papua New Gu	4,131	90(E)
114	Sierra Leone	4,087	90(E)
115	Laos	4,076	90(E)
116	Togo	3,961	90(E)
117	Lithuania	3,698	90(E)
118	Turkmenistan	3,659	90(E)
119	Armenia	3,545	90(E)
120	Puerto Rico	3,537	90(E)
121	Ireland	3,515	90(E)
122	New Zealand	3,452	90(E)
123	Albania	3,289	90(E)
124	Jordan	3,254	90(E)
125	Uruguay	3,106	90(E)
126	Singapore	3,047	90(E)
127	Costa Rica	3,032	90(E)
128	Cent. African Rep	3,008	90(E)
129	Eritrea	2,996	90(E)
130	Lebanon	2,974	90(E)
131	Latvia	2,713	90(E)
132	Congo, Rep	2,422	90(E)
133	Panama	2,411	90(E)
134	Jamaica	2,369	90(E)
135	Kuwait	2,141	90(E)
136	Liberia	2,137	90(E)
137	Mongolia	2,086	90(E)
138	Slovenia	1,998	90(E)
139	Mauritania	1,945	90(E)
140	Kosovo	1,930	90(E)
141	Macedonia	1,909	90(E)
142	Oman	1,843	90(E)
143	UAE	1,826	90(E)
144	Lesotho	1,601	90(E)
145	Estonia	1,569	90(E)
146	Namibia	1,417	90(E)
147	Botswana	1,367	90(E)
148	Trinidad/Tobago	1,235	90(E)
149	Mauritius	1,059	90(E)
150	West Bank	1,011	90(E)
151	Guinea-Bissau	996	90(E)
152	Gambia	962	90(E)
153	Gabon	918	90(E)
154	Swaziland	865	90(E)

155	Cyprus	751	90(E)
156	East Timor	740	90(E)
157	Guyana	731	90(E)
158	Fiji	724	90(E)
159	Gaza Strip	630	90(E)
160	Reunion	601	90(E)
161	Montenegro	591	90(E)
162	Bhutan	547	90(E)
163	Bahrain	503	90(E)
164	Qatar	467	90(E)
165	Comoros	433	90(E)
166	Suriname	402	90(E)
167	Luxembourg	382	90(E)
168	Djibouti	366	90(E)
169	Malta	360	90(E)
170	Martinique	360	90(E)
171	Cape Verde	355	90(E)
172	Guadeloupe	355	90(E)
173	Equatorial G	353	90(E)
174	Macao	352	90(E)
175	Solomon Is	314	90(E)
176	Barbados	271	90(E)
177	Brunei	258	90(E)
178	Bahamas	255	90(E)
179	Iceland	255	90(E)
180	W Sahara	221	90(E)
181	Maldives	215	90(E)
182	Fr Polynesia	197	90(E)
183	Belize	189	90(E)
184	Neth Antilles	188	90(E)
185	New Caledonia	171	90(E)
186	Samoa, W	161	90(E)
187	Vanuatu	149	90(E)
188	St Lucia	138	90(E)
189	Guam	134	90(E)
190	Guiana, Fr	116	90(E)
191	San Tome/Principe	115	90(E)
192	St Vincent	109	90(E)
193	Virgin I, US	102	90(E)
194	Micronesia	96	90(E)
195	Tonga	96	90(E)
196	Grenada	95	90(E)
197	Mayotte	89	90(E)
198	Jersey	84	90(E)
199	Dominica	73	90(E)
200	Kiribati	71	90(E)
201	Seychelles	70	90(E)
202	Isle of Man	69	90(E)
203	Antigua/Barbuda	63	90(E)
204	Aruba	63	90(E)
205	Guernsey	61	90(E)
206	Bermuda	59	90(E)
207	Greenland	56	90(E)
208	Andorra	53	90(E)
209	Faeroe Is	48	90(E)
210	Samoa, Ameri	47	90(E)

211	Marshall Is	44	90(E)
212	N Mariana Is	44	90(E)
213	St Kitts & Nevis	41	90(E)
214	Gibraltar	31	90(E)
215	Monaco	30	90(E)
216	Liechtenstein	29	90(E)
217	Cayman Is	26	90(E)
218	San Marino	23	90(E)
219	Cook Is	18	90(CIA)
220	Palau	15	90(E)
221	Wallis & Futuna	15	90(CIA)
222	Montserrat	12	90(CIA)
223	Virgin Is, Brit.	12	90(CIA)
224	Turks & Caicos	10	90(CIA)
225	Nauru	9	90(E)
226	Tuvalu	9	90(E)
227	Anguilla	7	CIA
228	St Helena	7	90(CIA)
229	St Pierre &	6	90(CIA)
230	Niue	2	90(CIA)
231	Falkland Is	2	90(E)
232	Tokelau	2	90(CIA)

TABLE 1.20 POPULATION IN THOUSANDS, YEAR 2000

OBS	COUNTRY	POP	SOURCE
1	China	1,268,853	00(E)
2	India	1,004,124	00(E)
3	US	282,430	00(E)
4	Indonesia	211,693	00(E)
5	Brazil	171,280	00(E)
6	Russia	146,710	00(E)
7	Pakistan	139,760	00(E)
8	Bangladesh	128,100	00(E)
9	Japan	126,861	00(E)
10	Nigeria	122,543	00(E)
11	Mexico	99,735	00(E)
12	Germany	82,203	00(E)
13	Vietnam	79,094	00(E)
14	Philippines	76,213	00(E)
15	Turkey	67,418	00(E)
16	Ethiopia	64,690	00(E)
17	Egypt	63,798	00(E)
18	Iran	63,696	00(E)
19	Thailand	60,666	00(E)
20	France	59,032	00(E)
21	UK	58,886	00(E)
22	Italy	57,645	00(E)
23	Congo, Dem R	50,689	00(E)
24	Ukraine	49,176	00(E)
25	Korea, South	47,008	00(E)
26	South Africa	44,510	00(E)
27	Burma	44,301	00(E)

28	Spain	40,264	00(E)
29	Colombia	40,044	00(E)
30	Poland	38,259	00(E)
31	Argentina	36,896	00(E)
32	Sudan	34,194	00(E)
33	Tanzania	33,712	00(E)
34	Canada	30,689	00(E)
35	Kenya	30,508	00(E)
36	Algeria	30,506	00(E)
37	Morocco	28,827	00(E)
38	Peru	25,663	00(E)
39	Iraq	25,052	00(E)
40	Uzbekistan	24,724	00(E)
41	Nepal	24,419	00(E)
42	Uganda	23,956	00(E)
43	Venezuela	23,493	00(E)
44	Malaysia	23,274	00(E)
45	Korea, North	22,946	00(E)
46	Taiwan	22,185	00(E)
47	Romania	22,072	00(E)
48	Afghanistan	20,737	00(E)
49	Saudi Arabia	20,474	00(E)
50	Ghana	19,736	00(E)
51	Australia	19,153	00(E)
52	Sri Lanka	18,467	00(E)
53	Mozambique	18,125	00(E)
54	Yemen	17,495	00(E)
55	Ivory Coast	17,049	00(E)
56	Madagascar	16,187	00(E)
57	Syria	16,106	00(E)
58	Netherlands	15,926	00(E)
59	Chile	15,398	00(E)
60	Cameroon	15,343	00(E)
61	Kazakhstan	14,884	00(E)
62	Ecuador	12,306	00(E)
63	Cambodia	12,251	00(E)
64	Zimbabwe	11,751	00(E)
65	Malawi	11,560	00(E)
66	Burkina Faso	11,309	00(E)
67	Cuba	11,142	00(E)
68	Niger	11,124	00(E)
69	Guatemala	11,085	00(E)
70	Greece	10,917	00(E)
71	Angola	10,377	00(E)
72	Senegal	10,332	00(E)
73	Czechia	10,273	00(E)
74	Belgium	10,251	00(E)
75	Portugal	10,239	00(E)
76	Hungary	10,211	00(E)
77	Zambia	10,205	00(E)
78	Mali	10,049	00(E)
79	Belarus	10,005	00(E)
80	Tunisia	9,564	00(E)
81	Sweden	8,872	00(E)
82	Haiti	8,573	00(E)
83	Dominican Rep	8,410	00(E)

84	Bolivia	8,317	00(E)
85	Chad	8,316	00(E)
86	Guinea	8,203	00(E)
87	Rwanda	8,176	00(E)
88	Austria	8,012	00(E)
89	Bulgaria	7,973	00(E)
90	Azerbaijan	7,809	00(E)
91	Serbia	7,661	00(E)
92	Switzerland	7,209	00(E)
93	Somalia	7,055	00(E)
94	Hong Kong	6,665	00(E)
95	Burundi	6,621	00(E)
96	Benin	6,426	00(E)
97	Honduras	6,348	00(E)
98	El Salvador	6,195	00(E)
99	Tajikistan	6,173	00(E)
100	Israel	6,098	00(E)
101	Togo	5,403	00(E)
102	Slovakia	5,401	00(E)
103	Papua New Gu	5,381	00(E)
104	Paraguay	5,349	00(E)
105	Denmark	5,337	00(E)
106	Laos	5,224	00(E)
107	Finland	5,176	00(E)
108	Libya	5,125	00(E)
109	Nicaragua	5,106	00(E)
110	Kyrgyzstan	4,946	00(E)
111	Jordan	4,799	00(E)
112	Georgia	4,654	00(E)
113	Sierra Leone	4,521	00(E)
114	Turkmenistan	4,520	00(E)
115	Norway	4,491	00(E)
116	Croatia	4,453	00(E)
117	Eritrea	4,357	00(E)
118	Moldova	4,145	00(E)
119	Singapore	4,028	00(E)
120	Costa Rica	3,881	00(E)
121	Central African Rep.	3,864	00(E)
122	New Zealand	3,850	00(E)
123	Puerto Rico	3,814	00(E)
124	Ireland	3,801	00(E)
125	Bosnia	3,781	00(E)
126	Lebanon	3,772	00(E)
127	Lithuania	3,500	00(E)
128	Uruguay	3,318	00(E)
129	UAE	3,219	00(E)
130	Congo, Rep	3,203	00(E)
131	Armenia	3,082	00(E)
132	Albania	3,080	00(E)
133	Liberia	3,071	00(E)
134	Panama	2,950	00(E)
135	Jamaica	2,589	00(E)
136	Mauritania	2,566	00(E)
137	Oman	2,402	00(E)
138	Mongolia	2,390	00(E)
139	Latvia	2,373	00(E)

140	Kuwait	2,236	00(E)
141	West Bank	2,202	00(E)
142	Macedonia	2,031	00(E)
143	Slovenia	1,990	00(E)
144	Kosovo	1,950	00(E)
145	Lesotho	1,886	00(E)
146	Namibia	1,879	00(E)
147	Botswana	1,729	00(E)
148	Gambia	1,384	00(E)
149	Estonia	1,370	00(E)
150	Guinea-Bissau	1,278	00(E)
151	Trinidad/Tobago	1,263	00(E)
152	Mauritius	1,187	00(E)
153	Gabon	1,182	00(E)
154	Gaza Strip	1,138	00(E)
155	Swaziland	1,058	00(E)
156	Cyprus	906	00(E)
157	East Timor	819	00(E)
158	Fiji	802	00(E)
159	Guyana	734	00(E)
160	Reunion	723	00(E)
161	Bahrain	629	00(E)
162	Qatar	617	00(E)
163	Montenegro	612	00(E)
164	Bhutan	559	00(E)
165	Comoros	539	00(E)
166	Suriname	465	00(E)
167	Equatorial G	449	00(E)
168	Luxembourg	436	00(E)
169	Cape Verde	435	00(E)
170	Djibouti	431	00(E)
171	Macao	431	00(E)
172	Solomon Is	415	00(E)
173	Guadeloupe	391	00(E)
174	Malta	390	00(E)
175	Martinique	385	00(E)
176	Brunei	324	00(E)
177	W Sahara	315	00(E)
178	Bahamas	303	00(E)
179	Barbados	286	00(E)
180	Iceland	281	00(E)
181	Maldives	271	00(E)
182	Belize	250	00(E)
183	Fr Polynesia	235	00(E)
184	New Caledonia	213	00(E)
185	Vanuatu	190	00(E)
186	Neth Antilles	179	00(E)
187	Samoa, W	175	00(E)
188	Guiana, Fr	165	00(E)
189	St Lucia	156	00(E)
190	Guam	155	00(E)
191	Mayotte	147	00(E)
192	San Tome & Principe	135	00(E)
193	St Vincent	112	00(E)
194	Virgin I, US	109	00(E)
195	Micronesia	107	00(E)

196	Grenada	101	00(E)
197	Tonga	99	00(E)
198	Aruba	91	00(E)
199	Jersey	87	00(E)
200	Kiribati	84	00(E)
201	Seychelles	81	00(E)
202	Isle of Man	76	00(E)
203	Antigua & Barbuda	75	00(E)
204	Dominica	72	00(E)
205	N Mariana Is	70	00(E)
206	Andorra	66	00(E)
207	Bermuda	63	00(E)
208	Guernsey	62	00(E)
209	Samoa, Ameri	58	00(E)
210	Greenland	56	00(E)
211	Marshall Is	52	00(E)
212	Faeroe Is	46	00(E)
213	St Kitts & Nevis	44	00(E)
214	Cayman Is	40	00(E)
215	Liechtenstein	33	00(E)
216	Monaco	32	00(E)
217	Gibraltar	29	00(CIA)
218	San Marino	27	00(E)
219	Cook Is	20	00(CIA)
220	Virgin Is, Brit.	20	00(CIA)
221	Palau	19	00(E)
222	Turks & Caicos	18	00(CIA)
223	Wallis & Futuna	15	00(CIA)
224	Anguilla	12	CIA
225	Nauru	10	00(E)
226	Tuvalu	9	00(E)
227	St Helena	7	00(CIA)
228	St Pierre &	7	00(CIA)
229	Montserrat	6	00(CIA)
230	Falkland Is	3	00(CIA)
231	Niue	2	00(CIA)
232	Tokelau	1	00(CIA)

TABLE 1.21 - POPULATION IN THOUSANDS, YEAR 2007			
OBS	COUNTRY	POP	SOURCE
1	China	1,317,925	07(E)
2	India	1,129,866	07(E)
3	US	302,633	07(E)
4	Indonesia	231,627	07(E)
5	Brazil	189,335	07(E)
6	Pakistan	159,060	07(E)
7	Nigeria	144,077	07(E)
8	Russia	141,378	07(E)
9	Bangladesh	140,661	07(E)
10	Japan	127,770	07(E)
11	Mexico	106,535	07(E)
12	Philippines	87,960	07(E)

13	Vietnam	87,375	07(E)
14	Germany	82,249	07(E)
15	Ethiopia	76,512	07(E)
16	Turkey	73,884	07(E)
17	Egypt	73,358	07(E)
18	Iran	71,243	07(E)
19	Thailand	63,884	07(E)
20	Congo, Dem R	62,636	07(E)
21	France	61,709	07(E)
22	UK	60,863	07(E)
23	Italy	59,051	07(E)
24	Korea, South	48,456	07(E)
25	South Africa	47,851	07(E)
26	Burma	47,374	07(E)
27	Ukraine	46,457	07(E)
28	Spain	45,321	07(E)
29	Colombia	42,870	07(E)
30	Argentina	39,531	07(E)
31	Tanzania	39,384	07(E)
32	Sudan	39,379	07(E)
33	Poland	38,110	07(E)
34	Kenya	36,914	07(E)
35	Algeria	33,858	07(E)
36	Canada	32,945	07(E)
37	Morocco	31,224	07(E)
38	Uganda	30,263	07(E)
39	Iraq	28,993	07(E)
40	Nepal	28,196	07(E)
41	Peru	27,903	07(E)
42	Uzbekistan	27,372	07(E)
43	Afghanistan	27,145	07(E)
44	Malaysia	26,572	07(E)
45	Venezuela	26,024	07(E)
46	Saudi Arabia	24,209	07(E)
47	Korea, North	23,790	07(E)
48	Ghana	22,931	07(E)
49	Taiwan	22,902	07(E)
50	Yemen	22,231	07(E)
51	Romania	21,549	07(E)
52	Mozambique	20,906	07(E)
53	Australia	20,857	07(E)
54	Sri Lanka	20,102	07(E)
55	Madagascar	19,683	07(E)
56	Ivory Coast	19,262	07(E)
57	Syria	19,048	07(E)
58	Cameroon	18,060	07(E)
59	Chile	16,598	07(E)
60	Netherlands	16,371	07(E)
61	Kazakhstan	15,472	07(E)
62	Burkina Faso	14,326	07(E)
63	Niger	14,226	07(E)
64	Cambodia	13,893	07(E)
65	Malawi	13,603	07(E)
66	Ecuador	13,341	07(E)
67	Guatemala	12,728	07(E)
68	Senegal	12,522	07(E)

69	Zimbabwe	12,311	07(E)
70	Angola	12,264	07(E)
71	Mali	11,995	07(E)
72	Zambia	11,477	07(E)
73	Cuba	11,238	07(E)
74	Greece	11,190	07(E)
75	Portugal	10,629	07(E)
76	Belgium	10,597	07(E)
77	Czechia	10,302	07(E)
78	Chad	10,239	07(E)
79	Tunisia	10,226	07(E)
80	Hungary	10,055	07(E)
81	Rwanda	9,725	07(E)
82	Belarus	9,692	07(E)
83	Haiti	9,598	07(E)
84	Bolivia	9,525	07(E)
85	Guinea	9,370	07(E)
86	Dominican Rep	9,366	07(E)
87	Sweden	9,142	07(E)
88	Somalia	8,699	07(E)
89	Burundi	8,391	07(E)
90	Austria	8,319	07(E)
91	Azerbaijan	8,120	07(E)
92	Benin	8,079	07(E)
93	Bulgaria	7,645	07(E)
94	Switzerland	7,607	07(E)
95	Honduras	7,484	07(E)
96	Serbia	7,402	07(E)
97	Hong Kong	6,924	07(E)
98	Israel	6,900	07(E)
99	El Salvador	6,857	07(E)
100	Tajikistan	6,736	07(E)
101	Togo	6,585	07(E)
102	Libya	6,342	07(E)
103	Papua New Gu	6,331	07(E)
104	Paraguay	6,127	07(E)
105	Jordan	5,924	07(E)
106	Sierra Leone	5,866	07(E)
107	Laos	5,859	07(E)
108	Nicaragua	5,602	07(E)
109	Denmark	5,454	07(E)
110	Slovakia	5,396	07(E)
111	Kyrgyzstan	5,317	07(E)
112	Finland	5,286	07(E)
113	Turkmenistan	5,097	07(E)
114	Eritrea	4,907	07(E)
115	Norway	4,702	07(E)
116	Georgia	4,613	07(E)
117	Singapore	4,564	07(E)
118	Costa Rica	4,445	07(E)
119	UAE	4,444	07(E)
120	Croatia	4,440	07(E)
121	Central African Rep.	4,343	07(E)
122	Ireland	4,330	07(E)
123	New Zealand	4,184	07(E)
124	Lebanon	4,099	07(E)

125	Puerto Rico	3,967	07(E)
126	Bosnia	3,855	07(E)
127	Moldova	3,794	07(E)
128	Congo, Rep	3,768	07(E)
129	Liberia	3,750	07(E)
130	Lithuania	3,375	07(E)
131	Panama	3,343	07(E)
132	Uruguay	3,340	07(E)
133	Kuwait	3,294	07(E)
134	Albania	3,176	07(E)
135	Mauritania	3,124	07(E)
136	Armenia	3,002	07(E)
137	West Bank	2,794	07(E)
138	Jamaica	2,680	07(E)
139	Mongolia	2,609	07(E)
140	Oman	2,595	07(E)
141	Latvia	2,274	07(E)
142	Kosovo	2,114	07(E)
143	Namibia	2,074	07(E)
144	Macedonia	2,044	07(E)
145	Slovenia	2,011	07(E)
146	Lesotho	2,008	07(E)
147	Botswana	1,882	07(E)
148	Gambia	1,709	07(E)
149	Gaza Strip	1,499	07(E)
150	Guinea-Bissau	1,472	07(E)
151	Estonia	1,338	07(E)
152	Gabon	1,331	07(E)
153	Trinidad/Tobago	1,303	07(E)
154	Mauritius	1,263	07(E)
155	East Timor	1,155	07(E)
156	Swaziland	1,141	07(E)
157	Cyprus	1,047	07(E)
158	Qatar	841	07(E)
159	Fiji	839	07(E)
160	Reunion	799	07(E)
161	Bahrain	749	07(E)
162	Guyana	738	07(E)
163	Bhutan	658	07(E)
164	Comoros	629	07(E)
165	Montenegro	624	07(E)
166	Macao	527	07(E)
167	Suriname	510	07(E)
168	Equatorial G	507	07(E)
169	Cape Verde	496	07(E)
170	Djibouti	496	07(E)
171	Solomon Is	495	07(E)
172	W Sahara	480	07(E)
173	Luxembourg	467	07(E)
174	Guadeloupe	413	07(E)
175	Malta	409	07(E)
176	Martinique	401	07(E)
177	Brunei	393	07(E)
178	Bahamas	331	07(E)
179	Iceland	310	07(E)
180	Belize	306	07(E)

181	Maldives	305	07(E)
182	Barbados	294	07(E)
183	Fr Polynesia	261	07(E)
184	New Caledonia	242	07(E)
185	Vanuatu	226	07(E)
186	Guiana, Fr	211	07(E)
187	Mayotte	194	07(E)
188	Neth Antilles	192	07(E)
189	Samoa, W	180	07(E)
190	Guam	173	07(E)
191	St Lucia	168	07(E)
192	San Tome & Principe	158	07(E)
193	Virgin I, US	113	07(E)
194	Micronesia	111	07(E)
195	Grenada	108	07(E)
196	St Vincent	106	07(E)
197	Aruba	105	07(E)
198	Tonga	101	07(E)
199	Kiribati	96	07(E)
200	Jersey	90	07(E)
201	Antigua & Barbuda	86	07(E)
202	N Mariana Is	85	07(E)
203	Seychelles	84	07(E)
204	Andorra	83	07(E)
205	Isle of Man	81	07(E)
206	Dominica	71	07(E)
207	Bermuda	65	07(E)
208	Samoa, Ameri	64	07(E)
209	Guernsey	64	07(E)
210	Greenland	57	07(E)
211	Marshall Is	57	07(E)
212	Cayman Is	56	07(E)
213	St Kitts & Nevis	50	07(E)
214	Faeroe Is	48	07(E)
215	Liechtenstein	35	07(E)
216	Monaco	34	07(E)
217	San Marino	31	07(E)
218	Gibraltar	28	07(CIA)
219	Virgin Is, Brit.	24	07(CIA)
220	Cook Is	22	07(CIA)
221	Turks & Caicos	22	07(CIA)
222	Palau	20	07(E)
223	Wallis & Futuna	16	07(CIA)
224	Anguilla	14	CIA
225	Nauru	10	07(E)
226	Tuvalu	10	07(E)
227	Montserrat	10	07(CIA)
228	St Helena	8	07(CIA)
229	St Pierre &	7	07(CIA)
230	Falkland Is	3	07(CIA)
231	Niue	1	07(CIA)
232	Tokelau	1	07(CIA)

CHAPTER 2. GDP AT PURCHASING POWER PARITIES PER CAPITA IN 2007 DOLLARS

OBS	COUNTRY	GPCPPP	SOURCE

<table>
<tr><td colspan="4" align="center">TABLE 2.1 - GDP AT PPP PER CAPITA, 2007 DOLLARS, YEAR 0001</td></tr>
<tr><td>OBS</td><td>COUNTRY</td><td>GPCPPP</td><td>SOURCE</td></tr>
<tr><td>1</td><td>Italy</td><td>1,189</td><td>0001(Maddison)</td></tr>
<tr><td>2</td><td>Lebanon</td><td>855</td><td>PROXY(W. Asia(Maddison))</td></tr>
<tr><td>3</td><td>Syria</td><td>855</td><td>PROXY(W. Asia(Maddison))</td></tr>
<tr><td>4</td><td>Greece</td><td>808</td><td>0001(Maddison)</td></tr>
<tr><td>5</td><td>Cyprus</td><td>808</td><td>0001(Maddison)</td></tr>
<tr><td>6</td><td>Israel</td><td>798</td><td>PROXY(W. Asia(Maddison))</td></tr>
<tr><td>7</td><td>Iran</td><td>780</td><td>PROXY(W. Asia(Maddison))</td></tr>
<tr><td>8</td><td>Turkey</td><td>780</td><td>PROXY(W. Asia(Maddison))</td></tr>
<tr><td>9</td><td>Jordan</td><td>764</td><td>PROXY(W. Asia(Maddison))</td></tr>
<tr><td>10</td><td>Iraq</td><td>743</td><td>PROXY(W. Asia(Maddison))</td></tr>
<tr><td>11</td><td>Egypt</td><td>735</td><td>0001(Maddison)</td></tr>
<tr><td>12</td><td>Spain</td><td>732</td><td>0001(Maddison)</td></tr>
<tr><td>13</td><td>Bahrain</td><td>715</td><td>PROXY(W. Asia(Maddison))</td></tr>
<tr><td>14</td><td>Kuwait</td><td>715</td><td>PROXY(W. Asia(Maddison))</td></tr>
<tr><td>15</td><td>Qatar</td><td>715</td><td>PROXY(W. Asia(Maddison))</td></tr>
<tr><td>16</td><td>Oman</td><td>715</td><td>PROXY(W. Asia(Maddison))</td></tr>
<tr><td>17</td><td>Saudi Arabia</td><td>715</td><td>PROXY(W. Asia(Maddison))</td></tr>
<tr><td>18</td><td>UAE</td><td>715</td><td>PROXY(W. Asia(Maddison))</td></tr>
<tr><td>19</td><td>Yemen</td><td>715</td><td>PROXY(W. Asia(Maddison))</td></tr>
<tr><td>20</td><td>Thailand</td><td>710</td><td>PROXY(Other E. Asia(Maddison))</td></tr>
<tr><td>21</td><td>France</td><td>695</td><td>0001(Maddison)</td></tr>
<tr><td>22</td><td>Malaysia</td><td>663</td><td>PROXY(Other E. Asia(Maddison))</td></tr>
<tr><td>23</td><td>China</td><td>661</td><td>0001(Maddison)</td></tr>
<tr><td>24</td><td>Korea, South</td><td>661</td><td>PROXY(China(Maddison))</td></tr>
<tr><td>25</td><td>Pakistan</td><td>661</td><td>0001(Undivided India(Maddison))</td></tr>
<tr><td>26</td><td>Bangladesh</td><td>661</td><td>0001(Undivided India(Maddison))</td></tr>
<tr><td>27</td><td>Korea, North</td><td>661</td><td>PROXY(China(Maddison))</td></tr>
<tr><td>28</td><td>Portugal</td><td>661</td><td>0001(Maddison)</td></tr>
<tr><td>29</td><td>Belgium</td><td>661</td><td>0001(Maddison)</td></tr>
<tr><td>30</td><td>Hong Kong</td><td>661</td><td>PROXY(China(Maddison))</td></tr>
<tr><td>31</td><td>India</td><td>661</td><td>0001(Undivided India(Maddison))</td></tr>
<tr><td>32</td><td>Philippines</td><td>642</td><td>PROXY(Other E. Asia(Maddison))</td></tr>
<tr><td>33</td><td>Indonesia</td><td>637</td><td>PROXY(Other E. Asia(Maddison))</td></tr>
<tr><td>34</td><td>Tunisia</td><td>632</td><td>PROXY(Other N. Africa(Maddison))</td></tr>
<tr><td>35</td><td>Algeria</td><td>632</td><td>PROXY(Other N. Africa(Maddison))</td></tr>
<tr><td>36</td><td>Libya</td><td>632</td><td>0001(Other N. Africa(Maddison))</td></tr>
<tr><td>37</td><td>Hungary</td><td>624</td><td>AVG(Danubian provinces(Maddison))</td></tr>
<tr><td>38</td><td>Bulgaria</td><td>624</td><td>AVG(Danubian provinces(Maddison))</td></tr>
<tr><td>39</td><td>Switzerland</td><td>624</td><td>0001(Maddison)</td></tr>
<tr><td>40</td><td>Austria</td><td>624</td><td>0001(Maddison)</td></tr>
<tr><td>41</td><td>Romania</td><td>624</td><td>AVG(Danubian provinces(Maddison))</td></tr>
<tr><td>42</td><td>Serbia</td><td>624</td><td>AVG(Danubian provinces(Maddison))</td></tr>
<tr><td>43</td><td>Netherlands</td><td>624</td><td>0001(Maddison)</td></tr>
<tr><td>44</td><td>Taiwan</td><td>605</td><td>PROXY(Other E. Asia(Maddison))</td></tr>
<tr><td>45</td><td>Sri Lanka</td><td>605</td><td>PROXY(Other E. Asia(Maddison))</td></tr>
<tr><td>46</td><td>Germany</td><td>599</td><td>0001(Maddison)</td></tr>
<tr><td>47</td><td>Croatia</td><td>588</td><td>MIN(EST)</td></tr>
</table>

48	Slovakia	588	MIN(EST)
49	Brazil	588	000I(Maddison)
50	Burma	588	MIN(PROXY(Other E. Asia(Maddison)))
51	Costa Rica	588	000I(Maddison)
52	Czechia	588	MIN(EST)
53	El Salvador	588	000I(Maddison)
54	Guinea	588	000I(Sahel & W. Africa(Maddison))
55	Somalia	588	000I(Rest of Africa(Maddison))
56	Sweden	588	000I(Maddison)
57	Afghanistan	588	MIN(PROXY(Other E. Asia(Maddison)))
58	Argentina	588	000I(Maddison)
59	Australia	588	000I(Maddison)
60	Cambodia	588	MIN(PROXY(Other E. Asia(Maddison)))
61	Canada	588	000I(Maddison)
62	Chile	588	000I(Maddison)
63	Denmark	588	000I(Maddison)
64	Ecuador	588	000I(Maddison)
65	Eritrea	588	000I(Sahel & W. Africa(Maddison))
66	Guinea-Bissau	588	000I(Sahel & W. Africa(Maddison))
67	Ireland	588	000I(UK(Maddison))
68	Kosovo	588	MIN(EST)
69	Kyrgyzstan	588	000I(Maddison)
70	Macedonia	588	MIN(EST)
71	Madagascar	588	000I(Rest of Africa(Maddison))
72	Malawi	588	000I(Rest of Africa(Maddison))
73	Mexico	588	000I(Maddison)
74	Moldova	588	000I(Maddison)
75	Montenegro	588	MIN(EST)
76	Morocco	588	000I(Maddison)
77	Namibia	588	000I(Rest of Africa(Maddison))
78	Nicaragua	588	000I(Maddison)
79	Norway	588	000I(Maddison)
80	Panama	588	000I(Maddison)
81	Poland	588	MIN(EST)
82	Puerto Rico	588	000I(Maddison)
83	Russia	588	000I(Maddison)
84	South Africa	588	000I(Rest of Africa(Maddison))
85	Sudan	588	000I(Sahel & W. Africa(Maddison))
86	Swaziland	588	000I(Rest of Africa(Maddison))
87	Turkmenistan	588	000I(Maddison)
88	Ukraine	588	000I(Maddison)
89	Uruguay	588	000I(Maddison)
90	Venezuela	588	000I(Maddison)
91	Vietnam	588	MIN(PROXY(Other E. Asia(Maddison)))
92	Zimbabwe	588	000I(Rest of Africa(Maddison))
93	Armenia	588	000I(Maddison)
94	Belarus	588	000I(Maddison)
95	Bosnia	588	MIN(EST)
96	Botswana	588	000I(Rest of Africa(Maddison))
97	Colombia	588	000I(Maddison)
98	Estonia	588	000I(Maddison)
99	Finland	588	000I(Maddison)
100	Georgia	588	000I(Maddison)
101	Guatemala	588	000I(Maddison)
102	Honduras	588	000I(Maddison)
103	Jamaica	588	000I(Maddison)

104	Japan	588	0001(Maddison)
105	Latvia	588	0001(Maddison)
106	Lesotho	588	0001(Rest of Africa(Maddison))
107	Mongolia	588	MIN(PROXY(Other E. Asia(Maddison)))
108	New Zealand	588	0001(Maddison)
109	Peru	588	0001(Maddison)
110	Sierra Leone	588	0001(Sahel & W. Africa(Maddison))
111	Slovenia	588	MIN(EST)
112	Tajikistan	588	0001(Maddison)
113	Trinidad/Tobago	588	0001(Maddison)
114	UK	588	0001(Maddison)
115	US	588	0001(Maddison)
116	Zambia	588	0001(Rest of Africa(Maddison))
117	Albania	588	MIN(EST)
118	Azerbaijan	588	0001(Maddison)
119	Bolivia	588	0001(Maddison)
120	Burundi	588	0001(Rest of Africa(Maddison))
121	Cuba	588	0001(Maddison)
122	Ethiopia	588	0001(Sahel & W. Africa(Maddison))
123	Haiti	588	0001(Maddison)
124	Kazakhstan	588	0001(Maddison)
125	Laos	588	MIN(PROXY(Other E. Asia(Maddison)))
126	Lithuania	588	0001(Maddison)
127	Nepal	588	MIN(PROXY(Other E. Asia(Maddison)))
128	Paraguay	588	0001(Maddison)
129	Singapore	588	MIN(PROXY(Other E. Asia(Maddison)))
130	Uzbekistan	588	0001(Maddison)
131	Dominican Rep	588	0001(Maddison)
132	Ghana	588	0001(Sahel & W. Africa(Maddison))
133	Mozambique	588	0001(Rest of Africa(Maddison))

TABLE 2.2 - GDP AT PPP PER CAPITA, 2007 DOLLARS, YEAR 1000			
OBS	COUNTRY	GPCPPP	SOURCE
1	Lebanon	1,017	PROXY(W. Asia(Maddison))
2	Syria	1,017	PROXY(W. Asia(Maddison))
3	Israel	949	PROXY(W. Asia(Maddison))
4	Iran	928	PROXY(W. Asia(Maddison))
5	Turkey	928	PROXY(W. Asia(Maddison))
6	Jordan	909	PROXY(W. Asia(Maddison))
7	Iraq	884	PROXY(W. Asia(Maddison))
8	Cyprus	881	1000(Maddison)
9	Bahrain	850	PROXY(W. Asia(Maddison))
10	Qatar	850	PROXY(W. Asia(Maddison))
11	Saudi Arabia	850	PROXY(W. Asia(Maddison))
12	Kuwait	850	PROXY(W. Asia(Maddison))
13	UAE	850	PROXY(W. Asia(Maddison))
14	Yemen	850	PROXY(W. Asia(Maddison))
15	Oman	850	PROXY(W. Asia(Maddison))
16	Egypt	735	1000(Maddison)

17	Thailand	710	PROXY(Other E. Asia(Maddison))
18	Malaysia	663	PROXY(Other E. Asia(Maddison))
19	China	661	1000(Maddison)
20	Italy	661	1000(Maddison)
21	Korea, South	661	PROXY(China(Maddison))
22	Pakistan	661	1000(Undivided India(Maddison))
23	Bangladesh	661	1000(Undivided India(Maddison))
24	Korea, North	661	PROXY(China(Maddison))
25	Spain	661	1000(Maddison)
26	Hong Kong	661	PROXY(China(Maddison))
27	India	661	1000(Undivided India(Maddison))
28	Philippines	642	PROXY(Other E. Asia(Maddison))
29	Indonesia	637	PROXY(Other E. Asia(Maddison))
30	Tunisia	632	PROXY(Other N. Africa(Maddison))
31	Algeria	632	PROXY(Other N. Africa(Maddison))
32	Morocco	632	1000(Maddison)
33	Libya	632	1000(Other N. Africa(Maddison))
34	Austria	624	1000(Maddison)
35	Belgium	624	1000(Maddison)
36	Portugal	624	1000(Maddison)
37	France	624	1000(Maddison)
38	Japan	624	1000(Maddison)
39	Netherlands	624	1000(Maddison)
40	Sudan	610	1000(Sahel & W. Africa(Maddison))
41	Ghana	610	PROXY(Sahel & W. Africa(Maddison))
42	Taiwan	605	PROXY(Other E. Asia(Maddison))
43	Sri Lanka	605	PROXY(Other E. Asia(Maddison))
44	Switzerland	602	1000(Maddison)
45	Germany	602	1000(Maddison)
46	Croatia	588	1000(Maddison)
47	Slovakia	588	1000(Maddison)
48	Brazil	588	1000(Maddison)
49	Burma	588	MIN(PROXY(Other E. Asia(Maddison)))
50	Costa Rica	588	1000(Maddison)
51	Czechia	588	1000(Maddison)
52	El Salvador	588	1000(Maddison)
53	Guinea	588	MIN(1950(Maddison))
54	Hungary	588	1000(Maddison)
55	Serbia	588	1000(Maddison)
56	Somalia	588	1000(Rest of Africa(Maddison))
57	Sweden	588	1000(Maddison)
58	Afghanistan	588	MIN(PROXY(Other E. Asia(Maddison)))
59	Argentina	588	1000(Maddison)
60	Australia	588	1000(Maddison)
61	Bulgaria	588	1000(Maddison)
62	Cambodia	588	MIN(PROXY(Other E. Asia(Maddison)))
63	Canada	588	1000(Maddison)
64	Chile	588	1000(Maddison)
65	Denmark	588	1000(Maddison)
66	Ecuador	588	1000(Maddison)
67	Eritrea	588	MIN(1950(Maddison))
68	Greece	588	1000(Maddison)
69	Guinea-Bissau	588	MIN(1950(Maddison))
70	Ireland	588	1000(UK(Maddison))

71	Kosovo	588	1000(Maddison)
72	Kyrgyzstan	588	1000(Maddison)
73	Macedonia	588	1000(Maddison)
74	Madagascar	588	1000(Rest of Africa(Maddison))
75	Malawi	588	1000(Rest of Africa(Maddison))
76	Mexico	588	1000(Maddison)
77	Moldova	588	1000(Maddison)
78	Montenegro	588	1000(Maddison)
79	Namibia	588	1000(Rest of Africa(Maddison))
80	Nicaragua	588	1000(Maddison)
81	Norway	588	1000(Maddison)
82	Panama	588	1000(Maddison)
83	Poland	588	1000(Maddison)
84	Puerto Rico	588	1000(Maddison)
85	Romania	588	1000(Maddison)
86	Russia	588	1000(Maddison)
87	South Africa	588	1000(Rest of Africa(Maddison))
88	Swaziland	588	1000(Rest of Africa(Maddison))
89	Turkmenistan	588	1000(Maddison)
90	Ukraine	588	1000(Maddison)
91	Uruguay	588	1000(Maddison)
92	Venezuela	588	1000(Maddison)
93	Vietnam	588	MIN(PROXY(Other E. Asia(Maddison)))
94	Zimbabwe	588	1000(Rest of Africa(Maddison))
95	Armenia	588	1000(Maddison)
96	Belarus	588	1000(Maddison)
97	Bosnia	588	1000(Maddison)
98	Botswana	588	1000(Rest of Africa(Maddison))
99	Colombia	588	1000(Maddison)
100	Estonia	588	1000(Maddison)
101	Finland	588	1000(Maddison)
102	Georgia	588	1000(Maddison)
103	Guatemala	588	1000(Maddison)
104	Honduras	588	1000(Maddison)
105	Jamaica	588	1000(Maddison)
106	Latvia	588	1000(Maddison)
107	Lesotho	588	1000(Rest of Africa(Maddison))
108	Mongolia	588	MIN(PROXY(Other E. Asia(Maddison)))
109	New Zealand	588	1000(Maddison)
110	Peru	588	1000(Maddison)
111	Sierra Leone	588	MIN(1950(Maddison))
112	Slovenia	588	1000(Maddison)
113	Tajikistan	588	1000(Maddison)
114	Trinidad/Tobago	588	1000(Maddison)
115	UK	588	1000(Maddison)
116	US	588	1000(Maddison)
117	Zambia	588	1000(Rest of Africa(Maddison))
118	Albania	588	1000(Maddison)
119	Azerbaijan	588	1000(Maddison)
120	Bolivia	588	1000(Maddison)
121	Burundi	588	1000(Rest of Africa(Maddison))
122	Cuba	588	1000(Maddison)
123	Ethiopia	588	MIN(1950(Maddison))
124	Haiti	588	1000(Maddison)

125	Kazakhstan	588	1000(Maddison)
126	Laos	588	MIN(PROXY(Other E. Asia(Maddison)))
127	Lithuania	588	1000(Maddison)
128	Nepal	588	MIN(PROXY(Other E. Asia(Maddison)))
129	Paraguay	588	1000(Maddison)
130	Singapore	588	MIN(PROXY(Other E. Asia(Maddison)))
131	Uzbekistan	588	1000(Maddison)
132	Dominican Rep	588	1000(Maddison)
133	Mozambique	588	1000(Rest of Africa(Maddison))

TABLE 2.3 - GDP AT PPP PER CAPITA, 2007 DOLLARS, YEAR 1500

OBS	COUNTRY	GPCPPP	SOURCE
1	Italy	1,616	1500(Maddison)
2	Belgium	1,285	1500(Maddison)
3	Netherlands	1,118	1500(Maddison)
4	Slovenia	1,095	INTERPOL(Maddison)
5	Denmark	1,084	1500(Maddison)
6	France	1,068	1500(Maddison)
7	UK	1,049	1500(Maddison)
8	Hungary	1,047	INTERPOL(Maddison)
9	Austria	1,039	1500(Maddison)
10	Estonia	1,031	INTERPOL(Maddison)
11	Sweden	1,021	1500(Maddison)
12	Germany	1,011	1500(Maddison)
13	Spain	971	1500(Maddison)
14	Lebanon	967	PROXY(Other W. Asia(Maddison))
15	Syria	967	PROXY(Other W. Asia(Maddison))
16	Poland	960	PROXY(E. Europe(Maddison))
17	Latvia	952	PROXY(USSR(Maddison))
18	Czechia	946	PROXY(E. Europe(Maddison))
19	Romania	945	PROXY(E. Europe(Maddison))
20	Norway	940	1500(Maddison)
21	Kazakhstan	940	PROXY(USSR(Maddison))
22	Switzerland	928	1500(Maddison)
23	Thailand	926	PROXY(Other E. Asia(Maddison))
24	Lithuania	920	PROXY(USSR(Maddison))
25	Israel	902	PROXY(Other W. Asia(Maddison))
26	Portugal	890	1500(Maddison)
27	China	881	1500(Maddison)
28	Iran	881	1500(Maddison)
29	Korea, South	881	1500(Maddison)
30	Turkey	881	1500(Maddison)
31	Korea, North	881	1500(Maddison)
32	Hong Kong	881	PROXY(China(Maddison))
33	Malaysia	864	PROXY(Other E. Asia(Maddison))
34	Jordan	864	PROXY(Other W. Asia(Maddison))
35	Bulgaria	853	PROXY(E. Europe(Maddison))
36	Iraq	840	PROXY(W. Asia(Maddison))
37	Philippines	837	PROXY(Other E. Asia(Maddison))
38	Indonesia	830	1500(Maddison)

39	Slovakia	826	PROXY(E. Europe(Maddison))
40	Bahrain	808	1500(Arabia(Maddison))
41	Qatar	808	1500(Arabia(Maddison))
42	Kuwait	808	1500(Arabia(Maddison))
43	Pakistan	808	1500(Undivided India(Maddison))
44	Bangladesh	808	1500(Undivided India(Maddison))
45	India	808	1500(Undivided India(Maddison))
46	Saudi Arabia	808	1500(Arabia(Maddison))
47	UAE	808	1500(Arabia(Maddison))
48	Oman	808	1500(Arabia(Maddison))
49	Yemen	808	1500(Arabia(Maddison))
50	Russia	797	PROXY(USSR(Maddison))
51	Taiwan	788	PROXY(Other E. Asia(Maddison))
52	Sri Lanka	788	PROXY(Other E. Asia(Maddison))
53	Croatia	773	PROXY(E. Europe(Maddison))
54	Ireland	773	1500(Maddison)
55	Vietnam	755	PROXY(Other E. Asia(Maddison))
56	Armenia	742	PROXY(USSR(Maddison))
57	Japan	735	1500(Maddison)
58	Afghanistan	732	PROXY(Other E. Asia(Maddison))
59	Burma	722	PROXY(Other E. Asia(Maddison))
60	Georgia	722	PROXY(USSR(Maddison))
61	Singapore	716	PROXY(Other E. Asia(Maddison))
62	Egypt	698	1500(Maddison)
63	Laos	696	PROXY(Other E. Asia(Maddison))
64	Serbia	668	PROXY(E. Europe(Maddison))
65	Finland	666	1500(Maddison)
66	Montenegro	657	PROXY(E. Europe(Maddison))
67	Moldova	649	PROXY(USSR(Maddison))
68	Greece	636	1500(Maddison)
69	Belarus	633	PROXY(USSR(Maddison))
70	Tunisia	632	PROXY(Other N. Africa(Maddison))
71	Algeria	632	PROXY(Other N. Africa(Maddison))
72	Morocco	632	1500(Maddison)
73	Libya	632	1500(Other N. Africa(Maddison))
74	Cyprus	625	PROXY(Greece(Maddison))
75	Mexico	624	1500(Maddison)
76	Uzbekistan	617	PROXY(USSR(Maddison))
77	Sudan	610	1500(Sahel & W. Africa(Maddison))
78	Ghana	610	PROXY(Sahel & W. Africa(Maddison))
79	Argentina	605	AVG(Other Sp. Am.(Maddison))
80	Chile	605	AVG(Other Sp. Am.(Maddison))
81	Uruguay	605	AVG(Other Sp. Am.(Maddison))
82	Ukraine	596	PROXY(USSR(Maddison))
83	Cambodia	588	PROXY(Other E. Asia(Maddison))
84	Brazil	588	1500(Maddison)
85	Costa Rica	588	MIN(PROXY(Other Sp. Am.(Maddison)))
86	El Salvador	588	MIN(PROXY(Other Sp. Am.(Maddison)))
87	Guinea	588	MIN(1950(Maddison))
88	Somalia	588	1500(Rest of Africa(Maddison))

89	Australia	588	1500(Maddison)
90	Canada	588	1500(Maddison)
91	Ecuador	588	MIN(PROXY(Other Sp. Am.(Maddison)))
92	Eritrea	588	MIN(1950(Maddison))
93	Guinea-Bissau	588	MIN(1950(Maddison))
94	Kosovo	588	MIN(PROXY(E. Europe(Maddison)))
95	Kyrgyzstan	588	MIN(PROXY(USSR(Maddison)))
96	Macedonia	588	MIN(PROXY(E. Europe(Maddison)))
97	Madagascar	588	1500(Rest of Africa(Maddison))
98	Malawi	588	1500(Rest of Africa(Maddison))
99	Namibia	588	1500(Rest of Africa(Maddison))
100	Nicaragua	588	MIN(PROXY(Other Sp. Am.(Maddison)))
101	Panama	588	MIN(PROXY(Other Sp. Am.(Maddison)))
102	Puerto Rico	588	1500(Caribbean cs(Maddison))
103	South Africa	588	1500(Rest of Africa(Maddison))
104	Swaziland	588	1500(Rest of Africa(Maddison))
105	Turkmenistan	588	MIN(PROXY(USSR(Maddison)))
106	Venezuela	588	MIN(PROXY(Other Sp. Am.(Maddison)))
107	Zimbabwe	588	1500(Rest of Africa(Maddison))
108	Bosnia	588	MIN(PROXY(E. Europe(Maddison)))
109	Botswana	588	1500(Rest of Africa(Maddison))
110	Colombia	588	MIN(PROXY(Other Sp. Am.(Maddison)))
111	Guatemala	588	MIN(PROXY(Other Sp. Am.(Maddison)))
112	Honduras	588	MIN(PROXY(Other Sp. Am.(Maddison)))
113	Jamaica	588	1500(Caribbean cs(Maddison))
114	Lesotho	588	1500(Rest of Africa(Maddison))
115	Mongolia	588	MIN(PROXY(Other E. Asia(Maddison)))
116	New Zealand	588	1500(Maddison)
117	Peru	588	MIN(PROXY(Other Sp. Am.(Maddison)))
118	Sierra Leone	588	MIN(1950(Maddison))
119	Tajikistan	588	MIN(PROXY(USSR(Maddison)))
120	Trinidad/Tobago	588	1500(Caribbean cs(Maddison))
121	US	588	1500(Maddison)
122	Zambia	588	1500(Rest of Africa(Maddison))
123	Albania	588	MIN(PROXY(E. Europe(Maddison)))
124	Azerbaijan	588	MIN(PROXY(USSR(Maddison)))
125	Bolivia	588	MIN(PROXY(Other Sp. Am.(Maddison)))
126	Burundi	588	1500(Rest of Africa(Maddison))
127	Cuba	588	1500(Caribbean cs(Maddison))
128	Ethiopia	588	MIN(1950(Maddison))
129	Haiti	588	1500(Caribbean cs(Maddison))
130	Nepal	588	MIN(PROXY(Other E. Asia(Maddison)))

131	Paraguay	588	MIN(PROXY(Other Sp. Am.(Maddison)))
132	Dominican Rep	588	1500(Caribbean cs(Maddison))
133	Mozambique	588	1500(Rest of Africa(Maddison))

TABLE 2.4 - GDP AT PPP PER CAPITA, 2007 DOLLARS, YEAR 1600

OBS	COUNTRY	GPCPPP	SOURCE
1	Netherlands	2,029	1600(Maddison)
2	Italy	1,616	1600(Maddison)
3	Belgium	1,434	1600(Maddison)
4	UK	1,431	1600(Maddison)
5	Denmark	1,285	1600(Maddison)
6	Spain	1,253	1600(Maddison)
7	Slovenia	1,241	INTERPOL(Maddison)
8	France	1,236	1600(Maddison)
9	Austria	1,230	1600(Maddison)
10	Sweden	1,211	1600(Maddison)
11	Hungary	1,175	INTERPOL(Maddison)
12	Germany	1,162	1600(Maddison)
13	Estonia	1,154	INTERPOL(Maddison)
14	Norway	1,117	1600(Maddison)
15	Switzerland	1,102	1600(Maddison)
16	Portugal	1,087	1600(Maddison)
17	Poland	1,061	PROXY(E. Europe(Maddison))
18	Latvia	1,053	PROXY(USSR(Maddison))
19	Czechia	1,046	PROXY(E. Europe(Maddison))
20	Romania	1,044	PROXY(E. Europe(Maddison))
21	Kazakhstan	1,040	PROXY(USSR(Maddison))
22	Lithuania	1,018	PROXY(USSR(Maddison))
23	Uruguay	1,011	INTERPOL(Maddison)
24	Lebanon	967	INTERPOL(Maddison)
25	Syria	967	INTERPOL(Maddison)
26	Thailand	942	PROXY(Other E. Asia(Maddison))
27	Bulgaria	942	PROXY(E. Europe(Maddison))
28	Slovakia	913	PROXY(E. Europe(Maddison))
29	Ireland	904	1600(Maddison)
30	Israel	902	INTERPOL(Maddison)
31	Russia	882	PROXY(USSR(Maddison))
32	China	881	1600(Maddison)
33	Iran	881	INTERPOL(Maddison)
34	Korea, South	881	INTERPOL(Maddison)
35	Turkey	881	INTERPOL(Maddison)
36	Korea, North	881	INTERPOL(Maddison)
37	Hong Kong	881	PROXY(China(Maddison))
38	Malaysia	880	PROXY(Other E. Asia(Maddison))
39	Jordan	864	INTERPOL(Maddison)
40	Argentina	863	INTERPOL(Maddison)
41	Croatia	854	PROXY(E. Europe(Maddison))
42	Philippines	852	PROXY(Other E. Asia(Maddison))
43	Iraq	841	PROXY(W. Asia(Maddison))
44	Indonesia	841	INTERPOL(Maddison)
45	Armenia	821	PROXY(USSR(Maddison))

46	Bahrain	808	INTERPOL(Maddison)
47	Qatar	808	INTERPOL(Maddison)
48	Kuwait	808	INTERPOL(Maddison)
49	Pakistan	808	1600(Undivided India(Maddison))
50	Bangladesh	808	1600(Undivided India(Maddison))
51	India	808	1600(Undivided India(Maddison))
52	Saudi Arabia	808	INTERPOL(Maddison)
53	UAE	808	INTERPOL(Maddison)
54	Oman	808	INTERPOL(Maddison)
55	Yemen	808	INTERPOL(Maddison)
56	Taiwan	802	PROXY(Other E. Asia(Maddison))
57	Sri Lanka	802	PROXY(Other E. Asia(Maddison))
58	Georgia	798	PROXY(USSR(Maddison))
59	Finland	790	1600(Maddison)
60	Jamaica	787	INTERPOL(Maddison)
61	Trinidad/ Tobago	772	INTERPOL(Maddison)
62	Vietnam	769	PROXY(Other E. Asia(Maddison))
63	Japan	764	1600(Maddison)
64	Afghanistan	745	PROXY(Other E. Asia(Maddison))
65	Serbia	738	PROXY(E. Europe(Maddison))
66	Burma	735	PROXY(Other E. Asia(Maddison))
67	Singapore	729	PROXY(Other E. Asia(Maddison))
68	Montenegro	726	PROXY(E. Europe(Maddison))
69	Moldova	718	PROXY(USSR(Maddison))
70	Chile	712	INTERPOL(Maddison)
71	Greece	710	1600(Maddison)
72	Laos	708	PROXY(Other E. Asia(Maddison))
73	Belarus	700	PROXY(USSR(Maddison)) PROXY(USSR(Maddison))
74	Egypt	698	1600(Maddison)
75	Cyprus	698	PROXY(Greece(Maddison))
76	Uzbekistan	682	PROXY(USSR(Maddison))
77	Mexico	667	1600(Maddison)
78	Ukraine	659	PROXY(USSR(Maddison))
79	Turkmenistan	646	PROXY(USSR(Maddison))
80	Tunisia	632	PROXY(Other N. Africa(Maddison))
81	Algeria	632	PROXY(Other N. Africa(Maddison))
82	Morocco	632	1600(Maddison)
83	Libya	632	1600(Other N. Africa(Maddison))
84	Brazil	629	1600(Maddison)
85	Somalia	610	1600(Rest of Africa(Maddison))
86	South Africa	610	1600(Rest of Africa(Maddison))
87	Zambia	610	1600(Rest of Africa(Maddison))
88	Zimbabwe	610	1600(Rest of Africa(Maddison))
89	Madagascar	610	1600(Rest of Africa(Maddison))
90	Namibia	610	1600(Rest of Africa(Maddison))
91	Sudan	610	1600(Sahel & W. Africa(Maddison))
92	Swaziland	610	1600(Rest of Africa(Maddison))
93	Ghana	610	PROXY(Sahel & W. Africa(Maddison))
94	Mozambique	610	1600(Rest of Africa(Maddison))
95	Cambodia	598	PROXY(Other E. Asia(Maddison))
96	Azerbaijan	593	PROXY(USSR(Maddison))
97	Costa Rica	588	MIN(PROXY(Other Sp. Am.(Maddison)))
98	El Salvador	588	MIN(PROXY(Other Sp. Am.(Maddison)))
99	Guinea	588	MIN(1950(Maddison))

100	Australia	588	1600(Maddison)
101	Canada	588	1600(Maddison)
102	Ecuador	588	MIN(PROXY(Other Sp. Am.(Maddison)))
103	Eritrea	588	MIN(1950(Maddison))
104	Guinea-Bissau	588	MIN(1950(Maddison))
105	Kosovo	588	MIN(PROXY(E. Europe(Maddison)))
106	Kyrgyzstan	588	MIN(PROXY(USSR(Maddison)))
107	Macedonia	588	MIN(PROXY(E. Europe(Maddison)))
108	Malawi	588	MIN(1950(Maddison))
109	Nicaragua	588	MIN(PROXY(Other Sp. Am.(Maddison)))
110	Panama	588	MIN(PROXY(Other Sp. Am.(Maddison)))
111	Puerto Rico	588	MIN(PROXY(Caribbean cs(Maddison)))
112	Venezuela	588	MIN(PROXY(Other Sp. Am.(Maddison)))
113	Bosnia	588	MIN(PROXY(E. Europe(Maddison)))
114	Botswana	588	MIN(1950(Maddison))
115	Colombia	588	MIN(PROXY(Other Sp. Am.(Maddison)))
116	Guatemala	588	MIN(PROXY(Other Sp. Am.(Maddison)))
117	Honduras	588	MIN(PROXY(Other Sp. Am.(Maddison)))
118	Lesotho	588	MIN(1950(Maddison))
119	Mongolia	588	MIN(PROXY(Other E. Asia(Maddison)))
120	New Zealand	588	1600(Maddison)
121	Peru	588	MIN(PROXY(Other Sp. Am.(Maddison)))
122	Sierra Leone	588	MIN(1950(Maddison))
123	Tajikistan	588	MIN(PROXY(USSR(Maddison)))
124	US	588	1600(Maddison)
125	Albania	588	MIN(PROXY(E. Europe(Maddison)))
126	Bolivia	588	MIN(PROXY(Other Sp. Am.(Maddison)))
127	Burundi	588	MIN(1950(Maddison))
128	Cuba	588	MIN(PROXY(Caribbean cs(Maddison)))
129	Ethiopia	588	MIN(1950(Maddison))
130	Haiti	588	MIN(PROXY(Caribbean cs(Maddison)))
131	Nepal	588	MIN(PROXY(Other E. Asia(Maddison)))
132	Paraguay	588	MIN(PROXY(Other Sp. Am.(Maddison)))
133	Dominican Rep	588	MIN(PROXY(Caribbean cs(Maddison)))

TABLE 2.5 - GDP AT PPP PER CAPITA 2007 DOLLARS, YEAR 1700

OBS	COUNTRY	GPCPPP	SOURCE
1	Netherlands	3,129	1700(Maddison)
2	UK	1,836	1700(Maddison)
3	Uruguay	1,690	INTERPOL(Maddison)
4	Belgium	1,681	1700(Maddison)
5	Italy	1,616	1700(Maddison)
6	Denmark	1,526	1700(Maddison)
7	Austria	1,459	1700(Maddison)
8	Sweden	1,435	1700(Maddison)
9	Slovenia	1,405	INTERPOL(Maddison)
10	Germany	1,337	1700(Maddison)

11	France	1,337	1700(Maddison)
12	Norway	1,322	1700(Maddison)
13	Hungary	1,318	INTERPOL(Maddison)
14	Switzerland	1,308	1700(Maddison)
15	Estonia	1,292	INTERPOL(Maddison)
16	Spain	1,253	1700(Maddison)
17	Argentina	1,229	INTERPOL(Maddison)
18	Portugal	1,203	1700(Maddison)
19	Poland	1,173	PROXY(E. Europe(Maddison))
20	Latvia	1,164	PROXY(USSR(Maddison))
21	Czechia	1,156	PROXY(E. Europe(Maddison))
22	Romania	1,154	PROXY(E. Europe(Maddison))
23	Kazakhstan	1,149	PROXY(USSR(Maddison))
24	Lithuania	1,125	PROXY(USSR(Maddison))
25	Jamaica	1,053	PROXY(Caribbean cs(Maddison))
26	Ireland	1,050	1700(Maddison)
27	Bulgaria	1,042	PROXY(E. Europe(Maddison))
28	Trinidad/Tobago	1,015	INTERPOL(Maddison)
29	Slovakia	1,009	PROXY(E. Europe(Maddison))
30	Russia	974	PROXY(USSR(Maddison))
31	Lebanon	967	PROXY(Other W. Asia(Maddison))
32	Syria	967	PROXY(Other W. Asia(Maddison))
33	Croatia	945	PROXY(E. Europe(Maddison))
34	Thailand	937	PROXY(Other E. Asia(Maddison))
35	Finland	937	1700(Maddison)
36	Armenia	907	PROXY(USSR(Maddison))
37	Israel	902	PROXY(Other W. Asia(Maddison))
38	Georgia	882	PROXY(USSR(Maddison))
39	China	881	1700(Maddison)
40	Iran	881	1700(Maddison)
41	Korea, South	881	1700(Maddison)
42	Turkey	881	1700(Maddison)
43	Korea, North	881	1700(Maddison)
44	Hong Kong	881	PROXY(China(Maddison))
45	Malaysia	875	PROXY(Other E. Asia(Maddison))
46	Jordan	864	PROXY(Other W. Asia(Maddison))
47	Indonesia	852	1700(Maddison)
48	Philippines	847	PROXY(Other E. Asia(Maddison))
49	Puerto Rico	842	PROXY(Caribbean cs(Maddison))
50	Iraq	841	PROXY(W. Asia(Maddison))
51	Chile	838	INTERPOL(Maddison)
52	Japan	837	1700(Maddison)
53	Mexico	834	1700(Maddison)
54	Serbia	816	PROXY(E. Europe(Maddison))
55	Bahrain	808	1700(Arabia(Maddison))
56	Qatar	808	1700(Arabia(Maddison))
57	Kuwait	808	1700(Arabia(Maddison))
58	Pakistan	808	1700(Undivided India(Maddison))
59	Bangladesh	808	1700(Undivided India(Maddison))
60	India	808	1700(Undivided India(Maddison))
61	Saudi Arabia	808	1700(Arabia(Maddison))
62	UAE	808	1700(Arabia(Maddison))
63	Oman	808	1700(Arabia(Maddison))
64	Yemen	808	1700(Arabia(Maddison))
65	Cuba	804	PROXY(Caribean cs(Maddison))

66	Montenegro	803	PROXY(E. Europe(Maddison))
67	Taiwan	798	PROXY(Other E. Asia(Maddison))
68	Sri Lanka	798	PROXY(Other E. Asia(Maddison))
69	Moldova	794	PROXY(USSR(Maddison))
70	Greece	779	1700(Maddison)
71	US	774	1700(Maddison)
72	Belarus	774	PROXY(USSR(Maddison))
73	Cyprus	765	PROXY(Greece(Maddison))
74	Vietnam	765	PROXY(Other E. Asia(Maddison))
75	Uzbekistan	754	PROXY(USSR(Maddison))
76	Afghanistan	741	PROXY(Other E. Asia(Maddison))
77	Burma	731	PROXY(Other E. Asia(Maddison))
78	Ukraine	729	PROXY(USSR(Maddison))
79	Singapore	726	PROXY(Other E. Asia(Maddison))
80	Turkmenistan	714	PROXY(USSR(Maddison))
81	Laos	704	PROXY(Other E. Asia(Maddison))
82	Egypt	698	1700(Maddison)
83	Brazil	674	1700(Maddison)
84	Azerbaijan	656	PROXY(USSR(Maddison))
85	Tunisia	632	PROXY(Other N. Africa(Maddison))
86	Canada	632	1700(Maddison)
87	Algeria	632	PROXY(Other N. Africa(Maddison))
88	Morocco	632	1700(Maddison)
89	Libya	632	1700(Other N. Africa(Maddison))
90	Colombia	611	PROXY(Other Sp. Am.(Maddison))
91	Somalia	610	1700(Rest of Africa(Maddison))
92	South Africa	610	1700(Rest of Africa(Maddison))
93	Zambia	610	1700(Rest of Africa(Maddison))
94	Zimbabwe	610	1700(Rest of Africa(Maddison))
95	Madagascar	610	1700(Rest of Africa(Maddison))
96	Namibia	610	1700(Rest of Africa(Maddison))
97	Sudan	610	1700(Sahel & W. Africa(Maddison))
98	Swaziland	610	1700(Rest of Africa(Maddison))
99	Ghana	610	PROXY(Sahel & W. Africa(Maddison))
100	Mozambique	610	1700(Rest of Africa(Maddison))
101	Tajikistan	606	PROXY(USSR(Maddison))
102	Cambodia	595	PROXY(Other E. Asia(Maddison))
103	Costa Rica	588	MIN(PROXY(Other Sp. Am.(Maddison)))
104	El Salvador	588	MIN(PROXY(Other Sp. Am.(Maddison)))
105	Guinea	588	MIN(1950(Maddison))
106	Australia	588	1700(Maddison)
107	Ecuador	588	MIN(PROXY(Other Sp. Am.(Maddison)))
108	Eritrea	588	MIN(1950(Maddison))
109	Guinea-Bissau	588	MIN(1950(Maddison))
110	Kosovo	588	MIN(PROXY(E. Europe(Maddison)))
111	Kyrgyzstan	588	MIN(PROXY(USSR(Maddison)))
112	Macedonia	588	MIN(PROXY(E. Europe(Maddison)))
113	Malawi	588	MIN(1950(Maddison))
114	Nicaragua	588	MIN(PROXY(Other Sp. Am.(Maddison)))
115	Panama	588	MIN(PROXY(Other Sp. Am.(Maddison)))
116	Venezuela	588	MIN(PROXY(Other Sp. Am.(Maddison)))
117	Bosnia	588	MIN(PROXY(E. Europe(Maddison)))
118	Botswana	588	MIN(1950(Maddison))
119	Guatemala	588	MIN(PROXY(Other Sp. Am.(Maddison)))
120	Honduras	588	MIN(PROXY(Other Sp. Am.(Maddison)))
121	Lesotho	588	MIN(1950(Maddison))

122	Mongolia	588	MIN(PROXY(Other E. Asia(Maddison)))
123	New Zealand	588	1700(Maddison)
124	Peru	588	MIN(PROXY(Other Sp. Am.(Maddison)))
125	Sierra Leone	588	MIN(1950(Maddison))
126	Albania	588	MIN(PROXY(E. Europe(Maddison)))
127	Bolivia	588	MIN(PROXY(Other Sp. Am.(Maddison)))
128	Burundi	588	MIN(1950(Maddison))
129	Ethiopia	588	MIN(1950(Maddison))
130	Haiti	588	MIN(PROXY(Caribbean cs(Maddison)))
131	Nepal	588	MIN(PROXY(Other E. Asia(Maddison)))
132	Paraguay	588	MIN(PROXY(Other Sp. Am.(Maddison)))
133	Dominican Rep	588	MIN(PROXY(Caribbean cs(Maddison)))

TABLE 2.6 - GDP AT PPP PER CAPITA, 2007 DOLLARS, YEAR 1820

OBS	COUNTRY	GPCPPP	SOURCE
1	Uruguay	3,128	PROXY(Other L. Am.(Maddison))
2	Netherlands	2,700	1820(Maddison)
3	UK	2,506	1820(Maddison)
4	Belgium	1,938	1820(Maddison)
5	Argentina	1,881	PROXY(Other L. Am.(Maddison))
6	Denmark	1,872	1820(Maddison)
7	US	1,847	1820(Maddison)
8	Austria	1,789	1820(Maddison)
9	Sweden	1,760	1820(Maddison)
10	France	1,667	1820(Maddison)
11	Italy	1,641	1820(Maddison)
12	Slovenia	1,632	INTERPOL(Maddison)
13	Norway	1,622	1820(Maddison)
14	Switzerland	1,601	1820(Maddison)
15	Germany	1,582	1820(Maddison)
16	Hungary	1,514	INTERPOL(Maddison)
17	Spain	1,481	1820(Maddison)
18	Estonia	1,478	PROXY(USSR(Maddison))
19	Trinidad/ Tobago	1,410	PROXY(Other L. Am.(Maddison))
20	Portugal	1,356	1820(Maddison)
21	Canada	1,328	1820(Maddison)
22	Poland	1,322	PROXY(E. Europe(Maddison))
23	Latvia	1,313	PROXY(USSR(Maddison))
24	Czechia	1,303	PROXY(Czechoslovakia(Maddison))
25	Romania	1,301	PROXY(E. Europe(Maddison))
26	Kazakhstan	1,296	PROXY(USSR(Maddison))
27	Ireland	1,288	1820(Maddison)
28	Lithuania	1,269	PROXY(USSR(Maddison))
29	Bulgaria	1,174	PROXY(E. Europe(Maddison))
30	Finland	1,147	1820(Maddison)
31	Slovakia	1,137	PROXY(Czechoslovakia(Maddison))
32	Mexico	1,115	1820(Maddison)
33	Russia	1,099	PROXY(USSR(Maddison))
34	Croatia	1,065	PROXY(E. Europe(Maddison))
35	Jamaica	1,028	1820(Maddison)
36	Armenia	1,023	PROXY(USSR(Maddison))

37	Chile	1,020	1820(Maddison)
38	Georgia	995	PROXY(USSR(Maddison))
39	Japan	983	1820(Maddison)
40	Lebanon	967	1820(Maddison)
41	Syria	967	1820(Maddison)
42	Brazil	949	1820(Maddison)
43	Thailand	949	1820(Maddison)
44	Turkey	945	1820(Maddison)
45	Greece	942	1820(Maddison)
46	Cyprus	926	PROXY(Greece(Maddison))
47	Serbia	920	PROXY(E. Europe(Maddison))
48	Montenegro	905	PROXY(E. Europe(Maddison))
49	Israel	902	1820(Palestine(Maddison))
50	Indonesia	899	1820(Maddison)
51	Moldova	895	PROXY(USSR(Maddison))
52	Malaysia	886	1820(Maddison)
53	China	881	1820(Maddison)
54	Korea, South	881	1820(Maddison)
55	Korea, North	881	1820(Maddison)
56	Hong Kong	881	1820(Maddison)
57	Belarus	873	PROXY(USSR(Maddison))
58	Iraq	864	1820(Maddison)
59	Iran	864	1820(Maddison)
60	Jordan	864	1820(Maddison)
61	Philippines	858	1820(Maddison)
62	Uzbekistan	853	PROXY(USSR(Maddison))
63	Colombia	835	PROXY(Other L. Am.(Maddison))
64	Puerto Rico	823	PROXY(Other L. Am.(Maddison))
65	Ukraine	822	PROXY(USSR(Maddison))
66	Bahrain	808	1820(Arabia(Maddison))
67	Qatar	808	1820(Arabia(Maddison))
68	Taiwan	808	1820(Maddison)
69	Kuwait	808	1820(Arabia(Maddison))
70	Saudi Arabia	808	1820(Arabia(Maddison))
71	Sri Lanka	808	1820(Maddison)
72	UAE	808	1820(Arabia(Maddison))
73	Oman	808	1820(Arabia(Maddison))
74	Yemen	808	1820(Arabia(Maddison))
75	Turkmenistan	805	PROXY(USSR(Maddison))
76	Guatemala	800	PROXY(Other L. Am.(Maddison))
77	Cuba	785	PROXY(Other L. Am.(Maddison))
78	Pakistan	780	1820(Maddison)
79	Bangladesh	780	1820(Maddison)
80	India	780	1820(Maddison)
81	Vietnam	774	1820(Maddison)
82	Australia	761	1820(Maddison)
83	Costa Rica	753	PROXY(Other L. Am.(Maddison))
84	Afghanistan	751	PROXY(26 E. Asian cs(Maddison))
85	Burma	740	1820(Maddison)
86	Azerbaijan	740	PROXY(USSR(Maddison))
87	Bolivia	736	PROXY(Other L. Am.(Maddison))
88	Panama	735	PROXY(Other L. Am.(Maddison))
89	Singapore	735	1820(Maddison)
90	Ecuador	715	PROXY(Other L. Am.(Maddison))
91	Laos	713	PROXY(26 E. Asian cs(Maddison))
92	Peru	700	PROXY(Other L. Am.(Maddison))

93	Egypt	698	1820(Maddison)
94	Tajikistan	683	PROXY(USSR(Maddison))
95	Venezuela	676	1820(Maddison)
96	Tunisia	632	1820(Maddison)
97	Algeria	632	1820(Maddison)
98	Morocco	632	1820(Maddison)
99	Libya	632	1820(Other N. Africa(Maddison))
100	Albania	623	PROXY(E. Europe(Maddison))
101	Kyrgyzstan	623	PROXY(USSR(Maddison))
102	Nicaragua	620	PROXY(Other L. Am.(Maddison))
103	Somalia	610	1820(Rest of Africa(Maddison))
104	South Africa	610	1820(Maddison)
105	Zambia	610	1820(Rest of Africa(Maddison))
106	Zimbabwe	610	1820(Rest of Africa(Maddison))
107	Madagascar	610	1820(Rest of Africa(Maddison))
108	Namibia	610	1820(Rest of Africa(Maddison))
109	Sudan	610	1820(Sahel & W. Africa(Maddison))
110	Swaziland	610	1820(Rest of Africa(Maddison))
111	Ghana	610	1820(Maddison)
112	Mozambique	610	1820(Rest of Africa(Maddison))
113	Paraguay	608	PROXY(Other L. Am.(Maddison))
114	Cambodia	603	PROXY(26 E. Asian cs(Maddison))
115	El Salvador	588	MIN(PROXY(Other L. Am.(Maddison)))
116	Guinea	588	MIN(1950(Maddison))
117	Eritrea	588	MIN(1950(Maddison))
118	Guinea-Bissau	588	MIN(1950(Maddison))
119	Kosovo	588	MIN(PROXY(E. Europe(Maddison)))
120	Macedonia	588	MIN(PROXY(E. Europe(Maddison)))
121	Malawi	588	MIN(1950(Maddison))
122	Bosnia	588	MIN(PROXY(E. Europe(Maddison)))
123	Botswana	588	MIN(1950(Maddison))
124	Honduras	588	MIN(PROXY(Other L. Am.(Maddison)))
125	Lesotho	588	MIN(1950(Maddison))
126	Mongolia	588	MIN(PROXY(26 E. Asian cs(Maddison)))
127	New Zealand	588	1820(Maddison)
128	Sierra Leone	588	MIN(1950(Maddison))
129	Burundi	588	MIN(1950(Maddison))
130	Ethiopia	588	MIN(1950(Maddison))
131	Haiti	588	MIN(PROXY(Other L. Am.(Maddison)))
132	Nepal	588	MIN(1820(Maddison))
133	Dominican Rep	588	MIN(PROXY(Other L. Am.(Maddison)))

TABLE 2.7 - GDP AT PPP PER CAPITA, 2007 DOLLARS, YEAR 1870			
OBS	COUNTRY	GPCPPP	SOURCE
1	Australia	4,808	1870(Maddison)
2	UK	4,687	1870(Maddison)
3	New Zealand	4,554	1870(Maddison)
4	Netherlands	4,050	1870(Maddison)
5	Belgium	3,955	1870(Maddison)
6	US	3,592	1870(Maddison)
7	Uruguay	3,204	1870(Maddison)
8	Switzerland	3,088	1870(Maddison)

9	Denmark	2,943	1870(Maddison)
10	France	2,756	1870(Maddison)
11	Austria	2,737	1870(Maddison)
12	Germany	2,702	1870(Maddison)
13	Ireland	2,608	1870(Maddison)
14	Canada	2,490	1870(Maddison)
15	Sweden	2,442	1870(Maddison)
16	Italy	2,202	1870(Maddison)
17	Norway	2,104	1870(Maddison)
18	Estonia	2,026	PROXY(USSR(Maddison))
19	Argentina	1,926	1870(Maddison)
20	Chile	1,895	1870(Maddison)
21	Latvia	1,799	PROXY(USSR(Maddison))
22	Czechia	1,787	PROXY(Czechoslovakia(Maddison))
23	Kazakhstan	1,777	PROXY(USSR(Maddison))
24	Spain	1,773	1870(Maddison)
25	Lithuania	1,740	PROXY(USSR(Maddison))
26	Slovenia	1,737	PROXY(Yugoslavia(Maddison))
27	Finland	1,675	1870(Maddison)
28	Hungary	1,604	1870(Maddison)
29	Slovakia	1,559	PROXY(Czechoslovakia(Maddison))
30	Russia	1,506	PROXY(USSR(Maddison))
31	Trinidad/ Tobago	1,444	PROXY(Other L. Am.(Maddison))
32	Portugal	1,432	1870(Maddison)
33	Armenia	1,402	PROXY(USSR(Maddison))
34	Poland	1,390	1870(Maddison)
35	Romania	1,368	1870(Maddison)
36	Georgia	1,364	PROXY(USSR(Maddison))
37	Greece	1,293	1870(Maddison)
38	Cyprus	1,271	PROXY(Greece(Maddison))
39	South Africa	1,261	1870(Maddison)
40	Sri Lanka	1,250	1870(Maddison)
41	Lebanon	1,240	1870(Maddison)
42	Syria	1,240	1870(Maddison)
43	Bulgaria	1,234	1870(Maddison)
44	Moldova	1,227	PROXY(USSR(Maddison))
45	Turkey	1,212	1870(Maddison)
46	Belarus	1,197	PROXY(USSR(Maddison))
47	Uzbekistan	1,165	PROXY(USSR(Maddison))
48	Namibia	1,150	INTERPOL(Maddison)
49	Ukraine	1,127	PROXY(USSR(Maddison))
50	Croatia	1,119	PROXY(Yugoslavia(Maddison))
51	Turkmenistan	1,103	PROXY(USSR(Maddison))
52	Israel	1,103	1870(Palestine(Maddison))
53	Japan	1,083	1870(Maddison)
54	Iran	1,056	1870(Maddison)
55	Iraq	1,056	1870(Maddison)
56	Jordan	1,056	1870(Maddison)
57	Algeria	1,050	1870(Maddison)
58	Brazil	1,047	1870(Maddison)
59	Thailand	1,046	1870(Maddison)
60	Azerbaijan	1,014	PROXY(USSR(Maddison))
61	Hong Kong	1,003	1870(Maddison)
62	Singapore	1,002	1870(Maddison)
63	Mexico	990	1870(Maddison)

64	Malaysia	974	1870(Maddison)
65	Serbia	967	PROXY(Yugoslavia(Maddison))
66	Indonesia	961	1870(Maddison)
67	Egypt	953	1870(Maddison)
68	Montenegro	951	PROXY(Yugoslavia(Maddison))
69	Tajikistan	936	PROXY(USSR(Maddison))
70	Tunisia	930	1870(Maddison)
71	Philippines	917	1870(Maddison)
72	Pakistan	916	INTERPOL(Maddison)
73	Mozambique	897	INTERPOL(Maddison)
74	Korea, North	887	1870(Maddison)
75	Korea, South	887	1870(Maddison)
76	Somalia	874	INTERPOL(Maddison)
77	Colombia	855	PROXY(Other L. Am.(Maddison))
78	Kyrgyzstan	854	PROXY(USSR(Maddison))
79	Bahrain	845	1870(Arabia(Maddison))
80	Qatar	845	1870(Arabia(Maddison))
81	Kuwait	845	1870(Arabia(Maddison))
82	Saudi Arabia	845	1870(Arabia(Maddison))
83	Yemen	845	1870(Arabia(Maddison))
84	Oman	845	1870(Arabia(Maddison))
85	UAE	845	1870(Arabia(Maddison))
86	Puerto Rico	843	PROXY(Other L. Am.(Maddison))
87	Madagascar	839	INTERPOL(Maddison)
88	Venezuela	836	1870(Maddison)
89	Morocco	827	1870(Maddison)
90	Bangladesh	825	INTERPOL(Maddison)
91	Libya	824	INTERPOL(Maddison)
92	India	820	1870(Maddison)
93	Guatemala	819	PROXY(Other L. Am.(Maddison))
94	Taiwan	808	1870(Maddison)
95	Cuba	804	PROXY(Other L. Am.(Maddison))
96	Sudan	793	INTERPOL(Maddison)
97	Jamaica	786	1870(Maddison)
98	China	779	1870(Maddison)
99	Costa Rica	771	PROXY(Other L. Am.(Maddison))
100	Bolivia	754	PROXY(Other L. Am.(Maddison))
101	Swaziland	754	INTERPOL(Maddison)
102	Panama	753	PROXY(Other L. Am.(Maddison))
103	Zimbabwe	746	INTERPOL(Maddison)
104	Vietnam	742	1870(Maddison)
105	Burma	740	1870(Maddison)
106	Ecuador	732	PROXY(Other L. Am.(Maddison))
107	Zambia	729	INTERPOL(Maddison)
108	Afghanistan	722	PROXY(26 E. Asian cs(Maddison))
109	Peru	717	PROXY(Other L. Am.(Maddison))
110	Laos	686	PROXY(26 E. Asian cs(Maddison))
111	Ghana	679	1870(Maddison)
112	Albania	655	1870(Maddison)
113	Nicaragua	635	PROXY(Other L. Am.(Maddison))
114	Paraguay	622	PROXY(Other L. Am.(Maddison))
115	Macedonia	595	PROXY(Yugoslavia(Maddison))
116	El Salvador	588	MIN(PROXY(Other L. Am.(Maddison)))
117	Guinea	588	MIN(1950(Maddison))
118	Cambodia	588	MIN(PROXY(26 E. Asian cs(Maddison)))
119	Eritrea	588	MIN(1950(Maddison))

120	Guinea-Bissau	588	MIN(1950(Maddison))
121	Kosovo	588	MIN(PROXY(Yugoslavia(Maddison)))
122	Malawi	588	MIN(1950(Maddison))
123	Bosnia	588	MIN(PROXY(Yugoslavia(Maddison)))
124	Botswana	588	MIN(1950(Maddison))
125	Honduras	588	MIN(PROXY(Other L. Am.(Maddison)))
126	Lesotho	588	MIN(1950(Maddison))
127	Mongolia	588	MIN(PROXY(26 E. Asian cs(Maddison)))
128	Sierra Leone	588	MIN(1950(Maddison))
129	Burundi	588	MIN(1950(Maddison))
130	Ethiopia	588	MIN(1950(Maddison))
131	Haiti	588	MIN(PROXY(Other L. Am.(Maddison)))
132	Nepal	588	MIN(1870(Maddison))
133	Dominican Rep	588	MIN(PROXY(Other L. Am.(Maddison)))

TABLE 2.8 - GDP AT PPP PER CAPITA ,2007 DOLLARS, YEAR 1880

OBS	COUNTRY	GPCPPP	SOURCE
1	Australia	6,295	1880(Maddison)
2	New Zealand	5,505	1880(Maddison)
3	UK	5,108	1880(Maddison)
4	Belgium	4,503	1880(Maddison)
5	Netherlands	4,475	1880(Maddison)
6	US	4,231	1880(Maddison)
7	Switzerland	3,599	1880(Maddison)
8	Denmark	3,204	1880(Maddison)
9	France	3,115	1880(Maddison)
10	Uruguay	3,059	1880(Maddison)
11	Austria	3,054	1880(Maddison)
12	Germany	2,925	1880(Maddison)
13	Ireland	2,884	INTERPOL(Maddison)
14	Sweden	2,712	1880(Maddison)
15	Canada	2,668	1880(Maddison)
16	Argentina	2,468	INTERPOL(Maddison)
17	Spain	2,418	1880(Maddison)
18	Norway	2,333	1880(Maddison)
19	Italy	2,323	1880(Maddison)
20	Chile	2,263	INTERPOL(Maddison)
21	Estonia	2,218	INTERPOL(Maddison)
22	Slovenia	2,060	INTERPOL(Maddison)
23	Czechia	2,032	INTERPOL(Maddison)
24	Latvia	1,970	INTERPOL(Maddison)
25	Kazakhstan	1,945	INTERPOL(Maddison)
26	Lithuania	1,904	INTERPOL(Maddison)
27	Hungary	1,863	INTERPOL(Maddison)
28	Slovakia	1,773	INTERPOL(Maddison)
29	Trinidad/ Tobago	1,720	INTERPOL(Maddison)
30	Finland	1,697	1880(Maddison)
31	Russia	1,649	INTERPOL(Maddison)
32	Poland	1,619	INTERPOL(Maddison)
33	Romania	1,582	INTERPOL(Maddison)
34	Armenia	1,535	INTERPOL(Maddison)

35	Greece	1,496	INTERPOL(Maddison)
36	Georgia	1,493	INTERPOL(Maddison)
37	Cyprus	1,470	PROXY(Greece(Maddison))
38	South Africa	1,458	INTERPOL(Maddison)
39	Bulgaria	1,432	INTERPOL(Maddison)
40	Portugal	1,391	1880(Maddison)
41	Lebanon	1,383	INTERPOL(Maddison)
42	Syria	1,383	INTERPOL(Maddison)
43	Moldova	1,343	INTERPOL(Maddison)
44	Croatia	1,328	INTERPOL(Maddison)
45	Turkey	1,326	INTERPOL(Maddison)
46	Belarus	1,310	INTERPOL(Maddison)
47	Namibia	1,305	INTERPOL(Maddison)
48	Uzbekistan	1,276	INTERPOL(Maddison)
49	Japan	1,268	1880(Maddison)
50	Israel	1,242	INTERPOL(Maddison)
51	Ukraine	1,233	INTERPOL(Maddison)
52	Sri Lanka	1,221	1880(Maddison)
53	Mexico	1,213	INTERPOL(Maddison)
54	Turkmenistan	1,208	INTERPOL(Maddison)
55	Algeria	1,164	1880(Maddison)
56	Hong Kong	1,161	INTERPOL(Maddison)
57	Singapore	1,160	INTERPOL(Maddison)
58	Serbia	1,147	INTERPOL(Maddison)
59	Iran	1,141	INTERPOL(Maddison)
60	Iraq	1,141	INTERPOL(Maddison)
61	Jordan	1,141	INTERPOL(Maddison)
62	Montenegro	1,128	INTERPOL(Maddison)
63	Azerbaijan	1,110	INTERPOL(Maddison)
64	Brazil	1,105	1880(Maddison)
65	Thailand	1,098	INTERPOL(Maddison)
66	Tajikistan	1,025	INTERPOL(Maddison)
67	Malaysia	1,020	INTERPOL(Maddison)
68	Colombia	1,015	INTERPOL(Maddison)
69	Egypt	1,013	INTERPOL(Maddison)
70	Tunisia	1,005	INTERPOL(Maddison)
71	Puerto Rico	1,004	INTERPOL(Maddison)
72	Guatemala	976	INTERPOL(Maddison)
73	Indonesia	973	1880(Maddison)
74	Mozambique	969	INTERPOL(Maddison)
75	Cuba	958	INTERPOL(Maddison)
76	Korea, North	953	INTERPOL(Maddison)
77	Korea, South	953	INTERPOL(Maddison)
78	Philippines	950	INTERPOL(Maddison)
79	Pakistan	946	INTERPOL(Maddison)
80	Venezuela	945	INTERPOL(Maddison)
81	Somalia	939	INTERPOL(Maddison)
82	Kyrgyzstan	934	INTERPOL(Maddison)
83	Costa Rica	919	INTERPOL(Maddison)
84	Bolivia	899	INTERPOL(Maddison)
85	Panama	897	INTERPOL(Maddison)
86	Madagascar	894	INTERPOL(Maddison)
87	Morocco	873	INTERPOL(Maddison)
88	Ecuador	872	INTERPOL(Maddison)
89	Libya	868	INTERPOL(Maddison)
90	Taiwan	862	INTERPOL(Maddison)

91	India	856	INTERPOL(Maddison)
92	Bahrain	853	INTERPOL(Maddison)
93	Kuwait	853	INTERPOL(Maddison)
94	Qatar	853	INTERPOL(Maddison)
95	Saudi Arabia	853	INTERPOL(Maddison)
96	Yemen	853	INTERPOL(Maddison)
97	UAE	853	INTERPOL(Maddison)
98	Oman	853	INTERPOL(Maddison)
99	Peru	852	INTERPOL(Maddison)
100	Sudan	835	INTERPOL(Maddison)
101	Bangladesh	835	INTERPOL(Maddison)
102	Jamaica	813	INTERPOL(Maddison)
103	Vietnam	808	INTERPOL(Maddison)
104	Burma	795	INTERPOL(Maddison)
105	Swaziland	787	INTERPOL(Maddison)
106	China	786	INTERPOL(Maddison)
107	Afghanistan	782	INTERPOL(Maddison)
108	Zimbabwe	777	INTERPOL(Maddison)
109	Albania	759	INTERPOL(Maddison)
110	Nicaragua	757	INTERPOL(Maddison)
111	Zambia	756	INTERPOL(Maddison)
112	Laos	743	INTERPOL(Maddison)
113	Paraguay	742	INTERPOL(Maddison)
114	Macedonia	705	INTERPOL(Maddison)
115	El Salvador	697	INTERPOL(Maddison)
116	Ghana	694	INTERPOL(Maddison)
117	Bosnia	675	PROXY(Yugoslavia(Maddison))
118	Cambodia	628	INTERPOL(Maddison)
119	Nepal	626	INTERPOL(Maddison)
120	Honduras	615	INTERPOL(Maddison)
121	Guinea	588	MIN(1950(Maddison))
122	Eritrea	588	MIN(1950(Maddison))
123	Guinea-Bissau	588	MIN(1950(Maddison))
124	Kosovo	588	MIN(INTERPOL(Maddison))
125	Malawi	588	MIN(1950(Maddison))
126	Botswana	588	MIN(1950(Maddison))
127	Lesotho	588	MIN(1950(Maddison))
128	Mongolia	588	MIN(INTERPOL(Maddison))
129	Sierra Leone	588	MIN(1950(Maddison))
130	Burundi	588	MIN(1950(Maddison))
131	Ethiopia	588	MIN(1950(Maddison))
132	Haiti	588	MIN(INTERPOL(Maddison))
133	Dominican Rep	588	MIN(INTERPOL(Maddison))

TABLE 2.9 - GDP AT PPP PER CAPITA, 2007 DOLLARS, YEAR 1890			
OBS	COUNTRY	GPCPPP	SOURCE
1	Australia	6,549	1890(Maddison)
2	UK	5,890	1890(Maddison)
3	New Zealand	5,517	1890(Maddison)
4	Belgium	5,036	1890(Maddison)
5	US	4,983	1890(Maddison)
6	Netherlands	4,882	1890(Maddison)

7	Switzerland	4,675	1890(Maddison)
8	Denmark	3,707	1890(Maddison)
9	Austria	3,589	1890(Maddison)
10	Germany	3,567	1890(Maddison)
11	Canada	3,494	1890(Maddison)
12	France	3,491	1890(Maddison)
13	Ireland	3,189	INTERPOL(Maddison)
14	Argentina	3,162	1890(Maddison)
15	Uruguay	3,154	1890(Maddison)
16	Sweden	3,065	1890(Maddison)
17	Chile	2,701	INTERPOL(Maddison)
18	Norway	2,611	1890(Maddison)
19	Italy	2,449	1890(Maddison)
20	Slovenia	2,444	PROXY(Yugoslavia(Maddison))
21	Estonia	2,428	INTERPOL(Maddison)
22	Spain	2,386	1890(Maddison)
23	Czechia	2,310	PROXY(Czechoslovakia(Maddison))
24	Hungary	2,164	1890(Maddison)
25	Latvia	2,156	INTERPOL(Maddison)
26	Kazakhstan	2,129	INTERPOL(Maddison)
27	Lithuania	2,085	INTERPOL(Maddison)
28	Trinidad/Tobago	2,050	INTERPOL(Maddison)
29	Finland	2,029	1890(Maddison)
30	Slovakia	2,016	PROXY(Czechoslovakia(Maddison))
31	Poland	1,886	1890(Maddison)
32	Romania	1,831	1890(Maddison)
33	Russia	1,805	INTERPOL(Maddison)
34	Greece	1,731	1890(Maddison)
35	Cyprus	1,701	PROXY(Greece(Maddison))
36	South Africa	1,685	INTERPOL(Maddison)
37	Armenia	1,680	INTERPOL(Maddison)
38	Bulgaria	1,662	1890(Maddison)
39	Portugal	1,657	1890(Maddison)
40	Georgia	1,635	INTERPOL(Maddison)
41	Croatia	1,575	PROXY(Yugoslavia(Maddison))
42	Lebanon	1,543	INTERPOL(Maddison)
43	Syria	1,543	INTERPOL(Maddison)
44	Sri Lanka	1,535	1890(Maddison)
45	Japan	1,487	1890(Maddison)
46	Mexico	1,485	1890(Maddison)
47	Namibia	1,482	INTERPOL(Maddison)
48	Moldova	1,470	INTERPOL(Maddison)
49	Turkey	1,450	INTERPOL(Maddison)
50	Belarus	1,434	INTERPOL(Maddison)
51	Israel	1,398	INTERPOL(Maddison)
52	Uzbekistan	1,397	INTERPOL(Maddison)
53	Serbia	1,361	PROXY(Yugoslavia(Maddison))
54	Ukraine	1,350	INTERPOL(Maddison)
55	Hong Kong	1,343	INTERPOL(Maddison)
56	Singapore	1,342	INTERPOL(Maddison)
57	Montenegro	1,338	PROXY(Yugoslavia(Maddison))
58	Turkmenistan	1,322	INTERPOL(Maddison)
59	Algeria	1,307	INTERPOL(Maddison)
60	Iran	1,231	INTERPOL(Maddison)
61	Iraq	1,231	INTERPOL(Maddison)
62	Jordan	1,231	INTERPOL(Maddison)

63	Azerbaijan	1,215	INTERPOL(Maddison)
64	Colombia	1,204	INTERPOL(Maddison)
65	Puerto Rico	1,196	INTERPOL(Maddison)
66	Brazil	1,166	1890(Maddison)
67	Guatemala	1,163	INTERPOL(Maddison)
68	Thailand	1,152	1890(Maddison)
69	Cuba	1,141	INTERPOL(Maddison)
70	Tajikistan	1,122	INTERPOL(Maddison)
71	Costa Rica	1,095	INTERPOL(Maddison)
72	Tunisia	1,086	INTERPOL(Maddison)
73	Egypt	1,084	INTERPOL(Maddison)
74	Bolivia	1,071	INTERPOL(Maddison)
75	Panama	1,069	INTERPOL(Maddison)
76	Malaysia	1,068	INTERPOL(Maddison)
77	Venezuela	1,067	INTERPOL(Maddison)
78	Mozambique	1,047	INTERPOL(Maddison)
79	Ecuador	1,039	INTERPOL(Maddison)
80	Korea, South	1,023	INTERPOL(Maddison)
81	Korea, North	1,023	INTERPOL(Maddison)
82	Kyrgyzstan	1,023	INTERPOL(Maddison)
83	Peru	1,011	INTERPOL(Maddison)
84	Somalia	1,009	INTERPOL(Maddison)
85	Philippines	984	INTERPOL(Maddison)
86	Pakistan	977	INTERPOL(Maddison)
87	Indonesia	970	1890(Maddison)
88	Madagascar	953	INTERPOL(Maddison)
89	Morocco	921	INTERPOL(Maddison)
90	Taiwan	920	INTERPOL(Maddison)
91	Libya	916	INTERPOL(Maddison)
92	Nicaragua	902	INTERPOL(Maddison)
93	India	893	1890(Maddison)
94	Paraguay	884	INTERPOL(Maddison)
95	Sudan	880	INTERPOL(Maddison)
96	Vietnam	879	INTERPOL(Maddison)
97	Albania	879	1890(Maddison)
98	Bahrain	862	INTERPOL(Maddison)
99	Qatar	862	INTERPOL(Maddison)
100	Kuwait	862	INTERPOL(Maddison)
101	Yemen	862	INTERPOL(Maddison)
102	UAE	862	INTERPOL(Maddison)
103	Oman	862	INTERPOL(Maddison)
104	Saudi Arabia	862	INTERPOL(Maddison)
105	Burma	854	INTERPOL(Maddison)
106	Afghanistan	846	INTERPOL(Maddison)
107	Bangladesh	844	INTERPOL(Maddison)
108	Jamaica	842	INTERPOL(Maddison)
109	Macedonia	837	PROXY(Yugoslavia(Maddison))
110	El Salvador	831	INTERPOL(Maddison)
111	Swaziland	821	INTERPOL(Maddison)
112	Zimbabwe	809	INTERPOL(Maddison)
113	Laos	804	INTERPOL(Maddison)
114	Bosnia	801	PROXY(Yugoslavia(Maddison))
115	China	793	1890(Maddison)
116	Zambia	783	INTERPOL(Maddison)
117	Honduras	732	INTERPOL(Maddison)
118	Ghana	709	INTERPOL(Maddison)

119	Dominican Rep	683	INTERPOL(Maddison)
120	Cambodia	679	INTERPOL(Maddison)
121	Nepal	672	INTERPOL(Maddison)
122	Guinea	588	MIN(1950(Maddison))
123	Eritrea	588	MIN(1950(Maddison))
124	Guinea-Bissau	588	MIN(1950(Maddison))
125	Kosovo	588	MIN(PROXY(Yugoslvaia(Maddison)))
126	Malawi	588	MIN(1950(Maddison))
127	Botswana	588	MIN(1950(Maddison))
128	Lesotho	588	MIN(1950(Maddison))
129	Mongolia	588	MIN(INTERPOL(Maddison))
130	Sierra Leone	588	MIN(1950(Maddison))
131	Burundi	588	MIN(1950(Maddison))
132	Ethiopia	588	MIN(1950(Maddison))
133	Haiti	588	MIN(INTERPOL(Maddison))

TABLE 2.10 - GDP AT PPP PER CAPITA, 2007 DOLLARS, YEAR 1900			
OBS	COUNTRY	GPCPPP	SOURCE
1	UK	6,599	1900(Maddison)
2	New Zealand	6,314	1900(Maddison)
3	US	6,010	1900(Maddison)
4	Australia	5,896	1900(Maddison)
5	Switzerland	5,631	1900(Maddison)
6	Belgium	5,481	1900(Maddison)
7	Netherlands	5,030	1900(Maddison)
8	Denmark	4,432	1900(Maddison)
9	Germany	4,385	1900(Maddison)
10	Canada	4,277	1900(Maddison)
11	Austria	4,234	1900(Maddison)
12	France	4,225	1900(Maddison)
13	Argentina	4,049	1900(Maddison)
14	Sweden	3,762	1900(Maddison)
15	Ireland	3,527	INTERPOL(Maddison)
16	Uruguay	3,260	1900(Maddison)
17	Chile	3,225	1900(Maddison)
18	Norway	2,846	1900(Maddison)
19	Estonia	2,658	PROXY(USSR(Maddison))
20	Czechia	2,654	PROXY(Czechoslovakia(Maddison))
21	Spain	2,624	1900(Maddison)
22	Italy	2,622	1900(Maddison)
23	Slovenia	2,615	PROXY(Yugoslavia(Maddison))
24	Hungary	2,471	1900(Maddison)
25	Finland	2,451	1900(Maddison)
26	Trinidad/ Tobago	2,442	INTERPOL(Maddison)
27	Latvia	2,360	PROXY(USSR(Maddison))
28	Kazakhstan	2,330	PROXY(USSR(Maddison))
29	Slovakia	2,316	PROXY(Czechoslovakia(Maddison))
30	Lithuania	2,282	PROXY(USSR(Maddison))
31	Poland	2,257	1900(Maddison)
32	Romania	2,079	1900(Maddison)
33	Mexico	2,007	1900(Maddison)

34	Greece	1,985	1900(Maddison)
35	Russia	1,976	PROXY(USSR(Maddison))
36	Cyprus	1,951	PROXY(Greece(Maddison))
37	South Africa	1,949	INTERPOL(Maddison)
38	Portugal	1,913	1900(Maddison)
39	Sri Lanka	1,895	1900(Maddison)
40	Armenia	1,839	PROXY(USSR(Maddison))
41	Bulgaria	1,797	1900(Maddison)
42	Georgia	1,789	PROXY(USSR(Maddison))
43	Japan	1,734	1900(Maddison)
44	Lebanon	1,721	INTERPOL(Maddison)
45	Syria	1,721	INTERPOL(Maddison)
46	Croatia	1,686	PROXY(Yugoslavia(Maddison))
47	Namibia	1,683	INTERPOL(Maddison)
48	Moldova	1,609	PROXY(USSR(Maddison))
49	Turkey	1,586	INTERPOL(Maddison)
50	Israel	1,574	INTERPOL(Maddison)
51	Belarus	1,570	PROXY(USSR(Maddison))
52	Hong Kong	1,554	INTERPOL(Maddison)
53	Singapore	1,554	INTERPOL(Maddison)
54	Uzbekistan	1,529	PROXY(USSR(Maddison))
55	Ukraine	1,478	PROXY(USSR(Maddison))
56	Algeria	1,469	INTERPOL(Maddison)
57	Serbia	1,456	PROXY(Yugoslavia(Maddison))
58	Turkmenistan	1,447	PROXY(USSR(Maddison))
59	Montenegro	1,432	PROXY(Yugoslavia(Maddison))
60	Colombia	1,429	1900(Maddison)
61	Puerto Rico	1,425	INTERPOL(Maddison)
62	Guatemala	1,386	INTERPOL(Maddison)
63	Cuba	1,360	INTERPOL(Maddison)
64	Azerbaijan	1,330	PROXY(USSR(Maddison))
65	Iran	1,330	INTERPOL(Maddison)
66	Iraq	1,330	INTERPOL(Maddison)
67	Jordan	1,330	INTERPOL(Maddison)
68	Costa Rica	1,305	INTERPOL(Maddison)
69	Bolivia	1,276	INTERPOL(Maddison)
70	Panama	1,274	INTERPOL(Maddison)
71	Ecuador	1,238	INTERPOL(Maddison)
72	Tajikistan	1,228	PROXY(USSR(Maddison))
73	Venezuela	1,206	1900(Maddison)
74	Peru	1,200	1900(Maddison)
75	Thailand	1,187	INTERPOL(Maddison)
76	Egypt	1,183	INTERPOL(Maddison)
77	Tunisia	1,173	INTERPOL(Maddison)
78	Mozambique	1,131	INTERPOL(Maddison)
79	Kyrgyzstan	1,120	PROXY(USSR(Maddison))
80	Malaysia	1,119	INTERPOL(Maddison)
81	Korea, North	1,098	INTERPOL(Maddison)
82	Korea, South	1,098	INTERPOL(Maddison)
83	Indonesia	1,092	1900(Maddison)
84	Somalia	1,084	INTERPOL(Maddison)
85	Nicaragua	1,074	INTERPOL(Maddison)
86	Paraguay	1,053	INTERPOL(Maddison)
87	Philippines	1,020	INTERPOL(Maddison)
88	Madagascar	1,016	INTERPOL(Maddison)
89	Pakistan	1,009	1900(Maddison)

90	Albania	1,006	1900(Maddison)
91	Brazil	996	1900(Maddison)
92	El Salvador	990	INTERPOL(Maddison)
93	Taiwan	981	INTERPOL(Maddison)
94	Morocco	972	INTERPOL(Maddison)
95	Libya	966	INTERPOL(Maddison)
96	Vietnam	957	INTERPOL(Maddison)
97	Sudan	928	INTERPOL(Maddison)
98	India	918	1900(Maddison)
99	Burma	917	INTERPOL(Maddison)
100	Afghanistan	916	INTERPOL(Maddison)
101	Macedonia	895	PROXY(Yugoslavia(Maddison))
102	Honduras	873	INTERPOL(Maddison)
103	Jamaica	871	INTERPOL(Maddison)
104	Laos	870	INTERPOL(Maddison)
105	Bahrain	870	INTERPOL(Maddison)
106	Qatar	870	INTERPOL(Maddison)
107	Kuwait	870	INTERPOL(Maddison)
108	Saudi Arabia	870	INTERPOL(Maddison)
109	UAE	870	INTERPOL(Maddison)
110	Yemen	870	INTERPOL(Maddison)
111	Oman	870	INTERPOL(Maddison)
112	Bosnia	857	PROXY(Yugoslavia(Maddison))
113	Swaziland	857	INTERPOL(Maddison)
114	Bangladesh	854	1900(Maddison)
115	Dominican Rep	848	INTERPOL(Maddison)
116	Zimbabwe	842	INTERPOL(Maddison)
117	Zambia	812	INTERPOL(Maddison)
118	China	801	1900(Maddison)
119	Ghana	776	INTERPOL(Maddison)
120	Cambodia	735	INTERPOL(Maddison)
121	Nepal	722	INTERPOL(Maddison)
122	Haiti	699	INTERPOL(Maddison)
123	Mongolia	618	INTERPOL(Maddison)
124	Guinea	588	MIN(1950(Maddison))
125	Eritrea	588	MIN(1950(Maddison))
126	Guinea-Bissau	588	MIN(1950(Maddison))
127	Kosovo	588	MIN(PROXY (Yugo(Maddison)))
128	Malawi	588	MIN(1950(Maddison))
129	Botswana	588	MIN(1950(Maddison))
130	Lesotho	588	MIN(1950(Maddison))
131	Sierra Leone	588	MIN(1950(Maddison))
132	Burundi	588	MIN(1950(Maddison))
133	Ethiopia	588	MIN(1950(Maddison))

TABLE 2.11 - GDP AT PURCHASING POWER PARITIES PER CAPITA 2007 DOLLARS YEAR 1913			
OBS	COUNTRY	GPCPPP	SOURCE
1	US	7,788	1913(Maddison)
2	Australia	7,576	1913(Maddison)
3	New Zealand	7,569	1913(Maddison)
4	UK	7,230	1913(Maddison)
5	Canada	6,533	1913(Maddison)

6	Switzerland	6,267	1913(Maddison)
7	Belgium	6,200	1913(Maddison)
8	Netherlands	5,948	1913(Maddison)
9	Denmark	5,747	1913(Maddison)
10	Argentina	5,578	1913(Maddison)
11	Germany	5,359	1913(Maddison)
12	France	5,120	1913(Maddison)
13	Austria	5,091	1913(Maddison)
14	Uruguay	4,863	1913(Maddison)
15	Sweden	4,548	1913(Maddison)
16	Chile	4,390	1913(Maddison)
17	Ireland	4,020	1913(Maddison)
18	Italy	3,767	1913(Maddison)
19	Norway	3,674	1913(Maddison)
20	Czechia	3,217	PROXY(Czechoslovakia(Maddison))
21	Estonia	3,198	PROXY(USSR(Maddison))
22	Finland	3,101	1913(Maddison)
23	Hungary	3,082	1913(Maddison)
24	Trinidad/Tobago	3,067	PROXY(Other L. Am.(Maddison))
25	Slovenia	3,064	PROXY(Yugoslavia(Maddison))
26	Spain	3,021	1913(Maddison)
27	Latvia	2,839	PROXY(USSR(Maddison))
28	Slovakia	2,808	PROXY(Czechoslovakia(Maddison))
29	Kazakhstan	2,803	PROXY(USSR(Maddison))
30	Lithuania	2,745	PROXY(USSR(Maddison))
31	Romania	2,558	1913(Maddison)
32	Poland	2,555	1913(Maddison)
33	Mexico	2,545	1913(Maddison)
34	Russia	2,377	PROXY(USSR(Maddison))
35	South Africa	2,354	1913(Maddison)
36	Greece	2,339	1913(Maddison)
37	Cyprus	2,299	PROXY(Greece(Maddison))
38	Bulgaria	2,254	1913(Maddison)
39	Armenia	2,212	PROXY(USSR(Maddison))
40	Georgia	2,152	PROXY(USSR(Maddison))
41	Japan	2,038	1913(Maddison)
42	Namibia	1,984	INTERPOL(Maddison)
43	Lebanon	1,983	1913(Maddison)
44	Syria	1,983	1913(Maddison)
45	Croatia	1,975	PROXY(Yugoslavia(Maddison))
46	Moldova	1,936	PROXY(USSR(Maddison))
47	Belarus	1,888	PROXY(USSR(Maddison))
48	Singapore	1,879	1913(Maddison)
49	Hong Kong	1,879	1913(Maddison)
50	Uzbekistan	1,839	PROXY(USSR(Maddison))
51	Portugal	1,836	1913(Maddison)
52	Israel	1,836	1913(Palestine(Maddison))
53	Colombia	1,816	1913(Maddison)
54	Sri Lanka	1,813	1913(Maddison)
55	Puerto Rico	1,790	PROXY(Other L. Am.(Maddison))
56	Turkey	1,782	1913(Maddison)
57	Ukraine	1,778	PROXY(USSR(Maddison))
58	Turkmenistan	1,741	PROXY(USSR(Maddison))
59	Guatemala	1,740	PROXY (Other L. Am.(Maddison))
60	Algeria	1,709	1913(Maddison)
61	Cuba	1,708	PROXY(Other L. Am.(Maddison))

62	Serbia	1,706	PROXY(Yugoslavia(Maddison))
63	Montenegro	1,678	PROXY(Yugoslavia(Maddison))
64	Costa Rica	1,639	PROXY(Other L. Am.(Maddison))
65	Venezuela	1,622	1913(Maddison)
66	Bolivia	1,602	PROXY(Other L. Am.(Maddison))
67	Azerbaijan	1,600	PROXY(USSR(Maddison))
68	Panama	1,599	PROXY(Other L. Am.(Maddison))
69	Ecuador	1,555	PROXY(Other L. Am.(Maddison))
70	Philippines	1,547	1913(Maddison)
71	Peru	1,523	1913(Maddison)
72	Tajikistan	1,477	PROXY(USSR(Maddison))
73	Iran	1,469	1913(Maddison)
74	Iraq	1,469	1913(Maddison)
75	Jordan	1,469	1913(Maddison)
76	Nicaragua	1,349	PROXY(Other L. Am.(Maddison))
77	Kyrgyzstan	1,347	PROXY(USSR(Maddison))
78	Indonesia	1,328	1913(Maddison)
79	Egypt	1,325	1913(Maddison)
80	Malaysia	1,322	1913(Maddison)
81	Paraguay	1,322	PROXY(Other L. Am.(Maddison))
82	Tunisia	1,297	1913(Maddison)
83	Mozambique	1,251	INTERPOL(Maddison)
84	El Salvador	1,243	PROXY(Other L. Am.(Maddison))
85	Thailand	1,236	1913(Maddison)
86	Korea, North	1,205	1913(Maddison)
87	Korea, South	1,205	1913(Maddison)
88	Brazil	1,191	1913(Maddison)
89	Albania	1,191	1913(Maddison)
90	Somalia	1,190	INTERPOL(Maddison)
91	Ghana	1,147	1913(Maddison)
92	Madagascar	1,103	INTERPOL(Maddison)
93	Taiwan	1,097	1913(Maddison)
94	Honduras	1,096	PROXY(Other L. Am.(Maddison))
95	Pakistan	1,071	1913(Maddison)
96	Vietnam	1,068	1913(Maddison)
97	Macedonia	1,049	PROXY(Yugoslavia(Maddison))
98	Morocco	1,043	1913(Maddison)
99	Libya	1,035	INTERPOL(Maddison)
100	Afghanistan	1,015	PROXY(26 E. Asian cs(Maddison))
101	Burma	1,006	1913(Maddison)
102	Bosnia	1,004	PROXY(Yugoslavia(Maddison))
103	Sudan	993	INTERPOL(Maddison)
104	India	974	1913(Maddison)
105	Laos	965	PROXY(26 E. Asian cs(Maddison))
106	Jamaica	911	1913(Maddison)
107	Bangladesh	906	1913(Maddison)
108	Swaziland	905	INTERPOL(Maddison)
109	Zimbabwe	887	INTERPOL(Maddison)
110	Bahrain	881	1913(Arabia(Maddison))
111	Qatar	881	1913(Arabia(Maddison))
112	Kuwait	881	1913(Arabia(Maddison))
113	Saudi Arabia	881	1913(Arabia(Maddison))
114	Yemen	881	1913(Arabia(Maddison))
115	Oman	881	1913(Arabia(Maddison))
116	UAE	881	1913(Arabia(Maddison))
117	Haiti	877	PROXY (Other L. Am.(Maddison))

118	Dominican Rep	857	PROXY(Other L. Am.(Maddison))
119	Zambia	851	INTERPOL(Maddison)
120	Cambodia	815	PROXY (26 E. Asian cs(Maddison))
121	China	811	1913(Maddison)
122	Nepal	792	1913(Maddison)
123	Mongolia	685	PROXY (26 E. Asian cs(Maddison))
124	Guinea	588	MIN(1950(Maddison))
125	Eritrea	588	MIN(1950(Maddison))
126	Guinea-Bissau	588	MIN(1950(Maddison))
127	Kosovo	588	MIN(PROXY (Yugoslavia(Maddison)))
128	Malawi	588	MIN(1950(Maddison))
129	Botswana	588	MIN(1950(Maddison))
130	Lesotho	588	MIN(1950(Maddison))
131	Sierra Leone	588	MIN(1950(Maddison))
132	Burundi	588	MIN(1950(Maddison))
133	Ethiopia	588	MIN(1950(Maddison))

TABLE 2.12 - GDP AT PPP PER CAPITA, 2007 DOLLARS, YEAR 1920

OBS	COUNTRY	GPCPPP	SOURCE
1	New Zealand	8,287	1920(Maddison)
2	US	8,157	1920(Maddison)
3	Australia	7,002	1920(Maddison)
4	UK	6,682	1920(Maddison)
5	Switzerland	6,338	1920(Maddison)
6	Netherlands	6,200	1920(Maddison)
7	Denmark	5,865	1920(Maddison)
8	Belgium	5,821	1920(Maddison)
9	Canada	5,672	1920(Maddison)
10	Argentina	5,102	1920(Maddison)
11	France	4,741	1920(Maddison)
12	Sweden	4,116	1920(Maddison)
13	Germany	4,108	1920(Maddison)
14	Norway	4,084	1920(Maddison)
15	Chile	4,021	1920(Maddison)
16	Uruguay	3,928	1920(Maddison)
17	Italy	3,801	1920(Maddison)
18	Ireland	3,757	INTERPOL(Maddison)
19	Austria	3,544	1920(Maddison)
20	Trinidad/Tobago	3,413	INTERPOL(Maddison)
21	Spain	3,198	1920(Maddison)
22	Slovenia	2,989	PROXY(Yugoslavia(Maddison))
23	Czechia	2,967	PROXY(Czechoslovakia(Maddison))
24	Estonia	2,796	PROXY(Finland(Maddison))
25	Poland	2,784	INTERPOL(Maddison)
26	Greece	2,753	INTERPOL(Maddison)
27	Finland	2,712	1920(Maddison)
28	Cyprus	2,706	PROXY(Greece(Maddison))
29	Mexico	2,678	1920(Maddison)
30	Slovakia	2,590	PROXY(Czechoslovakia(Maddison))
31	South Africa	2,567	INTERPOL(Maddison)
32	Hungary	2,511	1920(Maddison)
33	Japan	2,492	1920(Maddison)

34	Latvia	2,483	PROXY(Finland(Maddison))
35	Lithuania	2,400	PROXY(Finland(Maddison))
36	Costa Rica	2,386	1920(Maddison)
37	Lebanon	2,216	INTERPOL(Maddison)
38	Syria	2,213	INTERPOL(Maddison)
39	Namibia	2,169	INTERPOL(Maddison)
40	Israel	2,142	INTERPOL(Maddison)
41	Singapore	2,085	INTERPOL(Maddison)
42	Hong Kong	2,085	INTERPOL(Maddison)
43	Puerto Rico	1,992	INTERPOL(Maddison)
44	Peru	1,955	1920(Maddison)
45	Croatia	1,927	PROXY(Yugoslavia(Maddison))
46	Cuba	1,901	INTERPOL(Maddison)
47	Philippines	1,894	1920(Maddison)
48	Honduras	1,872	1920(Maddison)
49	Guatemala	1,869	1920(Maddison)
50	Nicaragua	1,857	1920(Maddison)
51	Algeria	1,856	1920(Maddison)
52	Qatar	1,852	INTERPOL(Maddison)
53	Colombia	1,844	1920(Maddison)
54	Kuwait	1,834	INTERPOL(Maddison)
55	Portugal	1,806	1920(Maddison)
56	Bolivia	1,783	INTERPOL(Maddison)
57	Panama	1,780	INTERPOL(Maddison)
58	Ecuador	1,731	INTERPOL(Maddison)
59	Venezuela	1,723	1920(Maddison)
60	Serbia	1,664	PROXY(Yugoslavia(Maddison))
61	Montenegro	1,637	PROXY(Yugoslavia(Maddison))
62	UAE	1,637	INTERPOL(Maddison)
63	Malaysia	1,631	1920(Maddison)
64	Iran	1,628	INTERPOL(Maddison)
65	Jordan	1,618	INTERPOL(Maddison)
66	Sri Lanka	1,604	1920(Maddison)
67	Iraq	1,558	INTERPOL(Maddison)
68	Romania	1,516	PROXY(Bulgaria(Maddison))
69	Korea, North	1,482	1920(Maddison)
70	Korea, South	1,482	1920(Maddison)
71	Paraguay	1,471	INTERPOL(Maddison)
72	Brazil	1,415	1920(Maddison)
73	Taiwan	1,409	1920(Maddison)
74	Indonesia	1,388	1920(Maddison)
75	El Salvador	1,369	1920(Maddison)
76	Tunisia	1,356	INTERPOL(Maddison)
77	Bulgaria	1,335	1924(Maddison)
78	Mozambique	1,320	INTERPOL(Maddison)
79	Egypt	1,306	INTERPOL(Maddison)
80	Georgia	1,275	PROXY(Bulgaria(Maddison))
81	Albania	1,263	INTERPOL(Maddison)
82	Somalia	1,252	INTERPOL(Maddison)
83	Ghana	1,229	INTERPOL(Maddison)
84	Thailand	1,204	INTERPOL(Maddison)
85	Morocco	1,195	INTERPOL(Maddison)
86	Madagascar	1,154	INTERPOL(Maddison)
87	Moldova	1,147	PROXY(Romania(Maddison))
88	Saudi Arabia	1,130	INTERPOL(Maddison)
89	Bahrain	1,118	INTERPOL(Maddison)

90	Kazakhstan	1,086	PROXY(USSR(Davies))
91	Burma	1,076	INTERPOL(Maddison)
92	Pakistan	1,075	INTERPOL(Maddison)
93	Libya	1,074	INTERPOL(Maddison)
94	Vietnam	1,048	INTERPOL(Maddison)
95	Turkey	1,046	1923(Maddison)
96	Jamaica	1,033	INTERPOL(Maddison)
97	Sudan	1,030	INTERPOL(Maddison)
98	Macedonia	1,023	PROXY(Yugoslavia(Maddison))
99	Afghanistan	1,002	INTERPOL(Maddison)
100	Bosnia	979	PROXY(Yugoslavia(Maddison))
101	Haiti	976	INTERPOL(Maddison)
102	Dominican Rep	954	INTERPOL(Maddison)
103	Yemen	954	INTERPOL(Maddison)
104	Laos	952	INTERPOL(Maddison)
105	Swaziland	932	INTERPOL(Maddison)
106	India	924	1920(Maddison)
107	Russia	921	PROXY(USSR(Davies))
108	Zimbabwe	913	INTERPOL(Maddison)
109	Bangladesh	908	INTERPOL(Maddison)
110	Oman	888	INTERPOL(Maddison)
111	Zambia	872	INTERPOL(Maddison)
112	Armenia	857	PROXY(USSR(Davies))
113	China	817	INTERPOL(Maddison)
114	Cambodia	805	INTERPOL(Maddison)
115	Nepal	780	INTERPOL(Maddison)
116	Belarus	732	PROXY(USSR(Davies))
117	Uzbekistan	713	PROXY(USSR(Davies))
118	Ukraine	689	PROXY(USSR(Davies))
119	Mongolia	676	INTERPOL(Maddison)
120	Turkmenistan	675	PROXY(USSR(Davies))
121	Azerbaijan	620	PROXY(USSR(Davies))
122	Guinea	588	MIN(1950(Maddison))
123	Eritrea	588	MIN(1950(Maddison))
124	Guinea-Bissau	588	MIN(1950(Maddison))
125	Kosovo	588	MIN(PROXY(Yugoslavia(Maddison)))
126	Kyrgyzstan	588	MIN(PROXY(USSR(Davies)))
127	Malawi	588	MIN(1950(Maddison))
128	Botswana	588	MIN(1950(Maddison))
129	Lesotho	588	MIN(1950(Maddison))
130	Sierra Leone	588	MIN(1950(Maddison))
131	Tajikistan	588	MIN(PROXY(USSR(Davies)))
132	Burundi	588	MIN(1950(Maddison))
133	Ethiopia	588	MIN(1950(Maddison))

TABLE 2.13 - GDP AT PPP PER CAPITA, 2007 DOLLARS, YEAR 1929			
OBS	COUNTRY	GPCPPP	SOURCE
1	US	10,136	1929(Maddison)
2	Switzerland	9,303	1929(Maddison)
3	Netherlands	8,358	1929(Maddison)
4	UK	8,085	1929(Maddison)
5	Australia	7,732	1929(Maddison)

6	New Zealand	7,731	1929(Maddison)
7	Denmark	7,456	1929(Maddison)
8	Canada	7,441	1929(Maddison)
9	Belgium	7,425	1929(Maddison)
10	France	6,920	1929(Maddison)
11	Argentina	6,416	1929(Maddison)
12	Germany	5,951	1929(Maddison)
13	Sweden	5,684	1929(Maddison)
14	Uruguay	5,652	1929(Maddison)
15	Chile	5,619	1929(Maddison)
16	Austria	5,434	1929(Maddison)
17	Norway	5,101	1929(Maddison)
18	Venezuela	5,033	1929(Maddison)
19	Qatar	4,812	INTERPOL(Maddison)
20	Kuwait	4,707	INTERPOL(Maddison)
21	Czechia	4,670	PROXY(Czechoslovakia(Maddison))
22	Italy	4,544	1929(Maddison)
23	Ireland	4,149	1929(Maddison)
24	Estonia	4,115	PROXY(Finland(Maddison))
25	Slovakia	4,075	PROXY(Czechoslovakia(Maddison))
26	Spain	4,024	1929(Maddison)
27	Finland	3,992	1929(Maddison)
28	Slovenia	3,954	PROXY(Yugoslavia(Maddison))
29	Trinidad/Tobago	3,916	INTERPOL(Maddison)
30	Latvia	3,654	PROXY(Finland(Maddison))
31	Hungary	3,638	1929(Maddison)
32	UAE	3,626	INTERPOL(Maddison)
33	Lithuania	3,533	PROXY(Finland(Maddison))
34	Greece	3,441	1929(Maddison)
35	Cyprus	3,382	PROXY(Greece(Maddison))
36	Poland	3,110	1929(Maddison)
37	Japan	2,976	1929(Maddison)
38	South Africa	2,870	INTERPOL(Maddison)
39	Kazakhstan	2,681	PROXY(USSR(Maddison))
40	Israel	2,610	INTERPOL(Maddison)
41	Mexico	2,581	1929(Maddison)
42	Nicaragua	2,571	1929(Maddison)
43	Lebanon	2,557	INTERPOL(Maddison)
44	Croatia	2,549	PROXY(Yugoslavia(Maddison))
45	Syria	2,548	INTERPOL(Maddison)
46	Guatemala	2,527	1929(Maddison)
47	Malaysia	2,471	1929(Maddison)
48	Namibia	2,431	INTERPOL(Maddison)
49	Cuba	2,408	1929(Maddison)
50	Singapore	2,385	INTERPOL(Maddison)
51	Hong Kong	2,384	INTERPOL(Maddison)
52	Peru	2,379	1929(Maddison)
53	Portugal	2,365	1929(Maddison)
54	Costa Rica	2,324	1929(Maddison)
55	Puerto Rico	2,285	INTERPOL(Maddison)
56	Russia	2,273	PROXY(USSR(Maddison))
57	Colombia	2,211	1929(Maddison)
58	Philippines	2,207	1929(Maddison)
59	Honduras	2,202	1929(Maddison)
60	Serbia	2,202	PROXY(Yugoslavia(Maddison))
61	Montenegro	2,165	PROXY(Yugoslavia(Maddison))

62	Armenia	2,116	PROXY(USSR(Maddison))
63	Georgia	2,059	PROXY(USSR(Maddison))
64	Bolivia	2,045	INTERPOL(Maddison)
65	Panama	2,042	INTERPOL(Maddison)
66	Algeria	2,006	INTERPOL(Maddison)
67	Ecuador	1,986	INTERPOL(Maddison)
68	Sri Lanka	1,963	1929(Maddison)
69	Iran	1,857	INTERPOL(Maddison)
70	Jordan	1,831	INTERPOL(Maddison)
71	Belarus	1,806	PROXY(USSR(Maddison))
72	Turkey	1,782	1929(Maddison)
73	Uzbekistan	1,759	PROXY(USSR(Maddison))
74	Bulgaria	1,734	1929(Maddison)
75	Indonesia	1,719	1929(Maddison)
76	Ukraine	1,700	PROXY(USSR(Maddison))
77	Romania	1,692	1929(Maddison)
78	Paraguay	1,688	INTERPOL(Maddison)
79	Taiwan	1,684	1929(Maddison)
80	Iraq	1,680	INTERPOL(Maddison)
81	Brazil	1,670	1929(Maddison)
82	Turkmenistan	1,665	PROXY(USSR(Maddison))
83	Saudi Arabia	1,555	INTERPOL(Maddison)
84	Azerbaijan	1,530	PROXY(USSR(Maddison))
85	El Salvador	1,529	1929(Maddison)
86	Bahrain	1,516	INTERPOL(Maddison)
87	Korea, North	1,490	1929(Maddison)
88	Korea, South	1,490	1929(Maddison)
89	Tunisia	1,435	INTERPOL(Maddison)
90	Morocco	1,423	INTERPOL(Maddison)
91	Mozambique	1,415	INTERPOL(Maddison)
92	Tajikistan	1,413	PROXY(USSR(Maddison))
93	Albania	1,360	1920(Maddison)
94	Macedonia	1,354	PROXY(Yugoslavia(Maddison))
95	Ghana	1,342	INTERPOL(Maddison)
96	Somalia	1,335	INTERPOL(Maddison)
97	Bosnia	1,296	PROXY(Yugoslavia(Maddison))
98	Kyrgyzstan	1,288	PROXY(USSR(Maddison))
99	Egypt	1,283	1929(Maddison)
100	Moldova	1,281	PROXY(Romania(Maddison))
101	Burma	1,272	INTERPOL(Maddison)
102	Madagascar	1,222	INTERPOL(Maddison)
103	Jamaica	1,215	INTERPOL(Maddison)
104	Thailand	1,165	1929(Maddison)
105	Libya	1,126	INTERPOL(Maddison)
106	Haiti	1,120	INTERPOL(Maddison)
107	Dominican Rep	1,095	INTERPOL(Maddison)
108	Sudan	1,080	INTERPOL(Maddison)
109	Pakistan	1,080	1929(Maddison)
110	Yemen	1,056	INTERPOL(Maddison)
111	Vietnam	1,023	INTERPOL(Maddison)
112	Afghanistan	985	INTERPOL(Maddison)
113	India	977	1929(Maddison)
114	Swaziland	969	INTERPOL(Maddison)
115	Zimbabwe	946	INTERPOL(Maddison)
116	Laos	936	INTERPOL(Maddison)
117	Bangladesh	909	1929(Maddison)

118	Zambia	901	INTERPOL(Maddison)
119	Oman	896	INTERPOL(Maddison)
120	China	826	1929(Maddison)
121	Cambodia	791	INTERPOL(Maddison)
122	Nepal	764	INTERPOL(Maddison)
123	Mongolia	665	INTERPOL(Maddison)
124	Guinea	588	MIN(1950(Maddison))
125	Eritrea	588	MIN(1950(Maddison))
126	Guinea-Bissau	588	MIN(1950(Maddison))
127	Kosovo	588	MIN(PROXY(Yugoslavia(Maddison)))
128	Malawi	588	MIN(1950(Maddison))
129	Botswana	588	MIN(1950(Maddison))
130	Lesotho	588	MIN(1950(Maddison))
131	Sierra Leone	588	MIN(1950(Maddison))
132	Burundi	588	MIN(1950(Maddison))
133	Ethiopia	588	MIN(1950(Maddison))

TABLE 2.14 - GDP AT PPP PER CAPITA, 2007, DOLLARS YEAR 1938			
OBS	COUNTRY	GPCPPP	SOURCE
1	Qatar	12,500	INTERPOL(Maddison)
2	Kuwait	12,078	INTERPOL(Maddison)
3	New Zealand	9,494	1938(Maddison)
4	Switzerland	9,388	1938(Maddison)
5	UK	9,206	1938(Maddison)
6	US	9,000	1938(Maddison)
7	Australia	8,647	1938(Maddison)
8	Denmark	8,465	1938(Maddison)
9	UAE	8,035	INTERPOL(Maddison)
10	Netherlands	7,713	1938(Maddison)
11	Germany	7,337	1938(Maddison)
12	Belgium	7,099	1938(Maddison)
13	Sweden	6,942	1938(Maddison)
14	Canada	6,679	1938(Maddison)
15	France	6,561	1938(Maddison)
16	Norway	6,372	1938(Maddison)
17	Venezuela	6,088	1938(Maddison)
18	Argentina	5,982	1938(Maddison)
19	Estonia	5,436	PROXY(Finland(Maddison))
20	Uruguay	5,401	1938(Maddison)
21	Finland	5,273	1938(Maddison)
22	Austria	5,229	1938(Maddison)
23	Chile	5,194	1938(Maddison)
24	Italy	4,872	1938(Maddison)
25	Latvia	4,827	PROXY(Finland(Maddison))
26	Lithuania	4,667	PROXY(Finland(Maddison))
27	Trinidad/Tobago	4,493	INTERPOL(Maddison)
28	Ireland	4,484	1938(Maddison)
29	Czechia	4,424	PROXY(37Czechoslovakia(Maddison))
30	Kazakhstan	4,159	PROXY(USSR(Maddison))
31	Greece	3,933	1938(Maddison)
32	Slovenia	3,931	PROXY(Yugoslavia(Maddison))
33	Hungary	3,901	1938(Maddison)

34	Cyprus	3,866	PROXY(Greece(Maddison))
35	Slovakia	3,861	PROXY(37Czechoslovakia(Maddison))
36	Japan	3,598	1938(Maddison)
37	Russia	3,526	PROXY(USSR(Maddison))
38	Armenia	3,282	PROXY(USSR(Maddison))
39	Guatemala	3,267	1938(Maddison)
40	South Africa	3,209	INTERPOL(Maddison)
41	Poland	3,206	1938(Maddison)
42	Georgia	3,193	PROXY(USSR(Maddison))
43	Israel	3,180	INTERPOL(Maddison)
44	Lebanon	2,950	INTERPOL(Maddison)
45	Syria	2,933	INTERPOL(Maddison)
46	Belarus	2,801	PROXY(USSR(Maddison))
47	Costa Rica	2,756	1938(Maddison)
48	Uzbekistan	2,728	PROXY(USSR(Maddison))
49	Singapore	2,727	INTERPOL(Maddison)
50	Hong Kong	2,726	INTERPOL(Maddison)
51	Namibia	2,725	INTERPOL(Maddison)
52	Colombia	2,708	1938(Maddison)
53	Ukraine	2,638	PROXY(USSR(Maddison))
54	Mexico	2,636	1938(Maddison)
55	Spain	2,630	1938(Maddison)
56	Puerto Rico	2,622	INTERPOL(Maddison)
57	Turkmenistan	2,583	PROXY(USSR(Maddison))
58	Peru	2,581	1938(Maddison)
59	Portugal	2,567	1938(Maddison)
60	Croatia	2,534	PROXY(Yugoslavia(Maddison))
61	Turkey	2,533	1938(Maddison)
62	Azerbaijan	2,373	PROXY(USSR(Maddison))
63	Bolivia	2,347	INTERPOL(Maddison)
64	Panama	2,343	INTERPOL(Maddison)
65	Bulgaria	2,343	1938(Maddison)
66	Ecuador	2,278	INTERPOL(Maddison)
67	Philippines	2,236	1938(Maddison)
68	Tajikistan	2,192	PROXY(USSR(Maddison))
69	Serbia	2,189	PROXY(Yugoslavia(Maddison))
70	Montenegro	2,153	PROXY(Yugoslavia(Maddison))
71	Korea, South	2,143	1938(Maddison)
72	Korea, North	2,143	1938(Maddison)
73	Saudi Arabia	2,141	INTERPOL(Maddison)
74	Iran	2,119	INTERPOL(Maddison)
75	Jordan	2,072	INTERPOL(Maddison)
76	Bahrain	2,058	INTERPOL(Maddison)
77	Algeria	2,016	INTERPOL(Maddison)
78	Malaysia	1,999	1938(Maddison)
79	Kyrgyzstan	1,998	PROXY(USSR(Maddison))
80	Cuba	1,995	1938(Maddison)
81	Paraguay	1,937	INTERPOL(Maddison)
82	Taiwan	1,913	1938(Maddison)
83	Brazil	1,875	1938(Maddison)
84	Romania	1,825	1938(Maddison)
85	Iraq	1,812	INTERPOL(Maddison)
86	Sri Lanka	1,800	1938(Maddison)
87	Indonesia	1,726	1938(Maddison)
88	Morocco	1,694	INTERPOL(Maddison)
89	Honduras	1,623	1938(Maddison)

90	Nicaragua	1,581	1938(Maddison)
91	Tunisia	1,519	INTERPOL(Maddison)
92	Mozambique	1,517	INTERPOL(Maddison)
93	Ghana	1,466	INTERPOL(Maddison)
94	El Salvador	1,435	1938(Maddison)
95	Jamaica	1,428	1938(Maddison)
96	Somalia	1,424	INTERPOL(Maddison)
97	Albania	1,407	INTERPOL(Maddison)
98	Moldova	1,381	PROXY(Romania(Maddison))
99	Macedonia	1,346	PROXY(Yugoslavia(Maddison))
100	Egypt	1,308	INTERPOL(Maddison)
101	Madagascar	1,294	INTERPOL(Maddison)
102	Bosnia	1,288	PROXY(Yugoslavia(Maddison))
103	Haiti	1,285	INTERPOL(Maddison)
104	Dominican Rep	1,256	INTERPOL(Maddison)
105	Thailand	1,213	1938(Maddison)
106	Libya	1,181	INTERPOL(Maddison)
107	Yemen	1,169	INTERPOL(Maddison)
108	Sudan	1,133	INTERPOL(Maddison)
109	Burma	1,087	1938(Maddison)
110	Swaziland	1,007	INTERPOL(Maddison)
111	Pakistan	999	1938(Maddison)
112	Vietnam	998	INTERPOL(Maddison)
113	Zimbabwe	981	INTERPOL(Maddison)
114	Afghanistan	969	INTERPOL(Maddison)
115	Zambia	930	INTERPOL(Maddison)
116	Laos	921	INTERPOL(Maddison)
117	India	909	1938(Maddison)
118	Oman	904	INTERPOL(Maddison)
119	Bangladesh	840	1938(Maddison)
120	China	826	1938(Maddison)
121	Cambodia	778	INTERPOL(Maddison)
122	Nepal	749	INTERPOL(Maddison)
123	Mongolia	653	INTERPOL(Maddison)
124	Guinea	588	MIN(1950(Maddison))
125	Eritrea	588	MIN(1950(Maddison))
126	Guinea-Bissau	588	MIN(1950(Maddison))
127	Kosovo	588	MIN(PROXY(Yugoslavia(Maddison)))
128	Malawi	588	MIN(1950(Maddison))
129	Botswana	588	MIN(1950(Maddison))
130	Lesotho	588	MIN(1950(Maddison))
131	Sierra Leone	588	MIN(1950(Maddison))
132	Burundi	588	MIN(1950(Maddison))
133	Ethiopia	588	MIN(1950(Maddison))

TABLE 2.15 - GDP AT PPP PER CAPITA, 2007 DOLLARS, YEAR 1950			
OBS	COUNTRY	GPCPPP	SOURCE
1	Qatar	44,642	50(Maddison)
2	Kuwait	42,425	50(Maddison)
3	UAE	23,209	50(Maddison)
4	Cayman Is	14,756	PROXY(8 Caribbean cs(Maddison))
5	Bahamas	14,059	50(Maddison)

6	US	14,046	50(Maddison)
7	Guam	13,951	PROXY(14 Pacific is(Maddison))
8	Switzerland	13,316	50(Maddison)
9	New Zealand	12,423	50(Maddison)
10	Luxembourg	12,314	50(Maddison)
11	Falkland Is	11,688	PROXY(8 Caribbean cs(Maddison))
12	N Mariana Is	10,991	PROXY(14 Pacific is(Maddison))
13	Venezuela	10,963	50(Maddison)
14	Aruba	10,906	PROXY(8 Caribbean cs(Maddison))
15	Australia	10,889	50(Maddison)
16	Canada	10,711	50(Maddison)
17	Denmark	10,200	50(Maddison)
18	UK	10,194	50(Maddison)
19	Sweden	9,900	50(Maddison)
20	Liechtenstein	9,710	PROXY(9 European cs(Maddison))
21	Nauru	9,219	PROXY(14 Pacific is(Maddison))
22	Jersey	9,146	PROXY(9 European cs(Maddison))
23	Netherlands	8,809	50(Maddison)
24	Virgin I, US	8,641	PROXY(8 Caribbean cs(Maddison))
25	Norway	8,026	50(Maddison)
26	Belgium	8,024	50(Maddison)
27	Iceland	7,828	50(Maddison)
28	Monaco	7,746	PROXY(9 European cs(Maddison))
29	France	7,744	50(Maddison)
30	Guiana, Fr	7,509	50(Maddison)
31	Argentina	7,327	50(Maddison)
32	Brunei	7,313	50(Maddison)
33	Guernsey	7,082	PROXY(9 European cs(Maddison))
34	Virgin Is, Brit.	7,007	PROXY(8 Caribbean cs(Maddison))
35	San Marino	6,977	PROXY(9 European cs(Maddison))
36	Uruguay	6,845	50(Maddison)
37	St Pierre &	6,501	PROXY(8 Caribbean cs(Maddison))
38	Fr Polynesia	6,453	PROXY(14 Pacific is(Maddison))
39	Greenland	6,396	PROXY(9 European cs(Maddison))
40	Finland	6,248	50(Maddison)
41	Faeroe Is	6,134	PROXY(9 European cs(Maddison))
42	Estonia	6,105	PROXY(USSR(Maddison))
43	Andorra	6,105	PROXY(9 European cs(Maddison))
44	New Caledonia	5,979	PROXY(14 Pacific is(Maddison))
45	Germany	5,702	50(Maddison)
46	Chile	5,614	50(Maddison)
47	Austria	5,445	50(Maddison)
48	Latvia	5,421	PROXY(USSR(Maddison))
49	Trinidad/Tobago	5,398	50(Maddison)
50	Czechia	5,374	PROXY(Czechoslovakia(Maddison))
51	Kazakhstan	5,352	PROXY(USSR(Maddison))
52	Lithuania	5,241	PROXY(USSR(Maddison))
53	Neth Antilles	5,155	50(Maddison)
54	Italy	5,145	50(Maddison)
55	Ireland	5,073	50(Maddison)
56	Slovakia	4,690	PROXY(Czechoslovakia(Maddison))
57	Gabon	4,566	50(Maddison)
58	Russia	4,538	PROXY(USSR(Maddison))
59	Isle of Man	4,522	PROXY(9 European cs(Maddison))
60	Slovenia	4,497	PROXY(Yugoslavia(Maddison))
61	Anguilla	4,491	PROXY(8 Caribbean cs(Maddison))

62	Palau	4,392	PROXY(14 Pacific is(Maddison))
63	Fiji	4,326	50(Maddison)
64	Armenia	4,224	PROXY(USSR(Maddison))
65	Israel	4,139	50(Maddison)
66	Georgia	4,110	PROXY(USSR(Maddison))
67	Turks & Caicos	3,900	PROXY(8 Caribbean cs(Maddison))
68	South Africa	3,724	50(Maddison)
69	Moldova	3,696	PROXY(USSR(Maddison))
70	Mauritius	3,658	50(Maddison)
71	Hungary	3,643	50(Maddison)
72	Belarus	3,605	PROXY(USSR(Maddison))
73	Poland	3,595	50(Maddison)
74	Lebanon	3,569	50(Maddison)
75	Syria	3,539	50(Maddison)
76	Uzbekistan	3,511	PROXY(USSR(Maddison))
77	Mexico	3,474	50(Maddison)
78	Ukraine	3,394	PROXY(USSR(Maddison))
79	Peru	3,325	50(Maddison)
80	Turkmenistan	3,324	PROXY(USSR(Maddison))
81	Saudi Arabia	3,278	50(Maddison)
82	Singapore	3,260	50(Maddison)
83	Hong Kong	3,259	50(Maddison)
84	Spain	3,216	50(Maddison)
85	Namibia	3,173	50(Maddison)
86	Colombia	3,163	50(Maddison)
87	Puerto Rico	3,150	50(Maddison)
88	Barbados	3,119	50(Maddison)
89	Bahrain	3,091	50(Maddison)
90	Portugal	3,065	50(Maddison)
91	Guatemala	3,063	50(Maddison)
92	Azerbaijan	3,054	PROXY(USSR(Maddison))
93	Cuba	3,006	50(Maddison)
94	Reunion	2,922	50(Maddison)
95	Croatia	2,898	PROXY(Yugoslavia(Maddison))
96	Costa Rica	2,884	50(Maddison)
97	Gibraltar	2,840	PROXY(9 European cs(Maddison))
98	Japan	2,822	50(Maddison)
99	Tajikistan	2,821	PROXY(USSR(Maddison))
100	Bolivia	2,819	50(Maddison)
101	Panama	2,815	50(Maddison)
102	Greece	2,813	50(Maddison)
103	Seychelles	2,809	50(Maddison)
104	Montserrat	2,795	PROXY(8 Caribbean cs(Maddison))
105	Cyprus	2,766	50(Maddison)
106	Cook Is	2,766	PROXY(14 Pacific is(Maddison))
107	Ecuador	2,737	50(Maddison)
108	Antigua/Barbuda	2,619	50(Maddison)
109	Samoa, Ameri	2,591	PROXY(14 Pacific is(Maddison))
110	Kyrgyzstan	2,572	PROXY(USSR(Maddison))
111	Guadeloupe	2,536	50(Maddison)
112	Iran	2,527	50(Maddison)
113	Serbia	2,504	PROXY(Yugoslavia(Maddison))
114	Montenegro	2,462	PROXY(Yugoslavia(Maddison))
115	Brazil	2,456	50(Maddison)
116	Bermuda	2,449	50(Maddison)
117	Jordan	2,443	50(Maddison)

118	Bulgaria	2,426	50(Maddison)
119	Turkey	2,384	50(Maddison)
120	Belize	2,377	50(Maddison)
121	Nicaragua	2,374	50(Maddison)
122	Dominica	2,362	50(Maddison)
123	Paraguay	2,327	50(Maddison)
124	Malaysia	2,290	50(Maddison)
125	Djibouti	2,204	50(Maddison)
126	El Salvador	2,188	50(Maddison)
127	Suriname	2,152	50(Maddison)
128	Morocco	2,138	50(Maddison)
129	Vanuatu	2,057	PROXY(14 Pacific is(Maddison))
130	Micronesia	2,029	PROXY(14 Pacific is(Maddison))
131	Algeria	2,005	50(Maddison)
132	Iraq	2,004	50(Maddison)
133	Jamaica	1,950	50(Maddison)
134	Martinique	1,939	50(Maddison)
135	Samoa, W	1,938	PROXY(14 Pacific is(Maddison))
136	Honduras	1,929	50(Maddison)
137	Congo, Rep	1,894	50(Maddison)
138	St Helena	1,870	PROXY(3 Afr. cs(Maddison))
139	Senegal	1,850	50(Maddison)
140	Sri Lanka	1,841	50(Maddison)
141	St Kitts & Nevis	1,829	50(Maddison)
142	Tonga	1,828	PROXY(14 Pacific is(Maddison))
143	Wallis & Futuna	1,757	PROXY(14 Pacific is(Maddison))
144	Romania	1,737	50(Maddison)
145	St Vincent	1,732	50(Maddison)
146	Mozambique	1,665	50(Maddison)
147	Ghana	1,648	50(Maddison)
148	Tunisia	1,638	50(Maddison)
149	Guyana	1,605	50(Maddison)
150	Benin	1,593	50(Maddison)
151	West Bank	1,578	PROXY(West Bank & Gaza(Maddison))
152	Philippines	1,572	50(Maddison)
153	Somalia	1,553	50(Maddison)
154	Liberia	1,550	50(Maddison)
155	Angola	1,546	50(Maddison)
156	Haiti	1,544	50(Maddison)
157	Macedonia	1,540	PROXY(Yugoslavia(Maddison))
158	Ivory Coast	1,529	50(Maddison)
159	Macao	1,519	PROXY(Maddison)
160	Dominican Rep	1,509	50(Maddison)
161	Bosnia	1,473	PROXY(Yugoslavia(Maddison))
162	Albania	1,471	50(Maddison)
163	Marshall Is	1,434	PROXY(14 Pacific is(Maddison))
164	Madagascar	1,397	50(Maddison)
165	Grenada	1,372	50(Maddison)
166	Taiwan	1,357	50(Maddison)
167	Yemen	1,338	50(Maddison)
168	Egypt	1,337	50(Maddison)
169	Malta	1,309	50(Maddison)
170	Libya	1,259	50(Maddison)
171	Indonesia	1,234	50(Maddison)
172	Sudan	1,206	50(Maddison)

173	San Tome & Principe	1,205	50(Maddison)
174	Thailand	1,200	50(Maddison)
175	Niger	1,194	50(Maddison)
176	Cent. African Rep	1,134	50(Maddison)
177	Korea, North	1,131	50(Maddison)
178	Korea, South	1,131	50(Maddison)
179	Papua New Gu	1,108	50(Maddison)
180	Niue	1,106	PROXY(14 Pacific is(Maddison))
181	Nigeria	1,106	50(Maddison)
182	St Lucia	1,080	50(Maddison)
183	Swaziland	1,059	50(Maddison)
184	Gaza Strip	1,052	PROXY(West Bank & Gaza(Maddison))
185	Zimbabwe	1,030	50(Maddison)
186	Uganda	1,009	50(Maddison)
187	Cameroon	986	50(Maddison)
188	Zambia	971	50(Maddison)
189	Vietnam	967	50(Maddison)
190	Kenya	956	50(Maddison)
191	Afghanistan	948	50(Maddison)
192	Pakistan	945	50(Maddison)
193	Tokelau	922	PROXY(14 Pacific is(Maddison))
194	Oman	915	50(Maddison)
195	India	909	50(Maddison)
196	Laos	901	50(Maddison)
197	Gambia	892	50(Maddison)
198	Solomon Is	871	PROXY(14 Pacific is(Maddison))
199	Kiribati	859	PROXY(14 Pacific is(Maddison))
200	Togo	843	50(Maddison)
201	Congo, Dem R	837	50(Maddison)
202	Comoros	823	50(Maddison)
203	Rwanda	804	50(Maddison)
204	Maldives	800	50(Maddison)
205	Bangladesh	793	50(Maddison)
206	Equatorial G	793	50(Maddison)
207	Cambodia	761	50(Maddison)
208	Bhutan	739	50(Maddison)
209	Tuvalu	738	PROXY(14 Pacific is(Maddison))
210	Nepal	729	50(Maddison)
211	Chad	699	50(Maddison)
212	Burkina Faso	696	50(Maddison)
213	Mauritania	682	50(Maddison)
214	Mali	671	50(Maddison)
215	Cape Verde	661	50(Maddison)
216	China	645	50(Maddison)
217	Mongolia	639	50(Maddison)
218	Tanzania	623	50(Maddison)
219	East Timor	615	PROXY(14 Pacific is(Maddison))
220	Burma	582	50(Maddison)
221	Kosovo	554	PROXY(Yugoslavia(Maddison))
222	Burundi	529	50(Maddison)
223	Lesotho	522	50(Maddison)
224	Botswana	513	50(Maddison)
225	Malawi	476	50(Maddison)
226	Mayotte	463	PROXY(3 Afr. cs(Maddison))
227	Sierra Leone	462	50(WB/Maddison)

228	Guinea	445	50(Maddison)
229	Guinea-Bissau	425	50(Maddison)
230	Eritrea	403	PROXY(Ethiopia & Eritr.(Maddison))
231	Ethiopia	392	PROXY(Ethiopia & Eritr.(Maddison))
232	W Sahara	338	PROXY(3 Afr. cs(Maddison))

TABLE 2.16 - GDP AT PPP PER CAPITA, 2007 DOLLARS, YEAR 1960

OBS	COUNTRY	GPCPPP	SOURCE
1	Qatar	48,634	60(Maddison)
2	Kuwait	42,418	60(Maddison)
3	UAE	32,866	60(Maddison)
4	Cayman Is	19,572	INTERPOL(8 Caribbean cs(Maddison))
5	Switzerland	19,209	60(Maddison)
6	Guam	17,222	INTERPOL(14 Pacific is(Maddison))
7	Bahamas	16,920	INTERPOL(Maddison)
8	Luxembourg	16,721	INTERPOL(Maddison)
9	US	16,642	60(Maddison)
10	Aruba	16,022	INTERPOL(8 Caribbean cs(Maddison))
11	Falkland Is	15,496	INTERPOL(8 Caribbean cs(Maddison))
12	Liechtenstein	13,854	INTERPOL(9 European cs(Maddison))
13	New Zealand	13,853	60(Maddison)
14	Jersey	13,136	INTERPOL(9 European cs(Maddison))
15	Canada	12,916	60(Maddison)
16	Sweden	12,881	60(Maddison)
17	Denmark	12,859	60(Maddison)
18	Australia	12,851	60(Maddison)
19	UK	12,699	60(Maddison)
20	Netherlands	12,428	60(Maddison)
21	N Mariana Is	12,084	INTERPOL(14 Pacific is(Maddison))
22	Venezuela	11,974	60(Maddison)
23	Germany	11,851	60(Maddison)
24	Monaco	11,552	INTERPOL(9 European cs(Maddison))
25	San Marino	11,168	INTERPOL(9 European cs(Maddison))
26	France	11,123	60(Maddison)
27	Norway	11,098	60(Maddison)
28	Iceland	10,971	INTERPOL(Maddison)
29	Virgin I, US	10,781	INTERPOL(8 Caribbean cs(Maddison))
30	Belgium	10,261	60(Maddison)
31	Guernsey	10,163	INTERPOL(9 European cs(Maddison))
32	Austria	10,065	60(Maddison)
33	Virgin Is, Brit.	9,347	INTERPOL(8 Caribbean cs(Maddison))
34	Greenland	9,258	INTERPOL(9 European cs(Maddison))
35	Finland	9,047	60(Maddison)
36	Faeroe Is	8,984	INTERPOL(9 European cs(Maddison))
37	Brunei	8,870	INTERPOL(Maddison)
38	Andorra	8,863	INTERPOL(9 European cs(Maddison))
39	Italy	8,847	60(Maddison)
40	St Pierre &	8,653	INTERPOL(8 Caribbean cs(Maddison))
41	Czechia	8,498	PROXY(Czechoslovakia(Maddison))
42	Trinidad/Tobago	8,202	60(Maddison)
43	Neth Antilles	8,010	INTERPOL(Maddison)
44	Argentina	7,998	60(Maddison)

45	Estonia	7,943	PROXY(USSR(Maddison))
46	Fr Polynesia	7,848	INTERPOL(14 Pacific is(Maddison))
47	Nauru	7,767	INTERPOL(14 Pacific is(Maddison))
48	Latvia	7,520	PROXY(USSR(Maddison))
49	Kazakhstan	7,419	PROXY(USSR(Maddison))
50	Lithuania	7,270	PROXY(USSR(Maddison))
51	Isle of Man	7,165	INTERPOL(9 European cs(Maddison))
52	Uruguay	7,154	60(Maddison)
53	Slovakia	7,136	PROXY(Czechoslovakia(Maddison))
54	Slovenia	7,132	PROXY(Yugoslavia(Maddison))
55	Guiana, Fr	7,043	INTERPOL(Maddison)
56	New Caledonia	6,937	INTERPOL(14 Pacific is(Maddison))
57	Israel	6,867	60(Maddison)
58	Saudi Arabia	6,770	60(Maddison)
59	Bahrain	6,408	60(Maddison)
60	Ireland	6,332	60(Maddison)
61	Russia	6,294	PROXY(USSR(Maddison))
62	Chile	6,173	60(Maddison)
63	Gabon	6,141	60(Maddison)
64	Hungary	5,847	60(Maddison)
65	Armenia	5,841	PROXY(USSR(Maddison))
66	Japan	5,822	60(Maddison)
67	Anguilla	5,793	INTERPOL(8 Caribbean cs(Maddison))
68	Barbados	5,694	INTERPOL(Maddison)
69	Georgia	5,655	PROXY(USSR(Maddison))
70	Gibraltar	5,494	INTERPOL(9 European cs(Maddison))
71	Palau	5,487	INTERPOL(14 Pacific is(Maddison))
72	Turks & Caicos	5,362	INTERPOL(8 Caribbean cs(Maddison))
73	Bermuda	5,174	INTERPOL(Maddison)
74	Moldova	5,150	PROXY(USSR(Maddison))
75	Serbia	5,097	PROXY(Yugoslavia(Maddison))
76	Montenegro	5,050	PROXY(Yugoslavia(Maddison))
77	Greece	5,027	60(Maddison)
78	Belarus	5,000	PROXY(USSR(Maddison))
79	Uzbekistan	4,894	PROXY(USSR(Maddison))
80	Poland	4,831	60(Maddison)
81	South Africa	4,784	60(Maddison)
82	Mexico	4,736	60(Maddison)
83	Croatia	4,711	PROXY(Yugoslavia(Maddison))
84	Ukraine	4,707	PROXY(USSR(Maddison))
85	Spain	4,670	60(Maddison)
86	Cyprus	4,647	INTERPOL(Maddison)
87	Turkmenistan	4,616	PROXY(USSR(Maddison))
88	Guadeloupe	4,616	INTERPOL(Maddison)
89	Hong Kong	4,604	60(Maddison)
90	Peru	4,593	60(Maddison)
91	Puerto Rico	4,530	60(Maddison)
92	Portugal	4,359	60(Maddison)
93	Fiji	4,348	INTERPOL(14 Pacific is(Maddison))
94	Jamaica	4,314	60(Maddison)
95	Azerbaijan	4,235	PROXY(USSR(Maddison))
96	Bulgaria	4,172	60(Maddison)
97	Samoa, Ameri	4,122	INTERPOL(14 Pacific is(Maddison))
98	Iraq	4,018	60(Maddison)
99	Costa Rica	3,938	60(Maddison)
100	Mauritius	3,936	60(Maddison)

101	Tajikistan	3,927	PROXY(USSR(Maddison))
102	Seychelles	3,867	60(Maddison)
103	Algeria	3,799	60(Maddison)
104	Martinique	3,751	INTERPOL(Maddison)
105	Syria	3,697	60(Maddison)
106	Ecuador	3,596	60(Maddison)
107	Kyrgyzstan	3,588	PROXY(USSR(Maddison))
108	Namibia	3,576	60(Maddison)
109	Colombia	3,530	60(Maddison)
110	Panama	3,522	60(Maddison)
111	Brazil	3,456	60(Maddison)
112	Lebanon	3,454	60(Maddison)
113	Singapore	3,405	60(Maddison)
114	St Kitts & Nevis	3,349	INTERPOL(Maddison)
115	Cook Is	3,343	INTERPOL(14 Pacific is(Maddison))
116	Turkey	3,309	60(Maddison)
117	Antigua & Barbuda	3,274	INTERPOL
118	Iran	3,249	60(Maddison)
119	Reunion	3,243	60(Maddison)
120	Guatemala	3,243	60(Maddison)
121	Romania	3,179	60(Maddison)
122	Suriname	3,108	INTERPOL(Maddison)
123	Montserrat	3,071	INTERPOL(8 Caribbean cs(Maddison))
124	Cuba	3,009	60(Maddison)
125	Jordan	3,005	60(Maddison)
126	Macao	2,942	INTERPOL(Maddison)
127	Libya	2,844	60(Maddison)
128	Belize	2,815	INTERPOL(Maddison)
129	Dominica	2,812	INTERPOL(Maddison)
130	Macedonia	2,805	PROXY(Yugoslavia(Maddison))
131	Nicaragua	2,792	60(Maddison)
132	El Salvador	2,774	60(Maddison)
133	Bosnia	2,520	PROXY(Yugoslavia(Maddison))
134	Somalia	2,491	60(Maddison)
135	St Helena	2,478	PROXY(3 Afr. cs(Maddison))
136	Liberia	2,452	60(Maddison)
137	Vanuatu	2,384	INTERPOL(14 Pacific is(Maddison))
138	Bolivia	2,362	60(Maddison)
139	Micronesia	2,351	INTERPOL(14 Pacific is(Maddison))
140	Djibouti	2,324	60(Maddison)
141	Paraguay	2,291	60(Maddison)
142	Malaysia	2,249	60(Maddison)
143	Samoa, W	2,247	INTERPOL(14 Pacific is(Maddison))
144	Albania	2,229	60(Maddison)
145	Congo, Rep	2,228	60(Maddison)
146	Malta	2,166	INTERPOL(Maddison)
147	Taiwan	2,140	60(Maddison)
148	Tonga	2,120	INTERPOL(14 Pacific is(Maddison))
149	St Vincent	2,115	INTERPOL(Maddison)
150	Honduras	2,068	60(Maddison)
151	Philippines	2,016	60(Maddison)
152	Morocco	1,998	60(Maddison)
153	Wallis & Futuna	1,978	INTERPOL(14 Pacific is(Maddison))
154	Tunisia	1,941	60(Maddison)

155	Dominican Rep	1,905	60(Maddison)
156	Grenada	1,891	INTERPOL(Maddison)
157	Sri Lanka	1,883	60(Maddison)
158	Angola	1,840	60(Maddison)
159	Guyana	1,826	INTERPOL(Maddison)
160	Madagascar	1,793	60(Maddison)
161	St Lucia	1,780	INTERPOL(Maddison)
162	Senegal	1,744	60(Maddison)
163	Ivory Coast	1,734	60(Maddison)
164	Benin	1,725	60(Maddison)
165	Zambia	1,683	60(Maddison)
166	Korea, North	1,623	60(Maddison)
167	Marshall Is	1,602	INTERPOL(14 Pacific is(Maddison))
168	Korea, South	1,600	60(Maddison)
169	Cent. African Rep.	1,561	60(Maddison)
170	Haiti	1,549	60(Maddison)
171	Sudan	1,510	60(Maddison)
172	Thailand	1,506	60(Maddison)
173	Papua New Gu	1,502	INTERPOL(Maddison)
174	Oman	1,497	60(Maddison)
175	West Bank	1,495	PROXY(West Bank & Gaza(Maddison))
176	Niger	1,477	60(Maddison)
177	Egypt	1,459	60(Maddison)
178	Ghana	1,455	60(Maddison)
179	Swaziland	1,447	60(Maddison)
180	Niue	1,443	INTERPOL(14 Pacific is(Maddison))
181	Indonesia	1,411	60(Maddison)
182	Mozambique	1,383	60(Maddison)
183	Yemen	1,377	60(Maddison)
184	Cameroon	1,299	60(Maddison)
185	Zimbabwe	1,292	60(Maddison)
186	San Tome & Principe	1,234	60(Maddison)
187	Nigeria	1,232	60(Maddison)
188	Congo, Dem R	1,174	60(Maddison)
189	Togo	1,143	60(Maddison)
190	Kosovo	1,128	PROXY(Yugoslavia(Maddison))
191	Vietnam	1,103	60(Maddison)
192	Equatorial G	1,089	60(Maddison)
193	Afghanistan	1,086	60(Maddison)
194	Tokelau	1,077	INTERPOL(14 Pacific is(Maddison))
195	India	1,047	60(Maddison)
196	Kenya	1,046	60(Maddison)
197	Comoros	1,043	60(Maddison)
198	Chad	1,027	60(Maddison)
199	Kiribati	1,023	INTERPOL(14 Pacific is(Maddison))
200	Solomon Is	1,010	INTERPOL(14 Pacific is(Maddison))
201	Uganda	1,000	60(Maddison)
202	Gambia	998	60(Maddison)
203	Gaza Strip	997	PROXY(West Bank & Gaza(Maddison))
204	Laos	983	60(Maddison)
205	Mauritania	956	60(Maddison)
206	Pakistan	949	60(Maddison)
207	Maldives	942	INTERPOL(Maddison)
208	Cambodia	933	60(Maddison)
209	Mongolia	912	60(Maddison)

210	China	902	60(Maddison)
211	Tuvalu	861	INTERPOL(14 Pacific is(Maddison))
212	Rwanda	821	60(Maddison)
213	Burkina Faso	816	60(Maddison)
214	Nepal	798	60(Maddison)
215	Bangladesh	797	60(Maddison)
216	Bhutan	786	INTERPOL(Maddison)
217	Cape Verde	743	60(Maddison)
218	Mali	739	60(Maddison)
219	Burma	695	60(Maddison)
220	Tanzania	694	60(Maddison)
221	East Timor	675	INTERPOL(14 Pacific is(Maddison))
222	Guinea	630	60(Maddison)
223	Mayotte	613	PROXY(3 Afr. cs(Maddison))
224	Lesotho	612	60(Maddison)
225	Botswana	607	60(Maddison)
226	Sierra Leone	602	60(WB/Maddison)
227	Malawi	537	60(Maddison)
228	Guinea-Bissau	468	60(Maddison)
229	W Sahara	448	PROXY(3 Afr. cs(Maddison))
230	Ethiopia	440	PROXY(Ethiopia & Eritr.(Maddison))
231	Eritrea	437	PROXY(Ethiopia & Eritr.(Maddison))
232	Burundi	425	60(Maddison)

TABLE 2.17 - GDP AT PPP PER CAPITA, 2007 DOLLARS, YEAR 1970			
OBS	COUNTRY	GPCPPP	SOURCE
1	Qatar	48,716	70(Maddison)
2	Kuwait	42,624	70(Maddison)
3	UAE	35,945	70(Maddison)
4	Switzerland	27,306	70(Maddison)
5	Cayman Is	25,959	INTERPOL(8 Caribbean cs(Maddison))
6	Aruba	23,536	INTERPOL(8 Caribbean cs(Maddison))
7	Luxembourg	22,705	INTERPOL(Maddison)
8	US	22,081	70(Maddison)
9	Guam	21,261	INTERPOL(14 Pacific is(Maddison))
10	Falkland Is	20,545	INTERPOL(8 Caribbean cs(Maddison))
11	Bahamas	20,363	INTERPOL(Maddison)
12	Liechtenstein	19,766	INTERPOL(9 European cs(Maddison))
13	Sweden	19,115	70(Maddison)
14	Jersey	18,868	INTERPOL(9 European cs(Maddison))
15	Saudi Arabia	18,757	70(Maddison)
16	Netherlands	18,373	70(Maddison)
17	Denmark	18,324	70(Maddison)
18	Canada	17,917	70(Maddison)
19	San Marino	17,876	INTERPOL(9 European cs(Maddison))
20	Australia	17,418	70(Maddison)
21	France	17,262	70(Maddison)
22	Monaco	17,230	INTERPOL(9 European cs(Maddison))
23	Germany	17,056	70(Maddison)
24	Norway	16,336	70(Maddison)
25	New Zealand	16,284	70(Maddison)
26	Libya	15,954	70(Maddison)
27	UK	15,813	70(Maddison)

28	Belgium	15,789	70(Maddison)
29	Austria	15,591	70(Maddison)
30	Iceland	15,374	INTERPOL(Maddison)
31	Italy	14,780	70(Maddison)
32	Guernsey	14,584	INTERPOL(9 European cs(Maddison))
33	Japan	14,086	70(Maddison)
34	Finland	13,726	70(Maddison)
35	Virgin I, US	13,452	INTERPOL(8 Caribbean cs(Maddison))
36	Greenland	13,400	INTERPOL(9 European cs(Maddison))
37	N Mariana Is	13,285	INTERPOL(14 Pacific is(Maddison))
38	Faeroe Is	13,159	INTERPOL(9 European cs(Maddison))
39	Andorra	12,868	INTERPOL(9 European cs(Maddison))
40	Bahrain	12,841	70(Maddison)
41	Virgin Is, Brit.	12,469	INTERPOL(8 Caribbean cs(Maddison))
42	Neth Antilles	12,445	INTERPOL(Maddison)
43	Venezuela	12,398	70(Maddison)
44	Israel	11,960	70(Maddison)
45	St Pierre &	11,517	INTERPOL(8 Caribbean cs(Maddison))
46	Isle of Man	11,355	INTERPOL(9 European cs(Maddison))
47	Czechia	11,354	PROXY(Czechoslovakia(Maddison))
48	Greece	11,135	70(Maddison)
49	Slovenia	11,089	PROXY(Yugoslavia(Maddison))
50	Bermuda	10,931	INTERPOL(Maddison)
51	Brunei	10,757	INTERPOL(Maddison)
52	Gibraltar	10,627	INTERPOL(9 European cs(Maddison))
53	Latvia	10,615	PROXY(USSR(Maddison))
54	Estonia	10,482	PROXY(USSR(Maddison))
55	Kazakhstan	10,465	PROXY(USSR(Maddison))
56	Barbados	10,394	INTERPOL(Maddison)
57	Spain	10,327	70(Maddison)
58	Lithuania	10,264	PROXY(USSR(Maddison))
59	Trinidad/Tobago	10,198	70(Maddison)
60	Serbia	10,063	PROXY(Yugoslavia(Maddison))
61	Montenegro	10,042	PROXY(Yugoslavia(Maddison))
62	Argentina	9,969	70(Maddison)
63	Fr Polynesia	9,544	INTERPOL(14 Pacific is(Maddison))
64	Slovakia	9,273	PROXY(Czechoslovakia(Maddison))
65	Ireland	9,269	70(Maddison)
66	Russia	8,885	PROXY(USSR(Maddison))
67	Hungary	8,658	70(Maddison)
68	Gabon	8,606	70(Maddison)
69	Guadeloupe	8,403	INTERPOL(Maddison)
70	Hong Kong	8,363	70(Maddison)
71	Armenia	8,218	PROXY(USSR(Maddison))
72	Oman	8,197	70(Maddison)
73	Portugal	8,126	70(Maddison)
74	New Caledonia	8,048	INTERPOL(14 Pacific is(Maddison))
75	Georgia	7,915	PROXY(USSR(Maddison))
76	Cyprus	7,808	INTERPOL(Maddison)
77	Croatia	7,497	PROXY(Yugoslavia(Maddison))
78	Anguilla	7,474	INTERPOL(8 Caribbean cs(Maddison))
79	Uruguay	7,380	70(Maddison)
80	Turks & Caicos	7,371	INTERPOL(8 Caribbean cs(Maddison))
81	Puerto Rico	7,329	70(Maddison)
82	Moldova	7,306	PROXY(USSR(Maddison))
83	Martinique	7,257	INTERPOL(Maddison)

84	Chile	7,224	70(Maddison)
85	South Africa	7,086	70(Maddison)
86	Belarus	7,057	PROXY(USSR(Maddison))
87	Uzbekistan	6,956	PROXY(USSR(Maddison))
88	Singapore	6,895	70(Maddison)
89	Palau	6,856	INTERPOL(14 Pacific is(Maddison))
90	Poland	6,832	70(Maddison)
91	Iran	6,808	70(Maddison)
92	Bulgaria	6,689	70(Maddison)
93	Mexico	6,639	70(Maddison)
94	Ukraine	6,639	PROXY(USSR(Maddison))
95	Jamaica	6,606	70(Maddison)
96	Guiana, Fr	6,605	INTERPOL(Maddison)
97	Samoa, Ameri	6,557	INTERPOL(14 Pacific is(Maddison))
98	Nauru	6,544	INTERPOL(14 Pacific is(Maddison))
99	Turkmenistan	6,524	PROXY(USSR(Maddison))
100	St Kitts & Nevis	6,132	INTERPOL(Maddison)
101	Azerbaijan	5,977	PROXY(USSR(Maddison))
102	Peru	5,941	70(Maddison)
103	Romania	5,754	70(Maddison)
104	Macao	5,698	INTERPOL(Maddison)
105	Panama	5,652	70(Maddison)
106	Tajikistan	5,564	PROXY(USSR(Maddison))
107	Costa Rica	5,376	70(Maddison)
108	Lebanon	5,330	70(Maddison)
109	Iraq	5,102	70(Maddison)
110	Kyrgyzstan	5,095	PROXY(USSR(Maddison))
111	Macedonia	4,979	PROXY(Yugoslavia(Maddison))
112	Ecuador	4,798	70(Maddison)
113	Reunion	4,759	70(Maddison)
114	Brazil	4,552	70(Maddison)
115	Turkey	4,543	70(Maddison)
116	Suriname	4,487	INTERPOL(Maddison)
117	Seychelles	4,374	70(Maddison)
118	Fiji	4,371	INTERPOL(14 Pacific is(Maddison))
119	Liberia	4,369	70(Maddison)
120	Algeria	4,248	70(Maddison)
121	Bosnia	4,211	PROXY(Yugoslavia(Maddison))
122	Namibia	4,149	70(Maddison)
123	Colombia	4,138	70(Maddison)
124	Taiwan	4,130	70(Maddison)
125	Mauritius	4,095	70(Maddison)
126	Antigua/Barbuda	4,093	INTERPOL
127	Cook Is	4,042	INTERPOL(14 Pacific is(Maddison))
128	Guatemala	3,862	70(Maddison)
129	Syria	3,810	70(Maddison)
130	El Salvador	3,748	70(Maddison)
131	Swaziland	3,685	70(Maddison)
132	Nicaragua	3,683	70(Maddison)
133	Malta	3,584	INTERPOL(Maddison)
134	Montserrat	3,374	INTERPOL(8 Caribbean cs(Maddison))
135	Dominica	3,347	INTERPOL(Maddison)
136	Belize	3,335	INTERPOL(Maddison)
137	Albania	3,199	70(Maddison)
138	Bolivia	3,195	70(Maddison)
139	Jordan	3,056	70(Maddison)

140	Malaysia	3,031	70(Maddison)
141	Cuba	2,938	70(Maddison)
142	St Lucia	2,934	INTERPOL(Maddison)
143	Korea, North	2,871	70(Maddison)
144	Korea, South	2,764	70(Maddison)
145	Vanuatu	2,763	INTERPOL(14 Pacific is(Maddison))
146	Micronesia	2,725	INTERPOL(14 Pacific is(Maddison))
147	Paraguay	2,678	70(Maddison)
148	Congo, Rep	2,657	70(Maddison)
149	Samoa, W	2,605	INTERPOL(14 Pacific is(Maddison))
150	Grenada	2,604	INTERPOL(Maddison)
151	Angola	2,593	70(Maddison)
152	St Vincent	2,583	INTERPOL(Maddison)
153	Tunisia	2,571	70(Maddison)
154	St Helena	2,546	PROXY(3 Afr. cs(Maddison))
155	Tonga	2,457	INTERPOL(14 Pacific is(Maddison))
156	Djibouti	2,443	70(Maddison)
157	Honduras	2,402	70(Maddison)
158	Philippines	2,314	70(Maddison)
159	Morocco	2,312	70(Maddison)
160	Dominican Rep.	2,278	70(Maddison)
161	Togo	2,237	70(Maddison)
162	Ivory Coast	2,234	70(Maddison)
163	Kosovo	2,227	PROXY(Yugoslavia(Maddison))
164	Wallis & Futuna	2,227	INTERPOL(14 Pacific is(Maddison))
165	Thailand	2,178	70(Maddison)
166	Guyana	2,079	INTERPOL(Maddison)
167	Sri Lanka	2,062	70(Maddison)
168	Madagascar	2,038	70(Maddison)
169	Papua New Gu	2,036	INTERPOL(Maddison)
170	Zambia	1,982	70(Maddison)
171	Equatorial G	1,890	70(Maddison)
172	Niue	1,883	INTERPOL(14 Pacific is(Maddison))
173	Somalia	1,868	70(Maddison)
174	Egypt	1,856	70(Maddison)
175	Marshall Is	1,789	INTERPOL(14 Pacific is(Maddison))
176	Senegal	1,749	70(Maddison)
177	Mauritania	1,740	70(Maddison)
178	Benin	1,661	70(Maddison)
179	Zimbabwe	1,649	70(Maddison)
180	Nigeria	1,638	70(Maddison)
181	Cameroon	1,607	70(Maddison)
182	Indonesia	1,575	70(Maddison)
183	Yemen	1,556	70(Maddison)
184	Niger	1,549	70(Maddison)
185	San Tome & Principe	1,537	70(Maddison)
186	Cent African Rep.	1,476	70(Maddison)
187	Comoros	1,470	70(Maddison)
188	Ghana	1,427	70(Maddison)
189	West Bank	1,419	PROXY(West Bank & Gaza(Maddison))
190	Haiti	1,364	70(Maddison)
191	Sudan	1,306	70(Maddison)
192	Mongolia	1,303	70(Maddison)
193	Pakistan	1,270	70(Maddison)
194	Kenya	1,263	70(Maddison)

195	Tokelau	1,258	INTERPOL(14 Pacific is(Maddison))
196	Congo, Dem R	1,224	70(Maddison)
197	Kiribati	1,219	INTERPOL(14 Pacific is(Maddison))
198	Solomon Is	1,171	INTERPOL(14 Pacific is(Maddison))
199	India	1,159	70(Maddison)
200	Gambia	1,134	70(Maddison)
201	Maldives	1,110	INTERPOL(Maddison)
202	Laos	1,069	70(Maddison)
203	Botswana	1,058	70(Maddison)
204	Vietnam	1,042	70(Maddison)
205	Afghanistan	1,042	70(Maddison)
206	China	1,017	70(Maddison)
207	Mozambique	1,006	70(Maddison)
208	Tuvalu	1,005	INTERPOL(14 Pacific is(Maddison))
209	Uganda	954	70(Maddison)
210	Gaza Strip	946	PROXY(West Bank & Gaza(Maddison))
211	Tanzania	923	70(Maddison)
212	Cambodia	904	70(Maddison)
213	Cape Verde	900	70(Maddison)
214	Burkina Faso	893	70(Maddison)
215	Bangladesh	870	70(Maddison)
216	Bhutan	837	INTERPOL(Maddison)
217	Rwanda	829	70(Maddison)
218	Nepal	825	70(Maddison)
219	Chad	822	70(Maddison)
220	Sierra Leone	792	70(WB/Maddison)
221	Guinea	789	70(Maddison)
222	Mali	783	70(Maddison)
223	Burma	742	70(Maddison)
224	East Timor	740	INTERPOL(14 Pacific is(Maddison))
225	Lesotho	728	70(Maddison)
226	Mayotte	630	PROXY(3 Afr. cs(Maddison))
227	Ethiopia	592	PROXY(Ethiopia & Eritr.(Maddison))
228	Malawi	582	70(Maddison)
229	Eritrea	535	PROXY(Ethiopia & Eritr.(Maddison))
230	Guinea-Bissau	517	70(Maddison)
231	W Sahara	460	PROXY(3 Afr. cs(Maddison))
232	Burundi	345	70(Maddison)

TABLE 2.18 - GDP AT PPP PER CAPITA, 2007 DOLLARS, YEAR 1980			
OBS	COUNTRY	GPCPPP	SOURCE
1	Qatar	43,416	80(Maddison)
2	Saudi Arabia	41,255	80(Maddison)
3	UAE	40,528	80(Maddison)
4	Kuwait	39,973	80(Maddison)
5	Cayman Is	30,886	INTERPOL(8 Caribbean cs(Maddison))
6	Switzerland	30,825	80(Maddison)
7	Aruba	29,819	INTERPOL(8 Caribbean cs(Maddison))
8	US	27,292	80(Maddison)
9	Norway	26,407	80(Maddison)
10	Liechtenstein	24,960	INTERPOL(9 European cs(Maddison))
11	Luxembourg	24,767	80(WB)

12	Falkland Is	24,438	INTERPOL(8 Caribbean cs(Maddison))
13	San Marino	24,344	INTERPOL(9 European cs(Maddison))
14	Canada	24,222	80(Maddison)
15	Jersey	23,931	INTERPOL(9 European cs(Maddison))
16	Guam	23,093	INTERPOL(14 Pacific is(Maddison))
17	Netherlands	22,875	80(Maddison)
18	Iceland	22,836	80(WB)
19	Austria	22,687	80(Maddison)
20	Germany	22,605	80(Maddison)
21	Sweden	22,584	80(Maddison)
22	France	22,409	80(Maddison)
23	Monaco	22,399	INTERPOL(9 European cs(Maddison))
24	Denmark	21,881	80(Maddison)
25	Belgium	21,656	80(Maddison)
26	Montenegro	21,508	PROXY(Yugoslavia(Maddison))
27	Serbia	21,384	PROXY(Yugoslavia(Maddison))
28	Bahamas	20,810	INTERPOL(Maddison)
29	Australia	20,767	80(Maddison)
30	Italy	20,201	80(Maddison)
31	Japan	19,421	80(Maddison)
32	UK	18,989	80(Maddison)
33	Guernsey	18,486	INTERPOL(9 European cs(Maddison))
34	Finland	18,389	80(Maddison)
35	Bahrain	18,334	80(Maddison)
36	Slovenia	18,086	PROXY(Yugoslavia(Maddison))
37	New Zealand	17,910	80(Maddison)
38	Greece	17,116	80(Maddison)
39	Greenland	17,082	INTERPOL(9 European cs(Maddison))
40	Faeroe Is	16,905	INTERPOL(9 European cs(Maddison))
41	Andorra	16,435	INTERPOL(9 European cs(Maddison))
42	Gibraltar	16,387	INTERPOL(9 European cs(Maddison))
43	Israel	16,240	80(Maddison)
44	Macao	15,949	82(WB)
45	Spain	15,620	80(Maddison)
46	Hong Kong	15,420	80(Maddison)
47	Virgin I, US	15,413	INTERPOL(8 Caribbean cs(Maddison))
48	Isle of Man	15,360	INTERPOL(9 European cs(Maddison))
49	Bermuda	15,307	INTERPOL(Maddison)
50	Singapore	14,897	80(Maddison)
51	Virgin Is, Brit.	14,888	INTERPOL(8 Caribbean cs(Maddison))
52	Czechia	14,678	PROXY(Czechoslovakia(Maddison))
53	Brunei	14,516	80(WB)
54	Trinidad/Tobago	14,046	80(Maddison)
55	N Mariana Is	13,788	INTERPOL(14 Pacific is(Maddison))
56	St Pierre &	13,732	INTERPOL(8 Caribbean cs(Maddison))
57	Barbados	13,696	INTERPOL(Maddison)
58	Ireland	12,895	80(Maddison)
59	Latvia	12,682	INTERPOL(Latvia(Maddison))
60	Croatia	12,546	PROXY(Yugoslavia(Maddison))
61	Libya	12,517	80(Maddison)
62	Venezuela	12,181	80(Maddison)
63	Neth Antilles	12,118	INTERPOL(Maddison)
64	Estonia	12,052	INTERPOL(Estonia(Maddison))
65	Portugal	11,994	80(Maddison)
66	Lithuania	11,762	INTERPOL(Lithuanua(Maddison))
67	Slovakia	11,718	PROXY(Czechoslovakia(Maddison))

68	Hungary	11,426	80(Maddison)
69	Kazakhstan	11,179	INTERPOL(Kazakhstan(Maddison))
70	Argentina	10,955	80(Maddison)
71	Guadeloupe	10,672	INTERPOL(Maddison)
72	Russia	10,336	INTERPOL(Russia(Maddison))
73	Fr Polynesia	10,306	INTERPOL(14 Pacific is(Maddison))
74	Cyprus	10,035	80(WB)
75	Mexico	9,940	80(Maddison)
76	Gabon	9,936	80(Maddison)
77	Romania	9,529	80(Maddison)
78	Georgia	9,463	INTERPOL(Georgia(Maddison))
79	Macedonia	9,403	PROXY(Yugoslavia(Maddison))
80	Seychelles	9,370	80(Maddison)
81	Iraq	9,369	80(Maddison)
82	Martinique	9,237	INTERPOL(Maddison)
83	Malta	9,193	80(WB)
84	Poland	9,049	80(Maddison)
85	Turks & Caicos	8,965	INTERPOL(8 Caribbean cs(Maddison))
86	Puerto Rico	8,928	80(Maddison)
87	Oman	8,917	80(Maddison)
88	Armenia	8,882	INTERPOL(Armenia(Maddison))
89	Anguilla	8,741	INTERPOL(8 Caribbean cs(Maddison))
90	Belarus	8,732	INTERPOL(Belarus(Maddison))
91	Uruguay	8,730	80(Maddison)
92	New Caledonia	8,531	INTERPOL(14 Pacific is(Maddison))
93	Moldova	8,421	INTERPOL(Moldova(Maddison))
94	Bulgaria	8,382	80(Maddison)
95	Lebanon	8,077	80(Maddison)
96	South Africa	7,931	80(Maddison)
97	Samoa, Ameri	7,867	INTERPOL(14 Pacific is(Maddison))
98	Taiwan	7,864	80(Maddison)
99	Ecuador	7,861	80(Maddison)
100	Ukraine	7,832	INTERPOL(Ukraine(Maddison))
101	Brazil	7,831	80(Maddison)
102	Chile	7,689	80(Maddison)
103	Panama	7,571	80(Maddison)
104	Palau	7,482	INTERPOL(14 Pacific is(Maddison))
105	Bosnia	7,439	PROXY(Yugoslavia(Maddison))
106	Algeria	7,026	80(Maddison)
107	Uzbekistan	6,996	INTERPOL(Uzbekistan(Maddison))
108	Costa Rica	6,959	80(Maddison)
109	Suriname	6,828	80(WB)
110	Peru	6,638	80(Maddison)
111	Azerbaijan	6,615	INTERPOL(Azerbaijan(Maddison))
112	Guiana, Fr	6,452	INTERPOL(Maddison)
113	Iran	6,416	80(Maddison)
114	Turkmenistan	6,303	INTERPOL(Turkmenistan(Maddison))
115	Nauru	6,118	INTERPOL(14 Pacific is(Maddison))
116	Turkey	5,937	80(Maddison)
117	Korea, South	5,647	80(Maddison)
118	Kyrgyzstan	5,462	INTERPOL(Kyrgyzstan(Maddison))
119	Mauritius	5,336	80(Maddison)
120	Tajikistan	5,303	INTERPOL(Tajikistan(Maddison))
121	Malaysia	5,250	80(Maddison)
122	Colombia	5,248	80(Maddison)
123	Jamaica	5,195	80(Maddison)

124	Antigua/Barbuda	5,118	80(WB)
125	Reunion	5,028	80(Maddison)
126	St Kitts & Nevis	4,840	80(WB)
127	Kosovo	4,732	PROXY(Yugoslavia(Maddison))
128	Namibia	4,723	80(Maddison)
129	Guatemala	4,557	80(Maddison)
130	Jordan	4,489	80(Maddison)
131	Swaziland	4,484	80(Maddison)
132	Fiji	4,385	INTERPOL(14 Pacific is(Maddison))
133	Cook Is	4,354	INTERPOL(14 Pacific is(Maddison))
134	Paraguay	4,318	80(Maddison)
135	Syria	4,282	80(Maddison)
136	Korea, North	4,174	80(Maddison)
137	El Salvador	4,155	80(Maddison)
138	Belize	4,023	80(WB)
139	Tunisia	3,975	80(Maddison)
140	Albania	3,818	80(Maddison)
141	Bolivia	3,773	80(Maddison)
142	St Lucia	3,601	80(WB)
143	Montserrat	3,575	INTERPOL(8 Caribbean cs(Maddison))
144	Congo, Rep	3,453	80(Maddison)
145	Dominican Rep	3,438	80(Maddison)
146	Botswana	3,376	80(Maddison)
147	Cuba	3,289	80(Maddison)
148	Dominica	3,232	80(WB)
149	Egypt	3,098	80(Maddison)
150	Grenada	3,072	80(WB)
151	St Vincent	3,049	80(WB)
152	Thailand	3,047	80(Maddison)
153	Nicaragua	2,983	80(Maddison)
154	Morocco	2,981	80(Maddison)
155	Honduras	2,954	80(Maddison)
156	Vanuatu	2,928	80(WB)
157	St Helena	2,928	PROXY(3 Afr. cs(Maddison))
158	Philippines	2,913	80(Maddison)
159	Micronesia	2,887	INTERPOL(14 Pacific is(Maddison))
160	Samoa, W	2,662	82(WB)
161	Guyana	2,481	80(WB)
162	Ivory Coast	2,464	80(Maddison)
163	Sri Lanka	2,335	80(Maddison)
164	Wallis & Futuna	2,333	INTERPOL(14 Pacific is(Maddison))
165	Djibouti	2,277	80(Maddison)
166	Tonga	2,217	81(WB)
167	Togo	2,151	80(Maddison)
168	Indonesia	2,149	80(Maddison)
169	Equatorial G	2,128	80(Maddison)
170	Yemen	2,125	80(Maddison)
171	Niue	2,090	INTERPOL(14 Pacific is(Maddison))
172	Papua New Gu	2,069	80(WB)
173	Cameroon	2,065	80(Maddison)
174	Liberia	1,934	80(Maddison)
175	Nigeria	1,885	80(Maddison)
176	Marshall Is	1,869	INTERPOL(14 Pacific is(Maddison))
177	Mongolia	1,860	80(Maddison)
178	Haiti	1,848	80(Maddison)

179	Senegal	1,824	80(Maddison)
180	San Tome/Principe	1,775	80(Maddison)
181	Zimbabwe	1,662	80(Maddison)
182	Maldives	1,654	INTERPOL(Maddison)
183	Mauritania	1,642	80(Maddison)
184	Madagascar	1,630	80(Maddison)
185	Ghana	1,618	80(Maddison)
186	Zambia	1,558	80(Maddison)
187	Benin	1,539	80(Maddison)
188	Mozambique	1,526	80(Maddison)
189	Somalia	1,480	80(Maddison)
190	Pakistan	1,475	80(Maddison)
191	Angola	1,414	80(Maddison)
192	Kenya	1,392	80(Maddison)
193	Sudan	1,371	80(Maddison)
194	West Bank	1,354	PROXY(West Bank & Gaza(Maddison))
195	Tokelau	1,337	INTERPOL(14 Pacific is(Maddison))
196	Niger	1,335	80(Maddison)
197	Kiribati	1,306	80(WB)
198	China	1,297	80(Maddison)
199	Gambia	1,264	80(Maddison)
200	Comoros	1,251	80(WB)
201	Solomon Is	1,240	80(WB)
202	India	1,226	80(Maddison)
203	Laos	1,224	80(Maddison)
204	Cape Verde	1,211	80(Maddison)
205	Cent. African Rep.	1,132	80(Maddison)
206	Tuvalu	1,067	INTERPOL(14 Pacific is(Maddison))
207	Vietnam	1,064	80(Maddison)
208	Cambodia	1,055	80(Maddison)
209	Uganda	1,053	80(Maddison)
210	Afghanistan	1,023	80(Maddison)
211	Lesotho	1,001	80(Maddison)
212	Guinea	998	80(Maddison)
213	Tanzania	981	80(Maddison)
214	Bhutan	980	80(WB)
215	Congo, Dem R	921	80(Maddison)
216	Gaza Strip	903	PROXY(West Bank & Gaza(Maddison))
217	Mali	897	80(Maddison)
218	Burkina Faso	863	80(Maddison)
219	Rwanda	856	80(Maddison)
220	Burma	840	80(Maddison)
221	Nepal	816	80(Maddison)
222	Bangladesh	800	80(Maddison)
223	Sierra Leone	785	80(WB/Maddison)
224	East Timor	767	INTERPOL(14 Pacific is(Maddison))
225	Malawi	727	80(Maddison)
226	Mayotte	725	PROXY(3 Afr. cs(Maddison))
227	Ethiopia	643	PROXY(Ethiopia & Eritr.(Maddison))
228	Eritrea	567	PROXY(Ethiopia & Eritr.(Maddison))
229	W Sahara	529	PROXY(3 Afr. cs(Maddison))
230	Guinea-Bissau	503	80(Maddison)
231	Chad	337	80(Maddison)
232	Burundi	296	80(Maddison)

OBS	COUNTRY	GPCPPP	SOURCE
	TABLE 2.19 - GDP AT PPP PER CAPITA, 2007 DOLLARS, YEAR 1990		
1	UAE	51,862	90(WB)
2	Luxembourg	42,138	90(Maddison)
3	Kuwait	37,673	90(Maddison)
4	Switzerland	35,992	90(Maddison)
5	Aruba	35,458	93(CIA)WEIGHT(US(Maddison))
6	Cayman Is	35,075	93(CIA)WEIGHT(US(Maddison))
7	US	34,085	90(Maddison)
8	Norway	33,337	90(Maddison)
9	San Marino	30,932	92(CIA)WEIGHT(US(Maddison))
10	Liechtenstein	29,910	90(CIA)
11	Jersey	28,775	99(CIA)WEIGHT(US(Maddison))
12	Austria	28,384	90(Maddison)
13	Canada	28,363	90(Maddison)
14	Falkland Is	27,747	95(CIA)WEIGHT(US(Maddison))
15	Monaco	27,454	93(CIA)WEIGHT(US(Maddison))
16	Netherlands	27,129	90(Maddison)
17	Japan	27,101	90(Maddison)
18	Sweden	26,918	90(Maddison)
19	France	26,885	90(Maddison)
20	Iceland	26,822	90(Maddison)
21	Denmark	26,372	90(Maddison)
22	Belgium	25,828	90(Maddison)
23	Hong Kong	25,748	90(Maddison)
24	Germany	25,719	90(Maddison)
25	Italy	25,245	90(Maddison)
26	Australia	24,527	90(Maddison)
27	Singapore	24,516	90(Maddison)
28	Saudi Arabia	24,170	90(Maddison)
29	UK	24,122	90(Maddison)
30	Finland	23,760	90(Maddison)
31	Guam	23,744	91(CIA)WEIGHT(US(Maddison))
32	Qatar	23,476	93(CIA)WEIGHT(US(WB))
33	Gibraltar	22,929	93(CIA)WEIGHT(US(Maddison))
34	Guernsey	22,217	97(CIA)WEIGHT(US(Maddison))
35	Macao	21,382	90(WB)
36	Spain	21,023	90(Maddison)
37	Greenland	20,621	95(CIA)WEIGHT(US(Maddison))
38	Faeroe Is	20,530	89(CIA)WEIGHT(US(Maddison))
39	Brunei	20,171	93(CIA)WEIGHT(US(Maddison))
40	New Zealand	20,095	90(Maddison)
41	Montenegro	19,929	PROXY(Serbia/Montenegro(Maddison))
42	Andorra	19,871	92(CIA)WEIGHT(US(Maddison))
43	Serbia	19,829	PROXY(Serbia/Montenegro(Maddison))
44	Bahamas	19,829	90(Maddison)
45	Isle of Man	19,417	94(CIA)WEIGHT(US(Maddison))
46	Greece	19,405	90(Maddison)
47	Israel	19,188	90(Maddison)
48	Ireland	18,019	90(Maddison)
49	Bermuda	17,969	90(Maddison)
50	Cyprus	17,943	90(Maddison)
51	Slovenia	17,221	90(Maddison)

52	Virgin I, US	17,029	87(CIA)WEIGHT(US(Maddison))
53	Virgin Is, Brit.	16,952	91(CIA)WEIGHT(US(Maddison))
54	Portugal	16,195	90(Maddison)
55	Gabon	16,021	90(WB)
56	Czechia	15,877	90(Maddison)
57	Barbados	15,694	90(Maddison)
58	Oman	15,659	90(Maddison)
59	St Pierre &	15,619	92(CIA)WEIGHT(US(Maddison))
60	Bahrain	15,591	90(Maddison)
61	Latvia	14,522	90(Maddison)
62	N Mariana Is	13,962	92(CIA)WEIGHT(US(Maddison))
63	Malta	13,955	90(Maddison)
64	Estonia	13,150	90(Maddison)
65	Taiwan	12,907	90(Maddison)
66	Lithuania	12,693	90(Maddison)
67	Slovakia	12,587	90(Maddison)
68	Antigua & Barbuda	12,540	90(Maddison)
69	Croatia	11,916	90(Maddison)
70	Seychelles	11,795	90(Maddison)
71	Hungary	11,767	90(Maddison)
72	Korea, South	11,591	90(Maddison)
73	Russia	11,395	90(Maddison)
74	Venezuela	11,377	90(Maddison)
75	Trinidad/Tobago	11,186	90(Maddison)
76	Guadeloupe	10,947	90(Maddison)
77	Kazakhstan	10,914	90(Maddison)
78	Georgia	10,882	90(Maddison)
79	Puerto Rico	10,871	90(Maddison)
80	Fr Polynesia	10,576	93(CIA)WEIGHT(US(Maddison))
81	Belarus	10,515	90(Maddison)
82	Turks & Caicos	10,346	92(CIA)WEIGHT(US(Maddison))
83	Martinique	9,825	90(Maddison)
84	Anguilla	9,804	93(CIA)WEIGHT(US(Maddison))
85	Neth Antilles	9,657	90(Maddison)
86	Mexico	9,652	90(Maddison)
87	Moldova	9,147	90(Maddison)
88	Argentina	9,003	90(Maddison)
89	Armenia	8,827	90(Maddison)
90	Macedonia	8,823	90(Maddison)
91	Ukraine	8,813	90(Maddison)
92	St Kitts & Nevis	8,797	90(Maddison)
93	New Caledonia	8,700	91(CIA)WEIGHT(US(Maddison))
94	Uruguay	8,633	90(Maddison)
95	Chile	8,369	90(Maddison)
96	Samoa, Ameri	8,364	91(CIA)WEIGHT(US(Maddison))
97	Turkey	8,068	90(Maddison)
98	Poland	7,984	90(Maddison)
99	Bulgaria	7,789	90(Maddison)
100	Palau	7,706	94(CIA)WEIGHT(US(Maddison))
101	Romania	7,629	90(Maddison)
102	Mauritius	7,418	90(Maddison)
103	Brazil	7,408	90(Maddison)
104	Malaysia	7,301	90(Maddison)
105	Ecuador	7,296	90(Maddison)
106	St Lucia	7,073	90(Maddison)
107	Bosnia	7,027	90(Maddison)

108	South Africa	6,896	90(Maddison)
109	Botswana	6,870	90(Maddison)
110	Azerbaijan	6,792	90(Maddison)
111	Costa Rica	6,736	90(Maddison)
112	Panama	6,646	90(Maddison)
113	Guiana, Fr	6,411	90(Maddison)
114	Algeria	6,283	90(Maddison)
115	Uzbekistan	6,271	90(Maddison)
116	Jamaica	6,136	90(Maddison)
117	Reunion	6,004	90(Maddison)
118	Nauru	5,981	93(CIA)WEIGHT(US(Maddison))
119	Colombia	5,764	90(Maddison)
120	Iran	5,538	90(Maddison)
121	Kyrgyzstan	5,346	90(Maddison)
122	Dominica	5,345	90(Maddison)
123	Turkmenistan	5,327	90(Maddison)
124	Grenada	5,255	90(Maddison)
125	Suriname	5,004	90(Maddison)
126	Libya	4,987	90(Maddison)
127	Thailand	4,954	90(Maddison)
128	St Vincent	4,824	90(Maddison)
129	Belize	4,819	90(Maddison)
130	Swaziland	4,567	90(Maddison)
131	Peru	4,478	90(Maddison)
132	Cook Is	4,464	93(CIA)WEIGHT(US(Maddison))
133	Tunisia	4,456	90(Maddison)
134	Fiji	4,395	90(Maddison)
135	Tajikistan	4,391	90(Maddison)
136	Kosovo	4,388	PROXY(Serbia/Montenegro(Maddison))
137	Paraguay	4,300	90(Maddison)
138	Syria	4,175	90(Maddison)
139	Korea, North	4,174	90(Maddison)
140	Namibia	4,115	90(Maddison)
141	Albania	4,087	90(Maddison)
142	Jordan	4,052	90(Maddison)
143	Guatemala	3,958	90(Maddison)
144	Egypt	3,793	90(Maddison)
145	Montserrat	3,729	92(CIA)WEIGHT(US(Maddison))
146	Iraq	3,611	90(Maddison)
147	Vanuatu	3,601	90(WB)
148	El Salvador	3,586	90(Maddison)
149	Dominican Rep	3,583	90(Maddison)
150	Congo, Rep	3,481	90(Maddison)
151	Angola	3,425	90(WB)
152	Cuba	3,416	90(Maddison)
153	Morocco	3,292	90(Maddison)
154	St Helena	3,252	PROXY(3 Afr. cs(Maddison))
155	Bolivia	3,225	90(Maddison)
156	Micronesia	2,944	90(WB)
157	Honduras	2,854	90(Maddison)
158	Samoa, W	2,815	90(WB)
159	Sri Lanka	2,772	90(Maddison)
160	Philippines	2,768	90(Maddison)
161	Maldives	2,726	90(Maddison)
162	Tonga	2,655	90(WB)
163	Indonesia	2,640	90(Maddison)

164	Mongolia	2,455	90(Maddison)
165	Wallis & Futuna	2,370	94(CIA)WEIGHT(US(Maddison))
166	Equatorial G	2,251	90(Maddison)
167	Nicaragua	2,183	90(Maddison)
168	Djibouti	2,179	90(Maddison)
169	Lebanon	2,175	90(Maddison)
170	Niue	2,165	93(CIA)WEIGHT(US(Maddison))
171	Cameroon	2,150	90(Maddison)
172	Yemen	2,117	90(Maddison)
173	Guyana	2,040	90(Maddison)
174	China	2,006	90(Maddison)
175	Bhutan	1,914	90(WB)
176	Marshall Is	1,896	92(CIA)WEIGHT(US(Maddison))
177	Pakistan	1,875	90(Maddison)
178	Papua New Gu	1,859	90(Maddison)
179	Ivory Coast	1,840	90(Maddison)
180	Senegal	1,788	90(Maddison)
181	Cape Verde	1,750	90(Maddison)
182	Zimbabwe	1,723	90(Maddison)
183	Solomon Is	1,718	90(WB)
184	Ghana	1,703	90(Maddison)
185	Mozambique	1,696	90(Maddison)
186	Somalia	1,650	90(Maddison)
187	Nigeria	1,603	90(Maddison)
188	India	1,558	90(Maddison)
189	Haiti	1,532	90(Maddison)
190	Benin	1,524	90(Maddison)
191	San Tome/Principe	1,513	90(Maddison)
192	Mauritania	1,483	90(Maddison)
193	Kenya	1,461	90(Maddison)
194	Liberia	1,422	90(Maddison)
195	Tokelau	1,365	93(CIA)WEIGHT(US(Maddison))
196	Zambia	1,327	90(Maddison)
197	Vietnam	1,319	90(Maddison)
198	Togo	1,297	90(Maddison)
199	Laos	1,292	90(Maddison)
200	West Bank	1,292	PROXY(West Bank & Gaza(Maddison))
201	Comoros	1,285	90(WB)
202	Kiribati	1,191	90(WB)
203	Gambia	1,123	90(Maddison)
204	Lesotho	1,120	90(Maddison)
205	Cambodia	1,104	90(Maddison)
206	Sudan	1,090	90(Maddison)
207	Tuvalu	1,089	93(CIA)WEIGHT(US(Maddison))
208	Madagascar	1,079	90(Maddison)
209	Uganda	1,046	90(Maddison)
210	Cent. African Rep.	971	90(Maddison)
211	Guinea	937	90(Maddison)
212	Burkina Faso	925	90(Maddison)
213	Nepal	908	90(Maddison)
214	Mali	895	90(Maddison)
215	Afghanistan	881	90(Maddison)
216	Bangladesh	879	90(Maddison)
217	Tanzania	864	90(Maddison)
218	Gaza Strip	861	PROXY(West Bank & Gaza(Madd
219	Rwanda	849	90(Maddison)

220	Burma	828	90(Maddison)
221	Mayotte	805	93(CIA)WEIGHT(US(Maddison))
222	East Timor	777	00(WB)WEIGHT(US(Maddison))
223	Congo, Dem R	759	90(Maddison)
224	Sierra Leone	720	90(WB)
225	Niger	695	90(Maddison)
226	Malawi	666	90(Maddison)
227	W Sahara	588	PROXY(3 Afr. cs(Maddison))
228	Ethiopia	582	90(WB)
229	Chad	537	90(Maddison)
230	Eritrea	529	90(WB)
231	Guinea-Bissau	508	90(Maddison)
232	Burundi	251	90(Maddison)

TABLE 2.20 - GDP AT PPP PER CAPITA, 2007 DOLLARS, YEAR 2000			
OBS	COUNTRY	GPCPPP	SOURCE
1	Luxembourg	64,786	00(WB)
2	Brunei	50,453	00(WB)
3	Norway	46,096	00(WB)
4	UAE	43,148	00(WB)
5	US	41,325	00(WB)
6	Singapore	39,248	00(WB)
7	Kuwait	39,179	00(WB)
8	Aruba	37,952	00(CIA)WEIGHT(US(WB))
9	San Marino	37,439	00(CIA)WEIGHT(US(WB))
10	Switzerland	37,042	00(WB)
11	Cayman Is	36,871	99(CIA)WEIGHT(US(WB))
12	Liechtenstein	34,550	99(CIA)WEIGHT(US(WB))
13	Netherlands	34,420	00(WB)
14	Austria	34,260	00(WB)
15	Ireland	34,202	00(WB)
16	Canada	33,492	00(WB)
17	Jersey	33,330	99(CIA)WEIGHT(US(WB))
18	Denmark	32,683	00(WB)
19	Monaco	32,289	00(CIA)WEIGHT(US(WB))
20	Hong Kong	31,555	00(WB)
21	Iceland	31,349	00(WB)
22	Belgium	31,264	00(WB)
23	Sweden	31,068	00(WB)
24	France	30,960	00(WB)
25	Australia	30,678	00(WB)
26	Japan	30,361	00(WB)
27	Germany	30,337	00(WB)
28	Gibraltar	29,969	00(CIA)WEIGHT(US(WB))
29	Guam	29,933	00(CIA)WEIGHT(US(WB))
30	Falkland Is	29,166	02(CIA)WEIGHT(US(WB))
31	Italy	29,138	00(WB)
32	UK	29,091	00(WB)
33	Finland	28,348	00(WB)
34	Spain	27,268	00(WB)
35	Bahrain	25,953	00(WB)
36	Guernsey	25,724	99(CIA)WEIGHT(US(WB))

37	Qatar	24,246	00(CIA)WEIGHT(US(WB))
38	Greece	24,153	00(WB)
39	Faeroe Is	23,969	00(CIA)WEIGHT(US(WB))
40	Greenland	23,960	00(CIA)WEIGHT(US(WB))
41	Israel	23,934	00(WB)
42	Cyprus	23,640	00(WB)
43	Macao	23,622	00(WB)
44	Isle of Man	23,406	01(CIA)WEIGHT(US(WB))
45	Bermuda	23,277	00(CIA)WEIGHT(US(WB))
46	Andorra	23,117	00(CIA)WEIGHT(US(WB))
47	New Zealand	23,021	00(WB)
48	Malta	21,492	00(WB)
49	Taiwan	21,172	00(CIA)WEIGHT(US(WB))
50	Portugal	21,035	00(WB)
51	Slovenia	20,394	00(WB)
52	Saudi Arabia	20,090	00(WB)
53	Bahamas	19,697	00(CIA)WEIGHT(US(WB))
54	Korea, South	18,717	00(WB)
55	New Caledonia	17,916	00(CIA)WEIGHT(US(WB))
56	Virgin Is, Brit.	17,837	00(CIA)WEIGHT(US(WB))
57	Virgin I, US	17,708	00(CIA)WEIGHT(US(WB))
58	Seychelles	16,968	00(WB)
59	Barbados	16,890	00(CIA)WEIGHT(US(WB))
60	Oman	16,881	00(WB)
61	St Pierre &	16,429	96(CIA)WEIGHT(US(WB))
62	Czechia	16,208	00(WB)
63	N Mariana Is	15,495	00(CIA)WEIGHT(US(WB))
64	Trinidad/Tobago	15,123	00(WB)
65	Gabon	14,668	00(WB)
66	Antigua & Barbuda	14,376	00(WB)
67	Samoa, Ameri	13,935	00(CIA)WEIGHT(US(WB))
68	Puerto Rico	13,638	00(CIA)WEIGHT(US(WB))
69	Guadeloupe	13,401	97(CIA)WEIGHT(US(WB))
70	Hungary	13,299	00(WB)
71	Estonia	13,222	00(WB)
72	Fr Polynesia	13,115	97(CIA)WEIGHT(US(WB))
73	Slovakia	12,721	00(WB)
74	St Kitts & Nevis	12,675	00(WB)
75	Libya	12,450	00(WB)
76	Martinique	11,733	01(CIA)WEIGHT(US(WB))
77	Chile	11,673	00(WB)
78	Poland	11,592	00(WB)
79	Mexico	11,527	00(WB)
80	Venezuela	11,425	00(WB)
81	Neth Antilles	11,394	00(CIA)WEIGHT(US(WB))
82	Argentina	11,318	00(WB)
83	Equatorial G	11,093	00(WB)
84	Malaysia	11,070	00(WB)
85	Turks & Caicos	10,945	00(CIA)WEIGHT(US(WB))
86	Croatia	10,668	00(WB)
87	Anguilla	10,255	99(CIA)WEIGHT(US(WB))
88	Lithuania	10,008	00(WB)
89	Botswana	9,908	00(WB)
90	Uruguay	9,898	00(WB)
91	Palau	9,844	98(CIA)WEIGHT(US(WB))
92	Turkey	9,789	00(WB)

93	Mauritius	9,717	00(WB)
94	Latvia	9,180	00(WB)
95	Russia	9,140	00(WB)
96	Costa Rica	8,670	00(WB)
97	Panama	8,613	00(WB)
98	St Lucia	8,601	00(WB)
99	Brazil	8,383	00(WB)
100	Iran	7,844	00(WB)
101	Guiana, Fr	7,596	98(CIA)WEIGHT(US(WB))
102	Lebanon	7,501	00(WB)
103	Bulgaria	7,480	00(WB)
104	South Africa	7,313	00(WB)
105	Grenada	7,112	00(WB)
106	Macedonia	7,048	00(WB)
107	Dominica	6,411	00(WB)
108	Thailand	6,403	00(WB)
109	Belarus	6,167	00(WB)
110	Romania	6,166	00(WB)
111	Belize	6,114	00(WB)
112	Reunion	6,095	99(CIA)WEIGHT(US(WB))
113	St Vincent	6,073	00(WB)
114	Jamaica	6,017	00(WB)
115	Colombia	5,988	00(WB)
116	Tunisia	5,900	00(WB)
117	Algeria	5,880	00(WB)
118	Kazakhstan	5,746	00(WB)
119	Peru	5,730	00(WB)
120	Serbia	5,615	00(WB)
121	Montenegro	5,569	00(WB)
122	Cook Is	5,500	99(CIA)WEIGHT(US(WB))
123	Ecuador	5,378	00(WB)
124	Dominican Rep	5,271	00(WB)
125	Turkmenistan	5,136	00(CIA)WEIGHT(US(WB))
126	El Salvador	5,076	00(WB)
127	Bosnia	4,968	00(WB)
128	Swaziland	4,957	00(WB)
129	Nauru	4,954	00(CIA)WEIGHT(US(WB))
130	Suriname	4,909	00(WB)
131	Namibia	4,508	00(WB)
132	Fiji	4,428	00(WB)
133	Egypt	4,407	00(WB)
134	Syria	4,398	00(WB)
135	Albania	4,376	00(WB)
136	Guatemala	4,308	00(WB)
137	Jordan	4,225	00(WB)
138	Paraguay	3,997	00(WB)
139	Ukraine	3,920	00(WB)
140	Maldives	3,838	00(WB)
141	Montserrat	3,792	99(CIA)WEIGHT(US(WB))
142	Bolivia	3,777	00(WB)
143	Vanuatu	3,707	00(WB)
144	Sri Lanka	3,536	00(WB)
145	Mayotte	3,409	98(CIA)WEIGHT(US(WB))
146	Morocco	3,351	00(WB)
147	Tonga	3,351	00(WB)
148	St Helena	3,278	98(CIA)WEIGHT(US(WB))

149	Samoa, W	3,267	00(WB)
150	China	3,244	00(WB)
151	Congo, Rep	3,207	00(WB)
152	Cuba	3,185	00(CIA)WEIGHT(US(WB))
153	Indonesia	3,122	00(WB)
154	Micronesia	3,074	00(WB)
155	Bhutan	3,038	00(WB)
156	Honduras	3,000	00(WB)
157	Iraq	2,986	00(CIA)WEIGHT(US(WB))
158	Philippines	2,922	00(WB)
159	Niue	2,900	00(CIA)WEIGHT(US(WB))
160	Angola	2,795	00(WB)
161	Guyana	2,765	00(WB)
162	Wallis & Futuna	2,700	00(CIA)WEIGHT(US(WB))
163	Azerbaijan	2,649	00(WB)
164	Georgia	2,525	00(WB)
165	Cape Verde	2,496	00(WB)
166	Armenia	2,452	00(WB)
167	Nicaragua	2,306	00(WB)
168	Yemen	2,260	00(WB)
169	Pakistan	2,155	00(WB)
170	Marshall Is	2,142	01(CIA)WEIGHT(US(WB))
171	Papua New Gu	2,080	00(WB)
172	India	2,044	00(WB)
173	Djibouti	1,997	00(WB)
174	Mongolia	1,980	00(WB)
175	Vietnam	1,943	00(WB)
176	Cameroon	1,892	00(WB)
177	Ivory Coast	1,798	00(WB)
178	Senegal	1,750	00(WB)
179	Uzbekistan	1,722	00(WB)
180	Mauritania	1,662	00(WB)
181	Solomon Is	1,656	00(WB)
182	Zimbabwe	1,647	00(CIA)WEIGHT(US(WB))
183	Tokelau	1,619	93(CIA)WEIGHT(US(WB))
184	Laos	1,611	00(WB)
185	Nigeria	1,597	00(WB)
186	Kyrgyzstan	1,585	00(WB)
187	Moldova	1,533	00(WB)
188	Ghana	1,522	00(WB)
189	Sudan	1,461	00(WB)
190	Kiribati	1,444	00(WB)
191	San Tome/Principe	1,433	00(WB)
192	Kenya	1,384	00(WB)
193	Benin	1,364	00(WB)
194	Lesotho	1,364	00(WB)
195	Cambodia	1,304	00(WB)
196	Tuvalu	1,291	00(CIA)WEIGHT(US(WB))
197	Mozambique	1,266	00(WB)
198	Kosovo	1,243	PROXY(Serbia)
199	Haiti	1,243	00(WB)
200	West Bank	1,237	00(CIA)WEIGHT(US(WB))
201	Korea, North	1,194	00(CIA)WEIGHT(US(WB))
202	Comoros	1,157	00(WB)
203	Gambia	1,147	00(WB)
204	Burma	1,079	00(WB)

205	Bangladesh	1,060	00(WB)
206	Tajikistan	1,057	00(WB)
207	Guinea	1,049	00(WB)
208	Burkina Faso	1,010	00(WB)
209	Nepal	998	00(WB)
210	Zambia	982	00(WB)
211	Uganda	976	00(WB)
212	Mali	973	00(WB)
213	Afghanistan	955	00(CIA)WEIGHT(US(WB))
214	Somalia	935	00(CIA)WEIGHT(US(WB))
215	Madagascar	897	00(WB)
216	East Timor	860	00(WB)
217	Togo	846	00(WB)
218	Rwanda	843	00(WB)
219	Central African Rep.	830	00(WB)
220	Tanzania	830	00(WB)
221	Gaza Strip	825	00(CIA)WEIGHT(US(WB))
222	Liberia	804	00(WB)
223	Malawi	751	00(WB)
224	W Sahara	592	PROXY(Maddison)WEIGHT(US(WB))
225	Niger	591	00(WB)
226	Ethiopia	558	00(WB)
227	Eritrea	556	00(WB)
228	Chad	545	00(WB)
229	Guinea-Bissau	494	00(WB)
230	Sierra Leone	405	00(WB)
231	Burundi	324	00(WB)
232	Congo, Dem R	264	00(WB)

TABLE 2.21 - GDP AT PPP PER CAPITA, 2007 DOLLARS, YEAR 2007

OBS	COUNTRY	GPCPPP	SOURCE
1	Liechtenstein	118,000	07(CIA)
2	Qatar	80,900	07(CIA)
3	Bermuda	80,623	04(CIA)WEIGHT(US(WB))
4	Luxembourg	78,986	07(WB)
5	Jersey	62,422	05(CIA)WEIGHT(US(WB))
6	Macao	57,344	07(WB 2005 prices) WEIGHT(US(WB))
7	Norway	53,332	07(WB)
8	Brunei	51,966	06(WB)WEIGHT(US(WB))
9	Cayman Is	50,519	04(CIA)WEIGHT(US(WB))
10	Singapore	50,304	07(WB)
11	Guernsey	48,842	05(CIA)WEIGHT(US(WB))
12	US	45,790	07(WB)
13	Falkland Is	44,833	02(CIA)WEIGHT(US(WB))
14	Virgin Is, Brit.	44,406	04(CIA)WEIGHT(US(WB))
15	Ireland	43,033	07(WB)
16	Andorra	42,500	07(CIA)
17	Hong Kong	42,322	07(WB)
18	San Marino	41,900	07(CIA)

19	Gibraltar	41,833	05(CIA)WEIGHT(US(WB))
20	Faeroe Is	40,183	01(CIA)WEIGHT(US(WB))
21	Switzerland	39,962	07(WB)
22	Kuwait	39,300	07(CIA)
23	Isle of Man	38,329	05(CIA)WEIGHT(US(WB))
24	Austria	38,153	07(WB)
25	Netherlands	37,960	07(WB)
26	Canada	37,529	07(WB)
27	UAE	37,300	07(CIA)
28	Iceland	37,173	07(WB)
29	Sweden	36,365	07(WB)
30	Denmark	35,787	07(WB)
31	Australia	34,882	07(WB)
32	Belgium	34,459	07(WB)
33	Finland	34,413	07(WB)
34	UK	33,535	07(WB)
35	Japan	33,525	07(WB)
36	France	33,414	07(WB)
37	Germany	33,154	07(WB)
38	Greece	33,073	07(WB)
39	Bahrain	32,100	07(CIA)
40	Spain	31,312	07(WB)
41	Monaco	31,243	06(CIA)WEIGHT(US(WB))
42	Equatorial G	30,637	07(WB)
43	Taiwan	30,202	06(CIA)WEIGHT(US(WB))
44	Italy	29,935	07(WB)
45	Cyprus	27,185	07(WB)
46	Slovenia	27,093	07(WB)
47	New Zealand	26,108	07(WB)
48	Greenland	25,924	01(CIA)WEIGHT(US(WB))
49	Israel	25,917	07(WB)
50	Aruba	25,144	04(CIA)WEIGHT(US(WB))
51	Bahamas	25,000	07(CIA)
52	Korea, South	24,712	07(WB)
53	Oman	24,000	07(CIA)
54	Trinidad/Tobago	23,498	07(WB)
55	Czechia	23,194	07(WB)
56	Saudi Arabia	22,907	07(WB)
57	Malta	22,615	06(WB)WEIGHT(US(WB))
58	Portugal	21,754	07(WB)
59	Puerto Rico	21,700	07(CIA)
60	Fr Polynesia	21,362	03(CIA)WEIGHT(US(WB))
61	Estonia	21,257	07(WB)
62	Slovakia	20,205	07(WB)
63	Barbados	19,300	07(CIA)
64	Hungary	18,680	07(WB)
65	Antigua & Barbuda	18,640	07(WB)
66	Neth Antilles	18,454	04(CIA)WEIGHT(US(WB))
67	New Caledonia	18,454	04(CIA)WEIGHT(US(WB))
68	Lithuania	17,673	07(WB)
69	Martinique	17,578	03(CIA)WEIGHT(US(WB))
70	Latvia	17,517	07(WB)
71	Virgin I, US	16,724	04(CIA)WEIGHT(US(WB))
72	N Mariana Is	16,543	00(CIA)WEIGHT(US(WB))
73	Guam	16,427	05(CIA)WEIGHT(US(WB))
74	Seychelles	16,400	07(WB)

75	Poland	15,811	07(WB)
76	Croatia	15,515	07(WB)
77	Gabon	15,175	07(WB)
78	Russia	14,743	07(WB)
79	St Kitts & Nevis	14,700	07(WB)
80	Turks & Caicos	14,564	02(CIA)WEIGHT(US(WB))
81	Libya	14,369	07(WB)
82	Chile	13,885	07(WB)
83	Botswana	13,415	07(WB)
84	Malaysia	13,380	07(WB)
85	Argentina	13,244	07(WB)
86	Mexico	12,780	07(WB)
87	Turkey	12,481	07(WB)
88	Venezuela	12,168	07(WB)
89	Romania	11,394	07(WB)
90	Panama	11,387	07(WB)
91	Bulgaria	11,298	07(WB)
92	Mauritius	11,278	07(WB)
93	Uruguay	11,238	07(WB)
94	Iran	10,934	07(WB)
95	Belarus	10,850	07(WB)
96	Kazakhstan	10,829	07(WB)
97	Costa Rica	10,638	07(WB)
98	Serbia	10,393	07(WB)
99	Montenegro	10,221	07(WB)
100	Anguilla	10,150	04(CIA)WEIGHT(US(WB))
101	Guiana, Fr	10,132	03(CIA)WEIGHT(US(WB))
102	Lebanon	10,112	07(WB)
103	St Lucia	9,999	07(WB)
104	Cook Is	9,966	05(CIA)WEIGHT(US(WB))
105	South Africa	9,736	07(WB)
106	Guadeloupe	9,644	03(CIA)WEIGHT(US(WB))
107	Brazil	9,570	07(WB)
108	St Pierre &	9,073	01(CIA)WEIGHT(US(WB))
109	Macedonia	8,543	07(WB)
110	Palau	8,323	05(CIA)WEIGHT(US(WB))
111	Thailand	8,138	07(WB)
112	Samoa, Ameri	8,000	07(CIA)
113	Dominica	7,948	07(WB)
114	Peru	7,842	07(WB)
115	Suriname	7,816	07(WB)
116	Algeria	7,743	07(WB)
117	St Vincent	7,694	07(WB)
118	Grenada	7,633	07(WB)
119	Tunisia	7,506	07(WB)
120	Azerbaijan	7,477	07(WB)
121	Bosnia	7,468	07(WB)
122	Ecuador	7,398	07(WB)
123	Niue	7,080	03(CIA)WEIGHT(US(WB))
124	Colombia	6,958	07(WB)
125	Ukraine	6,916	07(WB)
126	Belize	6,860	07(WB)
127	Reunion	6,790	05(CIA)WEIGHT(US(WB))
128	Dominican Rep	6,690	07(WB)
129	Jamaica	6,689	07(WB)

130	Albania	6,385	07(WB)
131	El Salvador	5,781	07(WB)
132	Armenia	5,711	07(WB)
133	Nauru	5,476	05(CIA)WEIGHT(US(WB))
134	Angola	5,467	07(WB)
135	Mayotte	5,366	05(CIA)WEIGHT(US(WB))
136	Egypt	5,352	07(WB)
137	China	5,345	07(WB)
138	Maldives	5,335	07(WB)
139	Turkmenistan	5,200	07(CIA)
140	Namibia	5,173	07(WB)
141	Swaziland	4,914	07(WB)
142	Jordan	4,903	07(WB)
143	Bhutan	4,838	07(WB)
144	Georgia	4,667	07(WB)
145	Guatemala	4,565	07(WB)
146	Syria	4,513	07(WB)
147	Fiji	4,438	07(WB)
148	Wallis & Futuna	4,383	04(CIA)WEIGHT(US(WB))
149	Paraguay	4,332	07(WB)
150	Montserrat	4,306	02(CIA)WEIGHT(US(WB))
151	Sri Lanka	4,259	07(WB)
152	Bolivia	4,208	07(WB)
153	Morocco	4,063	07(WB)
154	Cuba	4,062	06(CIA)WEIGHT(US(WB))
155	Samoa, W	4,018	07(WB)
156	Honduras	3,810	07(WB)
157	Indonesia	3,728	07(WB)
158	Vanuatu	3,667	07(WB)
159	St Helena	3,632	98(CIA)WEIGHT(US(WB))
160	Tonga	3,614	07(WB)
161	Iraq	3,600	07(CIA)
162	Congo, Rep	3,512	07(WB)
163	Philippines	3,410	07(WB)
164	Mongolia	3,222	07(WB)
165	Marshall Is	3,176	05(CIA)WEIGHT(US(WB))
166	Micronesia	3,057	07(WB)
167	Cape Verde	3,042	07(WB)
168	Guyana	3,012	07(WB)
169	India	2,753	07(WB)
170	Vietnam	2,600	07(WB)
171	Nicaragua	2,578	07(WB)
172	Moldova	2,560	07(WB)
173	Pakistan	2,525	07(WB)
174	Uzbekistan	2,425	07(WB)
175	Yemen	2,336	07(WB)
176	Kosovo	2,300	07(CIA)
177	Laos	2,140	07(WB)
178	Cameroon	2,124	07(WB)
179	Sudan	2,088	07(WB)
180	Papua New Gu	2,085	07(WB)
181	Djibouti	2,062	07(WB)
182	Tuvalu	2,026	02(CIA)WEIGHT(US(WB))
183	Kyrgyzstan	1,980	07(WB)
184	Nigeria	1,977	07(WB)
185	Mauritania	1,928	07(WB)

186	Burma	1,900	07(CIA)
187	Korea, North	1,875	06(CIA)WEIGHT(US(WB))
188	Tokelau	1,802	93(CIA)WEIGHT(US(WB))
189	Cambodia	1,802	07(WB)
190	Tajikistan	1,754	07(WB)
191	Solomon Is	1,681	07(WB)
192	Ivory Coast	1,673	07(WB)
193	Senegal	1,666	07(WB)
194	San Tome & Principe	1,639	07(WB)
195	Lesotho	1,542	07(WB)
196	Kenya	1,535	07(WB)
197	Kiribati	1,480	07(WB)
198	Chad	1,478	07(WB)
199	Zambia	1,359	07(WB)
200	Ghana	1,335	07(WB)
201	Benin	1,312	07(WB)
202	West Bank	1,296	06(CIA)WEIGHT(US(WB))
203	Bangladesh	1,242	07(WB)
204	Gambia	1,233	07(WB)
205	Tanzania	1,209	07(WB)
206	Haiti	1,155	07(WB)
207	Comoros	1,148	07(WB)
208	Guinea	1,140	07(WB)
209	Burkina Faso	1,124	07(WB)
210	Mali	1,084	07(WB)
211	Nepal	1,033	07(WB)
212	Uganda	939	07(WB)
213	Madagascar	935	07(WB)
214	Rwanda	867	07(WB)
215	Gaza Strip	864	06(CIA)WEIGHT(US(WB))
216	Togo	809	07(WB)
217	Afghanistan	800	07(CIA)
218	Mozambique	796	07(WB)
219	Ethiopia	779	07(WB)
220	Malawi	756	07(WB)
221	Centr. African Rep	714	07(WB)
222	East Timor	714	07(WB)
223	Sierra Leone	677	07(WB)
224	W Sahara	656	PROXY(Maddison) WEIGHT(US(WB))
225	Niger	628	07(WB)
226	Somalia	600	07(CIA)
227	Eritrea	520	07(WB)
228	Guinea-Bissau	478	07(WB)
229	Liberia	358	07(WB)
230	Burundi	341	07(WB)
231	Congo, Dem R	298	07(WB)
232	Zimbabwe	200	07(CIA)

CHAPTER 3. GROSS DOMESTIC PRODUCT AT PURCHASING POWER PARITIES IN MILLIONS OF 2007 DOLLARS

TABLE 3.1 - GDP AT PPP IN MILLIONS OF 2007 DOLLARS, YEAR 0001		
OBS	COUNTRY	GDPPPP
1	India	41,600
2	China	39,402
3	Italy	9,508
4	Turkey	5,355
5	Bangladesh	4,745
6	France	3,474
7	Iran	3,400
8	Pakistan	3,239
9	Egypt	2,938
10	Spain	2,744
11	Indonesia	2,066
12	Germany	1,798
13	Japan	1,763
14	Yemen	1,748
15	Greece	1,616
16	Saudi Arabia	1,409
17	Mexico	1,293
18	Algeria	1,263
19	Sudan	1,175
20	Syria	1,124
21	Korea, South	1,096
22	Russia	828
23	Iraq	810
24	Vietnam	683
25	Morocco	588
26	Korea, North	507
27	Tunisia	505
28	Romania	500
29	UK	439
30	Thailand	431
31	Czechia	423
32	Nepal	405
33	US	400
34	Burma	366
35	Afghanistan	342
36	Serbia	337
37	Bulgaria	312
38	Austria	312
39	Ukraine	309
40	Peru	295
41	Uzbekistan	290
42	Lebanon	279
43	Ethiopia	275
44	Kazakhstan	272
45	Colombia	271
46	Poland	264

47	Portugal	264
48	Libya	253
49	Bolivia	247
50	Cambodia	218
51	Oman	214
52	Croatia	208
53	Brazil	200
54	Belgium	198
55	Hungary	187
56	Switzerland	187
57	Sri Lanka	183
58	Chile	171
59	Slovakia	164
60	Jordan	163
61	Cyprus	162
62	Venezuela	161
63	Australia	145
64	Israel	144
65	Bosnia	144
66	Guatemala	133
67	Netherlands	125
68	Argentina	120
69	Somalia	118
70	Sweden	118
71	Albania	118
72	Ghana	117
73	Ecuador	112
74	Denmark	106
75	Philippines	97
76	Slovenia	79
77	Guinea	79
78	Ireland	68
79	Belarus	68
80	Kyrgyzstan	68
81	Tajikistan	68
82	Macedonia	67
83	Mongolia	65
84	Georgia	63
85	Sierra Leone	59
86	Norway	59
87	Turkmenistan	58
88	Azerbaijan	57
89	El Salvador	56
90	Kuwait	56
91	South Africa	55
92	Laos	49
93	Canada	47
94	Kosovo	45
95	Bahrain	42
96	Nicaragua	42
97	Taiwan	37
98	Malaysia	34
99	New Zealand	32
100	Paraguay	32
101	Honduras	30
102	Mozambique	29

103	UAE	28
104	Haiti	25
105	Namibia	24
106	Armenia	23
107	Lithuania	22
108	Montenegro	21
109	Panama	21
110	Cuba	21
111	Botswana	20
112	Eritrea	19
113	Moldova	18
114	Guinea-Bissau	17
115	Burundi	17
116	Zimbabwe	15
117	Malawi	15
118	Costa Rica	14
119	Latvia	14
120	Jamaica	14
121	Zambia	14
122	Uruguay	12
123	Finland	12
124	Qatar	10
125	Puerto Rico	8
126	Estonia	8
127	Dominican Rep	3
128	Lesotho	3
129	Trinidad/Tobago	2
130	Hong Kong	2
131	Swaziland	1
132	Madagascar	1
133	Singapore	1

Source: Calculated as POP*GPCPPP.

OBS	COUNTRY	GDPPPP
	TABLE 3.2 - GDP AT PPP IN MILLIONS OF 2007 DOLLARS, YEAR 1000	
1	India	41,600
2	China	39,005
3	Turkey	6,568
4	Bangladesh	4,745
5	Japan	4,683
6	Iran	4,170
7	France	4,058
8	Indonesia	3,824
9	Egypt	3,673
10	Italy	3,306
11	Pakistan	3,239
12	Mexico	2,644
13	Spain	2,644
14	Yemen	2,143
15	Germany	2,108
16	Korea, South	2,029
17	Sudan	1,829

18	Saudi Arabia	1,729
19	Russia	1,616
20	Syria	1,378
21	Vietnam	1,265
22	Algeria	1,263
23	Morocco	1,263
24	UK	1,097
25	Iraq	993
26	Korea, North	939
27	Thailand	797
28	US	764
29	Nepal	749
30	Poland	705
31	Burma	677
32	Greece	646
33	Afghanistan	633
34	Tunisia	632
35	Ukraine	619
36	Peru	600
37	Ethiopia	549
38	Colombia	549
39	Czechia	529
40	Bolivia	501
41	Uzbekistan	484
42	Bulgaria	470
43	Romania	470
44	Kazakhstan	454
45	Austria	437
46	Brazil	405
47	Cambodia	403
48	Portugal	375
49	Serbia	370
50	Chile	347
51	Lebanon	342
52	Sri Lanka	339
53	Venezuela	327
54	Libya	316
55	Hungary	294
56	Ghana	282
57	Guatemala	271
58	Oman	263
59	Belgium	250
60	Argentina	243
61	Croatia	242
62	Somalia	235
63	Sweden	235
64	Ecuador	228
65	Denmark	212
66	Slovakia	205
67	Jordan	200
68	Australia	188
69	Netherlands	187
70	Guinea	185
71	Switzerland	181
72	Philippines	180
73	Israel	177

74	Mozambique	176
75	Burundi	172
76	Ireland	170
77	Bosnia	168
78	South Africa	164
79	Sierra Leone	137
80	Belarus	135
81	Cyprus	132
82	Mongolia	120
83	Madagascar	118
84	Norway	118
85	Albania	118
86	El Salvador	113
87	Kyrgyzstan	113
88	Tajikistan	113
89	Georgia	106
90	Zimbabwe	102
91	Malawi	101
92	Turkmenistan	96
93	Azerbaijan	96
94	Canada	94
95	Slovenia	93
96	Zambia	91
97	Laos	91
98	Nicaragua	85
99	Macedonia	78
100	Kuwait	68
101	Taiwan	68
102	Paraguay	65
103	Malaysia	62
104	Honduras	61
105	Bahrain	52
106	Haiti	50
107	Kosovo	48
108	Lithuania	44
109	Panama	43
110	Cuba	42
111	New Zealand	42
112	Guinea-Bissau	40
113	Armenia	39
114	Eritrea	38
115	Moldova	37
116	UAE	34
117	Namibia	32
118	Costa Rica	29
119	Latvia	28
120	Jamaica	28
121	Botswana	27
122	Montenegro	25
123	Uruguay	25
124	Finland	24
125	Puerto Rico	17
126	Estonia	16
127	Qatar	12
128	Lesotho	9
129	Dominican Rep	6

130	Trinidad/Tobago	4
131	Swaziland	3
132	Hong Kong	2
133	Singapore	1

Source: Calculated as POP*GPCPPP.

TABLE 3.3 - GDP AT PPP IN MILLIONS OF 2007 DOLLARS, YEAR 1500		
OBS	COUNTRY	GDPPPP
1	China	90,792
2	India	74,571
3	Italy	16,968
4	France	16,021
5	Germany	12,129
6	Japan	11,312
7	Indonesia	8,882
8	Bangladesh	8,505
9	Spain	6,603
10	Russia	6,522
11	Pakistan	5,805
12	Turkey	5,553
13	Korea, South	4,822
14	Mexico	4,683
15	UK	3,861
16	Poland	3,840
17	Iran	3,526
18	Vietnam	2,896
19	Egypt	2,791
20	Sudan	2,439
21	Korea, North	2,230
22	Austria	2,077
23	Czechia	2,045
24	Romania	1,890
25	Ukraine	1,884
26	Thailand	1,851
27	Yemen	1,812
28	Belgium	1,800
29	Burma	1,482
30	Saudi Arabia	1,462
31	Afghanistan	1,406
32	Nepal	1,335
33	Hungary	1,308
34	US	1,175
35	Syria	1,165
36	Ethiopia	1,099
37	Netherlands	1,062
38	Kazakhstan	1,017
39	Algeria	948
40	Morocco	948
41	Portugal	890
42	Peru	869
43	Iraq	840

44	Colombia	796
45	Sri Lanka	788
46	Bolivia	726
47	Cambodia	719
48	Uzbekistan	711
49	Slovakia	693
50	Bulgaria	682
51	Denmark	651
52	Greece	636
53	Switzerland	604
54	Brazil	588
55	Mozambique	588
56	Sweden	562
57	Serbia	541
58	Chile	518
59	Tunisia	505
60	Venezuela	474
61	Somalia	470
62	Ghana	444
63	Ireland	440
64	Belarus	438
65	Philippines	418
66	Madagascar	411
67	Croatia	410
68	Guatemala	393
69	Argentina	363
70	Burundi	345
71	Ecuador	330
72	South Africa	328
73	Georgia	325
74	Libya	316
75	Guinea	291
76	Lebanon	289
77	Norway	282
78	Australia	264
79	Azerbaijan	240
80	Oman	222
81	Slovenia	222
82	Sierra Leone	216
83	Bosnia	216
84	Mongolia	213
85	Lithuania	206
86	Zimbabwe	204
87	Malawi	201
88	Finland	200
89	Laos	191
90	Zambia	182
91	Jordan	169
92	El Salvador	164
93	Kyrgyzstan	158
94	Tajikistan	158
95	Taiwan	158
96	Israel	149
97	Canada	147
98	Malaysia	145
99	Latvia	137

100	Turkmenistan	135
101	Nicaragua	123
102	Moldova	122
103	Armenia	122
104	Albania	118
105	Macedonia	100
106	Paraguay	94
107	Honduras	89
108	Estonia	83
109	Eritrea	76
110	Haiti	73
111	Guinea-Bissau	64
112	Namibia	63
113	Panama	62
114	Kosovo	62
115	Cuba	61
116	New Zealand	59
117	Kuwait	58
118	Botswana	54
119	Bahrain	44
120	Costa Rica	42
121	Cyprus	41
122	Jamaica	40
123	Uruguay	37
124	Montenegro	36
125	UAE	29
126	Puerto Rico	25
127	Lesotho	18
128	Qatar	10
129	Dominican Rep	9
130	Swaziland	7
131	Trinidad/Tobago	6
132	Hong Kong	5
133	Singapore	2

Source: Calculated as POP*GPCPPP.

TABLE 3.4 - GDP AT PPP IN MILLIONS OF 2007 DOLLARS, YEAR 1600		
OBS	COUNTRY	GDPPPP
1	China	141,036
2	India	91,519
3	France	22,857
4	Italy	21,170
5	Germany	18,593
6	Japan	14,133
7	Bangladesh	10,439
8	Spain	10,326
9	Indonesia	9,957
10	Russia	8,988
11	UK	8,244
12	Pakistan	7,125
13	Turkey	6,412
14	Korea, South	5,954

15	Poland	5,304
16	Iran	3,942
17	Egypt	3,489
18	Vietnam	3,419
19	Czechia	3,390
20	Austria	3,074
21	Netherlands	3,043
22	Korea, North	2,754
23	Ukraine	2,605
24	Sudan	2,561
25	Belgium	2,294
26	Thailand	2,107
27	Romania	2,088
28	Yemen	1,812
29	Burma	1,750
30	Mexico	1,667
31	Afghanistan	1,659
32	Nepal	1,548
33	Hungary	1,468
34	Saudi Arabia	1,462
35	Algeria	1,421
36	Morocco	1,421
37	Kazakhstan	1,286
38	Ethiopia	1,236
39	Portugal	1,196
40	Bulgaria	1,177
41	Slovakia	1,148
42	Syria	1,136
43	Switzerland	1,102
44	Greece	1,064
45	Sweden	920
46	Uzbekistan	899
47	US	881
48	Sri Lanka	879
49	Cambodia	849
50	Iraq	841
51	Denmark	836
52	Mozambique	762
53	Serbia	731
54	Philippines	674
55	Ireland	643
56	Tunisia	632
57	Belarus	605
58	Ghana	564
59	Croatia	553
60	Peru	521
61	Brazil	503
62	Somalia	488
63	Madagascar	488
64	Colombia	477
65	Norway	447
66	Bolivia	435
67	Georgia	431
68	Burundi	402
69	South Africa	398
70	Guinea	370

71	Chile	370
72	Taiwan	359
73	Finland	316
74	Libya	316
75	Argentina	310
76	Slovenia	307
77	Azerbaijan	296
78	Lithuania	285
79	Venezuela	284
80	Lebanon	282
81	Sierra Leone	275
82	Australia	264
83	Bosnia	264
84	Mongolia	247
85	Guatemala	236
86	Zimbabwe	233
87	Laos	226
88	Oman	222
89	Malawi	221
90	Zambia	208
91	Ecuador	198
92	Latvia	190
93	Kyrgyzstan	181
94	Tajikistan	180
95	Malaysia	171
96	Moldova	169
97	Turkmenistan	169
98	Jordan	165
99	Armenia	162
100	Canada	147
101	Israel	146
102	Macedonia	122
103	Albania	118
104	Estonia	116
105	El Salvador	98
106	Eritrea	86
107	Guinea-Bissau	81
108	Kosovo	76
109	Nicaragua	74
110	Cyprus	68
111	Namibia	66
112	New Zealand	59
113	Kuwait	58
114	Paraguay	57
115	Botswana	54
116	Honduras	53
117	Montenegro	49
118	Bahrain	44
119	Uruguay	37
120	Panama	37
121	Haiti	29
122	UAE	29
123	Costa Rica	25
124	Cuba	24
125	Jamaica	22
126	Lesotho	21

127	Puerto Rico	10
128	Qatar	10
129	Swaziland	8
130	Hong Kong	7
131	Dominican Rep	4
132	Trinidad/Tobago	3
133	Singapore	2

Source: Calculated as POP*GPCPPP.

TABLE 3.5 - GDP AT PPP IN MILLIONS OF 2007 DOLLARS, YEAR 1700		
OBS	COUNTRY	GDPPPP
1	China	121,644
2	India	111,857
3	France	28,705
4	Japan	22,610
5	Italy	21,493
6	Germany	20,054
7	UK	14,686
8	Russia	13,265
9	Bangladesh	12,758
10	Indonesia	11,162
11	Spain	10,990
12	Pakistan	8,708
13	Turkey	7,404
14	Korea, South	7,353
15	Poland	7,038
16	Netherlands	5,946
17	Iran	4,407
18	Vietnam	3,954
19	Ukraine	3,838
20	Mexico	3,755
21	Czechia	3,749
22	Austria	3,647
23	Korea, North	3,401
24	Belgium	3,361
25	Egypt	3,140
26	Romania	2,886
27	Sudan	2,683
28	Portugal	2,406
29	Thailand	2,343
30	Burma	2,024
31	Hungary	1,978
32	Afghanistan	1,919
33	Yemen	1,812
34	Sweden	1,809
35	Nepal	1,800
36	Kazakhstan	1,599
37	Switzerland	1,569
38	Saudi Arabia	1,462
39	Ireland	1,439
40	Ethiopia	1,374
41	Bulgaria	1,302

42	Slovakia	1,270
43	Greece	1,168
44	Uzbekistan	1,117
45	Syria	1,107
46	Algeria	1,106
47	Morocco	1,106
48	Denmark	1,068
49	Philippines	1,059
50	Cambodia	982
51	Sri Lanka	958
52	Mozambique	915
53	Belarus	892
54	Brazil	843
55	Iraq	841
56	Serbia	808
57	Taiwan	798
58	US	774
59	Ghana	726
60	Norway	661
61	Croatia	612
62	Madagascar	610
63	Peru	593
64	Somalia	579
65	South Africa	568
66	Colombia	565
67	Georgia	556
68	Tunisia	505
69	Argentina	503
70	Chile	495
71	Bolivia	495
72	Guinea	476
73	Burundi	460
74	Lithuania	419
75	Finland	375
76	Azerbaijan	374
77	Sierra Leone	353
78	Slovenia	348
79	Venezuela	323
80	Libya	316
81	Mongolia	287
82	Latvia	280
83	Lebanon	275
84	Guatemala	268
85	Australia	264
86	Bosnia	264
87	Laos	261
88	Zimbabwe	254
89	Moldova	249
90	Malawi	242
91	Zambia	227
92	Ecuador	225
93	Oman	222
94	Turkmenistan	210
95	Tajikistan	209
96	Armenia	209
97	Kyrgyzstan	203

98	Malaysia	198
99	Albania	176
100	Estonia	173
101	Jordan	161
102	Israel	142
103	Canada	126
104	Macedonia	122
105	El Salvador	112
106	Guinea-Bissau	104
107	Eritrea	95
108	Nicaragua	84
109	Cuba	83
110	Kosovo	76
111	Cyprus	75
112	Haiti	73
113	Jamaica	72
114	Uruguay	71
115	Namibia	66
116	Paraguay	64
117	Honduras	61
118	New Zealand	59
119	Kuwait	58
120	Botswana	54
121	Montenegro	54
122	Bahrain	44
123	Panama	42
124	Puerto Rico	36
125	Lesotho	29
126	UAE	29
127	Costa Rica	28
128	Swaziland	11
129	Trinidad/Tobago	10
130	Qatar	10
131	Dominican Rep	9
132	Hong Kong	6
133	Singapore	3

Source: Calculated as POP*GPCPPP.

TABLE 3.6 - GDP AT PPP IN MILLIONS OF 2007 DOLLARS, YEAR 1820		
OBS	COUNTRY	GDPPPP
1	China	335,843
2	India	136,791
3	France	52,108
4	UK	49,704
5	Germany	39,406
6	Russia	33,611
7	Italy	33,109
8	Japan	30,468
9	US	18,432
10	Spain	18,071
11	Indonesia	16,118

12	Bangladesh	15,602
13	Poland	13,784
14	Pakistan	10,649
15	Ukraine	9,559
16	Turkey	9,516
17	Romania	8,313
18	Korea, South	8,281
19	Mexico	7,345
20	Czechia	7,189
21	Belgium	6,654
22	Ireland	6,510
23	Netherlands	6,300
24	Hungary	6,278
25	Austria	6,028
26	Iran	5,667
27	Vietnam	5,072
28	Sweden	4,550
29	Portugal	4,471
30	Thailand	4,427
31	Brazil	4,277
32	Korea, North	3,830
33	Switzerland	3,180
34	Sudan	3,144
35	Egypt	3,066
36	Kazakhstan	2,697
37	Burma	2,596
38	Bulgaria	2,567
39	Afghanistan	2,462
40	Slovakia	2,434
41	Nepal	2,281
42	Belarus	2,221
43	Greece	2,177
44	Denmark	2,162
45	Yemen	2,095
46	Uzbekistan	1,892
47	Philippines	1,867
48	Ethiopia	1,733
49	Serbia	1,727
50	Algeria	1,699
51	Morocco	1,699
52	Saudi Arabia	1,690
53	Taiwan	1,616
54	Norway	1,573
55	Finland	1,341
56	Croatia	1,307
57	Syria	1,292
58	Mozambique	1,278
59	Cambodia	1,260
60	Canada	1,084
61	Lithuania	1,044
62	Madagascar	1,026
63	Colombia	1,007
64	Argentina	1,004
65	Sri Lanka	980
66	Iraq	944
67	Peru	922

68	South Africa	880
69	Georgia	870
70	Ghana	838
71	Bolivia	810
72	Chile	786
73	Slovenia	766
74	Latvia	697
75	Moldova	621
76	Somalia	610
77	Burundi	597
78	Azerbaijan	586
79	Tunisia	553
80	Guinea	549
81	Bosnia	500
82	Venezuela	485
83	Guatemala	476
84	Cuba	475
85	Estonia	438
86	Haiti	425
87	Jamaica	412
88	Sierra Leone	408
89	Mongolia	364
90	Ecuador	357
91	Turkmenistan	355
92	Tajikistan	353
93	Libya	340
94	Laos	335
95	Armenia	327
96	Kyrgyzstan	322
97	Lebanon	321
98	Zimbabwe	285
99	Albania	272
100	Malawi	271
101	Oman	257
102	Zambia	255
103	Malaysia	254
104	Australia	254
105	Macedonia	231
106	Puerto Rico	204
107	Jordan	187
108	Uruguay	172
109	Israel	166
110	El Salvador	146
111	Kosovo	144
112	Cyprus	140
113	Eritrea	120
114	Guinea-Bissau	120
115	Nicaragua	115
116	Montenegro	115
117	Paraguay	87
118	Trinidad/Tobago	85
119	Honduras	79
120	Namibia	72
121	Panama	69
122	Kuwait	67
123	Botswana	59

124	New Zealand	59
125	Dominican Rep	52
126	Bahrain	51
127	Costa Rica	47
128	Lesotho	46
129	UAE	33
130	Hong Kong	18
131	Swaziland	18
132	Qatar	11
133	Singapore	4

Source: Calculated as POP*GPCPPP.

TABLE 3.7 - GDP AT PPP IN MILLIONS OF 2007 DOLLARS, YEAR 1870		
OBS	COUNTRY	GDPPPP
1	China	278,752
2	India	173,947
3	US	144,546
4	UK	137,404
5	Germany	105,991
6	France	105,944
7	Russia	75,763
8	Italy	61,416
9	Japan	37,287
10	Spain	28,728
11	Indonesia	27,789
12	Poland	23,439
13	Ukraine	21,279
14	Bangladesh	20,401
15	Belgium	20,154
16	Pakistan	14,744
17	Netherlands	14,622
18	Turkey	14,293
19	Czechia	13,072
20	Romania	12,555
21	Austria	12,371
22	Brazil	10,262
23	Sweden	10,179
24	Ireland	10,055
25	Hungary	9,493
26	Canada	9,415
27	Mexico	9,129
28	Iran	8,889
29	Korea, South	8,654
30	Australia	8,535
31	Switzerland	8,199
32	Vietnam	7,811
33	Portugal	6,198
34	Egypt	6,096
35	Thailand	6,041
36	Denmark	5,556
37	Kazakhstan	4,990

38	Belarus	4,945
39	Sudan	4,851
40	Greece	4,728
41	Philippines	4,641
42	Slovakia	4,426
43	Korea, North	4,003
44	Algeria	3,966
45	Chile	3,686
46	Norway	3,650
47	Ethiopia	3,631
48	Uzbekistan	3,488
49	Sri Lanka	3,483
50	Argentina	3,459
51	South Africa	3,211
52	Bulgaria	3,191
53	Burma	3,143
54	Morocco	3,123
55	Afghanistan	3,038
56	Finland	2,938
57	Serbia	2,873
58	Mozambique	2,863
59	Nepal	2,761
60	Yemen	2,399
61	Lithuania	2,325
62	Georgia	2,251
63	Croatia	2,175
64	Colombia	2,045
65	Madagascar	2,013
66	Saudi Arabia	1,975
67	Syria	1,962
68	Taiwan	1,895
69	Peru	1,869
70	Iraq	1,669
71	Latvia	1,551
72	Azerbaijan	1,517
73	Moldova	1,383
74	Venezuela	1,382
75	Cambodia	1,375
76	New Zealand	1,325
77	Slovenia	1,290
78	Somalia	1,196
79	Bolivia	1,127
80	Uruguay	1,099
81	Tunisia	1,094
82	Cuba	1,070
83	Ghana	1,018
84	Estonia	976
85	Guatemala	885
86	Armenia	846
87	Burundi	826
88	Guinea	816
89	Bosnia	792
90	Malaysia	779
91	Ecuador	742
92	Zimbabwe	698
93	Haiti	676

94	Turkmenistan	656
95	Tajikistan	652
96	Zambia	611
97	Sierra Leone	606
98	Kyrgyzstan	596
99	Lebanon	590
100	Libya	544
101	Puerto Rico	543
102	Malawi	543
103	Laos	518
104	Albania	395
105	Mongolia	393
106	Jamaica	392
107	Macedonia	370
108	Oman	310
109	Cyprus	303
110	El Salvador	289
111	Jordan	281
112	Israel	262
113	Eritrea	252
114	Paraguay	239
115	Honduras	237
116	Namibia	234
117	Kosovo	227
118	Nicaragua	214
119	Montenegro	191
120	Trinidad/Tobago	179
121	Guinea-Bissau	179
122	Dominican Rep	142
123	Panama	133
124	Hong Kong	123
125	Lesotho	108
126	Costa Rica	106
127	Botswana	102
128	Singapore	84
129	Kuwait	70
130	Bahrain	53
131	Swaziland	52
132	UAE	35
133	Qatar	12

*Source: Calculated as POP*GPCPPP.*

TABLE 3.8 - GDP AT PPP IN MILLIONS OF 2007 DOLLARS, YEAR 1880		
OBS	COUNTRY	GDPPPP
1	China	289,231
2	US	213,492
3	India	184,111
4	UK	165,139
5	Germany	127,239
6	France	121,608
7	Russia	92,651

8	Italy	68,598
9	Japan	46,666
10	Spain	40,768
11	Indonesia	31,974
12	Poland	31,788
13	Ukraine	26,023
14	Belgium	24,950
15	Bangladesh	21,312
16	Netherlands	18,092
17	Turkey	16,533
18	Czechia	15,646
19	Pakistan	15,607
20	Romania	15,440
21	Austria	15,091
22	Australia	13,831
23	Brazil	13,030
24	Mexico	12,611
25	Sweden	12,399
26	Canada	11,696
27	Hungary	11,663
28	Ireland	10,676
29	Switzerland	10,219
30	Iran	10,213
31	Vietnam	9,793
32	Korea, South	9,337
33	Egypt	7,674
34	Thailand	6,812
35	Denmark	6,668
36	Portugal	6,414
37	Kazakhstan	6,103
38	Argentina	6,076
39	Greece	6,057
40	Belarus	6,048
41	Philippines	5,439
42	Slovakia	5,298
43	Sudan	5,290
44	Chile	5,138
45	Algeria	4,867
46	South Africa	4,557
47	Burma	4,484
48	Norway	4,477
49	Korea, North	4,381
50	Bulgaria	4,274
51	Uzbekistan	4,266
52	Ethiopia	4,210
53	Serbia	3,694
54	Sri Lanka	3,688
55	Morocco	3,537
56	Afghanistan	3,533
57	Finland	3,473
58	Mozambique	3,364
59	Nepal	3,093
60	Colombia	2,880
61	New Zealand	2,863
62	Lithuania	2,843
63	Croatia	2,796

64	Georgia	2,753
65	Peru	2,515
66	Yemen	2,506
67	Syria	2,309
68	Madagascar	2,303
69	Taiwan	2,087
70	Saudi Arabia	2,058
71	Iraq	2,026
72	Latvia	1,896
73	Azerbaijan	1,855
74	Venezuela	1,844
75	Moldova	1,692
76	Slovenia	1,658
77	Cambodia	1,565
78	Uruguay	1,419
79	Bolivia	1,401
80	Cuba	1,372
81	Somalia	1,369
82	Tunisia	1,316
83	Estonia	1,193
84	Malaysia	1,149
85	Guatemala	1,122
86	Ghana	1,089
87	Armenia	1,034
88	Bosnia	986
89	Ecuador	984
90	Guinea	884
91	Burundi	881
92	Zimbabwe	836
93	Turkmenistan	803
94	Tajikistan	798
95	Haiti	748
96	Puerto Rico	739
97	Kyrgyzstan	729
98	Zambia	728
99	Lebanon	708
100	Sierra Leone	656
101	Laos	646
102	Malawi	624
103	Libya	598
104	Albania	502
105	Macedonia	476
106	Jamaica	459
107	Mongolia	400
108	El Salvador	398
109	Cyprus	389
110	Israel	330
111	Oman	327
112	Jordan	323
113	Paraguay	298
114	Namibia	296
115	Eritrea	293
116	Nicaragua	286
117	Trinidad/Tobago	276
118	Honduras	267
119	Kosovo	246

120	Montenegro	246
121	Guinea-Bissau	193
122	Hong Kong	188
123	Dominican Rep	183
124	Panama	181
125	Costa Rica	163
126	Singapore	133
127	Lesotho	129
128	Botswana	114
129	Kuwait	74
130	Swaziland	64
131	Bahrain	56
132	UAE	37
133	Qatar	13

Source: Calculated as POP*GPCPPP.

TABLE 3.9 - GDP AT PPP IN MILLIONS OF 2007 DOLLARS, YEAR 1890		
OBS	COUNTRY	GDPPPP
1	US	315,452
2	China	301,465
3	India	208,404
4	UK	206,145
5	Germany	169,816
6	France	139,675
7	Russia	113,305
8	Italy	77,639
9	Japan	59,585
10	Poland	43,111
11	Spain	42,366
12	Indonesia	36,438
13	Ukraine	31,824
14	Belgium	30,700
15	Bangladesh	23,810
16	Netherlands	22,139
17	Australia	20,349
18	Austria	19,359
19	Turkey	19,125
20	Romania	18,988
21	Czechia	18,728
22	Pakistan	17,667
23	Mexico	17,421
24	Canada	17,181
25	Brazil	16,563
26	Sweden	14,649
27	Hungary	14,330
28	Switzerland	13,795
29	Vietnam	12,278
30	Iran	11,735
31	Ireland	10,706
32	Argentina	10,673
33	Korea, South	10,074
34	Egypt	9,517

35	Denmark	8,503
36	Portugal	8,332
37	Greece	7,757
38	Thailand	7,682
39	Kazakhstan	7,463
40	Belarus	7,396
41	Chile	7,161
42	South Africa	6,470
43	Burma	6,396
44	Philippines	6,373
45	Slovakia	6,342
46	Algeria	5,946
47	Sudan	5,770
48	Bulgaria	5,724
49	Uzbekistan	5,217
50	Norway	5,213
51	Sri Lanka	5,132
52	Ethiopia	4,881
53	Korea, North	4,804
54	Finland	4,796
55	Serbia	4,749
56	Afghanistan	4,110
57	Colombia	4,057
58	Morocco	4,005
59	Mozambique	3,952
60	New Zealand	3,669
61	Croatia	3,594
62	Nepal	3,491
63	Lithuania	3,477
64	Peru	3,383
65	Georgia	3,367
66	Syria	2,718
67	Madagascar	2,635
68	Yemen	2,618
69	Iraq	2,459
70	Venezuela	2,374
71	Latvia	2,319
72	Taiwan	2,300
73	Azerbaijan	2,268
74	Uruguay	2,164
75	Saudi Arabia	2,145
76	Slovenia	2,132
77	Moldova	2,069
78	Cambodia	1,804
79	Cuba	1,759
80	Bolivia	1,741
81	Malaysia	1,693
82	Tunisia	1,584
83	Somalia	1,566
84	Estonia	1,459
85	Guatemala	1,421
86	Ecuador	1,306
87	Bosnia	1,267
88	Armenia	1,265
89	Ghana	1,165
90	Puerto Rico	1,005

91	Zimbabwe	1,000
92	Turkmenistan	982
93	Tajikistan	976
94	Guinea	957
95	Burundi	941
96	Kyrgyzstan	891
97	Zambia	867
98	Lebanon	848
99	Haiti	828
100	Laos	806
101	Malawi	718
102	Sierra Leone	710
103	Libya	656
104	Albania	638
105	Macedonia	612
106	El Salvador	549
107	Jamaica	536
108	Cyprus	498
109	Trinidad/Tobago	425
110	Israel	417
111	Mongolia	408
112	Nicaragua	384
113	Namibia	374
114	Paraguay	372
115	Jordan	371
116	Oman	346
117	Honduras	341
118	Eritrea	339
119	Montenegro	316
120	Hong Kong	287
121	Dominican Rep	273
122	Kosovo	267
123	Costa Rica	251
124	Panama	246
125	Singapore	211
126	Guinea-Bissau	209
127	Lesotho	153
128	Botswana	127
129	Swaziland	79
130	Kuwait	79
131	Bahrain	60
132	UAE	39
133	Qatar	14

Source: Calculated as POP*GPCPPP.

TABLE 3.10 - GDP AT PPP IN MILLIONS OF 2007 DOLLARS, YEAR 1900		
OBS	COUNTRY	GDPPPP
1	US	459,125
2	China	320,270
3	UK	253,595
4	Germany	238,510

5	India	217,405
6	France	171,535
7	Russia	139,539
8	Italy	88,301
9	Japan	76,456
10	Poland	55,850
11	Spain	48,715
12	Indonesia	46,660
13	Ukraine	39,192
14	Belgium	36,829
15	Mexico	27,307
16	Netherlands	25,866
17	Austria	25,290
18	Bangladesh	24,893
19	Canada	23,338
20	Czechia	23,216
21	Romania	22,867
22	Turkey	22,122
23	Australia	22,055
24	Sweden	19,252
25	Argentina	19,002
26	Pakistan	18,717
27	Switzerland	18,583
28	Brazil	17,913
29	Hungary	17,611
30	Vietnam	15,394
31	Iran	13,483
32	Egypt	12,051
33	Denmark	11,351
34	Ireland	11,214
35	Korea, South	10,869
36	Portugal	10,337
37	Greece	9,849
38	Chile	9,591
39	Burma	9,332
40	Kazakhstan	9,191
41	South Africa	9,184
42	Belarus	9,108
43	Thailand	8,692
44	Slovakia	7,862
45	Philippines	7,468
46	Sri Lanka	7,414
47	Algeria	7,263
48	Bulgaria	7,187
49	Finland	6,484
50	Uzbekistan	6,425
51	Norway	6,346
52	Sudan	6,293
53	Serbia	5,859
54	Colombia	5,715
55	Ethiopia	5,659
56	Korea, North	5,247
57	New Zealand	5,096
58	Afghanistan	4,780
59	Mozambique	4,644
60	Peru	4,550

61	Morocco	4,535
62	Croatia	4,434
63	Lithuania	4,282
64	Georgia	4,146
65	Nepal	3,814
66	Syria	3,199
67	Venezuela	3,066
68	Madagascar	3,016
69	Iraq	2,984
70	Uruguay	2,983
71	Latvia	2,856
72	Taiwan	2,811
73	Azerbaijan	2,793
74	Yemen	2,735
75	Slovenia	2,630
76	Moldova	2,548
77	Malaysia	2,497
78	Cuba	2,255
79	Saudi Arabia	2,236
80	Bolivia	2,163
81	Cambodia	2,080
82	Tunisia	1,907
83	Guatemala	1,802
84	Estonia	1,797
85	Somalia	1,792
86	Ecuador	1,734
87	Bosnia	1,563
88	Armenia	1,557
89	Ghana	1,384
90	Puerto Rico	1,367
91	Turkmenistan	1,209
92	Tajikistan	1,202
93	Zimbabwe	1,197
94	Kyrgyzstan	1,098
95	Haiti	1,090
96	Guinea	1,036
97	Zambia	1,033
98	Lebanon	1,017
99	Laos	1,004
100	Burundi	1,004
101	Malawi	825
102	Albania	805
103	Sierra Leone	769
104	El Salvador	758
105	Macedonia	755
106	Libya	721
107	Trinidad/Tobago	654
108	Cyprus	632
109	Jamaica	627
110	Israel	526
111	Nicaragua	513
112	Hong Kong	476
113	Namibia	474
114	Paraguay	463
115	Mongolia	437
116	Dominican Rep	437

117	Honduras	436
118	Jordan	427
119	Eritrea	393
120	Montenegro	390
121	Costa Rica	388
122	Oman	365
123	Panama	335
124	Singapore	334
125	Kosovo	308
126	Guinea-Bissau	227
127	Lesotho	182
128	Botswana	142
129	Swaziland	98
130	Kuwait	85
131	Bahrain	64
132	UAE	42
133	Qatar	15

Source: Calculated as POP*GPCPPP.

TABLE 3.11 - GDP AT PPP IN MILLIONS OF 2007 DOLLARS, YEAR 1913		
OBS	COUNTRY	GDPPPP
1	US	760,140
2	China	354,502
3	Germany	348,670
4	UK	308,151
5	India	245,364
6	France	212,287
7	Russia	210,581
8	Italy	140,307
9	Japan	105,291
10	Poland	68,239
11	Indonesia	66,317
12	Spain	61,205
13	Ukraine	59,145
14	Canada	51,299
15	Belgium	47,527
16	Argentina	42,691
17	Mexico	38,092
18	Netherlands	36,667
19	Australia	36,525
20	Austria	34,448
21	Romania	32,041
22	Czechia	30,700
23	Bangladesh	28,812
24	Brazil	28,190
25	Turkey	26,731
26	Sweden	25,567
27	Switzerland	24,217
28	Hungary	24,165
29	Pakistan	21,428
30	Vietnam	20,655

31	Denmark	17,144
32	Iran	16,152
33	Egypt	16,148
34	Chile	15,061
35	Philippines	14,517
36	South Africa	14,481
37	Kazakhstan	13,870
38	Belarus	13,745
39	Korea, South	12,756
40	Greece	12,688
41	Ireland	12,430
42	Burma	12,404
43	Portugal	10,967
44	Thailand	10,736
45	Bulgaria	10,637
46	Slovakia	10,396
47	Uzbekistan	9,695
48	Colombia	9,433
49	Algeria	9,392
50	Finland	9,388
51	Norway	8,991
52	Sri Lanka	8,722
53	New Zealand	8,492
54	Serbia	8,350
55	Sudan	7,044
56	Ethiopia	6,859
57	Peru	6,610
58	Lithuania	6,462
59	Croatia	6,320
60	Georgia	6,257
61	Korea, North	5,899
62	Afghanistan	5,816
63	Mozambique	5,728
64	Uruguay	5,724
65	Morocco	5,331
66	Venezuela	4,661
67	Nepal	4,465
68	Latvia	4,310
69	Azerbaijan	4,215
70	Cuba	4,152
71	Malaysia	4,078
72	Syria	3,955
73	Moldova	3,845
74	Iraq	3,839
75	Taiwan	3,807
76	Slovenia	3,748
77	Madagascar	3,593
78	Bolivia	3,013
79	Yemen	2,895
80	Estonia	2,712
81	Ecuador	2,626
82	Guatemala	2,586
83	Cambodia	2,503
84	Tunisia	2,426
85	Saudi Arabia	2,359
86	Armenia	2,350

87	Ghana	2,344
88	Bosnia	2,228
89	Somalia	2,135
90	Puerto Rico	2,113
91	Turkmenistan	1,825
92	Tajikistan	1,813
93	Haiti	1,659
94	Kyrgyzstan	1,656
95	Zimbabwe	1,512
96	Laos	1,338
97	Zambia	1,297
98	Lebanon	1,287
99	El Salvador	1,253
100	Guinea	1,148
101	Burundi	1,092
102	Trinidad/Tobago	1,079
103	Macedonia	1,076
104	Albania	1,070
105	Malawi	989
106	Hong Kong	915
107	Sierra Leone	852
108	Libya	815
109	Cyprus	814
110	Paraguay	785
111	Nicaragua	780
112	Jamaica	762
113	Honduras	723
114	Israel	711
115	Namibia	643
116	Dominican Rep	643
117	Costa Rica	610
118	Singapore	607
119	Panama	557
120	Montenegro	556
121	Jordan	511
122	Mongolia	496
123	Eritrea	477
124	Oman	391
125	Kosovo	374
126	Guinea-Bissau	251
127	Lesotho	227
128	Botswana	163
129	Swaziland	130
130	Kuwait	92
131	Bahrain	70
132	UAE	46
133	Qatar	16

Source: Calculated as POP*GPCPPP.

OBS	COUNTRY	GDPPPP
	TABLE 3.12 - GDP AT PPP	
	IN MILLIONS OF 2007 DOLLARS,	
	YEAR 1920	
1	US	871,785
2	China	385,789
3	UK	292,106
4	Germany	250,133
5	India	234,078
6	France	184,894
7	Italy	142,136
8	Japan	139,078
9	Russia	80,766
10	Indonesia	74,585
11	Spain	67,906
12	Poland	66,736
13	Canada	49,905
14	Argentina	45,211
15	Belgium	43,958
16	Netherlands	42,456
17	Mexico	39,905
18	Brazil	38,770
19	Australia	37,516
20	Bangladesh	29,194
21	Czechia	27,744
22	Switzerland	24,572
23	Sweden	24,189
24	Austria	22,874
25	Ukraine	22,685
26	Pakistan	22,010
27	Vietnam	21,645
28	Philippines	20,310
29	Hungary	19,960
30	Iran	19,416
31	Denmark	19,014
32	Romania	18,703
33	South Africa	18,373
34	Korea, South	17,498
35	Egypt	17,273
36	Greece	15,692
37	Chile	15,387
38	Turkey	14,516
39	Burma	14,086
40	Thailand	11,803
41	Ireland	11,659
42	Colombia	11,455
43	Portugal	10,886
44	Algeria	10,734
45	Norway	10,721
46	New Zealand	10,285
47	Slovakia	9,395
48	Peru	9,126
49	Finland	8,497
50	Sri Lanka	8,423
51	Korea, North	8,267

52	Ethiopia	7,607
53	Sudan	7,485
54	Serbia	7,445
55	Morocco	6,789
56	Bulgaria	6,773
57	Mozambique	6,412
58	Afghanistan	6,137
59	Malaysia	5,781
60	Cuba	5,696
61	Croatia	5,635
62	Lithuania	5,593
63	Uruguay	5,386
64	Kazakhstan	5,320
65	Belarus	5,272
66	Taiwan	5,264
67	Venezuela	5,156
68	Syria	4,907
69	Nepal	4,768
70	Iraq	4,660
71	Madagascar	3,948
72	Bolivia	3,808
73	Latvia	3,730
74	Uzbekistan	3,719
75	Georgia	3,670
76	Yemen	3,363
77	Slovenia	3,342
78	Saudi Arabia	3,128
79	Ecuador	3,098
80	Ghana	3,006
81	Guatemala	2,984
82	Tunisia	2,857
83	Cambodia	2,652
84	Puerto Rico	2,613
85	Estonia	2,348
86	Somalia	2,346
87	Moldova	2,255
88	Haiti	2,074
89	Bosnia	1,987
90	Zimbabwe	1,714
91	Lebanon	1,673
92	Azerbaijan	1,617
93	El Salvador	1,602
94	Zambia	1,466
95	Hong Kong	1,351
96	Honduras	1,348
97	Laos	1,345
98	Trinidad/Tobago	1,328
99	Guinea	1,213
100	Nicaragua	1,188
101	Albania	1,177
102	Burundi	1,143
103	Malawi	1,090
104	Israel	1,040
105	Paraguay	1,029
106	Cyprus	1,007
107	Costa Rica	1,002

108	Macedonia	960
109	Armenia	901
110	Sierra Leone	901
111	Jamaica	883
112	Libya	870
113	Panama	867
114	Dominican Rep	839
115	Singapore	815
116	Namibia	759
117	Kyrgyzstan	715
118	Tajikistan	714
119	Turkmenistan	700
120	Jordan	596
121	Eritrea	529
122	Montenegro	495
123	Mongolia	493
124	Oman	396
125	Kosovo	342
126	Guinea-Bissau	265
127	Lesotho	257
128	Kuwait	204
129	Botswana	176
130	Swaziland	151
131	Bahrain	94
132	UAE	90
133	Qatar	36

Source: Calculated as POP*GPCPPP.

TABLE 3.13 - GDP AT PPP IN MILLIONS OF 2007 DOLLARS, YEAR 1929

OBS	COUNTRY	GDPPPP
1	US	1,239,015
2	China	402,317
3	Germany	385,290
4	UK	369,240
5	France	285,295
6	India	269,508
7	Russia	221,812
8	Japan	188,243
9	Italy	183,892
10	Indonesia	102,897
11	Spain	93,396
12	Poland	86,636
13	Canada	76,681
14	Argentina	74,371
15	Netherlands	65,041
16	Ukraine	62,300
17	Belgium	59,637
18	Brazil	54,946
19	Australia	49,454
20	Czechia	46,706
21	Mexico	43,559
22	Switzerland	37,415

23	Austria	36,214
24	Sweden	34,747
25	Bangladesh	31,308
26	Hungary	31,221
27	Philippines	28,443
28	Denmark	26,230
29	Turkey	26,205
30	South Africa	24,951
31	Pakistan	24,633
32	Iran	24,601
33	Chile	24,196
34	Romania	23,613
35	Vietnam	22,988
36	Greece	21,590
37	Korea, South	20,433
38	Egypt	18,728
39	Burma	18,269
40	Colombia	17,293
41	Venezuela	16,403
42	Portugal	15,850
43	Slovakia	15,816
44	Kazakhstan	14,610
45	Belarus	14,478
46	Norway	14,257
47	Thailand	14,048
48	Finland	13,667
49	Algeria	12,898
50	Peru	12,592
51	Ireland	12,185
52	New Zealand	11,372
53	Serbia	11,255
54	Sri Lanka	11,127
55	Malaysia	10,665
56	Bulgaria	10,315
57	Uzbekistan	10,213
58	Korea, North	9,820
59	Uruguay	9,523
60	Morocco	9,265
61	Lithuania	9,159
62	Cuba	9,010
63	Ethiopia	8,690
64	Croatia	8,518
65	Sudan	8,093
66	Taiwan	7,565
67	Mozambique	7,414
68	Georgia	6,591
69	Afghanistan	6,575
70	Syria	6,475
71	Latvia	6,109
72	Iraq	5,980
73	Nepal	5,181
74	Slovenia	5,052
75	Bolivia	4,848
76	Saudi Arabia	4,498
77	Madagascar	4,457
78	Azerbaijan	4,440

79	Guatemala	4,430
80	Ghana	4,139
81	Yemen	4,078
82	Estonia	3,845
83	Ecuador	3,828
84	Tunisia	3,526
85	Puerto Rico	3,487
86	Bosnia	3,003
87	Cambodia	2,858
88	Moldova	2,802
89	Haiti	2,677
90	Somalia	2,649
91	Armenia	2,476
92	Lebanon	2,344
93	El Salvador	2,156
94	Honduras	2,048
95	Zimbabwe	2,015
96	Turkmenistan	1,922
97	Tajikistan	1,910
98	Hong Kong	1,872
99	Nicaragua	1,748
100	Kyrgyzstan	1,745
101	Zambia	1,716
102	Israel	1,697
103	Trinidad/Tobago	1,559
104	Paraguay	1,452
105	Macedonia	1,451
106	Cyprus	1,386
107	Singapore	1,371
108	Laos	1,353
109	Albania	1,329
110	Dominican Rep	1,328
111	Guinea	1,303
112	Malawi	1,236
113	Burundi	1,212
114	Jamaica	1,196
115	Costa Rica	1,139
116	Panama	1,033
117	Sierra Leone	967
118	Libya	947
119	Namibia	938
120	Montenegro	749
121	Jordan	727
122	Eritrea	604
123	Kuwait	567
124	Mongolia	488
125	Oman	402
126	Kosovo	391
127	Lesotho	300
128	Guinea-Bissau	285
129	UAE	217
130	Botswana	195
131	Swaziland	184
132	Bahrain	139
133	Qatar	100

Source: Calculated as POP*GPCPPP.

TABLE 3.14 - GDP AT PPP IN MILLIONS OF 2007 DOLLARS, YEAR 1938

OBS	COUNTRY	GDPPPP
1	US	1,174,268
2	Germany	502,998
3	UK	437,209
4	China	423,836
5	Russia	377,047
6	India	281,397
7	France	275,305
8	Japan	258,613
9	Italy	211,521
10	Indonesia	117,609
11	Ukraine	105,901
12	Poland	99,573
13	Argentina	82,101
14	Canada	76,484
15	Brazil	74,009
16	Netherlands	66,987
17	Spain	66,477
18	Australia	59,701
19	Belgium	59,446
20	Mexico	51,935
21	Czechia	46,540
22	Sweden	43,718
23	Turkey	43,098
24	Switzerland	39,353
25	Hungary	35,756
26	Philippines	35,629
27	Austria	35,309
28	South Africa	33,885
29	Bangladesh	33,558
30	Korea, South	32,969
31	Denmark	31,973
32	Iran	31,171
33	Romania	28,466
34	Greece	27,770
35	Pakistan	26,692
36	Chile	25,528
37	Kazakhstan	24,835
38	Belarus	24,611
39	Vietnam	24,415
40	Colombia	23,562
41	Venezuela	22,057
42	Egypt	21,308
43	Finland	19,277
44	Portugal	19,218
45	Norway	18,707
46	Thailand	18,178
47	Burma	17,552
48	Uzbekistan	17,360
49	Korea, North	16,701
50	Slovakia	15,760

51	Peru	15,728
52	Bulgaria	15,381
53	New Zealand	15,228
54	Algeria	14,769
55	Lithuania	13,258
56	Ireland	13,169
57	Serbia	12,678
58	Morocco	12,644
59	Georgia	11,203
60	Sri Lanka	10,879
61	Taiwan	10,861
62	Uruguay	10,542
63	Malaysia	10,411
64	Ethiopia	9,928
65	Croatia	9,595
66	Latvia	8,843
67	Cuba	8,834
68	Sudan	8,751
69	Mozambique	8,572
70	Syria	8,545
71	Iraq	7,674
72	Azerbaijan	7,547
73	Afghanistan	7,045
74	Guatemala	6,894
75	Saudi Arabia	6,466
76	Bolivia	6,170
77	Ghana	5,700
78	Slovenia	5,691
79	Nepal	5,633
80	Estonia	5,565
81	Ecuador	5,366
82	Madagascar	5,032
83	Yemen	4,945
84	Puerto Rico	4,746
85	Tunisia	4,352
86	Armenia	4,208
87	Hong Kong	4,031
88	Haiti	3,447
89	Bosnia	3,383
90	Moldova	3,310
91	Lebanon	3,285
92	Turkmenistan	3,267
93	Tajikistan	3,247
94	Cambodia	3,080
95	Somalia	2,991
96	Kyrgyzstan	2,966
97	Israel	2,769
98	Zimbabwe	2,369
99	El Salvador	2,282
100	Trinidad/Tobago	2,058
101	Paraguay	2,055
102	Zambia	2,009
103	Dominican Rep	2,005
104	Singapore	1,936
105	Honduras	1,786
106	Cyprus	1,782

107	Jamaica	1,661
108	Macedonia	1,634
109	Costa Rica	1,626
110	Kuwait	1,575
111	Panama	1,500
112	Albania	1,463
113	Malawi	1,401
114	Guinea	1,399
115	Laos	1,361
116	Burundi	1,285
117	Nicaragua	1,233
118	Namibia	1,160
119	Sierra Leone	1,039
120	Libya	1,031
121	Jordan	886
122	Montenegro	843
123	Eritrea	690
124	UAE	520
125	Mongolia	483
126	Kosovo	443
127	Oman	409
128	Lesotho	350
129	Guinea-Bissau	306
130	Qatar	281
131	Swaziland	223
132	Botswana	215
133	Bahrain	204

Source: Calculated as POP*GPCPPP.

TABLE 3.15 - GDP AT PPP IN MILLIONS OF 2007 DOLLARS, YEAR 1950		
OBS	COUNTRY	GDPPPP
1	US	2,138,848
2	UK	512,670
3	Russia	462,545
4	Germany	389,864
5	China	362,834
6	India	336,365
7	France	323,194
8	Italy	242,345
9	Japan	236,006
10	Canada	147,143
11	Brazil	132,583
12	Argentina	125,650
13	Ukraine	125,266
14	Indonesia	98,155
15	Mexico	96,386
16	Spain	89,621
17	Australia	89,498
18	Poland	89,241
19	Netherlands	88,882
20	Sweden	69,442
21	Belgium	69,323

22	Switzerland	62,506
23	Venezuela	54,912
24	South Africa	50,959
25	Turkey	50,363
26	Czechia	47,965
27	Denmark	43,565
28	Iran	42,737
29	Colombia	39,753
30	Austria	37,758
31	Nigeria	37,568
32	Pakistan	37,265
33	Bangladesh	36,212
34	Kazakhstan	35,823
35	Chile	34,142
36	Hungary	34,022
37	Philippines	31,433
38	Romania	28,324
39	Belarus	27,919
40	Egypt	27,354
41	Vietnam	26,455
42	Norway	26,204
43	Portugal	25,874
44	Peru	25,374
45	Finland	25,049
46	Thailand	24,734
47	New Zealand	23,715
48	Uzbekistan	22,169
49	Korea, South	21,334
50	Greece	21,286
51	Morocco	19,138
52	Cuba	17,795
53	Bulgaria	17,588
54	Algeria	17,553
55	Slovakia	16,242
56	Uruguay	15,325
57	Ireland	15,061
58	Serbia	14,695
59	Georgia	14,494
60	Malaysia	13,994
61	Sri Lanka	13,887
62	Lithuania	13,380
63	Syria	12,369
64	Burma	11,338
65	Croatia	11,121
66	Korea, North	11,015
67	Iraq	10,701
68	Latvia	10,566
69	Saudi Arabia	10,492
70	Mozambique	10,403
71	Taiwan	10,343
72	Congo, Dem R	10,203
73	Sudan	9,711
74	Ecuador	9,270
75	Guatemala	9,094
76	Azerbaijan	8,812
77	Ghana	8,731

78	Moldova	8,652
79	Ethiopia	7,899
80	Afghanistan	7,724
81	Bolivia	7,651
82	Hong Kong	7,289
83	Puerto Rico	6,986
84	Estonia	6,691
85	Slovenia	6,596
86	Yemen	6,393
87	Angola	6,364
88	Nepal	6,298
89	Kuwait	6,152
90	Madagascar	5,915
91	Kenya	5,854
92	Tunisia	5,761
93	Armenia	5,719
94	Uganda	5,573
95	Israel	5,206
96	Lebanon	5,149
97	Haiti	4,973
98	Tanzania	4,943
99	Senegal	4,909
100	Cameroon	4,819
101	Kyrgyzstan	4,475
102	Tajikistan	4,322
103	El Salvador	4,268
104	Turkmenistan	4,003
105	Bosnia	3,921
106	Ivory Coast	3,831
107	Luxembourg	3,645
108	Trinidad/Tobago	3,606
109	Dominican Rep	3,550
110	Somalia	3,516
111	Paraguay	3,428
112	Cambodia	3,402
113	Singapore	3,332
114	Nicaragua	3,074
115	Burkina Faso	3,047
116	Zimbabwe	2,938
117	Honduras	2,760
118	Jamaica	2,735
119	Benin	2,664
120	Niger	2,637
121	Costa Rica	2,486
122	Zambia	2,479
123	Mali	2,476
124	Panama	2,421
125	Gabon	2,141
126	Papua New Gu	1,992
127	Macedonia	1,894
128	Chad	1,824
129	Albania	1,787
130	Mauritius	1,752
131	Rwanda	1,737
132	UAE	1,671
133	Namibia	1,539

134	Congo, Rep	1,530
135	Central African Rep.	1,490
136	Laos	1,372
137	Cyprus	1,366
138	Malawi	1,341
139	Libya	1,296
140	Liberia	1,277
141	Fiji	1,250
142	Burundi	1,250
143	West Bank	1,218
144	Guinea	1,166
145	Jordan	1,153
146	Togo	1,121
147	Iceland	1,119
148	Qatar	1,116
149	Bahamas	1,111
150	Montenegro	978
151	Sierra Leone	898
152	Guam	837
153	Reunion	713
154	Guyana	679
155	Barbados	658
156	Neth Antilles	577
157	Eritrea	565
158	Aruba	556
159	Guadeloupe	527
160	Jersey	521
161	Mongolia	477
162	Mauritania	472
163	Suriname	463
164	Martinique	430
165	Kosovo	423
166	Oman	417
167	Malta	408
168	Fr Polynesia	400
169	New Caledonia	389
170	Lesotho	383
171	Bahrain	340
172	Brunei	329
173	Guernsey	312
174	Macao	311
175	Swaziland	289
176	East Timor	266
177	Gambia	262
178	Gaza Strip	258
179	Isle of Man	249
180	Guinea-Bissau	243
181	Virgin I, US	233
182	Botswana	213
183	Guiana, Fr	203
184	Faeroe Is	190
185	Equatorial G	179
186	Belize	162
187	Samoa, W	159
188	Greenland	147
189	Monaco	139

190	Liechtenstein	136
191	Djibouti	132
192	Bhutan	124
193	Comoros	122
194	Antigua & Barbuda	120
195	Dominica	120
196	St Vincent	116
197	Grenada	104
198	Vanuatu	99
199	Cape Verde	97
200	Seychelles	96
201	Bermuda	95
202	Tonga	91
203	San Marino	91
204	St Kitts & Nevis	90
205	St Lucia	90
206	Cayman Is	89
207	Solomon Is	78
208	San Tome & Principe	72
209	N Mariana Is	66
210	Gibraltar	65
211	Micronesia	65
212	Maldives	63
213	Samoa, Ameri	49
214	Virgin Is, Brit.	40
215	Andorra	37
216	Palau	31
217	Kiribati	28
218	Nauru	28
219	Falkland Is	23
220	St Pierre &	19
221	Cook Is	18
222	Turks & Caicos	18
223	Montserrat	16
224	Marshall Is	16
225	Anguilla	14
226	St Helena	12
227	Wallis & Futuna	10
228	Mayotte	8
229	W Sahara	5
230	Tuvalu	4
231	Niue	1
232	Tokelau	1

Source: Calculated as POP*GPCPPP.

TABLE 3.16 - GDP AT PPP IN MILLIONS OF 2007 DOLLARS, YEAR 1960		
OBS	COUNTRY	GDPPPP
1	US	3,006,777
2	Germany	861,243
3	Russia	752,991
4	UK	665,048
5	China	587,196

6	Japan	547,787
7	France	508,136
8	India	466,288
9	Italy	444,109
10	Brazil	251,390
11	Canada	231,305
12	Ukraine	201,380
13	Mexico	179,389
14	Argentina	164,891
15	Netherlands	142,853
16	Poland	142,812
17	Spain	141,500
18	Indonesia	135,352
19	Australia	132,560
20	Switzerland	102,998
21	Sweden	96,353
22	Belgium	93,918
23	Turkey	93,363
24	Venezuela	90,477
25	South Africa	83,231
26	Czechia	81,065
27	Kazakhstan	74,056
28	Austria	70,929
29	Iran	70,514
30	Colombia	59,451
31	Denmark	58,909
32	Romania	58,512
33	Hungary	58,376
34	Philippines	54,540
35	Nigeria	52,195
36	Pakistan	47,821
37	Chile	47,179
38	Peru	45,612
39	Bangladesh	43,526
40	Uzbekistan	41,884
41	Greece	41,859
42	Thailand	41,631
43	Algeria	41,031
44	Belarus	40,949
45	Finland	40,077
46	Korea, South	40,014
47	Norway	39,742
48	Portugal	39,396
49	Egypt	38,052
50	Vietnam	37,106
51	Serbia	33,693
52	New Zealand	32,928
53	Bulgaria	32,819
54	Slovakia	29,580
55	Iraq	29,461
56	Saudi Arabia	27,588
57	Georgia	23,518
58	Morocco	23,227
59	Taiwan	22,832
60	Cuba	21,487
61	Lithuania	20,102

62	Croatia	19,012
63	Sri Lanka	18,631
64	Malaysia	18,306
65	Uruguay	18,156
66	Congo, Dem R	18,133
67	Ireland	17,944
68	Korea, North	17,770
69	Syria	16,757
70	Azerbaijan	16,442
71	Sudan	15,990
72	Ecuador	15,963
73	Latvia	15,950
74	Burma	15,872
75	Moldova	15,472
76	Israel	14,516
77	Hong Kong	14,156
78	Guatemala	13,295
79	Kuwait	12,386
80	Slovenia	11,269
81	Armenia	10,905
82	Puerto Rico	10,683
83	Ethiopia	10,644
84	Afghanistan	10,440
85	Mozambique	10,337
86	Ghana	10,126
87	Madagascar	9,632
88	Estonia	9,619
89	Angola	8,826
90	Kenya	8,533
91	Tajikistan	8,176
92	Yemen	8,085
93	Tunisia	8,055
94	Nepal	8,036
95	Bosnia	8,014
96	Bolivia	7,914
97	Kyrgyzstan	7,796
98	Turkmenistan	7,317
99	Cameroon	7,287
100	Uganda	7,264
101	El Salvador	7,150
102	Tanzania	7,116
103	Jamaica	7,028
104	Somalia	7,023
105	Trinidad/Tobago	6,791
106	Lebanon	6,520
107	Ivory Coast	6,168
108	Dominican Rep	6,156
109	Haiti	5,993
110	Senegal	5,701
111	Singapore	5,604
112	Zambia	5,475
113	Cambodia	5,375
114	Luxembourg	5,250
115	Zimbabwe	5,184
116	Nicaragua	4,926
117	Costa Rica	4,867

118	Niger	4,511
119	Paraguay	4,369
120	Honduras	4,036
121	Burkina Faso	3,971
122	Panama	3,966
123	Macedonia	3,904
124	Libya	3,836
125	Albania	3,590
126	Benin	3,545
127	UAE	3,385
128	Mali	3,321
129	Chad	3,125
130	Papua New Gu	3,124
131	Gabon	2,985
132	Jordan	2,693
133	Cyprus	2,663
134	Mauritius	2,606
135	Liberia	2,580
136	Central African Rep.	2,388
137	Rwanda	2,369
138	Montenegro	2,359
139	Congo, Rep	2,234
140	Qatar	2,189
141	Namibia	2,142
142	Guinea	1,965
143	Laos	1,953
144	Iceland	1,931
145	Bahamas	1,861
146	Malawi	1,853
147	Togo	1,797
148	Fiji	1,713
149	Sierra Leone	1,357
150	Barbados	1,315
151	Guadeloupe	1,228
152	West Bank	1,204
153	Burundi	1,196
154	Guam	1,154
155	Reunion	1,096
156	Neth Antilles	1,089
157	Kosovo	1,065
158	Martinique	1,058
159	Guyana	1,039
160	Bahrain	955
161	Aruba	913
162	Suriname	901
163	Mauritania	853
164	Mongolia	849
165	Oman	846
166	Jersey	828
167	Brunei	736
168	Malta	713
169	Eritrea	705
170	Fr Polynesia	659
171	Macao	547
172	New Caledonia	541
173	Lesotho	521

174	Swaziland	511
175	Guernsey	457
176	Gambia	359
177	Isle of Man	351
178	Virgin I, US	345
179	East Timor	338
180	Botswana	323
181	Faeroe Is	314
182	Gaza Strip	307
183	Greenland	296
184	Guinea-Bissau	289
185	Equatorial G	277
186	Belize	253
187	Samoa, W	247
188	Monaco	243
189	Guiana, Fr	232
190	Bermuda	228
191	Liechtenstein	222
192	Comoros	191
193	Djibouti	181
194	Antigua & Barbuda	180
195	Bhutan	176
196	St Vincent	171
197	St Kitts & Nevis	171
198	Grenada	170
199	Dominica	169
200	San Marino	168
201	Seychelles	162
202	St Lucia	160
203	Cayman Is	157
204	Vanuatu	153
205	Cape Verde	146
206	Tonga	138
207	Gibraltar	132
208	Solomon Is	119
209	N Mariana Is	109
210	Micronesia	106
211	Maldives	87
212	Samoa, Ameri	82
213	San Tome & Principe	79
214	Andorra	71
215	Virgin Is, Brit.	67
216	Palau	49
217	Kiribati	42
218	St Pierre &	32
219	Nauru	31
220	Falkland Is	31
221	Turks & Caicos	31
222	Cook Is	29
223	Marshall Is	24
224	Anguilla	23
225	Montserrat	22
226	St Helena	16
227	Mayotte	15
228	W Sahara	15
229	Wallis & Futuna	14

230	Tuvalu	4
231	Niue	1
232	Tokelau	1

Source: Calculated as POP*GPCPPP.

TABLE 3.17 - GDP AT PPP IN MILLIONS OF 2007 DOLLARS, YEAR 1970		
OBS	COUNTRY	GDPPPP
1	US	4,523,930
2	Japan	1,469,588
3	Germany	1,325,394
4	Russia	1,157,236
5	UK	879,706
6	France	876,395
7	China	833,978
8	Italy	795,476
9	India	642,234
10	Brazil	436,905
11	Canada	389,103
12	Spain	348,839
13	Mexico	345,421
14	Ukraine	314,114
15	Netherlands	239,218
16	Argentina	238,888
17	Poland	222,231
18	Australia	218,630
19	Iran	196,093
20	Indonesia	189,816
21	Switzerland	168,945
22	Turkey	162,431
23	South Africa	160,541
24	Sweden	153,720
25	Belgium	152,998
26	Kazakhstan	137,151
27	Venezuela	133,375
28	Romania	116,530
29	Austria	116,420
30	Czechia	111,324
31	Saudi Arabia	107,758
32	Greece	97,910
33	Colombia	93,097
34	Denmark	90,318
35	Hungary	89,502
36	Korea, South	89,127
37	Nigeria	88,049
38	Philippines	84,576
39	Pakistan	83,435
40	Uzbekistan	83,283
41	Thailand	81,137
42	Peru	78,377
43	Portugal	73,492
44	Serbia	71,980

45	Chile	69,130
46	Belarus	63,797
47	Norway	63,336
48	Finland	63,222
49	Egypt	61,857
50	Taiwan	60,229
51	Bangladesh	58,619
52	Algeria	58,393
53	Bulgaria	56,792
54	Iraq	51,594
55	New Zealand	45,920
56	Vietnam	44,702
57	Slovakia	41,988
58	Korea, North	40,898
59	Georgia	37,254
60	Morocco	35,392
61	Israel	35,378
62	Hong Kong	33,111
63	Malaysia	32,892
64	Lithuania	32,207
65	Kuwait	31,883
66	Libya	31,813
67	Croatia	31,524
68	Azerbaijan	30,894
69	Ecuador	28,642
70	Ireland	27,381
71	Moldova	26,266
72	Sri Lanka	25,808
73	Cuba	25,590
74	Congo, Dem R	25,215
75	Latvia	25,042
76	Syria	23,845
77	Uruguay	20,724
78	Armenia	20,692
79	Guatemala	20,331
80	Burma	20,318
81	Puerto Rico	19,949
82	Slovenia	19,151
83	Sudan	18,012
84	Ethiopia	17,444
85	Tajikistan	16,370
86	Kyrgyzstan	15,102
87	Bosnia	15,008
88	Angola	14,539
89	Singapore	14,306
90	Estonia	14,255
91	Turkmenistan	14,228
92	Kenya	14,205
93	Madagascar	14,121
94	El Salvador	13,484
95	Bolivia	13,456
96	Tunisia	13,111
97	Lebanon	13,022
98	Tanzania	12,747
99	Ghana	12,539
100	Jamaica	12,346

101	Afghanistan	12,333
102	Ivory Coast	11,860
103	Yemen	11,044
104	Cameroon	10,811
105	Dominican Rep	10,074
106	Nepal	10,024
107	Trinidad/Tobago	9,597
108	Costa Rica	9,451
109	Mozambique	9,355
110	Uganda	9,290
111	Zimbabwe	9,095
112	UAE	8,950
113	Nicaragua	8,821
114	Panama	8,511
115	Zambia	8,429
116	Macedonia	7,807
117	Luxembourg	7,697
118	Senegal	7,551
119	Albania	6,834
120	Somalia	6,724
121	Cambodia	6,684
122	Paraguay	6,652
123	Honduras	6,633
124	Niger	6,534
125	Haiti	6,430
126	Oman	6,123
127	Liberia	6,059
128	Qatar	5,408
129	Montenegro	5,222
130	Papua New Gu	5,199
131	Jordan	4,960
132	Cyprus	4,802
133	Togo	4,784
134	Burkina Faso	4,736
135	Gabon	4,552
136	Benin	4,351
137	Mali	4,340
138	Congo, Rep	3,515
139	Bahamas	3,462
140	Mauritius	3,395
141	Namibia	3,203
142	Iceland	3,136
143	Rwanda	3,130
144	Chad	3,065
145	Guinea	3,013
146	Central African Rep.	2,761
147	Laos	2,726
148	Kosovo	2,717
149	Bahrain	2,697
150	Malawi	2,624
151	Guadeloupe	2,605
152	Barbados	2,484
153	Martinique	2,359
154	Fiji	2,273
155	Sierra Leone	2,135
156	Reunion	2,127

157	Neth Antilles	2,029
158	Mauritania	2,001
159	Guam	1,807
160	Swaziland	1,673
161	Suriname	1,669
162	Mongolia	1,626
163	Macao	1,487
164	Guyana	1,474
165	Aruba	1,436
166	Brunei	1,377
167	Jersey	1,340
168	Burundi	1,214
169	Malta	1,168
170	Eritrea	1,157
171	Fr Polynesia	1,117
172	West Bank	863
173	Virgin I, US	847
174	New Caledonia	845
175	Lesotho	752
176	Guernsey	744
177	Botswana	742
178	Greenland	616
179	Isle of Man	590
180	Bermuda	579
181	Equatorial G	556
182	Gambia	547
183	Faeroe Is	513
184	East Timor	447
185	Liechtenstein	415
186	Monaco	414
187	Belize	400
188	Djibouti	386
189	Samoa, W	370
190	Gaza Strip	350
191	Comoros	347
192	San Marino	340
193	Guiana, Fr	324
194	Guinea-Bissau	320
195	St Lucia	305
196	St Kitts & Nevis	282
197	Gibraltar	276
198	Antigua & Barbuda	270
199	Cayman Is	260
200	Andorra	257
201	Bhutan	249
202	Grenada	247
203	Cape Verde	240
204	Vanuatu	238
205	Seychelles	236
206	Dominica	234
207	St Vincent	232
208	Tonga	197
209	Solomon Is	188
210	Samoa, Ameri	177
211	Micronesia	166
212	N Mariana Is	159

213	Maldives	128
214	San Tome & Principe	114
215	Virgin Is, Brit.	113
216	Palau	82
217	Kiribati	60
218	St Pierre &	54
219	Turks & Caicos	53
220	Cook Is	46
221	Nauru	46
222	Falkland Is	41
223	Marshall Is	39
224	Anguilla	38
225	W Sahara	35
226	Montserrat	31
227	Mayotte	22
228	Wallis & Futuna	21
229	St Helena	17
230	Tuvalu	6
231	Niue	2
232	Tokelau	1

Source: Calculated as POP*GPCPPP.

TABLE 3.18 - GDP AT PPP IN MILLIONS OF 2007 DOLLARS, YEAR 1980		
OBS	COUNTRY	GDPPPP
1	US	6,215,094
2	Japan	2,268,456
3	Germany	1,769,394
4	Russia	1,437,093
5	China	1,276,829
6	France	1,207,424
7	Italy	1,140,032
8	UK	1,069,624
9	Brazil	928,469
10	India	839,647
11	Mexico	689,124
12	Canada	593,823
13	Spain	587,857
14	Ukraine	391,889
15	Saudi Arabia	384,500
16	Indonesia	324,794
17	Netherlands	323,686
18	Poland	321,946
19	Argentina	307,773
20	Australia	300,525
21	Turkey	263,812
22	Iran	252,326
23	South Africa	231,102
24	Korea, South	215,296
25	Belgium	213,503
26	Romania	211,563
27	Switzerland	194,784
28	Sweden	187,674
29	Venezuela	179,893

30	Austria	171,261
31	Kazakhstan	167,316
32	Greece	165,045
33	Serbia	164,013
34	Czechia	151,563
35	Colombia	148,819
36	Thailand	142,626
37	Philippines	140,092
38	Taiwan	138,741
39	Nigeria	133,944
40	Algeria	132,161
41	Iraq	132,033
42	Pakistan	125,677
43	Egypt	125,601
44	Hungary	122,340
45	Portugal	117,276
46	Peru	115,004
47	Denmark	112,097
48	Uzbekistan	111,594
49	Norway	107,898
50	Finland	88,268
51	Chile	85,920
52	Belarus	84,266
53	Hong Kong	78,073
54	Bulgaria	74,284
55	Malaysia	72,258
56	Korea, North	71,951
57	Bangladesh	70,496
58	Israel	62,717
59	Ecuador	62,582
60	Morocco	58,325
61	Slovakia	58,309
62	Vietnam	56,400
63	New Zealand	56,308
64	Croatia	54,991
65	Kuwait	54,284
66	Georgia	48,007
67	Ireland	43,857
68	Azerbaijan	40,807
69	UAE	40,528
70	Lithuania	40,416
71	Libya	38,341
72	Syria	37,573
73	Singapore	35,962
74	Sri Lanka	34,436
75	Slovenia	34,381
76	Moldova	33,769
77	Cuba	32,303
78	Latvia	31,856
79	Guatemala	30,307
80	Bosnia	29,114
81	Puerto Rico	28,660
82	Burma	27,784
83	Armenia	27,500
84	Sudan	26,131
85	Congo, Dem R	25,853

86	Tunisia	25,609
87	Uruguay	25,438
88	Ethiopia	23,162
89	Kenya	22,740
90	Lebanon	22,495
91	Tajikistan	20,961
92	Ivory Coast	20,562
93	Bolivia	20,202
94	Kyrgyzstan	19,810
95	Dominican Rep	19,584
96	Yemen	19,410
97	El Salvador	19,053
98	Mozambique	18,475
99	Tanzania	18,310
100	Turkmenistan	18,120
101	Cameroon	18,097
102	Ghana	17,825
103	Estonia	17,801
104	Macedonia	16,879
105	Costa Rica	16,020
106	Trinidad/Tobago	15,198
107	Madagascar	14,767
108	Panama	14,757
109	Afghanistan	14,260
110	Paraguay	13,810
111	Uganda	13,070
112	Montenegro	12,453
113	Nepal	12,362
114	Zimbabwe	11,918
115	Jamaica	11,081
116	Oman	10,584
117	Senegal	10,534
118	Haiti	10,518
119	Albania	10,199
120	Honduras	10,050
121	Jordan	9,988
122	Qatar	9,942
123	Nicaragua	9,714
124	Somalia	9,601
125	Angola	9,532
126	Luxembourg	9,015
127	Zambia	8,879
128	Niger	7,720
129	Kosovo	7,358
130	Cambodia	7,246
131	Gabon	6,776
132	Papua New Gu	6,617
133	Cyprus	6,603
134	Congo, Rep	6,222
135	Bahrain	6,124
136	Mali	6,062
137	Togo	5,987
138	Burkina Faso	5,448
139	Benin	5,300
140	Iceland	5,207
141	Mauritius	5,155

142	Namibia	4,690
143	Guinea	4,565
144	Malawi	4,552
145	Rwanda	4,450
146	Bahamas	4,370
147	Macao	4,083
148	Laos	3,799
149	Liberia	3,612
150	Barbados	3,410
151	Guadeloupe	3,394
152	Botswana	3,363
153	Malta	3,346
154	Mongolia	3,093
155	Martinique	3,011
156	Fiji	2,780
157	Swaziland	2,757
158	Brunei	2,685
159	Central African Rep.	2,635
160	Reunion	2,549
161	Sierra Leone	2,540
162	Guam	2,471
163	Mauritania	2,467
164	Suriname	2,431
165	Neth Antilles	2,108
166	Guyana	1,888
167	Jersey	1,819
168	Aruba	1,789
169	Fr Polynesia	1,556
170	Chad	1,529
171	Virgin I, US	1,511
172	Eritrea	1,456
173	Lesotho	1,298
174	Burundi	1,273
175	New Caledonia	1,220
176	West Bank	992
177	Isle of Man	983
178	Guernsey	980
179	Greenland	854
180	Gambia	848
181	Bermuda	842
182	Faeroe Is	727
183	Liechtenstein	649
184	Djibouti	635
185	Monaco	605
186	Seychelles	590
187	Belize	587
188	Andorra	559
189	Cayman Is	525
190	San Marino	511
191	Gibraltar	492
192	Equatorial G	466
193	East Timor	446
194	Guiana, Fr	439
195	St Lucia	425
196	Comoros	418
197	Bhutan	415

198	Samoa, W	413
199	Gaza Strip	412
200	Guinea-Bissau	397
201	Antigua & Barbuda	353
202	Cape Verde	350
203	Vanuatu	343
204	St Vincent	305
205	Solomon Is	284
206	Grenada	273
207	Maldives	256
208	Samoa, Ameri	252
209	Dominica	242
210	N Mariana Is	234
211	St Kitts & Nevis	213
212	Micronesia	211
213	Tonga	204
214	San Tome & Principe	167
215	Virgin Is, Brit.	159
216	Palau	97
217	W Sahara	79
218	Turks & Caicos	76
219	Kiribati	76
220	St Pierre &	76
221	Cook Is	63
222	Marshall Is	58
223	Anguilla	52
224	Nauru	49
225	Falkland Is	49
226	Montserrat	39
227	Mayotte	38
228	Wallis & Futuna	28
229	St Helena	19
230	Tuvalu	9
231	Niue	3
232	Tokelau	2

Source: Calculated as POP*GPCPPP.

TABLE 3.19 - GDP AT PPP IN MILLIONS OF 2007 DOLLARS, YEAR 1990		
OBS	COUNTRY	GDPPPP
1	US	8,514,694
2	Japan	3,347,916
3	China	2,303,062
4	Germany	2,041,183
5	Russia	1,686,102
6	France	1,524,377
7	Italy	1,431,896
8	UK	1,380,692
9	India	1,305,630
10	Brazil	1,085,930
11	Spain	815,639
12	Mexico	810,785
13	Canada	785,690
14	Korea, South	496,879

15	Indonesia	482,792
16	Ukraine	457,312
17	Turkey	452,614
18	Australia	418,551
19	Netherlands	405,633
20	Saudi Arabia	367,071
21	Poland	303,632
22	Iran	299,771
23	Argentina	293,324
24	Thailand	268,962
25	Taiwan	261,751
26	South Africa	258,253
27	Belgium	257,426
28	Switzerland	245,966
29	Sweden	230,394
30	Venezuela	219,867
31	Austria	217,929
32	Pakistan	205,754
33	Colombia	201,008
34	Greece	197,177
35	Egypt	197,094
36	Kazakhstan	178,973
37	Romania	177,051
38	Philippines	169,476
39	Czechia	164,531
40	Portugal	160,698
41	Algeria	158,864
42	Serbia	155,342
43	Nigeria	151,449
44	Hong Kong	146,454
45	Norway	141,381
46	Denmark	135,554
47	Malaysia	132,162
48	Uzbekistan	128,647
49	Hungary	122,067
50	Finland	118,465
51	Chile	110,299
52	Belarus	107,101
53	Peru	97,444
54	Bangladesh	96,579
55	UAE	94,699
56	Israel	88,513
57	Vietnam	87,261
58	Korea, North	84,071
59	Morocco	81,680
60	Kuwait	80,659
61	Ecuador	74,943
62	Singapore	74,700
63	New Zealand	69,367
64	Bulgaria	67,904
65	Iraq	66,860
66	Slovakia	66,159
67	Ireland	63,335
68	Georgia	59,186
69	Croatia	53,717
70	Syria	51,920
71	Azerbaijan	48,905
72	Lithuania	46,940
73	Sri Lanka	45,094

74	Moldova	40,146
75	Latvia	39,398
76	Puerto Rico	38,449
77	Tunisia	36,338
78	Cuba	36,231
79	Guatemala	35,492
80	Slovenia	34,408
81	Kenya	34,123
82	Burma	32,512
83	Armenia	31,291
84	Bosnia	30,270
85	Oman	28,860
86	Congo, Dem R	28,785
87	Angola	28,419
88	Sudan	28,387
89	Ethiopia	28,050
90	Uruguay	26,814
91	Yemen	26,283
92	Ghana	26,253
93	Cameroon	25,553
94	Dominican Rep	25,379
95	Ivory Coast	23,513
96	Kyrgyzstan	23,497
97	Tajikistan	23,287
98	Tanzania	21,790
99	Libya	21,763
100	Bolivia	21,509
101	Mozambique	21,483
102	Estonia	20,632
103	Costa Rica	20,422
104	Turkmenistan	19,492
105	El Salvador	18,322
106	Paraguay	18,264
107	Uganda	18,264
108	Zimbabwe	17,493
109	Nepal	17,347
110	Macedonia	16,844
111	Luxembourg	16,097
112	Panama	16,023
113	Gabon	14,707
114	Jamaica	14,536
115	Senegal	14,027
116	Trinidad/Tobago	13,815
117	Honduras	13,678
118	Cyprus	13,475
119	Albania	13,443
120	Jordan	13,186
121	Madagascar	12,979
122	Montenegro	11,778
123	Afghanistan	11,159
124	Somalia	11,084
125	Qatar	10,963
126	Haiti	10,891
127	Zambia	10,585
128	Cambodia	10,329
129	Botswana	9,391
130	Nicaragua	9,041
131	Kosovo	8,469
132	Congo, Rep	8,430

133	Mauritius	7,855
134	Bahrain	7,842
135	Burkina Faso	7,708
136	Papua New Gu	7,679
137	Macao	7,526
138	Mali	7,240
139	Benin	7,127
140	Iceland	6,840
141	Lebanon	6,469
142	Malawi	6,348
143	Rwanda	6,190
144	Namibia	5,831
145	Guinea	5,654
146	Niger	5,439
147	Laos	5,268
148	Brunei	5,204
149	Togo	5,137
150	Mongolia	5,121
151	Bahamas	5,056
152	Malta	5,024
153	Barbados	4,253
154	Swaziland	3,950
155	Guadeloupe	3,886
156	Reunion	3,608
157	Martinique	3,537
158	Chad	3,233
159	Guam	3,182
160	Fiji	3,182
161	Liberia	3,038
162	Sierra Leone	2,943
163	Central African Rep.	2,921
164	Mauritania	2,885
165	Jersey	2,417
166	Aruba	2,234
167	Fr Polynesia	2,083
168	Suriname	2,011
169	Neth Antilles	1,816
170	Lesotho	1,793
171	Virgin I, US	1,737
172	Eritrea	1,585
173	Guyana	1,491
174	New Caledonia	1,488
175	Burundi	1,382
176	Guernsey	1,355
177	Isle of Man	1,340
178	West Bank	1,306
179	Greenland	1,155
180	Gambia	1,081
181	Bermuda	1,060
182	Andorra	1,053
183	Bhutan	1,047
184	Faeroe Is	985
185	St Lucia	976
186	Cayman Is	912
187	Belize	911
188	Liechtenstein	867
189	Seychelles	826
190	Monaco	824
191	Djibouti	797

192	Equatorial G	795
193	Antigua & Barbuda	790
194	Guiana, Fr	744
195	San Marino	711
196	Gibraltar	711
197	Cape Verde	621
198	N Mariana Is	614
199	Maldives	586
200	East Timor	575
201	Comoros	556
202	Gaza Strip	542
203	Solomon Is	539
204	Vanuatu	537
205	St Vincent	526
206	Guinea-Bissau	506
207	Grenada	499
208	Samoa, W	453
209	Samoa, Ameri	393
210	Dominica	390
211	St Kitts & Nevis	361
212	Micronesia	283
213	Tonga	255
214	Virgin Is, Brit.	208
215	San Tome & Principe	174
216	W Sahara	130
217	Palau	116
218	Turks & Caicos	101
219	St Pierre &	99
220	Kiribati	85
221	Marshall Is	83
222	Cook Is	81
223	Mayotte	72
224	Anguilla	67
225	Falkland Is	55
226	Nauru	54
227	Montserrat	46
228	Wallis & Futuna	35
229	St Helena	22
230	Tuvalu	10
231	Niue	4
232	Tokelau	2

Source: Calculated as POP*GPCPPP.

TABLE 3.20 - GDP AT PPP IN MILLIONS OF 2007 DOLLARS, YEAR 2000

OBS	COUNTRY	GDPPPP
1	US	11,671,444
2	China	4,116,227
3	Japan	3,851,632
4	Germany	2,493,832
5	India	2,052,149
6	France	1,827,616
7	UK	1,713,058
8	Italy	1,679,642
9	Brazil	1,435,795

10	Russia	1,340,880
11	Mexico	1,149,649
12	Spain	1,097,904
13	Canada	1,027,827
14	Korea, South	879,855
15	Indonesia	660,805
16	Turkey	659,926
17	Australia	587,576
18	Netherlands	548,175
19	Iran	499,630
20	Taiwan	469,707
21	Poland	443,483
22	Argentina	417,596
23	Saudi Arabia	411,333
24	Thailand	388,451
25	South Africa	325,518
26	Belgium	320,492
27	Pakistan	301,154
28	Egypt	281,142
29	Sweden	275,634
30	Austria	274,494
31	Venezuela	268,411
32	Switzerland	267,034
33	Greece	263,677
34	Malaysia	257,633
35	Colombia	239,782
36	Philippines	222,677
37	Portugal	215,377
38	Hong Kong	210,314
39	Norway	207,017
40	Nigeria	195,762
41	Ukraine	192,785
42	Chile	179,742
43	Algeria	179,376
44	Denmark	174,430
45	Czechia	166,506
46	Singapore	158,090
47	Vietnam	153,662
48	Peru	147,062
49	Finland	146,729
50	Israel	145,947
51	UAE	138,893
52	Romania	136,096
53	Hungary	135,796
54	Bangladesh	135,725
55	Ireland	130,000
56	Morocco	96,599
57	New Zealand	88,630
58	Kuwait	87,604
59	Kazakhstan	85,527
60	Iraq	74,803
61	Syria	70,839
62	Slovakia	68,704
63	Ecuador	66,184
64	Sri Lanka	65,297
65	Libya	63,805

66	Belarus	61,696
67	Bulgaria	59,639
68	Tunisia	56,432
69	Puerto Rico	52,014
70	Sudan	49,943
71	Burma	47,800
72	Guatemala	47,752
73	Croatia	47,504
74	Dominican Rep	44,331
75	Serbia	43,020
76	Uzbekistan	42,566
77	Kenya	42,209
78	Slovenia	40,583
79	Oman	40,548
80	Yemen	39,536
81	Ethiopia	36,080
82	Cuba	35,490
83	Lithuania	35,027
84	Costa Rica	33,649
85	Uruguay	32,842
86	El Salvador	31,446
87	Bolivia	31,413
88	Ivory Coast	30,659
89	Ghana	30,036
90	Cameroon	29,025
91	Angola	29,001
92	Lebanon	28,294
93	Luxembourg	28,247
94	Tanzania	27,971
95	Korea, North	27,406
96	Panama	25,407
97	Nepal	24,382
98	Uganda	23,390
99	Turkmenistan	23,214
100	Mozambique	22,937
101	Latvia	21,784
102	Cyprus	21,418
103	Paraguay	21,381
104	Azerbaijan	20,689
105	Jordan	20,277
106	Afghanistan	19,814
107	Zimbabwe	19,356
108	Trinidad/Tobago	19,100
109	Honduras	19,043
110	Bosnia	18,785
111	Estonia	18,114
112	Senegal	18,078
113	Gabon	17,338
114	Botswana	17,131
115	Brunei	16,347
116	Bahrain	16,324
117	Cambodia	15,979
118	Jamaica	15,579
119	Qatar	14,960
120	Madagascar	14,527
121	Macedonia	14,315

122	Albania	13,479
123	Congo, Dem R	13,386
124	Nicaragua	11,776
125	Georgia	11,752
126	Mauritius	11,534
127	Burkina Faso	11,422
128	Papua New Gu	11,191
129	Haiti	10,654
130	Congo, Rep	10,273
131	Macao	10,181
132	Zambia	10,021
133	Mali	9,782
134	Iceland	8,809
135	Benin	8,768
136	Malawi	8,686
137	Guinea	8,609
138	Namibia	8,471
139	Laos	8,416
140	Malta	8,382
141	Kyrgyzstan	7,840
142	Armenia	7,558
143	Rwanda	6,892
144	Somalia	6,599
145	Niger	6,575
146	Tajikistan	6,526
147	Moldova	6,352
148	Bahamas	5,968
149	Swaziland	5,245
150	Guadeloupe	5,240
151	Equatorial G	4,981
152	Barbados	4,831
153	Mongolia	4,733
154	Guam	4,640
155	Togo	4,569
156	Chad	4,532
157	Martinique	4,517
158	Reunion	4,407
159	Mauritania	4,265
160	New Caledonia	3,816
161	Fiji	3,552
162	Aruba	3,454
163	Montenegro	3,409
164	Central African Rep.	3,208
165	Fr Polynesia	3,082
166	Jersey	2,900
167	West Bank	2,725
168	Lesotho	2,572
169	Liberia	2,469
170	Kosovo	2,423
171	Eritrea	2,421
172	Suriname	2,283
173	Burundi	2,146
174	Neth Antilles	2,039
175	Guyana	2,030
176	Virgin I, US	1,930
177	Sierra Leone	1,833

178	Isle of Man	1,779
179	Bhutan	1,698
180	Guernsey	1,595
181	Gambia	1,588
182	Belize	1,529
183	Andorra	1,526
184	Cayman Is	1,475
185	Bermuda	1,466
186	Seychelles	1,374
187	Greenland	1,342
188	St Lucia	1,342
189	Guiana, Fr	1,253
190	Liechtenstein	1,140
191	Faeroe Is	1,103
192	Cape Verde	1,086
193	N Mariana Is	1,085
194	Antigua & Barbuda	1,078
195	Maldives	1,040
196	Monaco	1,033
197	San Marino	1,011
198	Gaza Strip	939
199	Gibraltar	884
200	Djibouti	861
201	Samoa, Ameri	808
202	Grenada	718
203	Vanuatu	704
204	East Timor	704
205	Solomon Is	687
206	St Vincent	680
207	Guinea-Bissau	632
208	Comoros	624
209	Samoa, W	572
210	St Kitts & Nevis	558
211	Mayotte	501
212	Dominica	462
213	Virgin Is, Brit.	350
214	Tonga	332
215	Micronesia	329
216	San Tome & Principe	194
217	Turks & Caicos	192
218	Palau	187
219	W Sahara	187
220	Kiribati	121
221	Anguilla	121
222	St Pierre &	113
223	Cook Is	112
224	Marshall Is	111
225	Falkland Is	82
226	Nauru	50
227	Wallis & Futuna	41
228	Montserrat	24
229	St Helena	24
230	Tuvalu	12
231	Niue	6
232	Tokelau	2

Source: Calculated as POP*GPCPPP.

TABLE 3.21 - GDP AT PPP IN MILLIONS OF 2007 DOLLARS, YEAR 2007		
OBS	COUNTRY	GDPPPP
1	US	13,857,565
2	China	7,044,309
3	Japan	4,283,489
4	India	3,110,521
5	Germany	2,726,883
6	Russia	2,084,336
7	France	2,061,945
8	UK	2,041,041
9	Brazil	1,811,936
10	Italy	1,767,692
11	Spain	1,419,091
12	Mexico	1,361,517
13	Canada	1,236,393
14	Korea, South	1,197,445
15	Turkey	922,146
16	Indonesia	863,505
17	Iran	778,971
18	Australia	727,534
19	Taiwan	691,680
20	Netherlands	621,443
21	Poland	602,557
22	Saudi Arabia	554,556
23	Argentina	523,549
24	Thailand	519,888
25	South Africa	465,877
26	Pakistan	401,627
27	Egypt	392,612
28	Greece	370,087
29	Belgium	365,162
30	Malaysia	355,533
31	Sweden	332,449
32	Ukraine	321,297
33	Austria	317,395
34	Venezuela	316,660
35	Switzerland	303,991
36	Philippines	299,944
37	Colombia	298,289
38	Hong Kong	293,038
39	Nigeria	284,840
40	Algeria	262,162
41	Norway	250,767
42	Romania	245,529
43	Czechia	238,945
44	Portugal	231,223
45	Chile	230,463
46	Singapore	229,587
47	Vietnam	227,175
48	Peru	218,815
49	Denmark	195,182
50	Hungary	187,827
51	Ireland	186,333

52	Finland	181,907
53	Israel	178,827
54	Bangladesh	174,701
55	Kazakhstan	167,546
56	UAE	165,761
57	Kuwait	129,454
58	Morocco	126,863
59	New Zealand	109,236
60	Slovakia	109,026
61	Belarus	105,158
62	Iraq	104,375
63	Ecuador	98,697
64	Libya	91,128
65	Burma	90,011
66	Bulgaria	86,373
67	Puerto Rico	86,084
68	Syria	85,964
69	Sri Lanka	85,614
70	Sudan	82,223
71	Serbia	76,929
72	Tunisia	76,756
73	Croatia	68,887
74	Qatar	68,037
75	Angola	67,047
76	Uzbekistan	66,377
77	Dominican Rep	62,659
78	Oman	62,280
79	Azerbaijan	60,713
80	Lithuania	59,646
81	Ethiopia	59,603
82	Guatemala	58,103
83	Kenya	56,663
84	Slovenia	54,484
85	Yemen	51,932
86	Tanzania	47,615
87	Costa Rica	47,286
88	Cuba	45,644
89	Korea, North	44,596
90	Lebanon	41,449
91	Bolivia	40,081
92	Latvia	39,834
93	El Salvador	39,640
94	Cameroon	38,359
95	Panama	38,067
96	Uruguay	37,535
97	Luxembourg	36,886
98	Ivory Coast	32,225
99	Trinidad/Tobago	30,618
100	Ghana	30,613
101	Macao	30,220
102	Nepal	29,126
103	Jordan	29,045
104	Bosnia	28,789
105	Honduras	28,514
106	Cyprus	28,463
107	Estonia	28,442

108	Uganda	28,417
109	Paraguay	26,542
110	Turkmenistan	26,504
111	Botswana	25,247
112	Cambodia	25,035
113	Bahrain	24,043
114	Afghanistan	21,716
115	Georgia	21,529
116	Senegal	20,862
117	Brunei	20,423
118	Albania	20,279
119	Gabon	20,198
120	Congo, Dem R	18,666
121	Madagascar	18,404
122	Jamaica	17,927
123	Macedonia	17,462
124	Armenia	17,144
125	Mozambique	16,641
126	Burkina Faso	16,102
127	Zambia	15,597
128	Equatorial G	15,533
129	Chad	15,133
130	Nicaragua	14,442
131	Mauritius	14,244
132	Congo, Rep	13,233
133	Papua New Gu	13,200
134	Mali	13,003
135	Laos	12,538
136	Tajikistan	11,815
137	Iceland	11,524
138	Haiti	11,086
139	Namibia	10,729
140	Guinea	10,682
141	Benin	10,600
142	Kyrgyzstan	10,528
143	Malawi	10,284
144	Moldova	9,713
145	Malta	9,249
146	Niger	8,934
147	Rwanda	8,432
148	Mongolia	8,406
149	Bahamas	8,275
150	Martinique	7,049
151	Montenegro	6,378
152	Mauritania	6,023
153	Barbados	5,674
154	Swaziland	5,607
155	Jersey	5,587
156	Fr Polynesia	5,576
157	Reunion	5,425
158	Togo	5,327
159	Bermuda	5,232
160	Somalia	5,219
161	Kosovo	4,862
162	New Caledonia	4,466
163	Liechtenstein	4,165

164	Suriname	3,986
165	Guadeloupe	3,983
166	Sierra Leone	3,971
167	Fiji	3,723
168	West Bank	3,622
169	Neth Antilles	3,543
170	Andorra	3,511
171	Bhutan	3,183
172	Guernsey	3,111
173	Isle of Man	3,105
174	Central African Rep.	3,101
175	Lesotho	3,096
176	Burundi	2,861
177	Guam	2,842
178	Cayman Is	2,839
179	Aruba	2,640
180	Eritrea	2,552
181	Zimbabwe	2,462
182	Guyana	2,223
183	Guiana, Fr	2,138
184	Gambia	2,107
185	Belize	2,099
186	Faeroe Is	1,945
187	Virgin I, US	1,890
188	St Lucia	1,680
189	Maldives	1,627
190	Antigua & Barbuda	1,601
191	Cape Verde	1,509
192	Greenland	1,478
193	N Mariana Is	1,398
194	Seychelles	1,383
195	Liberia	1,343
196	Gaza Strip	1,296
197	San Marino	1,278
198	Gibraltar	1,170
199	Monaco	1,062
200	Virgin Is, Brit.	1,046
201	Mayotte	1,041
202	Djibouti	1,023
203	Solomon Is	832
204	Vanuatu	829
205	East Timor	825
206	Grenada	824
207	St Vincent	816
208	St Kitts & Nevis	741
209	Samoa, W	723
210	Comoros	722
211	Guinea-Bissau	704
212	Dominica	561
213	Samoa, Ameri	515
214	Tonga	365
215	Micronesia	339
216	Turks & Caicos	317
217	W Sahara	315
218	San Tome & Principe	259
219	Cook Is	217

220	Marshall Is	180
221	Palau	168
222	Kiribati	141
223	Falkland Is	139
224	Anguilla	139
225	Wallis & Futuna	71
226	St Pierre &	64
227	Nauru	56
228	Montserrat	42
229	St Helena	27
230	Tuvalu	20
231	Niue	11
232	Tokelau	3

Source: Calculated as POP*GPCPPP.

CHAPTER 4. POPULATION GROWTH RATES

OBS	COUNTRY	GRPOP

TABLE 4.1 - POPULATION GROWTH RATES YEARS 0001-1000		
OBS	COUNTRY	GRPOP
1	Madagascar	0.53
2	Burundi	0.23
3	Zambia	0.19
4	Malawi	0.19
5	Zimbabwe	0.19
6	Mozambique	0.18
7	Swaziland	0.11
8	South Africa	0.11
9	Lesotho	0.11
10	Poland	0.10
11	Ireland	0.09
12	UK	0.09
13	Japan	0.09
14	Guinea	0.08
15	Ghana	0.08
16	Sierra Leone	0.08
17	Guinea-Bissau	0.08
18	Mexico	0.07
19	Trinidad/Tobago	0.07
20	Jamaica	0.07
21	Panama	0.07
22	Costa Rica	0.07
23	Puerto Rico	0.07
24	Haiti	0.07
25	Honduras	0.07
26	Cuba	0.07
27	Guatemala	0.07
28	Ecuador	0.07
29	Colombia	0.07
30	Brazil	0.07
31	Peru	0.07
32	Chile	0.07
33	Bolivia	0.07
34	Nicaragua	0.07
35	Venezuela	0.07
36	Argentina	0.07
37	Paraguay	0.07
38	El Salvador	0.07
39	Dominican Rep	0.07
40	Uruguay	0.07
41	Latvia	0.07
42	Eritrea	0.07
43	Belarus	0.07
44	Canada	0.07
45	Denmark	0.07
46	Estonia	0.07
47	Finland	0.07
48	Lithuania	0.07

49	Moldova	0.07
50	Morocco	0.07
51	Norway	0.07
52	Somalia	0.07
53	Sweden	0.07
54	Ukraine	0.07
55	Ethiopia	0.07
56	Russia	0.07
57	US	0.06
58	Singapore	0.06
59	Taiwan	0.06
60	Malaysia	0.06
61	Sri Lanka	0.06
62	Korea, North	0.06
63	Burma	0.06
64	Korea, South	0.06
65	Nepal	0.06
66	Indonesia	0.06
67	Afghanistan	0.06
68	Vietnam	0.06
69	Thailand	0.06
70	Cambodia	0.06
71	Mongolia	0.06
72	Philippines	0.06
73	Laos	0.06
74	Kazakhstan	0.05
75	Armenia	0.05
76	Hungary	0.05
77	Turkmenistan	0.05
78	Uzbekistan	0.05
79	Kyrgyzstan	0.05
80	Georgia	0.05
81	Tajikistan	0.05
82	Azerbaijan	0.05
83	Bulgaria	0.05
84	Netherlands	0.04
85	Portugal	0.04
86	Sudan	0.04
87	Austria	0.03
88	Botswana	0.03
89	Belgium	0.03
90	Namibia	0.03
91	France	0.03
92	Australia	0.03
93	New Zealand	0.03
94	Slovakia	0.02
95	Egypt	0.02
96	Libya	0.02
97	Tunisia	0.02
98	Czechia	0.02
99	Montenegro	0.02
100	Bosnia	0.02
101	Croatia	0.02
102	Germany	0.02
103	Serbia	0.02
104	Macedonia	0.02

105	Slovenia	0.02
106	Spain	0.01
107	Kosovo	0.01
108	Hong Kong	0.00
109	UAE	0.00
110	Jordan	0.00
111	Oman	0.00
112	Yemen	0.00
113	Saudi Arabia	0.00
114	Iraq	0.00
115	Syria	0.00
116	Turkey	0.00
117	Iran	0.00
118	Israel	0.00
119	Lebanon	0.00
120	Kuwait	0.00
121	Bahrain	0.00
122	Qatar	0.00
123	Albania	0.00
124	Algeria	0.00
125	Bangladesh	0.00
126	India	0.00
127	Pakistan	0.00
128	Romania	0.00
129	Switzerland	0.00
130	China	0.00
131	Cyprus	-0.03
132	Italy	-0.05
133	Greece	-0.06

Source: Calculated as (POP1000/POP0001)**(1/999) 1.

TABLE 4.2 - POPULATION GROWTH RATES YEARS 1000-1500		
OBS	COUNTRY	GRPOP
1	Finland	0.40
2	Belgium	0.25
3	Madagascar	0.25
4	Germany	0.25
5	Mozambique	0.24
6	Poland	0.24
7	Netherlands	0.23
8	Lithuania	0.22
9	Ukraine	0.22
10	Belarus	0.22
11	Latvia	0.22
12	Moldova	0.22
13	Estonia	0.22
14	Russia	0.22
15	Austria	0.21
16	Azerbaijan	0.18
17	Hungary	0.18
18	Romania	0.18
19	Georgia	0.18
20	Armenia	0.18

21	Czechia	0.18
22	Slovakia	0.18
23	France	0.17
24	Switzerland	0.15
25	Italy	0.15
26	Japan	0.14
27	Zambia	0.14
28	Burundi	0.14
29	Ethiopia	0.14
30	Botswana	0.14
31	Lesotho	0.14
32	Malawi	0.14
33	Namibia	0.14
34	Somalia	0.14
35	South Africa	0.14
36	Swaziland	0.14
37	Zimbabwe	0.14
38	Eritrea	0.14
39	Ireland	0.14
40	UK	0.14
41	Malaysia	0.12
42	Mongolia	0.12
43	Laos	0.12
44	Philippines	0.12
45	Sri Lanka	0.12
46	Taiwan	0.12
47	Thailand	0.12
48	Nepal	0.12
49	Burma	0.12
50	Indonesia	0.12
51	Afghanistan	0.12
52	Korea, South	0.12
53	Vietnam	0.12
54	Korea, North	0.12
55	Cambodia	0.12
56	Singapore	0.12
57	Hong Kong	0.11
58	China	0.11
59	Spain	0.11
60	Denmark	0.10
61	Mexico	0.10
62	Portugal	0.10
63	Sierra Leone	0.09
64	Guinea-Bissau	0.09
65	Ghana	0.09
66	Guinea	0.09
67	Canada	0.09
68	US	0.09
69	Norway	0.08
70	Bangladesh	0.08
71	Pakistan	0.08
72	India	0.08
73	Paraguay	0.07
74	Cuba	0.07
75	El Salvador	0.07
76	Haiti	0.07

77	Venezuela	0.07
78	Argentina	0.07
79	Bolivia	0.07
80	Chile	0.07
81	Peru	0.07
82	Brazil	0.07
83	Guatemala	0.07
84	Colombia	0.07
85	Nicaragua	0.07
86	Ecuador	0.07
87	Honduras	0.07
88	Uruguay	0.07
89	Costa Rica	0.07
90	Panama	0.07
91	Jamaica	0.07
92	Puerto Rico	0.07
93	Dominican Rep	0.07
94	Trinidad/Tobago	0.07
95	Australia	0.07
96	New Zealand	0.07
97	Uzbekistan	0.07
98	Kazakhstan	0.07
99	Turkmenistan	0.07
100	Kyrgyzstan	0.07
101	Tajikistan	0.07
102	Sweden	0.06
103	Sudan	0.06
104	Slovenia	0.05
105	Macedonia	0.05
106	Bosnia	0.05
107	Croatia	0.05
108	Serbia	0.05
109	Kosovo	0.05
110	Montenegro	0.05
111	Albania	0.00
112	Bulgaria	0.00
113	Libya	0.00
114	Greece	-0.02
115	Bahrain	-0.02
116	Kuwait	-0.02
117	Jordan	-0.02
118	Israel	-0.02
119	Iran	-0.02
120	Turkey	-0.02
121	Yemen	-0.02
122	Saudi Arabia	-0.02
123	Syria	-0.02
124	Iraq	-0.02
125	Lebanon	-0.02
126	Oman	-0.02
127	UAE	-0.02
128	Qatar	-0.02
129	Egypt	-0.04
130	Tunisia	-0.04
131	Algeria	-0.06
132	Morocco	-0.06

| 133 | Cyprus | -0.17 |

Source: Calculated as (POP1500/POP1000)**(1/500)-1.

TABLE 4.3 POPULATION GROWTH RATES YEARS 1500-1600		
OBS	COUNTRY	GRPOP
1	Taiwan	0.81
2	Philippines	0.46
3	Netherlands	0.46
4	UK	0.45
5	Bulgaria	0.45
6	China	0.44
7	Hong Kong	0.44
8	Switzerland	0.43
9	Slovakia	0.41
10	Czechia	0.41
11	Algeria	0.41
12	Cyprus	0.41
13	Greece	0.41
14	Morocco	0.41
15	Sweden	0.32
16	Finland	0.29
17	Germany	0.29
18	Norway	0.29
19	Sierra Leone	0.24
20	Guinea-Bissau	0.24
21	Ghana	0.24
22	Guinea	0.24
23	Moldova	0.22
24	Estonia	0.22
25	Belarus	0.22
26	Ireland	0.22
27	Ukraine	0.22
28	Austria	0.22
29	Egypt	0.22
30	Mozambique	0.22
31	Poland	0.22
32	Tunisia	0.22
33	Lithuania	0.22
34	Latvia	0.22
35	Italy	0.22
36	Russia	0.22
37	Korea, South	0.21
38	Korea, North	0.21
39	France	0.21
40	Pakistan	0.21
41	India	0.21
42	Bangladesh	0.21
43	Montenegro	0.20
44	Slovenia	0.20
45	Macedonia	0.20
46	Bosnia	0.20
47	Croatia	0.20

48	Serbia	0.20
49	Kosovo	0.20
50	Azerbaijan	0.20
51	Spain	0.19
52	Japan	0.18
53	Armenia	0.18
54	Georgia	0.18
55	Swaziland	0.15
56	South Africa	0.15
57	Burundi	0.15
58	Lesotho	0.15
59	Malaysia	0.15
60	Afghanistan	0.15
61	Burma	0.15
62	Cambodia	0.15
63	Vietnam	0.15
64	Nepal	0.15
65	Laos	0.15
66	Mongolia	0.15
67	Singapore	0.15
68	Turkey	0.14
69	Kyrgyzstan	0.13
70	Kazakhstan	0.13
71	Uzbekistan	0.13
72	Belgium	0.13
73	Madagascar	0.13
74	Turkmenistan	0.13
75	Tajikistan	0.13
76	Ethiopia	0.12
77	Eritrea	0.12
78	Iran	0.11
79	Thailand	0.11
80	Indonesia	0.10
81	Portugal	0.10
82	Zambia	0.10
83	Zimbabwe	0.10
84	Malawi	0.10
85	Sri Lanka	0.09
86	Denmark	0.08
87	Sudan	0.05
88	Albania	0.00
89	Australia	0.00
90	Bahrain	0.00
91	Botswana	0.00
92	Canada	0.00
93	Hungary	0.00
94	Iraq	0.00
95	Kuwait	0.00
96	Libya	0.00
97	Namibia	0.00
98	New Zealand	0.00
99	Oman	0.00
100	Qatar	0.00
101	Romania	0.00
102	Saudi Arabia	0.00
103	Somalia	0.00

104	UAE	0.00
105	Yemen	0.00
106	Lebanon	-0.03
107	Syria	-0.03
108	Jordan	-0.03
109	Israel	-0.03
110	Brazil	-0.22
111	US	-0.29
112	Chile	-0.50
113	El Salvador	-0.51
114	Nicaragua	-0.51
115	Ecuador	-0.51
116	Peru	-0.51
117	Argentina	-0.51
118	Costa Rica	-0.51
119	Guatemala	-0.51
120	Honduras	-0.51
121	Panama	-0.51
122	Colombia	-0.51
123	Venezuela	-0.51
124	Bolivia	-0.51
125	Paraguay	-0.51
126	Uruguay	-0.51
127	Haiti	-0.91
128	Cuba	-0.91
129	Jamaica	-0.91
130	Dominican Rep	-0.91
131	Puerto Rico	-0.91
132	Trinidad/Tobago	-0.91
133	Mexico	-1.09

Source: Calculated as (POP1600/POP1500)**(1/100)-1.

TABLE 4.4 POPULATION GROWTH RATES YEARS 1600-1700		
OBS	COUNTRY	GRPOP
1	Trinidad/Tobago	0.92
2	Puerto Rico	0.92
3	Dominican Rep	0.92
4	Jamaica	0.92
5	Cuba	0.92
6	Haiti	0.92
7	Taiwan	0.81
8	Ireland	0.66
9	Portugal	0.60
10	Mexico	0.59
11	Sweden	0.51
12	Philippines	0.46
13	Brazil	0.45
14	Albania	0.41
15	Japan	0.38
16	Lesotho	0.36
17	South Africa	0.36
18	Swaziland	0.36

19	UK	0.33
20	Russia	0.29
21	Estonia	0.29
22	Lithuania	0.29
23	Belarus	0.29
24	Ukraine	0.29
25	Moldova	0.29
26	Latvia	0.29
27	Guinea	0.25
28	Ghana	0.25
29	Guinea-Bissau	0.25
30	Sierra Leone	0.25
31	Netherlands	0.24
32	Belgium	0.22
33	Madagascar	0.22
34	Norway	0.22
35	Romania	0.22
36	Korea, South	0.21
37	Korea, North	0.21
38	Bangladesh	0.20
39	India	0.20
40	Pakistan	0.20
41	Hungary	0.18
42	Mozambique	0.18
43	Poland	0.18
44	Switzerland	0.18
45	Somalia	0.17
46	Armenia	0.15
47	Georgia	0.15
48	Singapore	0.15
49	Vietnam	0.15
50	Nepal	0.15
51	Burma	0.15
52	Afghanistan	0.15
53	Cambodia	0.15
54	Malaysia	0.15
55	Mongolia	0.15
56	Laos	0.15
57	France	0.15
58	Turkey	0.14
59	Azerbaijan	0.14
60	Burundi	0.13
61	Paraguay	0.13
62	Costa Rica	0.13
63	Panama	0.13
64	Honduras	0.13
65	Chile	0.13
66	Colombia	0.13
67	Venezuela	0.13
68	Bolivia	0.13
69	Ecuador	0.13
70	Peru	0.13
71	Guatemala	0.13
72	Nicaragua	0.13
73	Argentina	0.13
74	El Salvador	0.13

75	Uruguay	0.13
76	Tajikistan	0.12
77	Kyrgyzstan	0.12
78	Uzbekistan	0.12
79	Turkmenistan	0.12
80	Kazakhstan	0.12
81	Iran	0.11
82	Thailand	0.11
83	Ethiopia	0.11
84	Eritrea	0.11
85	Indonesia	0.10
86	Sri Lanka	0.09
87	Malawi	0.09
88	Zambia	0.09
89	Zimbabwe	0.09
90	Denmark	0.07
91	Spain	0.06
92	Sudan	0.05
93	Italy	0.02
94	Australia	0.00
95	Austria	0.00
96	Bahrain	0.00
97	Bosnia	0.00
98	Botswana	0.00
99	Bulgaria	0.00
100	Croatia	0.00
101	Cyprus	0.00
102	Czechia	0.00
103	Finland	0.00
104	Greece	0.00
105	Iraq	0.00
106	Kosovo	0.00
107	Kuwait	0.00
108	Libya	0.00
109	Macedonia	0.00
110	Montenegro	0.00
111	Namibia	0.00
112	New Zealand	0.00
113	Oman	0.00
114	Qatar	0.00
115	Saudi Arabia	0.00
116	Serbia	0.00
117	Slovakia	0.00
118	Slovenia	0.00
119	UAE	0.00
120	Yemen	0.00
121	Israel	-0.03
122	Jordan	-0.03
123	Syria	-0.03
124	Lebanon	-0.03
125	Germany	-0.06
126	Egypt	-0.11
127	China	-0.15
128	Hong Kong	-0.15
129	Canada	-0.22
130	Tunisia	-0.22

131	Algeria	-0.25
132	Morocco	-0.25
133	US	-0.40

Source: Calculated as (POP1700/POP1600)**(1/100)-1.

TABLE 4.5 - POPULATION GROWTH RATES YEARS 1700-1820		
OBS	COUNTRY	GRPOP
1	US	1.94
2	Dominican Rep	1.48
3	Cuba	1.48
4	Haiti	1.48
5	Jamaica	1.48
6	Puerto Rico	1.48
7	Trinidad/Tobago	1.48
8	Canada	1.18
9	Ireland	1.09
10	Brazil	1.07
11	Finland	0.90
12	Hungary	0.85
13	Hong Kong	0.85
14	China	0.85
15	Romania	0.78
16	UK	0.76
17	Russia	0.68
18	Latvia	0.66
19	Ukraine	0.66
20	Belarus	0.66
21	Lithuania	0.66
22	Moldova	'0.66
23	Estonia	0.66
24	Sweden	0.60
25	Taiwan	0.58
26	Norway	0.55
27	Kosovo	0.53
28	Serbia	0.53
29	Croatia	0.53
30	Macedonia	0.53
31	Bosnia	0.53
32	Slovenia	0.53
33	Montenegro	0.53
34	Thailand	0.52
35	Bulgaria	0.47
36	Philippines	0.46
37	Poland	0.46
38	Belgium	0.45
39	Czechia	0.44
40	Slovakia	0.44
41	Madagascar	0.43
42	Germany	0.42
43	Switzerland	0.42
44	Denmark	0.42
45	Portugal	0.42

46	South Africa	0.37
47	Lesotho	0.37
48	Swaziland	0.37
49	Greece	0.36
50	Cyprus	0.36
51	Algeria	0.36
52	Morocco	0.36
53	Italy	0.35
54	Turkmenistan	0.34
55	Kazakhstan	0.34
56	Uzbekistan	0.34
57	Kyrgyzstan	0.34
58	Tajikistan	0.34
59	Mexico	0.32
60	Albania	0.31
61	France	0.31
62	Mozambique	0.28
63	Spain	0.28
64	Azerbaijan	0.27
65	Georgia	0.27
66	Armenia	0.27
67	Indonesia	0.26
68	Austria	0.25
69	Iran	0.23
70	Uruguay	0.22
71	Costa Rica	0.22
72	Argentina	0.22
73	El Salvador	0.22
74	Nicaragua	0.22
75	Guatemala	0.22
76	Venezuela	0.22
77	Bolivia	0.22
78	Peru	0.22
79	Colombia	0.22
80	Honduras	0.22
81	Chile	0.22
82	Ecuador	0.22
83	Paraguay	0.22
84	Panama	0.22
85	Burundi	0.22
86	Laos	0.20
87	Mongolia	0.20
88	Cambodia	0.20
89	Afghanistan	0.20
90	Burma	0.20
91	Vietnam	0.20
92	Nepal	0.20
93	Malaysia	0.20
94	Singapore	0.20
95	Pakistan	0.20
96	India	0.20
97	Bangladesh	0.20
98	Eritrea	0.19
99	Ethiopia	0.19
100	Netherlands	0.17
101	Turkey	0.15

102	Sudan	0.13
103	Lebanon	0.13
104	Jordan	0.13
105	Syria	0.13
106	Israel	0.13
107	UAE	0.12
108	Qatar	0.12
109	Kuwait	0.12
110	Yemen	0.12
111	Saudi Arabia	0.12
112	Oman	0.12
113	Bahrain	0.12
114	Guinea-Bissau	0.12
115	Sierra Leone	0.12
116	Guinea	0.12
117	Ghana	0.12
118	Japan	0.12
119	Korea, North	0.10
120	Korea, South	0.10
121	Zimbabwe	0.10
122	Zambia	0.10
123	Malawi	0.10
124	Namibia	0.08
125	Botswana	0.08
126	Tunisia	0.07
127	Iraq	0.07
128	Libya	0.06
129	Somalia	0.04
130	Sri Lanka	0.01
131	New Zealand	0.00
132	Egypt	-0.02
133	Australia	-0.25

Source: Calculated as (POP1820/POP1700)**(1/120)-1.

TABLE 4.6 - POPULATION GROWTH RATES YEARS 1820-1870		
OBS	COUNTRY	GRPOP
1	Singapore	5.80
2	Uruguay	3.73
3	Hong Kong	3.70
4	Australia	3.40
5	Canada	3.11
6	US	2.83
7	Argentina	2.46
8	Honduras	2.22
9	New Zealand	2.16
10	Malaysia	2.07
11	Dominican Rep	2.02
12	Paraguay	2.00
13	Puerto Rico	1.93
14	Chile	1.87
15	Swaziland	1.74
16	Lesotho	1.74

17	Philippines	1.70
18	Venezuela	1.68
19	Sri Lanka	1.68
20	Cuba	1.59
21	Costa Rica	1.57
22	Brazil	1.57
23	Ethiopia	1.49
24	Eritrea	1.49
25	Trinidad/Tobago	1.46
26	Ecuador	1.42
27	Malawi	1.40
28	Zimbabwe	1.40
29	Zambia	1.40
30	El Salvador	1.38
31	Colombia	1.38
32	Peru	1.37
33	Armenia	1.28
34	Georgia	1.28
35	Azerbaijan	1.28
36	Panama	1.26
37	Guatemala	1.20
38	Nicaragua	1.20
39	Norway	1.17
40	South Africa	1.14
41	Botswana	1.09
42	Namibia	1.09
43	Russia	1.00
44	Denmark	0.99
45	Lithuania	0.97
46	Ukraine	0.97
47	Belarus	0.97
48	Latvia	0.97
49	Moldova	0.97
50	Estonia	0.97
51	Poland	0.97
52	Indonesia	0.96
53	Sweden	0.96
54	Vietnam	0.95
55	Laos	0.95
56	Haiti	0.93
57	Kosovo	0.92
58	Montenegro	0.92
59	Bosnia	0.92
60	Serbia	0.92
61	Croatia	0.92
62	Macedonia	0.92
63	Slovenia	0.92
64	Cyprus	0.92
65	Greece	0.92
66	Germany	0.91
67	Netherlands	0.88
68	Mozambique	0.84
69	Finland	0.81
70	Guinea-Bissau	0.80
71	Sierra Leone	0.80
72	Guinea	0.80

73	Belgium	0.79
74	UK	0.79
75	Egypt	0.75
76	Iraq	0.74
77	Romania	0.73
78	Lebanon	0.72
79	Hungary	0.71
80	Madagascar	0.71
81	Algeria	0.68
82	Morocco	0.68
83	Mexico	0.67
84	Burundi	0.65
85	Italy	0.65
86	Albania	0.65
87	Somalia	0.63
88	Bolivia	0.62
89	Tajikistan	0.60
90	Turkmenistan	0.60
91	Uzbekistan	0.60
92	Kazakhstan	0.60
93	Kyrgyzstan	0.60
94	Tunisia	0.59
95	Austria	0.59
96	Switzerland	0.58
97	Spain	0.57
98	Slovakia	0.57
99	Czechia	0.57
100	Portugal	0.55
101	Israel	0.52
102	Iran	0.50
103	Afghanistan	0.50
104	Jamaica	0.44
105	Thailand	0.43
106	Bangladesh	0.42
107	France	0.42
108	Libya	0.41
109	Jordan	0.41
110	Burma	0.38
111	Nepal	0.38
112	India	0.38
113	Sudan	0.34
114	Syria	0.34
115	Bulgaria	0.34
116	Pakistan	0.33
117	Taiwan	0.32
118	Turkey	0.32
119	Oman	0.29
120	Cambodia	0.23
121	Saudi Arabia	0.22
122	Japan	0.21
123	Yemen	0.18
124	Ghana	0.18
125	Mongolia	0.15
126	Korea, North	0.08
127	Korea, South	0.07
128	Bahrain	0.00

129	Kuwait	0.00
130	Qatar	0.00
131	UAE	0.00
132	China	-0.12
133	Ireland	-0.54

Source: Calculated as (POP1870/POP1820)**(1/50)-1.

TABLE 4.7 - POPULATION GROWTH RATES YEARS 1870-1880		
OBS	COUNTRY	GRPOP
1	New Zealand	5.98
2	Malaysia	3.48
3	Argentina	3.21
4	Singapore	3.18
5	Uruguay	3.07
6	Burma	2.88
7	Hong Kong	2.81
8	Costa Rica	2.61
9	Trinidad/Tobago	2.60
10	Dominican Rep	2.55
11	US	2.29
12	Australia	2.16
13	South Africa	2.07
14	Brazil	1.87
15	Swaziland	1.75
16	Lesotho	1.74
17	Colombia	1.73
18	Egypt	1.71
19	Venezuela	1.68
20	Chile	1.56
21	Finland	1.56
22	Poland	1.53
23	Canada	1.49
24	Eritrea	1.49
25	Ethiopia	1.49
26	El Salvador	1.49
27	Bulgaria	1.44
28	Laos	1.42
29	Vietnam	1.42
30	Zambia	1.40
31	Zimbabwe	1.40
32	Malawi	1.40
33	Panama	1.35
34	Puerto Rico	1.33
35	Indonesia	1.29
36	Peru	1.26
37	Philippines	1.24
38	Jamaica	1.23
39	Mexico	1.21
40	Iraq	1.18
41	Nicaragua	1.17
42	Netherlands	1.14
43	Israel	1.12

44	Ukraine	1.11
45	Estonia	1.11
46	Kyrgyzstan	1.11
47	Tajikistan	1.11
48	Azerbaijan	1.11
49	Kazakhstan	1.11
50	Moldova	1.11
51	Georgia	1.11
52	Belarus	1.11
53	Uzbekistan	1.11
54	Russia	1.11
55	Latvia	1.11
56	Lithuania	1.11
57	Armenia	1.11
58	Turkmenistan	1.11
59	Namibia	1.09
60	Botswana	1.09
61	Tunisia	1.08
62	Ecuador	1.08
63	Germany	1.04
64	Algeria	1.03
65	Cyprus	1.02
66	Greece	1.02
67	Haiti	1.02
68	Norway	1.01
69	UK	0.98
70	Denmark	0.98
71	Albania	0.93
72	Sweden	0.93
73	Austria	0.89
74	Mozambique	0.84
75	Belgium	0.84
76	Sri Lanka	0.81
77	Slovenia	0.81
78	Macedonia	0.81
79	Bosnia	0.81
80	Croatia	0.81
81	Serbia	0.81
82	Montenegro	0.81
83	Kosovo	0.81
84	Sierra Leone	0.80
85	Guinea	0.80
86	Guinea-Bissau	0.80
87	Cuba	0.73
88	Lebanon	0.72
89	Thailand	0.72
90	Afghanistan	0.72
91	Honduras	0.71
92	Madagascar	0.71
93	Morocco	0.71
94	Switzerland	0.67
95	Japan	0.67
96	Burundi	0.65
97	Portugal	0.64
98	Cambodia	0.63
99	Somalia	0.63

100	Jordan	0.63
101	Iran	0.62
102	Guatemala	0.62
103	Romania	0.61
104	Italy	0.58
105	Hungary	0.56
106	Turkey	0.56
107	Qatar	0.56
108	Kuwait	0.56
109	Bahrain	0.56
110	UAE	0.56
111	Syria	0.54
112	Czechia	0.51
113	Slovakia	0.51
114	Nepal	0.50
115	Ghana	0.45
116	Paraguay	0.45
117	Oman	0.44
118	Bolivia	0.42
119	Libya	0.41
120	Spain	0.40
121	Sudan	0.34
122	Yemen	0.34
123	Bangladesh	0.32
124	Taiwan	0.32
125	Saudi Arabia	0.31
126	China	0.28
127	Pakistan	0.25
128	Korea, North	0.19
129	Mongolia	0.19
130	France	0.16
131	India	0.14
132	Korea, South	0.05
133	Ireland	-0.41

Source: Calculated as (POP1880/POP1870)**(1/10)-1.

TABLE 4.8 - POPULATION GROWTH RATES YEARS 1880-1890		
OBS	COUNTRY	GRPOP
1	Uruguay	3.99
2	Australia	3.53
3	Malaysia	3.48
4	Argentina	3.21
5	Singapore	3.18
6	Burma	2.88
7	Hong Kong	2.81
8	Costa Rica	2.61
9	Trinidad/Tobago	2.60
10	Dominican Rep	2.55
11	New Zealand	2.49
12	US	2.29
13	South Africa	2.07
14	Brazil	1.87
15	Swaziland	1.75
16	Lesotho	1.74

17	Colombia	1.73
18	Chile	1.56
19	Poland	1.53
20	Eritrea	1.49
21	Ethiopia	1.49
22	El Salvador	1.49
23	Egypt	1.48
24	Finland	1.45
25	Bulgaria	1.44
26	Laos	1.42
27	Vietnam	1.42
28	Zambia	1.40
29	Malawi	1.40
30	Zimbabwe	1.40
31	Panama	1.35
32	Indonesia	1.35
33	Puerto Rico	1.33
34	Venezuela	1.31
35	Peru	1.26
36	Philippines	1.24
37	Jamaica	1.23
38	Mexico	1.21
39	Iraq	1.18
40	Nicaragua	1.17
41	Canada	1.16
42	Netherlands	1.16
43	Israel	1.15
44	Turkmenistan	1.11
45	Tajikistan	1.11
46	Latvia	1.11
47	Georgia	1.11
48	Armenia	1.11
49	Belarus	1.11
50	Kazakhstan	1.11
51	Russia	1.11
52	Uzbekistan	1.11
53	Lithuania	1.11
54	Azerbaijan	1.11
55	Moldova	1.11
56	Kyrgyzstan	1.11
57	Estonia	1.11
58	Ukraine	1.11
59	Botswana	1.09
60	Namibia	1.09
61	Tunisia	1.08
62	Ecuador	1.08
63	Haiti	1.02
64	Greece	1.02
65	Cyprus	1.02
66	Sri Lanka	1.02
67	Bangladesh	1.00
68	Denmark	0.98
69	Belgium	0.96
70	Albania	0.93
71	Pakistan	0.92
72	Germany	0.91

73	Austria	0.88
74	Portugal	0.87
75	Japan	0.85
76	Mozambique	0.84
77	Algeria	0.84
78	India	0.81
79	Montenegro	0.81
80	Serbia	0.81
81	Bosnia	0.81
82	Croatia	0.81
83	Macedonia	0.81
84	Slovenia	0.81
85	Kosovo	0.81
86	UK	0.80
87	Guinea	0.80
88	Sierra Leone	0.80
89	Guinea-Bissau	0.80
90	Cuba	0.73
91	Lebanon	0.72
92	Thailand	0.72
93	Afghanistan	0.72
94	Honduras	0.71
95	Madagascar	0.71
96	Italy	0.71
97	Morocco	0.71
98	Burundi	0.65
99	Cambodia	0.63
100	Somalia	0.63
101	Jordan	0.63
102	Iran	0.62
103	Guatemala	0.62
104	Romania	0.61
105	Hungary	0.56
106	Turkey	0.56
107	UAE	0.56
108	Kuwait	0.56
109	Bahrain	0.56
110	Qatar	0.56
111	Syria	0.54
112	Spain	0.52
113	Slovakia	0.51
114	Czechia	0.51
115	Nepal	0.50
116	Ghana	0.45
117	Paraguay	0.45
118	Sweden	0.45
119	Oman	0.44
120	Bolivia	0.42
121	Libya	0.41
122	Norway	0.40
123	Switzerland	0.39
124	Sudan	0.34
125	Yemen	0.34
126	China	0.32
127	Taiwan	0.32
128	Saudi Arabia	0.31

129	France	0.25
130	Korea, North	0.21
131	Mongolia	0.19
132	Korea, South	0.05
133	Ireland	-0.97

(POP1890/POP1880)**(1/10)-1.

TABLE 4.9 - POPULATION GROWTH RATES YEARS 1890-1900		
OBS	COUNTRY	GRPOP
1	Hong Kong	3.64
2	Malaysia	3.48
3	Argentina	3.35
4	Singapore	3.19
5	Burma	3.11
6	Uruguay	2.92
7	Costa Rica	2.61
8	Trinidad/Tobago	2.60
9	Dominican Rep	2.55
10	Brazil	2.39
11	South Africa	2.07
12	New Zealand	1.95
13	US	1.90
14	Australia	1.87
15	Lesotho	1.74
16	Swaziland	1.74
17	Colombia	1.73
18	Sri Lanka	1.58
19	Bulgaria	1.50
20	Egypt	1.50
21	Mexico	1.50
22	Ethiopia	1.49
23	Eritrea	1.49
24	El Salvador	1.49
25	Kosovo	1.44
26	Macedonia	1.44
27	Croatia	1.44
28	Serbia	1.44
29	Slovenia	1.44
30	Bosnia	1.44
31	Montenegro	1.44
32	Laos	1.42
33	Vietnam	1.42
34	Zimbabwe	1.40
35	Zambia	1.40
36	Malawi	1.40
37	Taiwan	1.37
38	Panama	1.35
39	Venezuela	1.35
40	Germany	1.34
41	Puerto Rico	1.33
42	Indonesia	1.30
43	Netherlands	1.26

44	Peru	1.26
45	Philippines	1.24
46	Jamaica	1.23
47	Azerbaijan	1.19
48	Lithuania	1.19
49	Latvia	1.19
50	Uzbekistan	1.19
51	Moldova	1.19
52	Kazakhstan	1.19
53	Russia	1.19
54	Ukraine	1.19
55	Estonia	1.19
56	Georgia	1.19
57	Kyrgyzstan	1.19
58	Belarus	1.19
59	Tajikistan	1.19
60	Armenia	1.19
61	Turkmenistan	1.19
62	Iraq	1.18
63	Nicaragua	1.17
64	Chile	1.16
65	Israel	1.15
66	Finland	1.13
67	Switzerland	1.12
68	Norway	1.11
69	Denmark	1.11
70	Botswana	1.09
71	Namibia	1.09
72	Tunisia	1.08
73	Ecuador	1.08
74	Canada	1.05
75	Austria	1.02
76	Greece	1.02
77	Cyprus	1.02
78	Haiti	1.02
79	Belgium	0.98
80	Albania	0.98
81	Japan	0.96
82	UK	0.94
83	Thailand	0.93
84	Mozambique	0.84
85	Algeria	0.84
86	Ghana	0.83
87	Poland	0.80
88	Sierra Leone	0.80
89	Guinea	0.80
90	Guinea-Bissau	0.80
91	Czechia	0.76
92	Slovakia	0.76
93	Hungary	0.74
94	Cuba	0.73
95	Portugal	0.72
96	Lebanon	0.72
97	Afghanistan	0.72
98	Honduras	0.71
99	Madagascar	0.71

100	Morocco	0.71
101	Sweden	0.68
102	Burundi	0.65
103	Cambodia	0.63
104	Somalia	0.63
105	Jordan	0.63
106	Iran	0.62
107	Guatemala	0.62
108	Italy	0.60
109	Romania	0.59
110	Turkey	0.56
111	Bahrain	0.56
112	Kuwait	0.56
113	UAE	0.56
114	Qatar	0.56
115	Syria	0.54
116	China	0.51
117	Paraguay	0.45
118	Spain	0.45
119	Oman	0.44
120	Bolivia	0.42
121	Libya	0.41
122	Sudan	0.34
123	Yemen	0.34
124	Bangladesh	0.33
125	Saudi Arabia	0.31
126	Pakistan	0.26
127	Mongolia	0.19
128	Nepal	0.17
129	Korea, North	0.17
130	India	0.15
131	France	0.14
132	Korea, South	0.05
133	Ireland	-0.54

Source: Calculated as $(POP1900/POP1890)^{**}(1/10)-1$

TABLE 4.10 - POPULATION GROWTH RATES YEARS 1900-1913		
OBS	COUNTRY	GRPOP
1	Argentina	3.83
2	Hong Kong	3.64
3	Singapore	3.18
4	Cuba	2.99
5	Dominican Rep	2.93
6	Canada	2.84
7	New Zealand	2.57
8	Malaysia	2.52
9	Paraguay	2.34
10	Panama	2.18
11	Honduras	2.16
12	El Salvador	2.13
13	Brazil	2.13
14	Trinidad/Tobago	2.12
15	South Africa	2.07

16	Colombia	2.04
17	Australia	1.97
18	Uruguay	1.96
19	Philippines	1.92
20	US	1.90
21	Turkmenistan	1.76
22	Armenia	1.76
23	Moldova	1.76
24	Belarus	1.76
25	Lithuania	1.76
26	Ukraine	1.76
27	Russia	1.76
28	Estonia	1.76
29	Georgia	1.76
30	Kazakhstan	1.76
31	Uzbekistan	1.76
32	Kyrgyzstan	1.76
33	Latvia	1.76
34	Tajikistan	1.76
35	Azerbaijan	1.76
36	Costa Rica	1.75
37	Swaziland	1.75
38	Lesotho	1.74
39	Puerto Rico	1.61
40	Sri Lanka	1.60
41	Montenegro	1.52
42	Bosnia	1.52
43	Slovenia	1.52
44	Serbia	1.52
45	Macedonia	1.52
46	Croatia	1.52
47	Kosovo	1.52
48	Haiti	1.49
49	Eritrea	1.49
50	Ethiopia	1.49
51	Burma	1.49
52	Taiwan	1.49
53	Nicaragua	1.47
54	Ecuador	1.45
55	Laos	1.42
56	Vietnam	1.42
57	Netherlands	1.40
58	Malawi	1.40
59	Zimbabwe	1.40
60	Zambia	1.40
61	Egypt	1.39
62	Germany	1.39
63	Thailand	1.33
64	Bulgaria	1.28
65	Japan	1.23
66	Switzerland	1.22
67	Indonesia	1.20
68	Denmark	1.18
69	Iraq	1.18
70	Jamaica	1.16
71	Israel	1.15

72	Chile	1.11
73	Namibia	1.09
74	Botswana	1.09
75	Tunisia	1.08
76	Ghana	1.05
77	Peru	1.04
78	Finland	1.04
79	Guatemala	1.03
80	Belgium	1.02
81	Romania	1.00
82	Austria	0.96
83	Venezuela	0.95
84	Albania	0.89
85	Mozambique	0.84
86	Algeria	0.82
87	UK	0.80
88	Bolivia	0.80
89	Guinea-Bissau	0.80
90	Guinea	0.80
91	Sierra Leone	0.80
92	Italy	0.78
93	Portugal	0.77
94	Mexico	0.74
95	Hungary	0.74
96	Sweden	0.73
97	Lebanon	0.72
98	Afghanistan	0.72
99	Norway	0.72
100	Madagascar	0.71
101	Morocco	0.71
102	Cyprus	0.69
103	Greece	0.69
104	China	0.69
105	Spain	0.68
106	Slovakia	0.67
107	Czechia	0.67
108	Bangladesh	0.66
109	Burundi	0.65
110	Cambodia	0.63
111	Somalia	0.63
112	Jordan	0.63
113	Iran	0.62
114	Poland	0.59
115	Pakistan	0.59
116	Turkey	0.56
117	Qatar	0.56
118	UAE	0.56
119	Kuwait	0.56
120	Bahrain	0.56
121	Syria	0.54
122	Korea, South	0.52
123	Nepal	0.50
124	India	0.48
125	Oman	0.44
126	Libya	0.41
127	Sudan	0.34

128	Yemen	0.34
129	Saudi Arabia	0.31
130	Korea, North	0.19
131	Mongolia	0.19
132	France	0.16
133	Ireland	-0.21

Source: Calculated as (POP1913/POP1900)**(1/13)-1

TABLE 4.11 - POPULATION GROWTH RATES YEARS 1913-1920		
OBS	COUNTRY	GRPOP
1	Panama	4.92
2	Hong Kong	4.16
3	Israel	3.30
4	Cuba	3.04
5	Singapore	2.77
6	Ghana	2.61
7	Colombia	2.59
8	Paraguay	2.35
9	Dominican Rep	2.29
10	Uruguay	2.20
11	South Africa	2.18
12	Lebanon	2.18
13	El Salvador	2.15
14	Brazil	2.12
15	Argentina	2.12
16	Malaysia	2.01
17	Iraq	1.95
18	Philippines	1.93
19	Korea, North	1.87
20	Bolivia	1.83
21	Costa Rica	1.75
22	Lesotho	1.74
23	Swaziland	1.74
24	Thailand	1.74
25	Tunisia	1.72
26	Haiti	1.67
27	Canada	1.64
28	Chile	1.57
29	Korea, South	1.56
30	Syria	1.53
31	Morocco	1.53
32	Australia	1.52
33	Netherlands	1.51
34	Puerto Rico	1.51
35	Eritrea	1.49
36	Ethiopia	1.49
37	Nicaragua	1.47
38	New Zealand	1.45
39	Trinidad/Tobago	1.44
40	Zambia	1.40
41	Malawi	1.40
42	Zimbabwe	1.40
43	US	1.31

44	Sri Lanka	1.26
45	Honduras	1.25
46	Denmark	1.20
47	Egypt	1.17
48	Iran	1.17
49	Nepal	1.16
50	Japan	1.11
51	China	1.10
52	Namibia	1.09
53	Botswana	1.09
54	Taiwan	1.06
55	Indonesia	1.05
56	Peru	1.05
57	Guatemala	1.03
58	Bulgaria	1.03
59	Cambodia	1.02
60	Yemen	1.02
61	Norway	1.01
62	Afghanistan	0.96
63	Vietnam	0.94
64	Qatar	0.89
65	Kuwait	0.89
66	Bahrain	0.89
67	UAE	0.89
68	Burma	0.87
69	Mozambique	0.84
70	Ecuador	0.83
71	Jordan	0.83
72	Sierra Leone	0.80
73	Guinea	0.80
74	Guinea-Bissau	0.80
75	Algeria	0.73
76	Madagascar	0.71
77	Greece	0.71
78	Cyprus	0.71
79	Spain	0.67
80	Burundi	0.65
81	Sweden	0.64
82	Somalia	0.63
83	Venezuela	0.58
84	Albania	0.53
85	Finland	0.49
86	Saudi Arabia	0.49
87	Libya	0.41
88	UK	0.36
89	Sudan	0.34
90	Pakistan	0.33
91	Jamaica	0.30
92	Laos	0.25
93	Hungary	0.20
94	Bangladesh	0.17
95	Portugal	0.14
96	Mongolia	0.08
97	India	0.08
98	Oman	0.07
99	Italy	0.06

100	Ireland	0.05
101	Switzerland	0.05
102	Mexico	-0.07
103	Turkmenistan	-0.15
104	Kyrgyzstan	-0.15
105	Georgia	-0.15
106	Armenia	-0.15
107	Kazakhstan	-0.15
108	Azerbaijan	-0.15
109	Uzbekistan	-0.15
110	Russia	-0.15
111	Ukraine	-0.15
112	Belarus	-0.15
113	Moldova	-0.15
114	Estonia	-0.15
115	Latvia	-0.15
116	Lithuania	-0.15
117	Tajikistan	-0.15
118	Belgium	-0.21
119	Romania	-0.21
120	Slovakia	-0.29
121	Czechia	-0.29
122	Austria	-0.67
123	France	-0.87
124	Germany	-0.94
125	Turkey	-1.11
126	Kosovo	-1.28
127	Macedonia	-1.28
128	Montenegro	-1.28
129	Serbia	-1.28
130	Slovenia	-1.28
131	Croatia	-1.28
132	Bosnia	-1.28
133	Poland	-1.54

Source: Calculated as (POP1920/POP1913)**(1/7)-1

TABLE 4.12 - POPULATION GROWTH RATES YEARS 1920-1929		
OBS	COUNTRY	GRPOP
1	Singapore	4.38
2	Dominican Rep	3.64
3	Israel	3.30
4	Argentina	3.03
5	Honduras	2.88
6	Ghana	2.61
7	Colombia	2.59
8	Cuba	2.50
9	Paraguay	2.33
10	Thailand	2.33
11	Uruguay	2.32
12	Malaysia	2.21
13	South Africa	2.18
14	Lebanon	2.18
15	Hong Kong	2.15

16	El Salvador	2.09
17	Taiwan	2.07
18	Philippines	2.06
19	Brazil	2.05
20	Australia	1.99
21	Iraq	1.95
22	New Zealand	1.91
23	Korea, North	1.87
24	Bulgaria	1.79
25	Canada	1.77
26	Swaziland	1.75
27	Lesotho	1.74
28	Costa Rica	1.73
29	Tunisia	1.72
30	Puerto Rico	1.69
31	Poland	1.68
32	Korea, South	1.68
33	Jamaica	1.59
34	Syria	1.53
35	Morocco	1.53
36	US	1.50
37	Montenegro	1.49
38	Bosnia	1.49
39	Slovenia	1.49
40	Kosovo	1.49
41	Croatia	1.49
42	Serbia	1.49
43	Macedonia	1.49
44	Ethiopia	1.49
45	Eritrea	1.49
46	Netherlands	1.43
47	Peru	1.41
48	Malawi	1.40
49	Zambia	1.40
50	Zimbabwe	1.40
51	Japan	1.40
52	Mexico	1.39
53	Romania	1.37
54	Haiti	1.32
55	Chile	1.32
56	Indonesia	1.21
57	Pakistan	1.21
58	Tajikistan	1.19
59	Estonia	1.19
60	Azerbaijan	1.19
61	Latvia	1.19
62	Uzbekistan	1.19
63	Kyrgyzstan	1.19
64	Belarus	1.19
65	Lithuania	1.19
66	Russia	1.19
67	Ukraine	1.19
68	Kazakhstan	1.19
69	Georgia	1.19
70	Moldova	1.19
71	Armenia	1.19

72	Turkmenistan	1.19
73	Algeria	1.18
74	Portugal	1.18
75	Iran	1.17
76	Bolivia	1.16
77	Nepal	1.16
78	Egypt	1.11
79	Botswana	1.09
80	Namibia	1.09
81	Cyprus	1.07
82	Greece	1.07
83	Guatemala	1.04
84	Burma	1.03
85	Cambodia	1.02
86	Yemen	1.02
87	Spain	0.99
88	Finland	0.99
89	Afghanistan	0.96
90	Venezuela	0.95
91	India	0.95
92	Vietnam	0.94
93	Denmark	0.91
94	Bahrain	0.89
95	UAE	0.89
96	Kuwait	0.89
97	Qatar	0.89
98	Italy	0.88
99	Sri Lanka	0.86
100	Hungary	0.85
101	Mozambique	0.84
102	Ecuador	0.83
103	Jordan	0.83
104	Sierra Leone	0.80
105	Guinea	0.80
106	Guinea-Bissau	0.80
107	Bangladesh	0.76
108	Slovakia	0.75
109	Czechia	0.75
110	Madagascar	0.71
111	Norway	0.70
112	Belgium	0.69
113	Germany	0.68
114	Nicaragua	0.68
115	Burundi	0.65
116	Turkey	0.65
117	Somalia	0.63
118	France	0.62
119	Albania	0.53
120	UK	0.49
121	Saudi Arabia	0.49
122	Sweden	0.44
123	Panama	0.43
124	Libya	0.41
125	Switzerland	0.41
126	Austria	0.35
127	China	0.35

128	Sudan	0.34
129	Laos	0.25
130	Trinidad/Tobago	0.25
131	Mongolia	0.08
132	Oman	0.07
133	Ireland	-0.61

Source: Calculated as (POP1929/POP1920)**(1/9)-1

TABLE 4.13 - POPULATION GROWTH RATES YEARS 1929-1938		
OBS	COUNTRY	GRPOP
1	Hong Kong	7.29
2	Israel	3.30
3	Dominican Rep	3.10
4	Panama	2.64
5	Taiwan	2.63
6	Ghana	2.61
7	Thailand	2.44
8	Philippines	2.38
9	Singapore	2.37
10	Paraguay	2.36
11	Ecuador	2.25
12	South Africa	2.18
13	Lebanon	2.18
14	Malaysia	2.11
15	Costa Rica	2.08
16	Guatemala	2.08
17	Brazil	2.05
18	Iraq	1.95
19	Puerto Rico	1.91
20	Argentina	1.89
21	Cuba	1.89
22	Honduras	1.88
23	Korea, North	1.87
24	Jamaica	1.86
25	Pakistan	1.77
26	Lesotho	1.74
27	Swaziland	1.74
28	Mexico	1.74
29	Tunisia	1.72
30	Bangladesh	1.66
31	Uruguay	1.65
32	Turkey	1.64
33	Peru	1.57
34	Trinidad/Tobago	1.57
35	Nicaragua	1.54
36	Syria	1.53
37	Morocco	1.53
38	Eritrea	1.49
39	Ethiopia	1.49
40	Chile	1.48
41	Algeria	1.46
42	Indonesia	1.45

43	Japan	1.43
44	Zambia	1.40
45	Malawi	1.40
46	Zimbabwe	1.40
47	Slovenia	1.40
48	Macedonia	1.40
49	Croatia	1.40
50	Serbia	1.40
51	Bosnia	1.40
52	Montenegro	1.40
53	Kosovo	1.40
54	El Salvador	1.34
55	Greece	1.32
56	Cyprus	1.32
57	Burma	1.31
58	Haiti	1.29
59	India	1.28
60	Korea, South	1.28
61	Romania	1.25
62	Portugal	1.24
63	Netherlands	1.23
64	Egypt	1.23
65	Poland	1.22
66	Colombia	1.19
67	Venezuela	1.18
68	Canada	1.18
69	Iran	1.17
70	Nepal	1.16
71	Bolivia	1.16
72	Bulgaria	1.10
73	Namibia	1.09
74	Botswana	1.09
75	Armenia	1.02
76	Moldova	1.02
77	Turkmenistan	1.02
78	Lithuania	1.02
79	Tajikistan	1.02
80	Kazakhstan	1.02
81	Azerbaijan	1.02
82	Belarus	1.02
83	Ukraine	1.02
84	Russia	1.02
85	Uzbekistan	1.02
86	Georgia	1.02
87	Kyrgyzstan	1.02
88	Latvia	1.02
89	Estonia	1.02
90	Cambodia	1.02
91	Yemen	1.02
92	New Zealand	0.97
93	Afghanistan	0.96
94	Spain	0.95
95	Vietnam	0.94
96	UAE	0.89
97	Qatar	0.89
98	Bahrain	0.89

99	Kuwait	0.89
100	Australia	0.85
101	Mozambique	0.84
102	Jordan	0.83
103	Guinea	0.80
104	Guinea-Bissau	0.80
105	Sierra Leone	0.80
106	Denmark	0.79
107	Italy	0.78
108	Hungary	0.73
109	Finland	0.73
110	US	0.73
111	Sri Lanka	0.72
112	Madagascar	0.71
113	Albania	0.70
114	Burundi	0.65
115	Germany	0.64
116	Somalia	0.63
117	China	0.58
118	Czechia	0.56
119	Slovakia	0.56
120	Norway	0.55
121	Saudi Arabia	0.49
122	Belgium	0.46
123	Switzerland	0.46
124	UK	0.44
125	Libya	0.41
126	Sudan	0.34
127	Sweden	0.33
128	Laos	0.25
129	France	0.20
130	Austria	0.15
131	Mongolia	0.08
132	Oman	0.07
133	Ireland	0.00

Source: Calculated as (POP1938/POP1929)**(1/9)-1

TABLE 4.14 - POPULATION GROWTH RATES YEARS 1938-1950		
OBS	COUNTRY	GRPOP
1	Nicaragua	4.32
2	Hong Kong	3.51
3	Pakistan	3.30
4	Dominican Rep	3.29
5	Costa Rica	3.21
6	Trinidad/Tobago	3.20
7	Israel	3.11
8	Colombia	3.11
9	Singapore	3.08
10	Ecuador	3.07
11	Mexico	2.89
12	Guatemala	2.89
13	Paraguay	2.77
14	Venezuela	2.74

15	Thailand	2.69
16	Brazil	2.64
17	Ghana	2.61
18	Panama	2.49
19	Taiwan	2.48
20	Cuba	2.45
21	Honduras	2.22
22	South Africa	2.18
23	Lebanon	2.18
24	Iraq	1.95
25	Egypt	1.92
26	Philippines	1.91
27	Peru	1.89
28	Korea, North	1.87
29	Argentina	1.87
30	Sri Lanka	1.86
31	Turkey	1.82
32	Chile	1.79
33	Lesotho	1.74
34	Swaziland	1.74
35	Tunisia	1.72
36	El Salvador	1.72
37	Korea, South	1.71
38	Puerto Rico	1.71
39	Burma	1.58
40	Jamaica	1.58
41	Haiti	1.54
42	Syria	1.53
43	Canada	1.53
44	Morocco	1.53
45	India	1.50
46	Algeria	1.49
47	Ethiopia	1.49
48	Eritrea	1.49
49	Australia	1.46
50	New Zealand	1.46
51	Zimbabwe	1.40
52	Malawi	1.40
53	Zambia	1.40
54	Libya	1.38
55	Malaysia	1.34
56	Kyrgyzstan	1.33
57	Albania	1.30
58	Indonesia	1.30
59	US	1.30
60	Japan	1.27
61	Netherlands	1.26
62	Iran	1.17
63	Nepal	1.16
64	Uruguay	1.15
65	Bangladesh	1.12
66	Botswana	1.09
67	Namibia	1.09
68	Denmark	1.03
69	Cambodia	1.02
70	Yemen	1.02

71	Portugal	1.01
72	Afghanistan	0.96
73	Kazakhstan	0.96
74	Switzerland	0.95
75	Vietnam	0.94
76	Sweden	0.90
77	Norway	0.89
78	Kuwait	0.89
79	Bahrain	0.89
80	UAE	0.89
81	Qatar	0.89
82	Mozambique	0.84
83	Bulgaria	0.83
84	Jordan	0.83
85	Spain	0.82
86	Guinea-Bissau	0.80
87	Sierra Leone	0.80
88	Guinea	0.80
89	Finland	0.77
90	China	0.77
91	Madagascar	0.71
92	Italy	0.68
93	Burundi	0.65
94	Somalia	0.63
95	Cyprus	0.58
96	Greece	0.58
97	Estonia	0.57
98	Latvia	0.52
99	Saudi Arabia	0.49
100	UK	0.48
101	Armenia	0.46
102	Romania	0.37
103	Sudan	0.34
104	Tajikistan	0.28
105	Bolivia	0.27
106	Belgium	0.26
107	Laos	0.25
108	Austria	0.22
109	Hungary	0.15
110	Montenegro	0.11
111	Macedonia	0.11
112	Kosovo	0.11
113	Croatia	0.11
114	Serbia	0.11
115	Bosnia	0.11
116	Slovenia	0.11
117	Ireland	0.09
118	Mongolia	0.08
119	Oman	0.07
120	Georgia	0.04
121	Germany	-0.02
122	France	-0.04
123	Uzbekistan	-0.06
124	Moldova	-0.20
125	Russia	-0.40
126	Turkmenistan	-0.41

127	Ukraine	-0.70
128	Azerbaijan	-0.81
129	Lithuania	-0.89
130	Belarus	-1.05
131	Czechia	-1.36
132	Slovakia	-1.36
133	Poland	-1.85

Source: Calculated as (POP1950/POP1938)**(1/12)-1

TABLE 4.15 - POPULATION GROWTH RATES YEARS 1950-1960		
OBS	COUNTRY	GRPOP
1	W Sahara	8.95
2	Kuwait	7.25
3	Jordan	6.62
4	Brunei	6.31
5	Qatar	6.05
6	Israel	5.33
7	Singapore	4.88
8	Venezuela	4.20
9	N Mariana Is	4.14
10	Kazakhstan	4.08
11	Mayotte	3.93
12	Costa Rica	3.67
13	UAE	3.65
14	Ivory Coast	3.57
15	Micronesia	3.47
16	Zimbabwe	3.47
17	Taiwan	3.42
18	Bahamas	3.37
19	Greenland	3.36
20	Reunion	3.31
21	Niger	3.29
22	Mauritius	3.29
23	Guatemala	3.28
24	Armenia	3.26
25	Hong Kong	3.23
26	Dominican Rep	3.22
27	Iraq	3.22
28	Mexico	3.16
29	Honduras	3.15
30	Marshall Is	3.15
31	Fiji	3.15
32	Nicaragua	3.14
33	Tajikistan	3.12
34	Uzbekistan	3.09
35	Fr Polynesia	3.08
36	Bahrain	3.08
37	Philippines	3.07
38	Suriname	3.04
39	Brazil	3.03
40	Azerbaijan	3.01
41	Guyana	3.01

42	Cape Verde	2.99
43	Thailand	2.98
44	Samoa, W	2.98
45	Colombia	2.97
46	Turkey	2.94
47	Rwanda	2.93
48	Andorra	2.92
49	Bhutan	2.92
50	Cayman Is	2.92
51	Nauru	2.92
52	Vanuatu	2.92
53	Kenya	2.91
54	Malaysia	2.91
55	Korea, South	2.86
56	Albania	2.86
57	Belize	2.84
58	El Salvador	2.83
59	Turkmenistan	2.79
60	Sudan	2.78
61	Uganda	2.78
62	Ghana	2.77
63	Tokelau	2.75
64	Sri Lanka	2.75
65	Niue	2.75
66	Solomon Is	2.75
67	Wallis & Futuna	2.75
68	Cook Is	2.74
69	Libya	2.74
70	Ecuador	2.74
71	Panama	2.73
72	Lebanon	2.72
73	Canada	2.69
74	Laos	2.68
75	Peru	2.67
76	Djibouti	2.66
77	Tonga	2.66
78	Morocco	2.65
79	Syria	2.63
80	Paraguay	2.62
81	Swaziland	2.60
82	Tanzania	2.60
83	Mauritania	2.57
84	Cambodia	2.57
85	Palau	2.54
86	Iran	2.53
87	Moldova	2.53
88	Botswana	2.49
89	Guadeloupe	2.49
90	Pakistan	2.48
91	Liberia	2.47
92	Egypt	2.46
93	Zambia	2.46
94	Saudi Arabia	2.44
95	South Africa	2.43
96	Martinique	2.42
97	Madagascar	2.41

98	Congo, Dem R	2.40
99	Gaza Strip	2.31
100	Chile	2.31
101	Australia	2.30
102	St Pierre &	2.29
103	Turks & Caicos	2.29
104	Anguilla	2.29
105	Montserrat	2.29
106	Virgin Is, Brit.	2.29
107	Kyrgyzstan	2.25
108	Nigeria	2.23
109	Mongolia	2.23
110	New Zealand	2.22
111	Somalia	2.22
112	Kiribati	2.19
113	Congo, Rep	2.19
114	Trinidad/Tobago	2.17
115	Oman	2.17
116	Comoros	2.15
117	Kosovo	2.14
118	Seychelles	2.14
119	Namibia	2.13
120	Bolivia	2.13
121	Algeria	2.12
122	Senegal	2.11
123	Iceland	2.10
124	Vietnam	2.09
125	Yemen	2.09
126	Benin	2.08
127	Malawi	2.05
128	Gambia	2.05
129	Guiana, Fr	2.03
130	Mali	2.00
131	Neth Antilles	1.96
132	St Vincent	1.92
133	Cuba	1.89
134	Indonesia	1.89
135	India	1.88
136	Argentina	1.86
137	Haiti	1.85
138	New Caledonia	1.84
139	Ethiopia	1.82
140	Slovakia	1.81
141	Bangladesh	1.81
142	Antigua & Barbuda	1.80
143	Mozambique	1.80
144	Bosnia	1.80
145	Burundi	1.77
146	Poland	1.76
147	Guinea	1.76
148	US	1.72
149	Virgin I, US	1.71
150	Grenada	1.71
151	Togo	1.69
152	Afghanistan	1.67
153	Tunisia	1.67

154	Georgia	1.66
155	Dominica	1.64
156	Montenegro	1.64
157	Russia	1.61
158	Burma	1.60
159	Monaco	1.55
160	Chad	1.55
161	Nepal	1.54
162	Angola	1.54
163	Maldives	1.54
164	Central African Rep.	1.53
165	Jamaica	1.50
166	Sierra Leone	1.50
167	Cyprus	1.49
168	Lesotho	1.49
169	Ukraine	1.49
170	East Timor	1.47
171	Papua New Gu	1.47
172	China	1.47
173	San Marino	1.44
174	Eritrea	1.42
175	Cameroon	1.39
176	Liechtenstein	1.34
177	Switzerland	1.34
178	Netherlands	1.31
179	Uruguay	1.26
180	Macedonia	1.24
181	Faeroe Is	1.22
182	Romania	1.22
183	Bermuda	1.21
184	Serbia	1.20
185	Japan	1.19
186	Korea, North	1.18
187	Equatorial G	1.17
188	Aruba	1.12
189	Guam	1.11
190	Burkina Faso	1.07
191	Jersey	1.01
192	Finland	1.00
193	Estonia	1.00
194	Greece	0.96
195	Norway	0.93
196	Barbados	0.91
197	France	0.91
198	Latvia	0.85
199	Spain	0.84
200	Bulgaria	0.82
201	St Lucia	0.81
202	Lithuania	0.80
203	Slovenia	0.74
204	Guinea-Bissau	0.74
205	Denmark	0.70
206	Portugal	0.68
207	Hungary	0.67
208	Czechia	0.67
209	San Tome & Principe	0.65

210	Sweden	0.65
211	Italy	0.64
212	Puerto Rico	0.61
213	Germany	0.61
214	Luxembourg	0.59
215	Belgium	0.58
216	Belarus	0.56
217	Malta	0.53
218	Samoa, Ameri	0.51
219	Croatia	0.51
220	Gibraltar	0.43
221	West Bank	0.42
222	UK	0.41
223	St Kitts & Nevis	0.40
224	Gabon	0.36
225	Guernsey	0.22
226	Austria	0.16
227	Falkland Is	0.00
228	St Helena	0.00
229	Tuvalu	0.00
230	Ireland	-0.46
231	Macao	-0.97
232	Isle of Man	-1.15

Source: Calculated as (POP1960/POP1950)**(1/10)-1

TABLE 4.16 - POPULATION GROWTH RATES YEARS 1960-1970		
OBS	COUNTRY	GRPOP
1	Kuwait	9.86
2	Andorra	9.60
3	Qatar	9.45
4	UAE	9.23
5	W Sahara	8.84
6	Djibouti	7.31
7	Virgin I, US	7.01
8	Jordan	6.12
9	Nauru	5.76
10	Bahamas	4.45
11	Brunei	4.43
12	Ivory Coast	4.09
13	Guiana, Fr	4.03
14	Libya	3.99
15	Marshall Is	3.90
16	Greenland	3.70
17	Venezuela	3.60
18	Costa Rica	3.59
19	Honduras	3.53
20	Tajikistan	3.52
21	Saudi Arabia	3.49
22	Bahrain	3.49
23	Macao	3.45
24	Mayotte	3.42
25	Israel	3.42
26	Uzbekistan	3.41

27	El Salvador	3.39
28	Fr Polynesia	3.37
29	Niger	3.28
30	Syria	3.28
31	Iraq	3.27
32	Kenya	3.26
33	Turkmenistan	3.24
34	Zimbabwe	3.24
35	Mexico	3.23
36	Dominican Rep	3.19
37	Taiwan	3.18
38	Solomon Is	3.16
39	Kyrgyzstan	3.15
40	Cape Verde	3.14
41	Togo	3.12
42	Nicaragua	3.11
43	Micronesia	3.09
44	Philippines	3.05
45	Samoa, Ameri	3.05
46	Armenia	3.04
47	Thailand	3.02
48	New Caledonia	3.02
49	Tanzania	3.01
50	Ecuador	3.01
51	Vanuatu	3.00
52	Uganda	2.98
53	Mongolia	2.97
54	Gambia	2.96
55	Panama	2.95
56	Eritrea	2.95
57	Colombia	2.94
58	Belize	2.92
59	N Mariana Is	2.92
60	Palau	2.92
61	Malaysia	2.92
62	Congo, Dem R	2.92
63	Azerbaijan	2.90
64	Bhutan	2.90
65	Peru	2.88
66	Iran	2.87
67	Albania	2.86
68	Reunion	2.83
69	Oman	2.83
70	Senegal	2.82
71	Fiji	2.81
72	Brazil	2.81
73	Congo, Rep	2.81
74	Liberia	2.80
75	Botswana	2.80
76	Morocco	2.79
77	Kazakhstan	2.76
78	Liechtenstein	2.76
79	Niue	2.75
80	Wallis & Futuna	2.75
81	Cook Is	2.75
82	Tokelau	2.74

83	Rwanda	2.72
84	Zambia	2.71
85	Malawi	2.71
86	Pakistan	2.69
87	Paraguay	2.68
88	South Africa	2.68
89	Sudan	2.67
90	Korea, North	2.67
91	Lebanon	2.61
92	Kosovo	2.60
93	Samoa, W	2.59
94	Madagascar	2.58
95	Comoros	2.58
96	Mauritania	2.57
97	Korea, South	2.57
98	Namibia	2.57
99	Hong Kong	2.56
100	Swaziland	2.55
101	Seychelles	2.54
102	Laos	2.54
103	Guatemala	2.53
104	Cambodia	2.53
105	Suriname	2.52
106	Egypt	2.48
107	Somalia	2.48
108	Benin	2.46
109	Vietnam	2.46
110	Algeria	2.44
111	Nigeria	2.41
112	Guam	2.41
113	Turkey	2.40
114	San Marino	2.39
115	Sri Lanka	2.37
116	Ghana	2.36
117	China	2.35
118	Singapore	2.34
119	Bolivia	2.31
120	Indonesia	2.31
121	Virgin Is, Brit.	2.29
122	Montserrat	2.29
123	Anguilla	2.29
124	Turks & Caicos	2.29
125	St Pierre &	2.29
126	Mauritius	2.28
127	Chile	2.27
128	Burundi	2.27
129	Cayman Is	2.26
130	Maldives	2.26
131	Guyana	2.22
132	Mozambique	2.22
133	India	2.20
134	Bangladesh	2.12
135	Mali	2.12
136	Afghanistan	2.10
137	Tonga	2.10
138	Tunisia	2.08

139	Papua New Gu	2.07
140	Chad	2.06
141	Guinea	2.05
142	Central African Rep.	2.03
143	Cuba	2.01
144	Ethiopia	2.00
145	Haiti	1.99
146	Australia	1.98
147	Lesotho	1.96
148	Canada	1.95
149	Yemen	1.91
150	Nepal	1.90
151	East Timor	1.89
152	Bermuda	1.88
153	Gaza Strip	1.85
154	Antigua & Barbuda	1.84
155	Tuvalu	1.84
156	Burma	1.83
157	Cameroon	1.83
158	Neth Antilles	1.83
159	Moldova	1.81
160	Sierra Leone	1.80
161	Kiribati	1.80
162	New Zealand	1.72
163	Angola	1.57
164	Dominica	1.55
165	Guadeloupe	1.54
166	Argentina	1.52
167	Iceland	1.49
168	Equatorial G	1.47
169	San Tome & Principe	1.46
170	St Lucia	1.46
171	Puerto Rico	1.45
172	Switzerland	1.44
173	Martinique	1.43
174	Jamaica	1.38
175	Monaco	1.34
176	Trinidad/Tobago	1.29
177	Lithuania	1.27
178	US	1.27
179	Guernsey	1.26
180	Netherlands	1.25
181	Georgia	1.25
182	Jersey	1.20
183	Macedonia	1.20
184	Estonia	1.17
185	Bosnia	1.15
186	Spain	1.09
187	Faeroe Is	1.09
188	Montenegro	1.08
189	Latvia	1.07
190	France	1.06
191	St Vincent	1.06
192	Japan	1.04
193	Uruguay	1.02
194	Ukraine	1.01

195	Belarus	0.99
196	Poland	0.96
197	Romania	0.96
198	Slovenia	0.89
199	Slovakia	0.89
200	Burkina Faso	0.87
201	Russia	0.85
202	Gabon	0.85
203	Gibraltar	0.80
204	Norway	0.80
205	Serbia	0.79
206	Luxembourg	0.77
207	Bulgaria	0.77
208	Denmark	0.73
209	Sweden	0.73
210	Cyprus	0.71
211	Italy	0.70
212	Aruba	0.68
213	Germany	0.67
214	UK	0.61
215	Isle of Man	0.60
216	Austria	0.58
217	Belgium	0.57
218	Greece	0.55
219	Grenada	0.54
220	Ireland	0.42
221	Croatia	0.41
222	Finland	0.39
223	Hungary	0.35
224	Barbados	0.34
225	Czechia	0.28
226	Guinea-Bissau	0.05
227	Portugal	0.01
228	Falkland Is	0.00
229	St Helena	0.00
230	Malta	-0.09
231	St Kitts & Nevis	-1.03
232	West Bank	-2.77

Source: Calculated as $(POP1970/POP1960)**(1/10)-1$

TABLE 4.17 - POPULATION GROWTH RATES YEARS 1970-1980		
OBS	COUNTRY	GRPOP
1	UAE	14.92
2	Qatar	7.51
3	W Sahara	6.90
4	Kuwait	6.15
5	Somalia	6.06
6	Djibouti	5.85
7	Andorra	5.45
8	Cayman Is	5.45
9	Saudi Arabia	4.96
10	Bahrain	4.75
11	Oman	4.74

12	Ivory Coast	4.62
13	Virgin I, US	4.52
14	Libya	4.39
15	Mayotte	4.04
16	Kenya	3.80
17	Brunei	3.75
18	Solomon Is	3.59
19	Botswana	3.57
20	Bhutan	3.56
21	N Mariana Is	3.54
22	Comoros	3.53
23	Marshall Is	3.49
24	Syria	3.44
25	Iraq	3.38
26	Gambia	3.36
27	Malawi	3.34
28	Guiana, Fr	3.33
29	Sudan	3.29
30	Rwanda	3.25
31	Venezuela	3.22
32	Niger	3.21
33	Jordan	3.21
34	Algeria	3.19
35	Iran	3.16
36	Congo, Dem R	3.14
37	Congo, Rep	3.14
38	New Caledonia	3.14
39	Vanuatu	3.13
40	Nicaragua	3.12
41	Swaziland	3.08
42	Tanzania	3.06
43	Maldives	3.03
44	Liberia	3.02
45	Tajikistan	3.00
46	Zambia	2.97
47	Senegal	2.95
48	Ecuador	2.92
49	Tuvalu	2.92
50	Mongolia	2.91
51	Mexico	2.91
52	Uzbekistan	2.91
53	Nigeria	2.83
54	Turkmenistan	2.80
55	Philippines	2.78
56	Benin	2.77
57	Peru	2.76
58	Costa Rica	2.73
59	Madagascar	2.72
60	Mauritania	2.71
61	Bangladesh	2.71
62	Israel	2.70
63	Cameroon	2.68
64	Togo	2.68
65	Mozambique	2.66
66	Zimbabwe	2.66
67	Pakistan	2.63

68	Panama	2.61
69	Fr Polynesia	2.58
70	Gabon	2.57
71	Dominican Rep	2.56
72	Paraguay	2.56
73	Yemen	2.55
74	Namibia	2.55
75	South Africa	2.55
76	Hong Kong	2.49
77	Morocco	2.48
78	El Salvador	2.46
79	Kosovo	2.46
80	Uganda	2.45
81	Guinea-Bissau	2.44
82	Tokelau	2.44
83	Niue	2.44
84	Wallis & Futuna	2.44
85	Cook Is	2.44
86	Bolivia	2.43
87	San Tome & Principe	2.42
88	Malaysia	2.40
89	Tunisia	2.37
90	Guatemala	2.36
91	Colombia	2.34
92	Guam	2.33
93	Thailand	2.31
94	Lesotho	2.29
95	Indonesia	2.29
96	Ghana	2.29
97	Papua New Gu	2.28
98	Albania	2.26
99	Nepal	2.23
100	Central African Rep.	2.21
101	Turkey	2.20
102	Liechtenstein	2.16
103	India	2.15
104	Vietnam	2.14
105	Bahamas	2.14
106	Brazil	2.13
107	Gaza Strip	2.11
108	Honduras	2.11
109	Isle of Man	2.10
110	Armenia	2.09
111	Kyrgyzstan	2.04
112	Ethiopia	2.03
113	Burundi	2.02
114	Fiji	2.00
115	Mali	2.00
116	Chad	1.99
117	Belize	1.98
118	Egypt	1.98
119	Laos	1.98
120	Korea, North	1.92
121	Taiwan	1.92
122	Haiti	1.90
123	Burma	1.90

124	West Bank	1.89
125	Angola	1.86
126	China	1.84
127	Sierra Leone	1.84
128	Guinea	1.82
129	Micronesia	1.81
130	Azerbaijan	1.78
131	Burkina Faso	1.76
132	Eritrea	1.75
133	Samoa, Ameri	1.71
134	Kiribati	1.70
135	Korea, South	1.69
136	Anguilla	1.68
137	Turks & Caicos	1.68
138	St Pierre &	1.67
139	Montserrat	1.67
140	Virgin Is, Brit.	1.67
141	Puerto Rico	1.66
142	Sri Lanka	1.66
143	Afghanistan	1.65
144	Argentina	1.60
145	Chile	1.56
146	Seychelles	1.55
147	Mauritius	1.54
148	Singapore	1.52
149	Gibraltar	1.44
150	Australia	1.43
151	Ireland	1.42
152	Tonga	1.41
153	Trinidad/Tobago	1.41
154	Macedonia	1.36
155	Nauru	1.34
156	Kazakhstan	1.34
157	Jamaica	1.33
158	Lebanon	1.32
159	St Lucia	1.27
160	Reunion	1.27
161	Canada	1.22
162	Cuba	1.21
163	Monaco	1.18
164	Japan	1.14
165	Iceland	1.12
166	Malta	1.11
167	Moldova	1.10
168	New Zealand	1.09
169	Spain	1.09
170	Montenegro	1.08
171	US	1.06
172	St Vincent	1.06
173	San Marino	1.01
174	Faeroe Is	0.98
175	Slovenia	0.96
176	Slovakia	0.95
177	Bosnia	0.94
178	Greece	0.93
179	Romania	0.92

180	Lithuania	0.91
181	Poland	0.90
182	Samoa, W	0.88
183	Greenland	0.84
184	Netherlands	0.84
185	Estonia	0.83
186	Palau	0.80
187	Cape Verde	0.79
188	Portugal	0.78
189	Georgia	0.75
190	Luxembourg	0.71
191	Guyana	0.71
192	Serbia	0.70
193	Dominica	0.69
194	Jersey	0.68
195	Cyprus	0.68
196	Russia	0.66
197	Neth Antilles	0.66
198	Belarus	0.66
199	Latvia	0.63
200	France	0.60
201	Ukraine	0.56
202	Norway	0.53
203	Czechia	0.52
204	Italy	0.48
205	Antigua & Barbuda	0.45
206	Bulgaria	0.43
207	Croatia	0.42
208	Finland	0.41
209	Barbados	0.41
210	Denmark	0.39
211	Guernsey	0.39
212	Uruguay	0.37
213	Bermuda	0.37
214	Hungary	0.35
215	Sweden	0.33
216	Guadeloupe	0.26
217	Switzerland	0.21
218	Belgium	0.17
219	UK	0.12
220	Austria	0.11
221	Germany	0.07
222	Martinique	0.03
223	Falkland Is	0.00
224	St Helena	0.00
225	Aruba	-0.17
226	Macao	-0.19
227	East Timor	-0.39
228	Suriname	-0.44
229	St Kitts & Nevis	-0.44
230	Grenada	-0.65
231	Cambodia	-0.74
232	Equatorial G	-2.90

Source: Calculated as (POP1980/POP1970)**(1/10)-1

OBS	COUNTRY	GRPOP
\multicolumn{3}{c}{TABLE 4.18 - POPULATION GROWTH RATES YEARS 1980-1990}
1	N Mariana Is	9.98
2	Qatar	7.39
3	UAE	6.21
4	Mayotte	5.52
5	Guiana, Fr	5.49
6	Saudi Arabia	5.00
7	Equatorial G	4.89
8	Kuwait	4.66
9	Andorra	4.54
10	Oman	4.50
11	Ivory Coast	4.36
12	Cayman Is	4.34
13	Malawi	4.30
14	Bahrain	4.18
15	W Sahara	3.95
16	Samoa, Ameri	3.92
17	Jordan	3.87
18	Gambia	3.67
19	Kenya	3.64
20	Namibia	3.62
21	Libya	3.60
22	Togo	3.59
23	Marshall Is	3.56
24	Syria	3.55
25	Zimbabwe	3.54
26	Honduras	3.49
27	Swaziland	3.47
28	Uganda	3.47
29	Rwanda	3.45
30	Zambia	3.42
31	Ghana	3.42
32	Brunei	3.38
33	Maldives	3.33
34	Gaza Strip	3.29
35	West Bank	3.27
36	Iran	3.25
37	Macao	3.24
38	Botswana	3.22
39	Solomon Is	3.21
40	Sudan	3.17
41	Cambodia	3.14
42	Yemen	3.12
43	Senegal	3.11
44	Benin	3.11
45	Cameroon	3.09
46	Niger	3.06
47	Congo, Dem R	3.06
48	Tanzania	3.05
49	Guatemala	3.03
50	Gabon	3.02
51	Congo, Rep	3.00
52	Algeria	3.00

53	Tajikistan	2.98
54	Ethiopia	2.95
55	Nigeria	2.89
56	Paraguay	2.88
57	Madagascar	2.88
58	Chad	2.86
59	Burkina Faso	2.82
60	Guinea	2.80
61	Costa Rica	2.79
62	Malaysia	2.78
63	Micronesia	2.78
64	Iraq	2.77
65	Laos	2.77
66	Djibouti	2.75
67	Venezuela	2.73
68	Fr Polynesia	2.69
69	Comoros	2.63
70	Belize	2.62
71	Mauritania	2.61
72	Bhutan	2.60
73	Central African Rep.	2.59
74	Papua New Gu	2.59
75	Ecuador	2.58
76	Pakistan	2.56
77	Uzbekistan	2.55
78	South Africa	2.54
79	Egypt	2.51
80	Burundi	2.50
81	East Timor	2.45
82	Vanuatu	2.45
83	Philippines	2.44
84	Turkmenistan	2.44
85	Nicaragua	2.43
86	Morocco	2.40
87	Tunisia	2.38
88	Sierra Leone	2.36
89	Turkey	2.36
90	Guinea-Bissau	2.36
91	Singapore	2.36
92	Nepal	2.35
93	Peru	2.31
94	Cook Is	2.30
95	Wallis & Futuna	2.30
96	Niue	2.30
97	Tokelau	2.30
98	Mongolia	2.29
99	Guam	2.28
100	Haiti	2.25
101	Vietnam	2.24
102	Bangladesh	2.24
103	Bolivia	2.22
104	Dominican Rep	2.20
105	Kosovo	2.18
106	Panama	2.15
107	Brazil	2.14
108	Lesotho	2.14

109	Albania	2.10
110	Angola	2.10
111	Colombia	2.09
112	Cape Verde	2.08
113	Kiribati	2.04
114	India	2.04
115	San Tome & Principe	2.04
116	Bahamas	1.96
117	Kyrgyzstan	1.94
118	Mexico	1.94
119	Indonesia	1.92
120	Mali	1.81
121	New Caledonia	1.80
122	Israel	1.79
123	Burma	1.73
124	Reunion	1.72
125	Chile	1.66
126	Australia	1.66
127	St Lucia	1.58
128	Korea, North	1.57
129	Azerbaijan	1.56
130	Eritrea	1.55
131	China	1.55
132	Thailand	1.49
133	Argentina	1.49
134	Palau	1.44
135	Guernsey	1.42
136	St Pierre &	1.41
137	Virgin Is, Brit.	1.41
138	Anguilla	1.41
139	Montserrat	1.41
140	Turks & Caicos	1.41
141	Taiwan	1.40
142	Armenia	1.36
143	Liberia	1.35
144	Fiji	1.34
145	Trinidad/Tobago	1.33
146	Cyprus	1.33
147	Canada	1.23
148	Suriname	1.22
149	Nauru	1.18
150	Tuvalu	1.18
151	Korea, South	1.18
152	Hong Kong	1.17
153	Greenland	1.14
154	Iceland	1.13
155	Guadeloupe	1.11
156	Faeroe Is	1.11
157	Liechtenstein	1.10
158	El Salvador	1.09
159	Monaco	1.06
160	Seychelles	1.06
161	Jamaica	1.05
162	Jersey	1.01
163	Martinique	1.00
164	Sri Lanka	0.99

165	Puerto Rico	0.97
166	Bosnia	0.96
167	New Zealand	0.94
168	US	0.93
169	Mauritius	0.92
170	Kazakhstan	0.92
171	San Marino	0.91
172	Moldova	0.91
173	St Vincent	0.87
174	Barbados	0.85
175	Switzerland	0.79
176	Neth Antilles	0.78
177	Latvia	0.77
178	Cuba	0.77
179	Isle of Man	0.76
180	Lithuania	0.74
181	Bermuda	0.70
182	Georgia	0.70
183	Poland	0.67
184	Lebanon	0.66
185	Grenada	0.65
186	Uruguay	0.64
187	Russia	0.62
188	Macedonia	0.62
189	Estonia	0.61
190	Japan	0.56
191	Netherlands	0.55
192	Slovakia	0.55
193	Belarus	0.54
194	Greece	0.52
195	France	0.51
196	Slovenia	0.50
197	Aruba	0.49
198	Luxembourg	0.48
199	Mozambique	0.46
200	Romania	0.44
201	Tonga	0.43
202	Virgin I, US	0.40
203	Finland	0.38
204	Samoa, W	0.38
205	Norway	0.37
206	Ukraine	0.37
207	Somalia	0.35
208	Ireland	0.33
209	Gibraltar	0.33
210	Spain	0.30
211	Sweden	0.30
212	Croatia	0.28
213	Serbia	0.21
214	Montenegro	0.21
215	Austria	0.17
216	UK	0.16
217	Portugal	0.15
218	Germany	0.14
219	Belgium	0.11
220	Italy	0.05

221	Czechia	0.04
222	Denmark	0.03
223	Falkland Is	0.00
224	St Helena	0.00
225	Malta	-0.11
226	Bulgaria	-0.16
227	Dominica	-0.27
228	Hungary	-0.32
229	Guyana	-0.40
230	St Kitts & Nevis	-0.70
231	Antigua & Barbuda	-0.91
232	Afghanistan	-0.96

Source: Calculated as (POP1990/POP1980)**(1/10)-1

TABLE 4.19 - POPULATION GROWTH RATES YEARS 1990-2000

OBS	COUNTRY	GRPOP
1	West Bank	8.10
2	Gaza Strip	6.09
3	Turks & Caicos	6.01
4	UAE	5.83
5	Anguilla	5.54
6	Mayotte	5.15
7	Afghanistan	5.06
8	Virgin Is, Brit.	4.81
9	N Mariana Is	4.75
10	Cayman Is	4.40
11	Jordan	3.96
12	Eritrea	3.82
13	Aruba	3.75
14	Gambia	3.70
15	Liberia	3.69
16	Mozambique	3.65
17	W Sahara	3.61
18	Guiana, Fr	3.59
19	Niger	3.58
20	Falkland Is	3.52
21	Yemen	3.49
22	Chad	3.28
23	Benin	3.23
24	Uganda	3.22
25	Togo	3.15
26	Guinea	3.12
27	Burkina Faso	3.10
28	Iraq	3.07
29	Saudi Arabia	3.03
30	Madagascar	3.01
31	Ethiopia	2.99
32	Tanzania	2.95
33	Congo, Dem R	2.94
34	Ivory Coast	2.92
35	Namibia	2.86
36	Honduras	2.85
37	Belize	2.84

38	Congo, Rep	2.83
39	Singapore	2.83
40	Israel	2.83
41	Solomon Is	2.83
42	Qatar	2.82
43	Mauritania	2.81
44	Senegal	2.79
45	Sudan	2.76
46	Cambodia	2.73
47	Kenya	2.71
48	Oman	2.68
49	Papua New Gu	2.68
50	Nigeria	2.64
51	Syria	2.62
52	Cameroon	2.59
53	Gabon	2.56
54	Malaysia	2.54
55	Central African Rep.	2.54
56	Guinea-Bissau	2.52
57	Laos	2.51
58	Ghana	2.50
59	Costa Rica	2.50
60	Zambia	2.49
61	Nepal	2.48
62	Vanuatu	2.46
63	Pakistan	2.45
64	Equatorial G	2.43
65	Lebanon	2.41
66	Palau	2.39
67	Botswana	2.38
68	Maldives	2.34
69	Paraguay	2.33
70	Brunei	2.30
71	Angola	2.26
72	Bahrain	2.26
73	Bolivia	2.23
74	New Caledonia	2.22
75	Andorra	2.22
76	Comoros	2.21
77	Philippines	2.21
78	Mali	2.20
79	Guatemala	2.14
80	Turkmenistan	2.14
81	Samoa, Ameri	2.13
82	Nicaragua	2.12
83	Egypt	2.07
84	Cape Verde	2.05
85	Macao	2.05
86	Panama	2.04
87	Swaziland	2.03
88	Venezuela	1.97
89	El Salvador	1.94
90	Malawi	1.94
91	Algeria	1.90
92	Cyprus	1.89
93	Haiti	1.89

94	Uzbekistan	1.88
95	Reunion	1.87
96	Burundi	1.86
97	Turkey	1.86
98	Ecuador	1.82
99	India	1.82
100	Vietnam	1.80
101	Fr Polynesia	1.78
102	Antigua & Barbuda	1.76
103	South Africa	1.74
104	Bahamas	1.74
105	Dominican Rep	1.73
106	Mexico	1.73
107	Kiribati	1.70
108	Marshall Is	1.68
109	Peru	1.66
110	Lesotho	1.65
111	Djibouti	1.65
112	Iran	1.64
113	Libya	1.62
114	San Marino	1.62
115	San Tome & Principe	1.62
116	Tunisia	1.61
117	Hong Kong	1.60
118	Brazil	1.57
119	Chile	1.57
120	Bangladesh	1.54
121	Tajikistan	1.53
122	Morocco	1.51
123	Indonesia	1.48
124	Zimbabwe	1.47
125	Seychelles	1.47
126	Guam	1.47
127	Suriname	1.47
128	Colombia	1.39
129	Mongolia	1.37
130	Luxembourg	1.33
131	Korea, North	1.31
132	Liechtenstein	1.30
133	Sri Lanka	1.28
134	Argentina	1.25
135	US	1.24
136	St Lucia	1.23
137	Burma	1.22
138	Kyrgyzstan	1.19
139	Australia	1.16
140	Cook Is	1.16
141	Rwanda	1.15
142	Mauritius	1.15
143	Thailand	1.12
144	New Zealand	1.10
145	Micronesia	1.09
146	Nauru	1.06
147	Canada	1.03
148	Fiji	1.03
149	East Timor	1.02

150	Sierra Leone	1.01
151	China	1.00
152	Iceland	0.98
153	Isle of Man	0.97
154	Guadeloupe	0.97
155	Korea, South	0.93
156	Taiwan	0.90
157	Jamaica	0.89
158	St Pierre &	0.86
159	Samoa, W	0.84
160	Azerbaijan	0.82
161	St Helena	0.80
162	Malta	0.80
163	Ireland	0.79
164	Puerto Rico	0.76
165	Greece	0.72
166	St Kitts & Nevis	0.71
167	Martinique	0.67
168	Virgin I, US	0.67
169	Uruguay	0.66
170	Bermuda	0.66
171	Monaco	0.65
172	Netherlands	0.63
173	Macedonia	0.62
174	Grenada	0.61
175	Norway	0.57
176	Barbados	0.54
177	Switzerland	0.54
178	Cuba	0.50
179	Somalia	0.49
180	Niue	0.46
181	Kuwait	0.44
182	Austria	0.43
183	France	0.40
184	Denmark	0.38
185	Finland	0.37
186	Spain	0.37
187	Sweden	0.36
188	Germany	0.35
189	Jersey	0.35
190	Montenegro	0.35
191	Portugal	0.31
192	Tonga	0.31
193	UK	0.28
194	Belgium	0.28
195	Slovakia	0.27
196	St Vincent	0.27
197	Japan	0.27
198	Wallis & Futuna	0.25
199	Trinidad/Tobago	0.22
200	Bhutan	0.22
201	Guernsey	0.16
202	Italy	0.16
203	Kosovo	0.10
204	Poland	0.06
205	Guyana	0.04

206	Greenland	0.00
207	Tuvalu	0.00
208	Slovenia	-0.04
209	Russia	-0.09
210	Czechia	-0.09
211	Croatia	-0.12
212	Dominica	-0.14
213	Hungary	-0.16
214	Belarus	-0.18
215	Serbia	-0.22
216	Faeroe Is	-0.42
217	Neth Antilles	-0.49
218	Romania	-0.50
219	Gibraltar	-0.50
220	Ukraine	-0.54
221	Lithuania	-0.55
222	Moldova	-0.57
223	Albania	-0.65
224	Bulgaria	-0.89
225	Kazakhstan	-0.96
226	Bosnia	-1.30
227	Latvia	-1.33
228	Estonia	-1.35
229	Armenia	-1.39
230	Tokelau	-1.52
231	Georgia	-1.55
232	Montserrat	-6.44

Source: Calculated as (POP2000/POP1990)**(1/10)-1

TABLE 4.20 - POPULATION GROWTH RATES YEARS 2000-2007		
OBS	COUNTRY	GRPOP
1	W Sahara	6.20
2	Montserrat	6.00
3	Kuwait	5.69
4	East Timor	5.03
5	Cayman Is	4.98
6	UAE	4.71
7	Qatar	4.52
8	Mayotte	4.04
9	Gaza Strip	4.01
10	Afghanistan	3.92
11	Sierra Leone	3.79
12	Niger	3.58
13	Guiana, Fr	3.58
14	Yemen	3.48
15	West Bank	3.46
16	Burundi	3.44
17	Burkina Faso	3.44
18	Uganda	3.40
19	Benin	3.32
20	Andorra	3.26
21	Turks & Caicos	3.15
22	Libya	3.09
23	Congo, Dem R	3.07

24	Gambia	3.06
25	Jordan	3.05
26	Somalia	3.04
27	Chad	3.02
28	Belize	2.93
29	Macao	2.91
30	Liberia	2.89
31	Togo	2.87
32	Mauritania	2.85
33	Madagascar	2.83
34	Brunei	2.80
35	Senegal	2.78
36	Kenya	2.76
37	N Mariana Is	2.73
38	Virgin Is, Brit.	2.65
39	Mali	2.56
40	Solomon Is	2.55
41	Bahrain	2.53
42	Vanuatu	2.51
43	Rwanda	2.51
44	Ethiopia	2.43
45	Syria	2.43
46	Saudi Arabia	2.42
47	Angola	2.42
48	Honduras	2.38
49	Bhutan	2.36
50	Cameroon	2.36
51	Malawi	2.35
52	Papua New Gu	2.35
53	Congo, Rep	2.35
54	Nigeria	2.34
55	San Tome & Principe	2.27
56	Tanzania	2.25
57	Comoros	2.23
58	Ghana	2.17
59	Anguilla	2.13
60	Iraq	2.11
61	Cyprus	2.09
62	Nepal	2.08
63	Philippines	2.07
64	Aruba	2.07
65	Mozambique	2.06
66	Guinea-Bissau	2.04
67	Sudan	2.04
68	Djibouti	2.03
69	Egypt	2.01
70	Guatemala	1.99
71	St Kitts & Nevis	1.96
72	Paraguay	1.96
73	Antigua & Barbuda	1.96
74	Costa Rica	1.96
75	Bolivia	1.96
76	Guinea	1.92
77	Malaysia	1.91
78	Cape Verde	1.89
79	Ireland	1.88

80	Pakistan	1.87
81	Kiribati	1.85
82	New Caledonia	1.84
83	Cambodia	1.81
84	Panama	1.80
85	Singapore	1.80
86	Israel	1.78
87	Ivory Coast	1.76
88	San Marino	1.76
89	Equatorial G	1.75
90	Turkmenistan	1.73
91	Eritrea	1.71
92	Gabon	1.71
93	Spain	1.70
94	Maldives	1.70
95	India	1.70
96	Zambia	1.69
97	Central African Rep.	1.68
98	Laos	1.65
99	Haiti	1.63
100	Iran	1.61
101	Guam	1.58
102	Dominican Rep	1.55
103	Fr Polynesia	1.51
104	Samoa, Ameri	1.51
105	Algeria	1.50
106	Venezuela	1.47
107	Uzbekistan	1.46
108	El Salvador	1.46
109	Brazil	1.44
110	Reunion	1.44
111	Vietnam	1.43
112	Namibia	1.42
113	Iceland	1.41
114	Falkland Is	1.35
115	Bangladesh	1.35
116	Nicaragua	1.33
117	Suriname	1.33
118	Turkey	1.32
119	Indonesia	1.29
120	Bahamas	1.27
121	Mongolia	1.26
122	Tajikistan	1.25
123	Australia	1.23
124	Sri Lanka	1.22
125	Botswana	1.22
126	Marshall Is	1.22
127	Peru	1.20
128	New Zealand	1.20
129	Lebanon	1.19
130	Ecuador	1.16
131	Kosovo	1.16
132	Morocco	1.15
133	Oman	1.11
134	Swaziland	1.08
135	Chile	1.08

136	Tuvalu	1.08
137	St Lucia	1.06
138	South Africa	1.04
139	Kyrgyzstan	1.04
140	Canada	1.02
141	Neth Antilles	1.01
142	US	0.99
143	Argentina	0.99
144	Luxembourg	0.99
145	Colombia	0.98
146	Liechtenstein	0.97
147	Burma	0.96
148	Grenada	0.96
149	Tunisia	0.96
150	Mexico	0.95
151	Wallis & Futuna	0.93
152	Cook Is	0.91
153	Isle of Man	0.91
154	Lesotho	0.90
155	Mauritius	0.89
156	Palau	0.88
157	Monaco	0.87
158	Guadeloupe	0.79
159	Switzerland	0.77
160	Thailand	0.74
161	Faeroe Is	0.73
162	Malta	0.68
163	Zimbabwe	0.67
164	Norway	0.66
165	Fiji	0.65
166	France	0.64
167	Martinique	0.58
168	Seychelles	0.57
169	St Helena	0.56
170	Puerto Rico	0.56
171	Azerbaijan	0.56
172	Kazakhstan	0.56
173	Hong Kong	0.55
174	China	0.54
175	Austria	0.54
176	Portugal	0.54
177	Micronesia	0.53
178	Korea, North	0.52
179	Virgin I, US	0.52
180	Jamaica	0.49
181	Belgium	0.48
182	UK	0.47
183	Taiwan	0.46
184	Trinidad/Tobago	0.45
185	Albania	0.44
186	Korea, South	0.43
187	Sweden	0.43
188	Bermuda	0.43
189	Jersey	0.41
190	Samoa, W	0.40
191	Barbados	0.39

192	Netherlands	0.39
193	Guernsey	0.39
194	Greece	0.35
195	Italy	0.34
196	Denmark	0.31
197	Finland	0.30
198	St Pierre &	0.29
199	Tonga	0.29
200	Nauru	0.28
201	Montenegro	0.28
202	Bosnia	0.28
203	Greenland	0.25
204	Slovenia	0.15
205	Cuba	0.12
206	Japan	0.10
207	Uruguay	0.09
208	Macedonia	0.09
209	Guyana	0.08
210	Czechia	0.04
211	Germany	0.01
212	Slovakia	-0.01
213	Croatia	-0.04
214	Poland	-0.06
215	Tokelau	-0.09
216	Georgia	-0.13
217	Hungary	-0.22
218	Dominica	-0.28
219	Estonia	-0.34
220	Romania	-0.34
221	Armenia	-0.38
222	Belarus	-0.45
223	Serbia	-0.49
224	Lithuania	-0.52
225	Russia	-0.53
226	Bulgaria	-0.60
227	Latvia	-0.61
228	Gibraltar	-0.75
229	St Vincent	-0.78
230	Ukraine	-0.81
231	Moldova	-1.26
232	Niue	-4.85

Source: Calculated as (POP2007/POP2000)**(1/7)-1.

CHAPTER 5. GDP PER CAPITA GROWTH RATES

TABLE 5.1 - GDP PER CAPITA GROWTH RATES YEARS 0001-1000		
OBS	COUNTRY	GRPCRL
1	Israel	0.02
2	Bahrain	0.02
3	Kuwait	0.02
4	Oman	0.02
5	Qatar	0.02
6	Saudi Arabia	0.02
7	UAE	0.02
8	Yemen	0.02
9	Iran	0.02
10	Turkey	0.02
11	Lebanon	0.02
12	Syria	0.02
13	Iraq	0.02
14	Jordan	0.02
15	Cyprus	0.01
16	Morocco	0.01
17	Japan	0.01
18	Ghana	0.00
19	Sudan	0.00
20	Germany	0.00
21	Afghanistan	0.00
22	Albania	0.00
23	Algeria	0.00
24	Argentina	0.00
25	Armenia	0.00
26	Australia	0.00
27	Austria	0.00
28	Azerbaijan	0.00
29	Bangladesh	0.00
30	Belarus	0.00
31	Bolivia	0.00
32	Bosnia	0.00
33	Botswana	0.00
34	Brazil	0.00
35	Burma	0.00
36	Burundi	0.00
37	Cambodia	0.00
38	Canada	0.00
39	Chile	0.00
40	China	0.00
41	Colombia	0.00
42	Costa Rica	0.00
43	Croatia	0.00
44	Cuba	0.00
45	Czechia	0.00
46	Denmark	0.00
47	Dominican Rep	0.00
48	Ecuador	0.00
49	Egypt	0.00

50	El Salvador	0.00
51	Eritrea	0.00
52	Estonia	0.00
53	Ethiopia	0.00
54	Finland	0.00
55	Georgia	0.00
56	Guatemala	0.00
57	Guinea	0.00
58	Guinea-Bissau	0.00
59	Haiti	0.00
60	Honduras	0.00
61	Hong Kong	0.00
62	India	0.00
63	Indonesia	0.00
64	Ireland	0.00
65	Jamaica	0.00
66	Kazakhstan	0.00
67	Korea, North	0.00
68	Korea, South	0.00
69	Kosovo	0.00
70	Kyrgyzstan	0.00
71	Laos	0.00
72	Latvia	0.00
73	Lesotho	0.00
74	Libya	0.00
75	Lithuania	0.00
76	Macedonia	0.00
77	Madagascar	0.00
78	Malawi	0.00
79	Malaysia	0.00
80	Mexico	0.00
81	Moldova	0.00
82	Mongolia	0.00
83	Montenegro	0.00
84	Mozambique	0.00
85	Namibia	0.00
86	Nepal	0.00
87	Netherlands	0.00
88	New Zealand	0.00
89	Nicaragua	0.00
90	Norway	0.00
91	Pakistan	0.00
92	Panama	0.00
93	Paraguay	0.00
94	Peru	0.00
95	Philippines	0.00
96	Poland	0.00
97	Puerto Rico	0.00
98	Russia	0.00
99	Sierra Leone	0.00
100	Singapore	0.00
101	Slovakia	0.00
102	Slovenia	0.00
103	Somalia	0.00
104	South Africa	0.00
105	Sri Lanka	0.00

106	Swaziland	0.00
107	Sweden	0.00
108	Taiwan	0.00
109	Tajikistan	0.00
110	Thailand	0.00
111	Trinidad/Tobago	0.00
112	Tunisia	0.00
113	Turkmenistan	0.00
114	UK	0.00
115	US	0.00
116	Ukraine	0.00
117	Uruguay	0.00
118	Uzbekistan	0.00
119	Venezuela	0.00
120	Vietnam	0.00
121	Zambia	0.00
122	Zimbabwe	0.00
123	Switzerland	0.00
124	Belgium	-0.01
125	Portugal	-0.01
126	Bulgaria	-0.01
127	Hungary	-0.01
128	Romania	-0.01
129	Serbia	-0.01
130	Spain	-0.01
131	France	-0.01
132	Greece	-0.03
133	Italy	-0.06

Source: Calculated as (GPCPPP1000/GPCPPP0001)**(1/999)-1.

TABLE 5.2 - GDP PER CAPITA GROWTH RATES YEARS 1000-1500		
OBS	COUNTRY	GRPCRL
1	Italy	0.18
2	Belgium	0.14
3	Slovenia	0.12
4	Denmark	0.12
5	Netherlands	0.12
6	UK	0.12
7	Hungary	0.12
8	Estonia	0.11
9	Sweden	0.11
10	France	0.11
11	Germany	0.10
12	Austria	0.10
13	Poland	0.10
14	Latvia	0.10
15	Czechia	0.10
16	Romania	0.10
17	Norway	0.09
18	Kazakhstan	0.09
19	Lithuania	0.09

20	Switzerland	0.09
21	Spain	0.08
22	Bulgaria	0.07
23	Portugal	0.07
24	Slovakia	0.07
25	Russia	0.06
26	China	0.06
27	Hong Kong	0.06
28	Korea, North	0.06
29	Korea, South	0.06
30	Croatia	0.05
31	Ireland	0.05
32	Philippines	0.05
33	Thailand	0.05
34	Malaysia	0.05
35	Sri Lanka	0.05
36	Taiwan	0.05
37	Indonesia	0.05
38	Vietnam	0.05
39	Armenia	0.05
40	Afghanistan	0.04
41	Burma	0.04
42	Georgia	0.04
43	Bangladesh	0.04
44	India	0.04
45	Pakistan	0.04
46	Singapore	0.04
47	Laos	0.03
48	Japan	0.03
49	Serbia	0.03
50	Finland	0.02
51	Montenegro	0.02
52	Moldova	0.02
53	Greece	0.02
54	Belarus	0.01
55	Mexico	0.01
56	Uzbekistan	0.01
57	Argentina	0.01
58	Chile	0.01
59	Uruguay	0.01
60	Ukraine	0.00
61	Cambodia	0.00
62	Albania	0.00
63	Algeria	0.00
64	Australia	0.00
65	Azerbaijan	0.00
66	Bolivia	0.00
67	Bosnia	0.00
68	Botswana	0.00
69	Brazil	0.00
70	Burundi	0.00
71	Canada	0.00
72	Colombia	0.00
73	Costa Rica	0.00
74	Cuba	0.00
75	Dominican Rep	0.00

76	Ecuador	0.00
77	El Salvador	0.00
78	Eritrea	0.00
79	Ethiopia	0.00
80	Ghana	0.00
81	Guatemala	0.00
82	Guinea	0.00
83	Guinea-Bissau	0.00
84	Haiti	0.00
85	Honduras	0.00
86	Jamaica	0.00
87	Kosovo	0.00
88	Kyrgyzstan	0.00
89	Lesotho	0.00
90	Libya	0.00
91	Macedonia	0.00
92	Madagascar	0.00
93	Malawi	0.00
94	Mongolia	0.00
95	Morocco	0.00
96	Mozambique	0.00
97	Namibia	0.00
98	Nepal	0.00
99	New Zealand	0.00
100	Nicaragua	0.00
101	Panama	0.00
102	Paraguay	0.00
103	Peru	0.00
104	Puerto Rico	0.00
105	Sierra Leone	0.00
106	Somalia	0.00
107	South Africa	0.00
108	Sudan	0.00
109	Swaziland	0.00
110	Tajikistan	0.00
111	Trinidad/Tobago	0.00
112	Tunisia	0.00
113	Turkmenistan	0.00
114	US	0.00
115	Venezuela	0.00
116	Zambia	0.00
117	Zimbabwe	0.00
118	Jordan	-0.01
119	Lebanon	-0.01
120	Syria	-0.01
121	Israel	-0.01
122	Iraq	-0.01
123	Bahrain	-0.01
124	Kuwait	-0.01
125	Oman	-0.01
126	Qatar	-0.01
127	Saudi Arabia	-0.01
128	UAE	-0.01
129	Yemen	-0.01
130	Iran	-0.01
131	Turkey	-0.01

132	Egypt	-0.01
133	Cyprus	-0.07

Source: Calculated as (GPCPPP1500/GPCPPP1000)**(1/500)-1

TABLE 5.3 GDP PER CAPITA GROWTH RATES YEARS 1500-1600		
OBS	COUNTRY	GRPCRL
1	Netherlands	0.60
2	Uruguay	0.51
3	Argentina	0.35
4	UK	0.31
5	Jamaica	0.29
6	Trinidad/Tobago	0.27
7	Spain	0.26
8	Portugal	0.20
9	Finland	0.17
10	Norway	0.17
11	Switzerland	0.17
12	Denmark	0.17
13	Sweden	0.17
14	Austria	0.17
15	Chile	0.16
16	Ireland	0.16
17	France	0.15
18	Germany	0.14
19	Slovenia	0.12
20	Hungary	0.12
21	Estonia	0.11
22	Cyprus	0.11
23	Greece	0.11
24	Belgium	0.11
25	Georgia	0.10
26	Belarus	0.10
27	Kazakhstan	0.10
28	Armenia	0.10
29	Moldova	0.10
30	Lithuania	0.10
31	Russia	0.10
32	Latvia	0.10
33	Ukraine	0.10
34	Uzbekistan	0.10
35	Romania	0.10
36	Czechia	0.10
37	Montenegro	0.10
38	Poland	0.10
39	Croatia	0.10
40	Slovakia	0.10
41	Bulgaria	0.10
42	Serbia	0.10
43	Turkmenistan	0.09
44	Brazil	0.07
45	Mexico	0.07
46	Japan	0.04
47	Madagascar	0.04

48	Mozambique	0.04
49	Namibia	0.04
50	Somalia	0.04
51	South Africa	0.04
52	Swaziland	0.04
53	Zambia	0.04
54	Zimbabwe	0.04
55	Sri Lanka	0.02
56	Taiwan	0.02
57	Laos	0.02
58	Vietnam	0.02
59	Philippines	0.02
60	Thailand	0.02
61	Singapore	0.02
62	Burma	0.02
63	Afghanistan	0.02
64	Cambodia	0.02
65	Malaysia	0.02
66	Indonesia	0.01
67	Azerbaijan	0.01
68	Iraq	0.00
69	Albania	0.00
70	Algeria	0.00
71	Australia	0.00
72	Bahrain	0.00
73	Bangladesh	0.00
74	Bolivia	0.00
75	Bosnia	0.00
76	Botswana	0.00
77	Burundi	0.00
78	Canada	0.00
79	China	0.00
80	Colombia	0.00
81	Costa Rica	0.00
82	Cuba	0.00
83	Dominican Rep	0.00
84	Ecuador	0.00
85	Egypt	0.00
86	El Salvador	0.00
87	Eritrea	0.00
88	Ethiopia	0.00
89	Ghana	0.00
90	Guatemala	0.00
91	Guinea	0.00
92	Guinea-Bissau	0.00
93	Haiti	0.00
94	Honduras	0.00
95	Hong Kong	0.00
96	India	0.00
97	Iran	0.00
98	Israel	0.00
99	Italy	0.00
100	Jordan	0.00
101	Korea, North	0.00
102	Korea, South	0.00
103	Kosovo	0.00

104	Kuwait	0.00
105	Kyrgyzstan	0.00
106	Lebanon	0.00
107	Lesotho	0.00
108	Libya	0.00
109	Macedonia	0.00
110	Malawi	0.00
111	Mongolia	0.00
112	Morocco	0.00
113	Nepal	0.00
114	New Zealand	0.00
115	Nicaragua	0.00
116	Oman	0.00
117	Pakistan	0.00
118	Panama	0.00
119	Paraguay	0.00
120	Peru	0.00
121	Puerto Rico	0.00
122	Qatar	0.00
123	Saudi Arabia	0.00
124	Sierra Leone	0.00
125	Sudan	0.00
126	Syria	0.00
127	Tajikistan	0.00
128	Tunisia	0.00
129	Turkey	0.00
130	UAE	0.00
131	US	0.00
132	Venezuela	0.00
133	Yemen	0.00

Source: Calculated as (GPCPPP1600/GPCPPP1500)**(1/100)-1.

TABLE 5.4 - GDP PER CAPITA GROWTH RATES YEARS 1600-1700		
OBS	COUNTRY	GRPCRL
1	Uruguay	0.51
2	Netherlands	0.43
3	Puerto Rico	0.36
4	Argentina	0.35
5	Cuba	0.31
6	Jamaica	0.29
7	US	0.28
8	Trinidad/Tobago	0.27
9	UK	0.25
10	Mexico	0.22
11	Denmark	0.17
12	Switzerland	0.17
13	Austria	0.17
14	Finland	0.17
15	Sweden	0.17
16	Norway	0.17
17	Chile	0.16
18	Belgium	0.16
19	Ireland	0.15

20	Germany	0.14
21	Slovenia	0.12
22	Hungary	0.12
23	Estonia	0.11
24	Portugal	0.10
25	Bulgaria	0.10
26	Slovakia	0.10
27	Romania	0.10
28	Serbia	0.10
29	Poland	0.10
30	Montenegro	0.10
31	Croatia	0.10
32	Czechia	0.10
33	Uzbekistan	0.10
34	Ukraine	0.10
35	Latvia	0.10
36	Russia	0.10
37	Moldova	0.10
38	Turkmenistan	0.10
39	Armenia	0.10
40	Georgia	0.10
41	Kazakhstan	0.10
42	Lithuania	0.10
43	Belarus	0.10
44	Azerbaijan	0.10
45	Greece	0.09
46	Cyprus	0.09
47	Japan	0.09
48	France	0.08
49	Canada	0.07
50	Brazil	0.07
51	Colombia	0.04
52	Tajikistan	0.03
53	Indonesia	0.01
54	Albania	0.00
55	Algeria	0.00
56	Australia	0.00
57	Bahrain	0.00
58	Bangladesh	0.00
59	Bolivia	0.00
60	Bosnia	0.00
61	Botswana	0.00
62	Burundi	0.00
63	China	0.00
64	Costa Rica	0.00
65	Dominican Rep	0.00
66	Ecuador	0.00
67	Egypt	0.00
68	El Salvador	0.00
69	Eritrea	0.00
70	Ethiopia	0.00
71	Ghana	0.00
72	Guatemala	0.00
73	Guinea	0.00
74	Guinea-Bissau	0.00
75	Haiti	0.00

76	Honduras	0.00
77	Hong Kong	0.00
78	India	0.00
79	Iran	0.00
80	Iraq	0.00
81	Israel	0.00
82	Italy	0.00
83	Jordan	0.00
84	Korea, North	0.00
85	Korea, South	0.00
86	Kosovo	0.00
87	Kuwait	0.00
88	Kyrgyzstan	0.00
89	Lebanon	0.00
90	Lesotho	0.00
91	Libya	0.00
92	Macedonia	0.00
93	Madagascar	0.00
94	Malawi	0.00
95	Mongolia	0.00
96	Morocco	0.00
97	Mozambique	0.00
98	Namibia	0.00
99	Nepal	0.00
100	New Zealand	0.00
101	Nicaragua	0.00
102	Oman	0.00
103	Pakistan	0.00
104	Panama	0.00
105	Paraguay	0.00
106	Peru	0.00
107	Qatar	0.00
108	Saudi Arabia	0.00
109	Sierra Leone	0.00
110	Somalia	0.00
111	South Africa	0.00
112	Spain	0.00
113	Sudan	0.00
114	Swaziland	0.00
115	Syria	0.00
116	Tunisia	0.00
117	Turkey	0.00
118	UAE	0.00
119	Venezuela	0.00
120	Yemen	0.00
121	Zambia	0.00
122	Zimbabwe	0.00
123	Laos	-0.01
124	Malaysia	-0.01
125	Vietnam	-0.01
126	Burma	-0.01
127	Thailand	-0.01
128	Singapore	-0.01
129	Afghanistan	-0.01
130	Cambodia	-0.01
131	Sri Lanka	-0.01

| 132 | Taiwan | -0.01 |
| 133 | Philippines | -0.01 |

Source: Calculated as (GPCPPP1700/GPCPPP1600)**(1/100)-1

TABLE 5.5 - GDP PER CAPITA GROWTH RATES YEARS 1700-1820		
OBS	COUNTRY	GRPCRL
1	US	0.73
2	Canada	0.62
3	Uruguay	0.51
4	Argentina	0.35
5	Brazil	0.29
6	Trinidad/Tobago	0.27
7	Colombia	0.26
8	UK	0.26
9	Guatemala	0.26
10	Mexico	0.24
11	Australia	0.22
12	Costa Rica	0.21
13	Bolivia	0.19
14	Panama	0.19
15	France	0.18
16	Norway	0.17
17	Austria	0.17
18	Ireland	0.17
19	Sweden	0.17
20	Denmark	0.17
21	Switzerland	0.17
22	Finland	0.17
23	Ecuador	0.16
24	Chile	0.16
25	Greece	0.16
26	Cyprus	0.16
27	Peru	0.15
28	Germany	0.14
29	Spain	0.14
30	Japan	0.13
31	Slovenia	0.12
32	Belgium	0.12
33	Venezuela	0.12
34	Hungary	0.12
35	Estonia	0.11
36	Uzbekistan	0.10
37	Tajikistan	0.10
38	Belarus	0.10
39	Armenia	0.10
40	Lithuania	0.10
41	Ukraine	0.10
42	Azerbaijan	0.10
43	Kazakhstan	0.10
44	Moldova	0.10
45	Russia	0.10
46	Latvia	0.10
47	Georgia	0.10

48	Turkmenistan	0.10
49	Serbia	0.10
50	Montenegro	0.10
51	Czechia	0.10
52	Poland	0.10
53	Romania	0.10
54	Croatia	0.10
55	Slovakia	0.10
56	Bulgaria	0.10
57	Portugal	0.10
58	Turkey	0.06
59	Albania	0.05
60	Kyrgyzstan	0.05
61	Indonesia	0.04
62	Nicaragua	0.04
63	Paraguay	0.03
64	Iraq	0.02
65	Italy	0.01
66	Cambodia	0.01
67	Afghanistan	0.01
68	Philippines	0.01
69	Sri Lanka	0.01
70	Taiwan	0.01
71	Thailand	0.01
72	Malaysia	0.01
73	Burma	0.01
74	Singapore	0.01
75	Laos	0.01
76	Vietnam	0.01
77	Algeria	0.00
78	Bahrain	0.00
79	Bosnia	0.00
80	Botswana	0.00
81	Burundi	0.00
82	China	0.00
83	Dominican Rep	0.00
84	Egypt	0.00
85	El Salvador	0.00
86	Eritrea	0.00
87	Ethiopia	0.00
88	Ghana	0.00
89	Guinea	0.00
90	Guinea-Bissau	0.00
91	Haiti	0.00
92	Honduras	0.00
93	Hong Kong	0.00
94	Israel	0.00
95	Jordan	0.00
96	Korea, North	0.00
97	Korea, South	0.00
98	Kosovo	0.00
99	Kuwait	0.00
100	Lebanon	0.00
101	Lesotho	0.00
102	Libya	0.00
103	Macedonia	0.00

104	Madagascar	0.00
105	Malawi	0.00
106	Mongolia	0.00
107	Morocco	0.00
108	Mozambique	0.00
109	Namibia	0.00
110	Nepal	0.00
111	New Zealand	0.00
112	Oman	0.00
113	Qatar	0.00
114	Saudi Arabia	0.00
115	Sierra Leone	0.00
116	Somalia	0.00
117	South Africa	0.00
118	Sudan	0.00
119	Swaziland	0.00
120	Syria	0.00
121	Tunisia	0.00
122	UAE	0.00
123	Yemen	0.00
124	Zambia	0.00
125	Zimbabwe	0.00
126	Iran	-0.02
127	Cuba	-0.02
128	Puerto Rico	-0.02
129	Jamaica	-0.02
130	Bangladesh	-0.03
131	India	-0.03
132	Pakistan	-0.03
133	Netherlands	-0.12

Source: Calculated as (GPCPPP1820/GPCPPP1700)**(1/120)-1

TABLE 5.6 - GDP PER CAPITA GROWTH RATES YEARS 1820-1870		
OBS	COUNTRY	GRPCRL
1	New Zealand	4.18
2	Australia	3.76
3	South Africa	1.46
4	Belgium	1.44
5	Ireland	1.42
6	US	1.34
7	Switzerland	1.32
8	Namibia	1.28
9	Canada	1.27
10	UK	1.26
11	Chile	1.25
12	Germany	1.08
13	Algeria	1.02
14	France	1.01
15	Denmark	0.91
16	Sri Lanka	0.88
17	Austria	0.85
18	Netherlands	0.81
19	Tunisia	0.78

20	Mozambique	0.78
21	Finland	0.76
22	Somalia	0.72
23	Sweden	0.66
24	Madagascar	0.64
25	Cyprus	0.64
26	Greece	0.64
27	Czechia	0.63
28	Slovakia	0.63
29	Moldova	0.63
30	Latvia	0.63
31	Kyrgyzstan	0.63
32	Georgia	0.63
33	Kazakhstan	0.63
34	Estonia	0.63
35	Russia	0.63
36	Turkmenistan	0.63
37	Belarus	0.63
38	Lithuania	0.63
39	Ukraine	0.63
40	Azerbaijan	0.63
41	Armenia	0.63
42	Tajikistan	0.63
43	Egypt	0.63
44	Uzbekistan	0.63
45	Singapore	0.62
46	Italy	0.59
47	Morocco	0.54
48	Libya	0.53
49	Sudan	0.53
50	Norway	0.52
51	Turkey	0.50
52	Lebanon	0.50
53	Syria	0.50
54	Venezuela	0.43
55	Swaziland	0.43
56	Zimbabwe	0.40
57	Israel	0.40
58	Iran	0.40
59	Iraq	0.40
60	Jordan	0.40
61	Spain	0.36
62	Zambia	0.36
63	Pakistan	0.32
64	Hong Kong	0.26
65	Ghana	0.21
66	Brazil	0.20
67	Thailand	0.19
68	Japan	0.19
69	Malaysia	0.19
70	Indonesia	0.13
71	Philippines	0.13
72	Slovenia	0.12
73	Hungary	0.12
74	Bangladesh	0.11
75	Portugal	0.11

76	Bulgaria	0.10
77	Albania	0.10
78	Croatia	0.10
79	Romania	0.10
80	Poland	0.10
81	Montenegro	0.10
82	Serbia	0.10
83	India	0.10
84	Bahrain	0.09
85	Kuwait	0.09
86	Oman	0.09
87	Qatar	0.09
88	Saudi Arabia	0.09
89	UAE	0.09
90	Yemen	0.09
91	Ecuador	0.05
92	Peru	0.05
93	Uruguay	0.05
94	Costa Rica	0.05
95	Guatemala	0.05
96	Bolivia	0.05
97	Argentina	0.05
98	Colombia	0.05
99	Panama	0.05
100	Trinidad/Tobago	0.05
101	Puerto Rico	0.05
102	Cuba	0.05
103	Paraguay	0.05
104	Nicaragua	0.05
105	Macedonia	0.02
106	Korea, North	0.01
107	Korea, South	0.01
108	Bosnia	0.00
109	Botswana	0.00
110	Burma	0.00
111	Burundi	0.00
112	Dominican Rep	0.00
113	El Salvador	0.00
114	Eritrea	0.00
115	Ethiopia	0.00
116	Guinea	0.00
117	Guinea-Bissau	0.00
118	Haiti	0.00
119	Honduras	0.00
120	Kosovo	0.00
121	Lesotho	0.00
122	Malawi	0.00
123	Mongolia	0.00
124	Nepal	0.00
125	Sierra Leone	0.00
126	Taiwan	0.00
127	Cambodia	-0.05
128	Afghanistan	-0.08
129	Laos	-0.08
130	Vietnam	-0.09
131	Mexico	-0.24

| 132 | China | -0.25 |
| 133 | Jamaica | -0.54 |

Source: Calculated as (GPCPPP1870/GPCPPP1820)**(1/50)-1.

TABLE 5.7 - GDP PER CAPITA GROWTH RATES YEARS 1870-1880		
OBS	COUNTRY	GRPCRL
1	Spain	3.15
2	Australia	2.73
3	Argentina	2.51
4	Mexico	2.05
5	New Zealand	1.91
6	Chile	1.79
7	Bolivia	1.77
8	Nicaragua	1.77
9	Paraguay	1.77
10	Ecuador	1.77
11	Guatemala	1.77
12	Puerto Rico	1.77
13	Costa Rica	1.77
14	Cuba	1.77
15	Trinidad/Tobago	1.77
16	Panama	1.77
17	Peru	1.73
18	Colombia	1.73
19	El Salvador	1.72
20	Serbia	1.72
21	Croatia	1.72
22	Slovenia	1.72
23	Montenegro	1.72
24	Macedonia	1.72
25	US	1.65
26	Japan	1.59
27	Switzerland	1.54
28	Poland	1.54
29	Hungary	1.51
30	Bulgaria	1.50
31	Albania	1.48
32	Singapore	1.47
33	Hong Kong	1.47
34	Greece	1.47
35	Cyprus	1.47
36	Romania	1.47
37	South Africa	1.46
38	Bosnia	1.40
39	Belgium	1.31
40	Czechia	1.29
41	Slovakia	1.29
42	Namibia	1.28
43	France	1.23
44	Venezuela	1.23
45	Israel	1.19
46	Austria	1.10
47	Lebanon	1.10

48	Syria	1.10
49	Sweden	1.06
50	Norway	1.04
51	Algeria	1.03
52	Ireland	1.01
53	Netherlands	1.00
54	Azerbaijan	0.91
55	Kyrgyzstan	0.91
56	Tajikistan	0.91
57	Russia	0.91
58	Turkmenistan	0.91
59	Latvia	0.91
60	Armenia	0.91
61	Lithuania	0.91
62	Moldova	0.91
63	Ukraine	0.91
64	Georgia	0.91
65	Uzbekistan	0.91
66	Kazakhstan	0.91
67	Estonia	0.91
68	Belarus	0.91
69	Turkey	0.90
70	UK	0.87
71	Denmark	0.86
72	Vietnam	0.85
73	Germany	0.80
74	Laos	0.80
75	Afghanistan	0.79
76	Tunisia	0.78
77	Mozambique	0.78
78	Iran	0.77
79	Iraq	0.77
80	Jordan	0.77
81	Somalia	0.72
82	Burma	0.72
83	Korea, North	0.71
84	Korea, South	0.71
85	Canada	0.69
86	Cambodia	0.66
87	Taiwan	0.65
88	Madagascar	0.64
89	Nepal	0.64
90	Egypt	0.60
91	Morocco	0.54
92	Italy	0.53
93	Brazil	0.53
94	Libya	0.53
95	Sudan	0.53
96	Thailand	0.48
97	Malaysia	0.46
98	Honduras	0.45
99	India	0.43
100	Swaziland	0.43
101	Zimbabwe	0.40
102	Zambia	0.36
103	Philippines	0.36

104	Jamaica	0.34
105	Pakistan	0.32
106	Ghana	0.22
107	Finland	0.13
108	Indonesia	0.12
109	Bangladesh	0.11
110	Bahrain	0.10
111	Kuwait	0.10
112	Oman	0.10
113	Qatar	0.10
114	Saudi Arabia	0.10
115	UAE	0.10
116	Yemen	0.10
117	China	0.09
118	Botswana	0.00
119	Burundi	0.00
120	Dominican Rep	0.00
121	Eritrea	0.00
122	Ethiopia	0.00
123	Guinea	0.00
124	Guinea-Bissau	0.00
125	Haiti	0.00
126	Kosovo	0.00
127	Lesotho	0.00
128	Malawi	0.00
129	Mongolia	0.00
130	Sierra Leone	0.00
131	Sri Lanka	-0.24
132	Portugal	-0.29
133	Uruguay	-0.46

Source: Calculated as (GPCPPP1880/GPCPPP1870)**(1/10)-1.

TABLE 5.8 - GDP PER CAPITA GROWTH RATES YEARS 1880-1890		
OBS	COUNTRY	GRPCRL
1	Canada	2.73
2	Switzerland	2.65
3	Argentina	2.51
4	Sri Lanka	2.32
5	Mexico	2.05
6	Germany	2.00
7	Finland	1.80
8	Chile	1.79
9	El Salvador	1.77
10	Puerto Rico	1.77
11	Trinidad/Tobago	1.77
12	Ecuador	1.77
13	Costa Rica	1.77
14	Panama	1.77
15	Paraguay	1.77
16	Guatemala	1.77
17	Cuba	1.77
18	Nicaragua	1.77
19	Bolivia	1.77

20	Honduras	1.77
21	Portugal	1.76
22	Peru	1.73
23	Colombia	1.73
24	Macedonia	1.72
25	Bosnia	1.72
26	Slovenia	1.72
27	Serbia	1.72
28	Croatia	1.72
29	Montenegro	1.72
30	US	1.65
31	Austria	1.63
32	Japan	1.61
33	Poland	1.54
34	Dominican Rep	1.51
35	Hungary	1.51
36	Bulgaria	1.50
37	Albania	1.48
38	Singapore	1.47
39	Hong Kong	1.47
40	Greece	1.47
41	Cyprus	1.47
42	Romania	1.47
43	Denmark	1.47
44	South Africa	1.46
45	UK	1.43
46	Slovakia	1.29
47	Czechia	1.29
48	Namibia	1.28
49	Sweden	1.23
50	Venezuela	1.23
51	Israel	1.19
52	Algeria	1.17
53	France	1.15
54	Norway	1.13
55	Belgium	1.13
56	Lebanon	1.10
57	Syria	1.10
58	Ireland	1.01
59	Belarus	0.91
60	Lithuania	0.91
61	Tajikistan	0.91
62	Kazakhstan	0.91
63	Russia	0.91
64	Turkmenistan	0.91
65	Latvia	0.91
66	Uzbekistan	0.91
67	Kyrgyzstan	0.91
68	Estonia	0.91
69	Ukraine	0.91
70	Armenia	0.91
71	Georgia	0.91
72	Moldova	0.91
73	Azerbaijan	0.91
74	Turkey	0.90
75	Netherlands	0.87

76	Vietnam	0.85
77	Cambodia	0.79
78	Afghanistan	0.79
79	Laos	0.79
80	Tunisia	0.78
81	Mozambique	0.78
82	Iran	0.77
83	Iraq	0.77
84	Jordan	0.77
85	Somalia	0.72
86	Burma	0.72
87	Korea, North	0.71
88	Korea, South	0.71
89	Nepal	0.71
90	Egypt	0.69
91	Taiwan	0.65
92	Madagascar	0.64
93	Brazil	0.54
94	Morocco	0.54
95	Libya	0.53
96	Italy	0.53
97	Sudan	0.53
98	Thailand	0.48
99	Malaysia	0.46
100	India	0.43
101	Swaziland	0.43
102	Zimbabwe	0.40
103	Australia	0.40
104	Zambia	0.36
105	Philippines	0.36
106	Jamaica	0.34
107	Pakistan	0.32
108	Uruguay	0.31
109	Ghana	0.22
110	Bangladesh	0.11
111	Bahrain	0.10
112	Kuwait	0.10
113	Oman	0.10
114	Qatar	0.10
115	Saudi Arabia	0.10
116	UAE	0.10
117	Yemen	0.10
118	China	0.09
119	New Zealand	0.02
120	Botswana	0.00
121	Burundi	0.00
122	Eritrea	0.00
123	Ethiopia	0.00
124	Guinea	0.00
125	Guinea-Bissau	0.00
126	Haiti	0.00
127	Kosovo	0.00
128	Lesotho	0.00
129	Malawi	0.00
130	Mongolia	0.00
131	Sierra Leone	0.00

| 132 | Indonesia | -0.03 |
| 133 | Spain | -0.13 |

Source: Calculated as (GPCPPP1890/GPCPPP1880)**(1/10)-1.

TABLE 5.9 - GDP PER CAPITA GROWTH RATES YEARS 1890-1900		
OBS	COUNTRY	GRPCRL
1	Mexico	3.06
2	Argentina	2.50
3	Dominican Rep	2.19
4	Sri Lanka	2.13
5	Germany	2.09
6	Sweden	2.07
7	Canada	2.04
8	France	1.93
9	Finland	1.91
10	US	1.89
11	Switzerland	1.88
12	Poland	1.81
13	Denmark	1.80
14	Chile	1.79
15	Cuba	1.77
16	Honduras	1.77
17	Nicaragua	1.77
18	Guatemala	1.77
19	Costa Rica	1.77
20	Bolivia	1.77
21	Panama	1.77
22	Paraguay	1.77
23	Trinidad/Tobago	1.77
24	El Salvador	1.77
25	Puerto Rico	1.77
26	Ecuador	1.77
27	Haiti	1.74
28	Peru	1.73
29	Colombia	1.73
30	Austria	1.67
31	Japan	1.55
32	Singapore	1.47
33	Hong Kong	1.47
34	South Africa	1.46
35	Portugal	1.44
36	Czechia	1.40
37	Slovakia	1.40
38	Cyprus	1.38
39	Greece	1.38
40	Albania	1.37
41	New Zealand	1.36
42	Hungary	1.34
43	Romania	1.28
44	Namibia	1.28
45	Venezuela	1.23
46	Israel	1.19
47	Indonesia	1.19

48	Algeria	1.17
49	UK	1.14
50	Lebanon	1.10
51	Syria	1.10
52	Ireland	1.01
53	Spain	0.96
54	Kyrgyzstan	0.91
55	Armenia	0.91
56	Moldova	0.91
57	Ukraine	0.91
58	Azerbaijan	0.91
59	Lithuania	0.91
60	Turkmenistan	0.91
61	Estonia	0.91
62	Latvia	0.91
63	Georgia	0.91
64	Russia	0.91
65	Tajikistan	0.91
66	Uzbekistan	0.91
67	Kazakhstan	0.91
68	Belarus	0.91
69	Turkey	0.90
70	Ghana	0.89
71	Egypt	0.88
72	Norway	0.87
73	Vietnam	0.85
74	Belgium	0.85
75	Afghanistan	0.80
76	Laos	0.79
77	Cambodia	0.79
78	Bulgaria	0.79
79	Tunisia	0.78
80	Mozambique	0.78
81	Iran	0.77
82	Iraq	0.77
83	Jordan	0.77
84	Somalia	0.72
85	Burma	0.72
86	Nepal	0.71
87	Korea, North	0.71
88	Korea, South	0.71
89	Italy	0.69
90	Montenegro	0.68
91	Croatia	0.68
92	Serbia	0.68
93	Bosnia	0.68
94	Slovenia	0.68
95	Macedonia	0.68
96	Taiwan	0.65
97	Madagascar	0.64
98	Morocco	0.54
99	Libya	0.53
100	Sudan	0.53
101	Mongolia	0.50
102	Malaysia	0.46
103	Swaziland	0.43

104	Zimbabwe	0.40
105	Zambia	0.36
106	Philippines	0.36
107	Jamaica	0.34
108	Uruguay	0.33
109	Pakistan	0.32
110	Thailand	0.31
111	Netherlands	0.30
112	India	0.28
113	Bangladesh	0.11
114	Bahrain	0.10
115	Kuwait	0.10
116	Oman	0.10
117	Qatar	0.10
118	Saudi Arabia	0.10
119	UAE	0.10
120	Yemen	0.10
121	China	0.09
122	Botswana	0.00
123	Burundi	0.00
124	Eritrea	0.00
125	Ethiopia	0.00
126	Guinea	0.00
127	Guinea-Bissau	0.00
128	Kosovo	0.00
129	Lesotho	0.00
130	Malawi	0.00
131	Sierra Leone	0.00
132	Australia	-1.05
133	Brazil	-1.57

Source: Calculated as (GPCPPP1900/GPCPPP1890)**(1/10)-1.

TABLE 5.10 - GDP PER CAPITA GROWTH RATES YEARS 1900-1913		
OBS	COUNTRY	GRPCRL
1	Canada	3.31
2	Philippines	3.26
3	Uruguay	3.12
4	Ghana	3.06
5	Italy	2.82
6	Argentina	2.50
7	Chile	2.40
8	Venezuela	2.30
9	Denmark	2.02
10	US	2.01
11	Norway	1.99
12	Australia	1.95
13	Colombia	1.86
14	Peru	1.85
15	Mexico	1.84
16	Finland	1.83
17	Haiti	1.77
18	Paraguay	1.77

19	Nicaragua	1.77
20	Puerto Rico	1.77
21	El Salvador	1.77
22	Ecuador	1.77
23	Guatemala	1.77
24	Bolivia	1.77
25	Trinidad/Tobago	1.77
26	Panama	1.77
27	Costa Rica	1.77
28	Honduras	1.77
29	Cuba	1.77
30	Bulgaria	1.76
31	Hungary	1.71
32	Romania	1.61
33	Germany	1.55
34	Indonesia	1.52
35	Slovakia	1.49
36	Czechia	1.49
37	France	1.49
38	Singapore	1.47
39	Sweden	1.47
40	Hong Kong	1.47
41	South Africa	1.46
42	Turkmenistan	1.43
43	Azerbaijan	1.43
44	Belarus	1.43
45	Estonia	1.43
46	Georgia	1.43
47	Kazakhstan	1.43
48	Ukraine	1.43
49	Latvia	1.43
50	Armenia	1.43
51	Uzbekistan	1.43
52	Russia	1.43
53	Lithuania	1.43
54	Tajikistan	1.43
55	Moldova	1.43
56	Kyrgyzstan	1.43
57	Austria	1.43
58	New Zealand	1.40
59	Brazil	1.39
60	Albania	1.31
61	Netherlands	1.30
62	Malaysia	1.29
63	Namibia	1.28
64	Greece	1.27
65	Cyprus	1.27
66	Japan	1.25
67	Bosnia	1.23
68	Croatia	1.23
69	Slovenia	1.23
70	Macedonia	1.23
71	Serbia	1.23
72	Montenegro	1.23
73	Israel	1.19
74	Algeria	1.17

75	Lebanon	1.10
76	Syria	1.10
77	Spain	1.09
78	Ireland	1.01
79	Poland	0.96
80	Belgium	0.95
81	Turkey	0.90
82	Egypt	0.88
83	Taiwan	0.86
84	Vietnam	0.85
85	Switzerland	0.83
86	Cambodia	0.80
87	Mongolia	0.79
88	Laos	0.79
89	Afghanistan	0.79
90	Tunisia	0.78
91	Mozambique	0.78
92	Iran	0.77
93	Iraq	0.77
94	Jordan	0.77
95	Somalia	0.72
96	Burma	0.72
97	Nepal	0.71
98	Korea, North	0.71
99	Korea, South	0.71
100	UK	0.70
101	Madagascar	0.64
102	Morocco	0.54
103	Libya	0.53
104	Sudan	0.53
105	Bangladesh	0.46
106	Pakistan	0.46
107	India	0.46
108	Swaziland	0.43
109	Zimbabwe	0.40
110	Zambia	0.36
111	Jamaica	0.34
112	Thailand	0.31
113	Bahrain	0.10
114	Kuwait	0.10
115	Oman	0.10
116	Qatar	0.10
117	Saudi Arabia	0.10
118	UAE	0.10
119	Yemen	0.10
120	China	0.10
121	Dominican Rep	0.09
122	Botswana	0.00
123	Burundi	0.00
124	Eritrea	0.00
125	Ethiopia	0.00
126	Guinea	0.00
127	Guinea-Bissau	0.00
128	Kosovo	0.00
129	Lesotho	0.00
130	Malawi	0.00

131	Sierra Leone	0.00
132	Portugal	-0.31
133	Sri Lanka	-0.34

Source: Calculated as (GPCPPP1913/GPCPPP1900)**(1/13)-1.

TABLE 5.11 - GDP PER CAPITA GROWTH RATES YEARS 1913-1920		
OBS	COUNTRY	GRPCRL
1	Qatar	11.19
2	Kuwait	11.04
3	UAE	9.24
4	Honduras	7.95
5	Costa Rica	5.51
6	Nicaragua	4.67
7	Taiwan	3.63
8	Peru	3.63
9	Saudi Arabia	3.61
10	Bahrain	3.45
11	Malaysia	3.04
12	Korea, North	3.01
13	Korea, South	3.01
14	Philippines	2.93
15	Japan	2.91
16	Brazil	2.48
17	Greece	2.36
18	Cyprus	2.36
19	Israel	2.22
20	Morocco	1.96
21	Jamaica	1.81
22	Lebanon	1.60
23	Syria	1.58
24	Paraguay	1.54
25	Cuba	1.54
26	Trinidad/Tobago	1.54
27	Panama	1.54
28	Haiti	1.54
29	Ecuador	1.54
30	Dominican Rep	1.54
31	Bolivia	1.54
32	Puerto Rico	1.54
33	Norway	1.52
34	Singapore	1.50
35	Hong Kong	1.50
36	Iran	1.48
37	El Salvador	1.39
38	Jordan	1.38
39	New Zealand	1.30
40	Namibia	1.28
41	South Africa	1.25
42	Poland	1.24
43	Algeria	1.19
44	Yemen	1.14
45	Guatemala	1.02
46	Ghana	0.98

47	Burma	0.95
48	Venezuela	0.87
49	Iraq	0.84
50	Albania	0.83
51	Spain	0.82
52	Mozambique	0.78
53	Mexico	0.73
54	Somalia	0.72
55	US	0.66
56	Madagascar	0.64
57	Indonesia	0.64
58	Tunisia	0.63
59	Netherlands	0.59
60	Libya	0.53
61	Sudan	0.53
62	Swaziland	0.43
63	Zimbabwe	0.40
64	Zambia	0.36
65	Denmark	0.29
66	Colombia	0.22
67	Switzerland	0.16
68	Italy	0.13
69	China	0.11
70	Oman	0.10
71	Pakistan	0.05
72	Bangladesh	0.02
73	Botswana	0.00
74	Burundi	0.00
75	Eritrea	0.00
76	Ethiopia	0.00
77	Guinea	0.00
78	Guinea-Bissau	0.00
79	Kosovo	0.00
80	Lesotho	0.00
81	Malawi	0.00
82	Sierra Leone	0.00
83	Laos	-0.19
84	Afghanistan	-0.19
85	Cambodia	-0.19
86	Mongolia	-0.19
87	Egypt	-0.20
88	Nepal	-0.22
89	Portugal	-0.24
90	Vietnam	-0.27
91	Serbia	-0.36
92	Slovenia	-0.36
93	Macedonia	-0.36
94	Montenegro	-0.36
95	Croatia	-0.36
96	Bosnia	-0.36
97	Thailand	-0.37
98	India	-0.75
99	Belgium	-0.90
100	Ireland	-0.96
101	France	-1.09
102	UK	-1.12

103	Australia	-1.12
104	Czechia	-1.15
105	Slovakia	-1.15
106	Chile	-1.25
107	Argentina	-1.27
108	Sweden	-1.42
109	Sri Lanka	-1.73
110	Estonia	-1.90
111	Finland	-1.90
112	Latvia	-1.90
113	Lithuania	-1.90
114	Canada	-2.00
115	Hungary	-2.89
116	Uruguay	-3.00
117	Germany	-3.73
118	Austria	-5.04
119	Bulgaria	-7.20
120	Georgia	-7.20
121	Romania	-7.20
122	Moldova	-7.20
123	Turkey	-7.33
124	Kyrgyzstan	-11.17
125	Tajikistan	-12.34
126	Ukraine	-12.67
127	Uzbekistan	-12.67
128	Kazakhstan	-12.67
129	Armenia	-12.67
130	Belarus	-12.67
131	Russia	-12.67
132	Azerbaijan	-12.67
133	Turkmenistan	-12.67

Source: Calculated as (GPCPPP1920/GPCPPP1913)**(1/7)-1.

TABLE 5.12 - GDP PER CAPITA GROWTH RATES YEARS 1920-1929

OBS	COUNTRY	GRPCRL
1	Venezuela	12.65
2	Qatar	11.19
3	Kuwait	11.04
4	Azerbaijan	10.56
5	Turkmenistan	10.56
6	Belarus	10.56
7	Armenia	10.56
8	Russia	10.56
9	Kazakhstan	10.56
10	Uzbekistan	10.56
11	Ukraine	10.56
12	Tajikistan	10.24
13	UAE	9.24
14	Kyrgyzstan	9.11
15	Turkey	6.10
16	Georgia	5.46
17	Slovakia	5.17
18	Czechia	5.17

19	Austria	4.87
20	Malaysia	4.73
21	Lithuania	4.39
22	Latvia	4.39
23	Finland	4.39
24	Estonia	4.39
25	Switzerland	4.36
26	France	4.29
27	Germany	4.21
28	Hungary	4.21
29	Uruguay	4.12
30	Chile	3.79
31	Nicaragua	3.68
32	Sweden	3.65
33	Saudi Arabia	3.61
34	Bahrain	3.45
35	Guatemala	3.41
36	Netherlands	3.37
37	Macedonia	3.16
38	Montenegro	3.16
39	Croatia	3.16
40	Slovenia	3.16
41	Serbia	3.16
42	Bosnia	3.16
43	Canada	3.06
44	Portugal	3.05
45	Bulgaria	2.94
46	Belgium	2.74
47	Denmark	2.70
48	Cuba	2.66
49	Spain	2.58
50	Argentina	2.58
51	Greece	2.51
52	Cyprus	2.51
53	Norway	2.50
54	US	2.44
55	Indonesia	2.40
56	Sri Lanka	2.27
57	Israel	2.22
58	Peru	2.20
59	UK	2.14
60	Colombia	2.04
61	Italy	2.00
62	Taiwan	2.00
63	Japan	2.00
64	Morocco	1.96
65	Burma	1.88
66	Brazil	1.86
67	Honduras	1.82
68	Jamaica	1.81
69	Philippines	1.71
70	Lebanon	1.60
71	Syria	1.58
72	Puerto Rico	1.54
73	Haiti	1.54
74	Ecuador	1.54

75	Panama	1.54
76	Bolivia	1.54
77	Trinidad/Tobago	1.54
78	Paraguay	1.54
79	Dominican Rep	1.54
80	Singapore	1.50
81	Hong Kong	1.50
82	Iran	1.48
83	Jordan	1.38
84	Namibia	1.28
85	South Africa	1.25
86	Poland	1.24
87	El Salvador	1.24
88	Romania	1.23
89	Moldova	1.23
90	Yemen	1.13
91	Australia	1.11
92	Ireland	1.11
93	Ghana	0.98
94	Algeria	0.87
95	Iraq	0.84
96	Albania	0.83
97	Mozambique	0.78
98	Somalia	0.72
99	Madagascar	0.64
100	Tunisia	0.63
101	India	0.62
102	Libya	0.53
103	Sudan	0.53
104	Swaziland	0.43
105	Zimbabwe	0.40
106	Zambia	0.36
107	China	0.11
108	Oman	0.10
109	Korea, North	0.05
110	Korea, South	0.05
111	Pakistan	0.05
112	Bangladesh	0.02
113	Botswana	0.00
114	Burundi	0.00
115	Eritrea	0.00
116	Ethiopia	0.00
117	Guinea	0.00
118	Guinea-Bissau	0.00
119	Kosovo	0.00
120	Lesotho	0.00
121	Malawi	0.00
122	Sierra Leone	0.00
123	Afghanistan	-0.19
124	Mongolia	-0.19
125	Cambodia	-0.19
126	Laos	-0.19
127	Egypt	-0.20
128	Nepal	-0.23
129	Vietnam	-0.27
130	Costa Rica	-0.29

131	Thailand	-0.37
132	Mexico	-0.41
133	New Zealand	-0.77

Source: Calculated as (GPCPPP1929/GPCPPP1920)**(1/9)-1.

TABLE 5.13 - GDP PER CAPITA GROWTH RATES YEARS 1929-1938

OBS	COUNTRY	GRPCRL
1	Qatar	11.19
2	Kuwait	11.04
3	UAE	9.24
4	Ukraine	5.00
5	Russia	5.00
6	Uzbekistan	5.00
7	Georgia	5.00
8	Belarus	5.00
9	Kazakhstan	5.00
10	Azerbaijan	5.00
11	Turkmenistan	5.00
12	Kyrgyzstan	5.00
13	Tajikistan	5.00
14	Armenia	5.00
15	Korea, North	4.13
16	Korea, South	4.13
17	Turkey	3.98
18	Saudi Arabia	3.61
19	Bahrain	3.45
20	Bulgaria	3.41
21	Lithuania	3.14
22	Finland	3.14
23	Estonia	3.14
24	Latvia	3.14
25	Guatemala	2.90
26	Norway	2.50
27	Germany	2.35
28	New Zealand	2.31
29	Colombia	2.28
30	Sweden	2.25
31	Israel	2.22
32	Venezuela	2.14
33	Japan	2.13
34	Morocco	1.96
35	Costa Rica	1.91
36	Jamaica	1.81
37	Lebanon	1.60
38	Syria	1.58
39	Panama	1.54
40	Ecuador	1.54
41	Bolivia	1.54
42	Dominican Rep	1.54
43	Trinidad/Tobago	1.54
44	Puerto Rico	1.54
45	Paraguay	1.54
46	Haiti	1.54

47	Singapore	1.50
48	Hong Kong	1.50
49	Cyprus	1.50
50	Greece	1.50
51	Iran	1.48
52	UK	1.45
53	Taiwan	1.43
54	Denmark	1.42
55	Jordan	1.38
56	Brazil	1.29
57	Namibia	1.28
58	Australia	1.25
59	South Africa	1.25
60	Yemen	1.14
61	Ghana	0.98
62	Peru	0.91
63	Portugal	0.91
64	Ireland	0.87
65	Iraq	0.84
66	Moldova	0.84
67	Romania	0.84
68	Hungary	0.78
69	Italy	0.78
70	Mozambique	0.78
71	Somalia	0.72
72	Madagascar	0.64
73	Tunisia	0.63
74	Libya	0.53
75	Sudan	0.53
76	Thailand	0.45
77	Swaziland	0.43
78	Zimbabwe	0.40
79	Albania	0.37
80	Zambia	0.36
81	Poland	0.34
82	Mexico	0.23
83	Egypt	0.22
84	Philippines	0.15
85	Oman	0.10
86	Switzerland	0.10
87	Algeria	0.06
88	Indonesia	0.05
89	Botswana	0.00
90	Burundi	0.00
91	China	0.00
92	Eritrea	0.00
93	Ethiopia	0.00
94	Guinea	0.00
95	Guinea-Bissau	0.00
96	Kosovo	0.00
97	Lesotho	0.00
98	Malawi	0.00
99	Sierra Leone	0.00
100	Bosnia	-0.07
101	Croatia	-0.07
102	Montenegro	-0.07

103	Slovenia	-0.07
104	Serbia	-0.07
105	Macedonia	-0.07
106	Cambodia	-0.19
107	Laos	-0.19
108	Mongolia	-0.19
109	Afghanistan	-0.19
110	Nepal	-0.22
111	Vietnam	-0.27
112	Austria	-0.43
113	Belgium	-0.50
114	Uruguay	-0.50
115	France	-0.59
116	Czechia	-0.60
117	Slovakia	-0.60
118	El Salvador	-0.70
119	Argentina	-0.77
120	India	-0.79
121	Pakistan	-0.86
122	Chile	-0.87
123	Bangladesh	-0.87
124	Netherlands	-0.89
125	Sri Lanka	-0.96
126	Canada	-1.19
127	US	-1.31
128	Burma	-1.73
129	Cuba	-2.07
130	Malaysia	-2.33
131	Honduras	-3.33
132	Spain	-4.62
133	Nicaragua	-5.26

Source: Calculated as (GPCPPP1938/GPCPPP1929)**(1/9)-1.

TABLE 5.14 - GDP PER CAPITA GROWTH RATES YEARS 1938-1950		
OBS	COUNTRY	GRPCRL
1	Qatar	11.19
2	Kuwait	11.04
3	UAE	9.24
4	Moldova	8.55
5	Venezuela	5.02
6	Canada	4.02
7	US	3.78
8	Saudi Arabia	3.61
9	El Salvador	3.57
10	Cuba	3.47
11	Bahrain	3.45
12	Nicaragua	3.45
13	Sweden	3.00
14	Switzerland	2.96
15	Jamaica	2.63
16	Mexico	2.33
17	Brazil	2.28
18	New Zealand	2.27
19	Israel	2.22

20	Peru	2.13
21	Armenia	2.12
22	Tajikistan	2.12
23	Georgia	2.12
24	Turkmenistan	2.12
25	Kyrgyzstan	2.12
26	Kazakhstan	2.12
27	Russia	2.12
28	Belarus	2.12
29	Ukraine	2.12
30	Uzbekistan	2.12
31	Azerbaijan	2.12
32	Uruguay	1.99
33	Morocco	1.96
34	Norway	1.94
35	Australia	1.94
36	Argentina	1.70
37	Spain	1.69
38	Slovakia	1.63
39	Czechia	1.63
40	Lebanon	1.60
41	Syria	1.58
42	Denmark	1.57
43	Haiti	1.54
44	Puerto Rico	1.54
45	Paraguay	1.54
46	Panama	1.54
47	Trinidad/Tobago	1.54
48	Ecuador	1.54
49	Bolivia	1.54
50	Dominican Rep	1.54
51	Singapore	1.50
52	Hong Kong	1.50
53	Portugal	1.49
54	Iran	1.48
55	Honduras	1.45
56	Finland	1.42
57	France	1.39
58	Jordan	1.38
59	Colombia	1.30
60	Namibia	1.28
61	South Africa	1.25
62	Malaysia	1.14
63	Yemen	1.14
64	Macedonia	1.13
65	Bosnia	1.13
66	Serbia	1.13
67	Slovenia	1.13
68	Croatia	1.13
69	Montenegro	1.13
70	Netherlands	1.11
71	Ireland	1.03
72	Belgium	1.03
73	Ghana	0.98
74	Latvia	0.97
75	Estonia	0.97

76	Lithuania	0.97
77	Poland	0.96
78	UK	0.85
79	Iraq	0.84
80	Mozambique	0.78
81	Somalia	0.72
82	Chile	0.65
83	Madagascar	0.64
84	Tunisia	0.63
85	Libya	0.53
86	Sudan	0.53
87	Italy	0.46
88	Swaziland	0.43
89	Zimbabwe	0.40
90	Costa Rica	0.38
91	Albania	0.37
92	Zambia	0.36
93	Austria	0.34
94	Bulgaria	0.29
95	Sri Lanka	0.19
96	Egypt	0.18
97	Oman	0.10
98	India	0.00
99	Algeria	-0.04
100	Thailand	-0.09
101	Cambodia	-0.19
102	Mongolia	-0.19
103	Afghanistan	-0.19
104	Laos	-0.19
105	Nepal	-0.22
106	Vietnam	-0.27
107	Romania	-0.41
108	Pakistan	-0.47
109	Bangladesh	-0.48
110	Kosovo	-0.49
111	Turkey	-0.50
112	Guatemala	-0.54
113	Hungary	-0.57
114	Burundi	-0.87
115	Lesotho	-0.99
116	Botswana	-1.13
117	Malawi	-1.74
118	Sierra Leone	-1.98
119	Japan	-2.00
120	China	-2.04
121	Germany	-2.08
122	Guinea	-2.29
123	Guinea-Bissau	-2.67
124	Cyprus	-2.75
125	Greece	-2.75
126	Indonesia	-2.76
127	Taiwan	-2.82
128	Philippines	-2.89
129	Eritrea	-3.10
130	Ethiopia	-3.33
131	Burma	-5.08

| 132 | Korea, North | -5.19 |
| 133 | Korea, South | -5.19 |

Source: Calculated as (GPCPPP1950/GPCPPP1938)**(1/12)-1.

TABLE 5.15 - GDP PER CAPITA GROWTH RATES YEARS 1950-1960		
OBS	COUNTRY	GRPCRL
1	Libya	8.49
2	Jamaica	8.27
3	Bermuda	7.77
4	Germany	7.59
5	Bahrain	7.56
6	Saudi Arabia	7.52
7	Japan	7.51
8	Montenegro	7.45
9	Serbia	7.37
10	Kosovo	7.37
11	Iraq	7.20
12	Macao	6.83
13	Martinique	6.82
14	Gibraltar	6.82
15	Algeria	6.60
16	Austria	6.34
17	St Kitts & Nevis	6.24
18	Romania	6.23
19	Barbados	6.20
20	Macedonia	6.18
21	Guadeloupe	6.17
22	Greece	5.98
23	Zambia	5.65
24	Bulgaria	5.57
25	Italy	5.57
26	Bosnia	5.51
27	Cyprus	5.33
28	Israel	5.19
29	Malta	5.16
30	St Lucia	5.13
31	Oman	5.05
32	Croatia	4.98
33	Hungary	4.84
34	Somalia	4.84
35	San Marino	4.82
36	Samoa, Ameri	4.75
37	Slovenia	4.72
38	Isle of Man	4.71
39	Liberia	4.70
40	Czechia	4.69
41	Taiwan	4.66
42	Neth Antilles	4.51
43	Slovakia	4.29
44	Trinidad/Tobago	4.27
45	Albania	4.24
46	Monaco	4.08
47	Aruba	3.92

48	Chad	3.92
49	Faeroe Is	3.89
50	Spain	3.80
51	Andorra	3.80
52	Finland	3.77
53	Greenland	3.77
54	Suriname	3.74
55	Switzerland	3.73
56	Puerto Rico	3.70
57	France	3.69
58	Jersey	3.69
59	Korea, North	3.68
60	Guernsey	3.68
61	Mongolia	3.62
62	Liechtenstein	3.62
63	Portugal	3.59
64	UAE	3.54
65	Guinea	3.54
66	Korea, South	3.53
67	Hong Kong	3.52
68	Netherlands	3.50
69	Brazil	3.47
70	Mauritania	3.44
71	Congo, Dem R	3.43
72	Iceland	3.43
73	China	3.42
74	Kyrgyzstan	3.39
75	Uzbekistan	3.38
76	Moldova	3.37
77	Tajikistan	3.36
78	Turkmenistan	3.34
79	Turkey	3.33
80	Lithuania	3.33
81	Latvia	3.33
82	Russia	3.33
83	Belarus	3.33
84	Ukraine	3.32
85	Azerbaijan	3.32
86	Kazakhstan	3.32
87	Norway	3.29
88	Armenia	3.29
89	Peru	3.28
90	Grenada	3.25
91	Seychelles	3.25
92	Central African Rep.	3.25
93	Georgia	3.24
94	Turks & Caicos	3.23
95	Equatorial G	3.22
96	Swaziland	3.17
97	Costa Rica	3.16
98	Mexico	3.15
99	Luxembourg	3.11
100	Togo	3.09
101	Papua New Gu	3.09
102	Gabon	3.01
103	Poland	3.00

104	Virgin Is, Brit.	2.92
105	St Pierre &	2.90
106	Cayman Is	2.86
107	Falkland Is	2.86
108	W Sahara	2.86
109	St Helena	2.86
110	Mayotte	2.86
111	Cameroon	2.80
112	Ecuador	2.77
113	Niue	2.70
114	Sierra Leone	2.67
115	Estonia	2.67
116	Sweden	2.67
117	Anguilla	2.58
118	Iran	2.55
119	South Africa	2.54
120	Madagascar	2.53
121	Philippines	2.52
122	Belgium	2.49
123	El Salvador	2.40
124	Comoros	2.40
125	Dominican Rep	2.36
126	Denmark	2.34
127	Zimbabwe	2.30
128	Thailand	2.29
129	Sudan	2.27
130	Panama	2.27
131	Antigua & Barbuda	2.26
132	Palau	2.25
133	Ireland	2.24
134	Virgin I, US	2.24
135	UK	2.22
136	Niger	2.15
137	Guam	2.13
138	Jordan	2.09
139	Cambodia	2.06
140	St Vincent	2.02
141	Fr Polynesia	1.98
142	Brunei	1.95
143	Cook Is	1.92
144	Canada	1.89
145	Bahamas	1.87
146	Burma	1.79
147	Kiribati	1.77
148	Angola	1.76
149	Dominica	1.76
150	Tunisia	1.71
151	US	1.71
152	Belize	1.71
153	Botswana	1.70
154	Australia	1.67
155	Maldives	1.65
156	Congo, Rep	1.64
157	Nicaragua	1.64
158	Lesotho	1.61
159	Burkina Faso	1.60

160	Tokelau	1.57
161	Tuvalu	1.56
162	New Caledonia	1.50
163	Samoa, W	1.49
164	Tonga	1.49
165	Solomon Is	1.49
166	Vanuatu	1.49
167	Micronesia	1.48
168	India	1.42
169	Afghanistan	1.37
170	Indonesia	1.35
171	Vietnam	1.33
172	Guyana	1.30
173	Ivory Coast	1.26
174	Malawi	1.21
175	Namibia	1.20
176	Wallis & Futuna	1.19
177	Ethiopia	1.18
178	Cape Verde	1.18
179	Gambia	1.13
180	Marshall Is	1.11
181	Colombia	1.10
182	New Zealand	1.10
183	Nigeria	1.08
184	Tanzania	1.08
185	Reunion	1.05
186	Guinea-Bissau	0.98
187	Mali	0.96
188	Chile	0.95
189	N Mariana Is	0.95
190	Montserrat	0.94
191	East Timor	0.93
192	Nepal	0.91
193	Kenya	0.90
194	Venezuela	0.89
195	Laos	0.88
196	Argentina	0.88
197	Egypt	0.88
198	Qatar	0.86
199	Eritrea	0.81
200	Benin	0.80
201	Mauritius	0.74
202	Honduras	0.70
203	Bhutan	0.63
204	Guatemala	0.57
205	Djibouti	0.53
206	Uruguay	0.44
207	Syria	0.44
208	Singapore	0.44
209	Yemen	0.28
210	San Tome & Principe	0.24
211	Sri Lanka	0.23
212	Rwanda	0.21
213	Fiji	0.05
214	Pakistan	0.05
215	Bangladesh	0.04

216	Haiti	0.03
217	Cuba	0.01
218	Kuwait	0.00
219	Uganda	-0.09
220	Paraguay	-0.16
221	Malaysia	-0.18
222	Lebanon	-0.33
223	West Bank	-0.54
224	Gaza Strip	-0.54
225	Senegal	-0.59
226	Guiana, Fr	-0.64
227	Morocco	-0.67
228	Ghana	-1.24
229	Nauru	-1.70
230	Bolivia	-1.76
231	Mozambique	-1.83
232	Burundi	-2.17

Source: Calculated as (GPCPPP1960/GPCPPP1950)**(1/10)-1.

TABLE 5.16 - GDP PER CAPITA GROWTH RATES YEARS 1960-1970

OBS	COUNTRY	GRPCRL
1	Libya	18.82
2	Oman	18.53
3	Saudi Arabia	10.73
4	Swaziland	9.80
5	Japan	9.24
6	Greece	8.28
7	Spain	8.26
8	Bermuda	7.77
9	Iran	7.68
10	Singapore	7.31
11	Bahrain	7.20
12	Montenegro	7.11
13	Serbia	7.04
14	Kosovo	7.04
15	Togo	6.95
16	Macao	6.83
17	Martinique	6.82
18	Gibraltar	6.82
19	Taiwan	6.79
20	Portugal	6.43
21	St Kitts & Nevis	6.24
22	Barbados	6.20
23	Guadeloupe	6.17
24	Mauritania	6.17
25	Hong Kong	6.15
26	Romania	6.11
27	Liberia	5.94
28	Macedonia	5.91
29	Korea, North	5.87
30	Botswana	5.72
31	Israel	5.71
32	Equatorial G	5.67

33	Korea, South	5.62
34	Cyprus	5.33
35	Bosnia	5.27
36	Italy	5.27
37	Malta	5.16
38	St Lucia	5.13
39	Puerto Rico	4.93
40	Panama	4.84
41	Bulgaria	4.84
42	San Marino	4.82
43	Croatia	4.76
44	Samoa, Ameri	4.75
45	Isle of Man	4.71
46	Slovenia	4.51
47	Neth Antilles	4.51
48	France	4.49
49	Austria	4.47
50	Lebanon	4.44
51	Belgium	4.40
52	Jamaica	4.35
53	Finland	4.26
54	Monaco	4.08
55	Sweden	4.03
56	South Africa	4.01
57	Hungary	4.00
58	Netherlands	3.99
59	Norway	3.94
60	Aruba	3.92
61	Reunion	3.91
62	Faeroe Is	3.89
63	Ireland	3.88
64	Andorra	3.80
65	Greenland	3.77
66	Thailand	3.76
67	Suriname	3.74
68	Germany	3.71
69	Jersey	3.69
70	Albania	3.68
71	Guernsey	3.68
72	Mongolia	3.63
73	Liechtenstein	3.62
74	Denmark	3.60
75	Switzerland	3.58
76	Uzbekistan	3.58
77	Kyrgyzstan	3.57
78	Moldova	3.56
79	Tajikistan	3.55
80	Poland	3.53
81	Turkmenistan	3.52
82	Lithuania	3.51
83	Latvia	3.51
84	Russia	3.51
85	Belarus	3.51
86	Azerbaijan	3.50
87	Kazakhstan	3.50
88	Ukraine	3.50

89	Comoros	3.50
90	Angola	3.49
91	Armenia	3.47
92	Mexico	3.44
93	Iceland	3.43
94	Gabon	3.43
95	Georgia	3.42
96	Canada	3.33
97	Grenada	3.25
98	Turks & Caicos	3.23
99	Turkey	3.22
100	Costa Rica	3.16
101	Luxembourg	3.11
102	Papua New Gu	3.09
103	Australia	3.09
104	Bolivia	3.07
105	El Salvador	3.06
106	Malaysia	3.03
107	Ethiopia	3.00
108	Pakistan	2.95
109	Czechia	2.94
110	Ecuador	2.92
111	Virgin Is, Brit.	2.92
112	Tanzania	2.90
113	St Pierre &	2.90
114	Nigeria	2.88
115	US	2.87
116	Cayman Is	2.86
117	Falkland Is	2.86
118	Tunisia	2.85
119	Estonia	2.81
120	Nicaragua	2.81
121	Brazil	2.79
122	Sierra Leone	2.78
123	Niue	2.69
124	Slovakia	2.65
125	Peru	2.61
126	Anguilla	2.58
127	Ivory Coast	2.56
128	Zimbabwe	2.47
129	Egypt	2.44
130	Iraq	2.42
131	Guinea	2.27
132	Antigua & Barbuda	2.26
133	Palau	2.25
134	Virgin I, US	2.24
135	Argentina	2.23
136	San Tome & Principe	2.22
137	UK	2.22
138	Trinidad/Tobago	2.20
139	Cameroon	2.15
140	Guam	2.13
141	Eritrea	2.06
142	St Vincent	2.02
143	Fr Polynesia	1.98
144	Brunei	1.95

145	Cape Verde	1.93
146	Cook Is	1.92
147	Kenya	1.90
148	Bahamas	1.87
149	Dominican Rep	1.80
150	Congo, Rep	1.78
151	Kiribati	1.77
152	Guatemala	1.76
153	Dominica	1.76
154	Lesotho	1.75
155	Belize	1.71
156	Maldives	1.65
157	Zambia	1.65
158	New Zealand	1.63
159	Colombia	1.60
160	Chile	1.58
161	Paraguay	1.57
162	Tokelau	1.57
163	Tuvalu	1.56
164	Honduras	1.51
165	Namibia	1.50
166	New Caledonia	1.50
167	Samoa, W	1.49
168	Tonga	1.49
169	Solomon Is	1.49
170	Vanuatu	1.49
171	Micronesia	1.48
172	Morocco	1.47
173	Philippines	1.39
174	Guyana	1.30
175	Gambia	1.29
176	Madagascar	1.29
177	Seychelles	1.24
178	Yemen	1.23
179	China	1.20
180	Wallis & Futuna	1.19
181	Algeria	1.12
182	Marshall Is	1.11
183	Indonesia	1.10
184	India	1.03
185	Guinea-Bissau	0.99
186	N Mariana Is	0.95
187	Montserrat	0.94
188	East Timor	0.93
189	Sri Lanka	0.92
190	Burkina Faso	0.90
191	UAE	0.90
192	Bangladesh	0.88
193	Laos	0.84
194	Malawi	0.81
195	Burma	0.65
196	Bhutan	0.63
197	Mali	0.58
198	Djibouti	0.50
199	Niger	0.48
200	Congo, Dem R	0.42

201	Mauritius	0.40
202	Venezuela	0.35
203	Nepal	0.33
204	Uruguay	0.31
205	Syria	0.30
206	Mayotte	0.27
207	St Helena	0.27
208	W Sahara	0.27
209	Jordan	0.17
210	Rwanda	0.10
211	Fiji	0.05
212	Kuwait	0.05
213	Senegal	0.03
214	Qatar	0.02
215	Ghana	-0.20
216	Cuba	-0.24
217	Cambodia	-0.32
218	Benin	-0.38
219	Afghanistan	-0.41
220	Uganda	-0.48
221	Gaza Strip	-0.52
222	West Bank	-0.52
223	Central African Rep.	-0.56
224	Vietnam	-0.56
225	Guiana, Fr	-0.64
226	Haiti	-1.26
227	Sudan	-1.44
228	Nauru	-1.70
229	Burundi	-2.06
230	Chad	-2.21
231	Somalia	-2.84
232	Mozambique	-3.14

Source: Calculated as (GPCPPP1970/GPCPPP1960)**(1/10)-1.

TABLE 5.17 - GDP PER CAPITA GROWTH RATES YEARS 1970-1980		
OBS	COUNTRY	GRPCRL
1	Botswana	12.30
2	Macao	10.84
3	Malta	9.88
4	Saudi Arabia	8.20
5	Singapore	8.01
6	Seychelles	7.92
7	Montenegro	7.91
8	Serbia	7.83
9	Kosovo	7.83
10	Korea, South	7.40
11	Taiwan	6.65
12	Macedonia	6.57
13	Hong Kong	6.31
14	Iraq	6.27
15	Bosnia	5.85
16	Malaysia	5.65
17	Brazil	5.58

18	Croatia	5.28
19	Egypt	5.26
20	Romania	5.17
21	Algeria	5.16
22	Ecuador	5.06
23	Slovenia	5.01
24	Norway	4.92
25	Paraguay	4.89
26	Tunisia	4.45
27	Gibraltar	4.43
28	Greece	4.39
29	Suriname	4.29
30	Mozambique	4.26
31	Lebanon	4.24
32	Spain	4.22
33	Dominican Rep	4.20
34	Mexico	4.12
35	Maldives	4.07
36	Iceland	4.04
37	Portugal	3.97
38	Jordan	3.92
39	Austria	3.82
40	Korea, North	3.81
41	Bahrain	3.63
42	Mongolia	3.62
43	Bermuda	3.42
44	Thailand	3.41
45	Ireland	3.36
46	Japan	3.26
47	Trinidad/Tobago	3.25
48	Lesotho	3.24
49	Belgium	3.21
50	Italy	3.17
51	Yemen	3.17
52	Indonesia	3.16
53	San Marino	3.14
54	Israel	3.11
55	Haiti	3.08
56	Isle of Man	3.07
57	Canada	3.06
58	Brunei	3.04
59	Cape Verde	3.01
60	Finland	2.97
61	Panama	2.97
62	Germany	2.86
63	Poland	2.85
64	Hungary	2.81
65	Barbados	2.80
66	Turkey	2.71
67	Mauritius	2.68
68	Monaco	2.66
69	Congo, Rep	2.65
70	France	2.64
71	Costa Rica	2.61
72	Czechia	2.60
73	Morocco	2.57

74	Cyprus	2.54
75	Cameroon	2.54
76	Faeroe Is	2.54
77	Andorra	2.48
78	China	2.46
79	Greenland	2.46
80	Martinique	2.44
81	Guadeloupe	2.42
82	Colombia	2.41
83	Jersey	2.41
84	Guernsey	2.40
85	Aruba	2.39
86	Guinea	2.38
87	Slovakia	2.37
88	Liechtenstein	2.36
89	Philippines	2.33
90	Bulgaria	2.28
91	Antigua & Barbuda	2.26
92	Malawi	2.25
93	Netherlands	2.22
94	Belarus	2.15
95	US	2.14
96	Honduras	2.09
97	St Lucia	2.07
98	Puerto Rico	1.99
99	Swaziland	1.98
100	Turks & Caicos	1.98
101	Belize	1.90
102	UK	1.85
103	Samoa, Ameri	1.84
104	Georgia	1.80
105	Latvia	1.79
106	Denmark	1.79
107	Virgin Is, Brit.	1.79
108	Albania	1.78
109	Guyana	1.78
110	St Pierre &	1.77
111	Australia	1.77
112	Cayman Is	1.75
113	Falkland Is	1.75
114	Uruguay	1.69
115	Sweden	1.68
116	Bolivia	1.68
117	St Vincent	1.67
118	Guatemala	1.67
119	Ukraine	1.67
120	Grenada	1.66
121	Bhutan	1.60
122	Anguilla	1.58
123	Cambodia	1.56
124	Russia	1.52
125	Pakistan	1.51
126	San Tome & Principe	1.45
127	Gabon	1.45
128	Moldova	1.43
129	Nigeria	1.42

130	Estonia	1.41
131	W Sahara	1.40
132	St Helena	1.40
133	Mayotte	1.40
134	Mali	1.37
135	Lithuania	1.37
136	Virgin I, US	1.37
137	Laos	1.37
138	Namibia	1.30
139	Ghana	1.27
140	Burma	1.26
141	Sri Lanka	1.25
142	Switzerland	1.22
143	UAE	1.21
144	Equatorial G	1.19
145	Syria	1.17
146	Cuba	1.13
147	South Africa	1.13
148	Peru	1.12
149	Gambia	1.09
150	Niue	1.05
151	El Salvador	1.04
152	Azerbaijan	1.02
153	Uganda	1.00
154	Ivory Coast	0.99
155	Kenya	0.98
156	New Zealand	0.96
157	Argentina	0.95
158	Palau	0.88
159	Luxembourg	0.87
160	Oman	0.85
161	Guam	0.83
162	Ethiopia	0.83
163	Armenia	0.78
164	Fr Polynesia	0.77
165	Cook Is	0.75
166	Kyrgyzstan	0.70
167	Kiribati	0.69
168	Kazakhstan	0.66
169	Chile	0.63
170	Tokelau	0.61
171	Tanzania	0.61
172	Tuvalu	0.61
173	New Caledonia	0.58
174	Solomon Is	0.58
175	Vanuatu	0.58
176	Montserrat	0.58
177	Micronesia	0.58
178	Eritrea	0.57
179	India	0.56
180	Reunion	0.55
181	Sudan	0.48
182	Wallis & Futuna	0.47
183	Marshall Is	0.44
184	Senegal	0.42
185	N Mariana Is	0.37

186	East Timor	0.36
187	Rwanda	0.33
188	Bahamas	0.22
189	Samoa, W	0.22
190	Vietnam	0.21
191	Papua New Gu	0.16
192	Zimbabwe	0.08
193	Uzbekistan	0.06
194	Fiji	0.03
195	Sierra Leone	-0.09
196	Nepal	-0.11
197	Venezuela	-0.18
198	Afghanistan	-0.18
199	Guiana, Fr	-0.23
200	Guinea-Bissau	-0.26
201	Neth Antilles	-0.27
202	Burkina Faso	-0.34
203	Turkmenistan	-0.34
204	Dominica	-0.35
205	Togo	-0.39
206	West Bank	-0.47
207	Gaza Strip	-0.47
208	Tajikistan	-0.48
209	Mauritania	-0.58
210	Iran	-0.59
211	Kuwait	-0.64
212	Nauru	-0.67
213	Djibouti	-0.70
214	Benin	-0.76
215	Bangladesh	-0.83
216	Tonga	-1.02
217	Qatar	-1.15
218	Niger	-1.48
219	Burundi	-1.51
220	Comoros	-1.60
221	Nicaragua	-2.09
222	Madagascar	-2.21
223	Somalia	-2.30
224	St Kitts & Nevis	-2.34
225	Jamaica	-2.37
226	Zambia	-2.38
227	Libya	-2.40
228	Central African Rep.	-2.62
229	Congo, Dem R	-2.81
230	Angola	-5.89
231	Liberia	-7.83
232	Chad	-8.54

Source: Calculated as (GPCPPP1980/GPCPPP1970)**(1/10)-1.

TABLE 5.18 - GDP PER CAPITA GROWTH RATES YEARS 1980-1990		
OBS	COUNTRY	GRPCRL
1	Antigua & Barbuda	9.38

2	Angola	9.25
3	Korea, South	7.46
4	Botswana	7.36
5	St Lucia	6.98
6	Bhutan	6.92
7	St Kitts & Nevis	6.16
8	Cyprus	5.98
9	Oman	5.79
10	Grenada	5.52
11	Luxembourg	5.46
12	Hong Kong	5.26
13	Dominica	5.16
14	Maldives	5.12
15	Singapore	5.11
16	Taiwan	5.08
17	Thailand	4.98
18	Gabon	4.89
19	Chad	4.78
20	St Vincent	4.70
21	China	4.46
22	Malta	4.26
23	Cape Verde	3.75
24	Gibraltar	3.42
25	Ireland	3.40
26	Japan	3.39
27	Malaysia	3.35
28	Mauritius	3.35
29	Brunei	3.34
30	Solomon Is	3.31
31	Turkey	3.12
32	Portugal	3.05
33	Spain	3.02
34	Macao	2.97
35	Mongolia	2.82
36	Finland	2.60
37	UAE	2.50
38	Pakistan	2.43
39	San Marino	2.42
40	India	2.42
41	UK	2.42
42	Isle of Man	2.37
43	Norway	2.36
44	Seychelles	2.33
45	Austria	2.27
46	Italy	2.25
47	US	2.25
48	Vietnam	2.17
49	Vanuatu	2.09
50	Indonesia	2.08
51	Monaco	2.06
52	Egypt	2.05
53	Puerto Rico	1.99
54	Faeroe Is	1.96
55	Andorra	1.92
56	Greenland	1.90
57	Denmark	1.88

58	Belarus	1.87
59	Jersey	1.86
60	Guernsey	1.86
61	France	1.84
62	Liechtenstein	1.83
63	Belize	1.82
64	Tonga	1.82
65	Reunion	1.79
66	Belgium	1.78
67	Sweden	1.77
68	Aruba	1.75
69	Sri Lanka	1.73
70	Netherlands	1.72
71	Israel	1.68
72	Jamaica	1.68
73	Australia	1.68
74	Iceland	1.62
75	Bermuda	1.62
76	Canada	1.59
77	Switzerland	1.56
78	Turks & Caicos	1.44
79	Georgia	1.41
80	Barbados	1.37
81	Latvia	1.36
82	Virgin Is, Brit.	1.31
83	Germany	1.30
84	St Pierre &	1.30
85	Cayman Is	1.28
86	Falkland Is	1.28
87	Greece	1.26
88	Ukraine	1.19
89	New Zealand	1.16
90	Anguilla	1.15
91	Tunisia	1.15
92	Lesotho	1.12
93	Somalia	1.09
94	Nepal	1.08
95	Mozambique	1.06
96	W Sahara	1.06
97	Mayotte	1.06
98	St Helena	1.06
99	Virgin I, US	1.00
100	Morocco	1.00
101	Russia	0.98
102	Colombia	0.94
103	Bangladesh	0.94
104	Estonia	0.88
105	Chile	0.85
106	Moldova	0.83
107	Czechia	0.79
108	Lithuania	0.76
109	Slovakia	0.72
110	Burkina Faso	0.70
111	Albania	0.68
112	Martinique	0.62
113	Samoa, Ameri	0.61

114	Equatorial G	0.56
115	Samoa, W	0.56
116	Laos	0.54
117	Ghana	0.51
118	Kenya	0.48
119	Cambodia	0.46
120	Montserrat	0.42
121	Dominican Rep	0.42
122	Cameroon	0.40
123	Cuba	0.38
124	Zimbabwe	0.36
125	Niue	0.35
126	Palau	0.29
127	Hungary	0.29
128	Guam	0.28
129	Azerbaijan	0.27
130	Comoros	0.26
131	Fr Polynesia	0.26
132	Guadeloupe	0.25
133	Cook Is	0.25
134	Tokelau	0.21
135	Tuvalu	0.20
136	New Caledonia	0.20
137	Micronesia	0.19
138	Swaziland	0.18
139	Wallis & Futuna	0.16
140	Marshall Is	0.15
141	N Mariana Is	0.13
142	East Timor	0.12
143	Guinea-Bissau	0.10
144	Congo, Rep	0.08
145	Fiji	0.02
146	Korea, North	0.00
147	Mali	-0.02
148	Yemen	-0.04
149	Paraguay	-0.04
150	Uganda	-0.06
151	Armenia	-0.06
152	Guiana, Fr	-0.06
153	Rwanda	-0.09
154	Benin	-0.10
155	Uruguay	-0.11
156	Burma	-0.14
157	Senegal	-0.20
158	Kyrgyzstan	-0.21
159	Nauru	-0.23
160	Kazakhstan	-0.24
161	Syria	-0.25
162	Mexico	-0.29
163	Costa Rica	-0.33
164	Honduras	-0.34
165	Djibouti	-0.44
166	Gaza Strip	-0.47
167	West Bank	-0.47
168	Bahamas	-0.48
169	Slovenia	-0.49

170	Philippines	-0.51
171	Croatia	-0.51
172	Brazil	-0.55
173	Bosnia	-0.57
174	Kuwait	-0.59
175	Guinea	-0.62
176	Macedonia	-0.63
177	Venezuela	-0.68
178	Eritrea	-0.68
179	Bulgaria	-0.73
180	Ecuador	-0.74
181	Kosovo	-0.75
182	Serbia	-0.75
183	Montenegro	-0.76
184	Sierra Leone	-0.86
185	Malawi	-0.88
186	Kiribati	-0.92
187	Ethiopia	-0.99
188	Mauritania	-1.01
189	Jordan	-1.02
190	Papua New Gu	-1.06
191	Uzbekistan	-1.09
192	Algeria	-1.11
193	Gambia	-1.18
194	Poland	-1.24
195	Tanzania	-1.26
196	Panama	-1.30
197	Namibia	-1.37
198	South Africa	-1.39
199	Guatemala	-1.40
200	Iran	-1.46
201	El Salvador	-1.46
202	Afghanistan	-1.47
203	Central African Rep.	-1.52
204	Bolivia	-1.56
205	San Tome & Principe	-1.58
206	Zambia	-1.59
207	Nigeria	-1.60
208	Bahrain	-1.61
209	Burundi	-1.63
210	Turkmenistan	-1.67
211	Haiti	-1.86
212	Tajikistan	-1.87
213	Congo, Dem R	-1.92
214	Guyana	-1.94
215	Argentina	-1.94
216	Romania	-2.20
217	Neth Antilles	-2.24
218	Trinidad/Tobago	-2.25
219	Sudan	-2.27
220	Ivory Coast	-2.88
221	Liberia	-3.03
222	Suriname	-3.06
223	Nicaragua	-3.07
224	Peru	-3.86
225	Madagascar	-4.05

226	Togo	-4.93
227	Saudi Arabia	-5.21
228	Qatar	-5.96
229	Niger	-6.31
230	Libya	-8.79
231	Iraq	-9.09
232	Lebanon	-12.29

Source: Calculated as (GPCPPP1990/GPCPPP1980)**(1/10)-1.

TABLE 5.19 - GDP PER CAPITA GROWTH RATES YEARS 1990-2000		
OBS	COUNTRY	GRPCRL
1	Equatorial G	17.29
2	Mayotte	15.53
3	Lebanon	13.18
4	Brunei	9.60
5	Libya	9.58
6	New Caledonia	7.49
7	Ireland	6.62
8	Samoa, Ameri	5.24
9	Bahrain	5.23
10	Taiwan	5.07
11	China	4.93
12	Korea, South	4.91
13	Singapore	4.82
14	Bhutan	4.73
15	Malta	4.41
16	Luxembourg	4.40
17	Malaysia	4.25
18	Vietnam	3.95
19	Dominican Rep	3.94
20	Poland	3.80
21	Botswana	3.73
22	St Kitts & Nevis	3.72
23	Seychelles	3.70
24	Cape Verde	3.61
25	Iran	3.54
26	El Salvador	3.54
27	Maldives	3.48
28	Chile	3.38
29	Norway	3.29
30	Guyana	3.09
31	Grenada	3.07
32	Trinidad/Tobago	3.06
33	Sudan	2.97
34	Niue	2.97
35	Tunisia	2.85
36	Cyprus	2.80
37	India	2.75
38	Mauritius	2.74
39	Gibraltar	2.71
40	Burma	2.68
41	Portugal	2.65

42	Spain	2.64
43	Panama	2.63
44	Bermuda	2.62
45	Thailand	2.60
46	Burundi	2.59
47	Costa Rica	2.56
48	Peru	2.50
49	Palau	2.48
50	Sri Lanka	2.46
51	Belize	2.41
52	Netherlands	2.41
53	Tonga	2.35
54	Guam	2.34
55	St Vincent	2.33
56	Argentina	2.32
57	Puerto Rico	2.29
58	Australia	2.26
59	Israel	2.23
60	Laos	2.23
61	Greece	2.21
62	Fr Polynesia	2.17
63	Denmark	2.17
64	Cook Is	2.11
65	Hong Kong	2.05
66	Guadeloupe	2.04
67	Lesotho	1.99
68	St Lucia	1.97
69	Turkey	1.95
70	Kiribati	1.95
71	US	1.94
72	Belgium	1.93
73	San Marino	1.93
74	Austria	1.90
75	UK	1.89
76	Bangladesh	1.89
77	Isle of Man	1.89
78	Dominica	1.83
79	Mexico	1.79
80	Martinique	1.79
81	Finland	1.78
82	Tokelau	1.72
83	Tuvalu	1.71
84	Guiana, Fr	1.71
85	Slovenia	1.71
86	Indonesia	1.69
87	Cambodia	1.68
88	Canada	1.68
89	Neth Antilles	1.67
90	Germany	1.67
91	Monaco	1.64
92	Bolivia	1.59
93	Iceland	1.57
94	Faeroe Is	1.56
95	Andorra	1.52
96	Greenland	1.51
97	Egypt	1.51

98	Samoa, W	1.50
99	Jersey	1.48
100	Guernsey	1.48
101	Liechtenstein	1.45
102	Italy	1.44
103	Sweden	1.44
104	France	1.42
105	Pakistan	1.40
106	Uruguay	1.38
107	Antigua & Barbuda	1.38
108	New Zealand	1.37
109	Wallis & Futuna	1.31
110	Brazil	1.24
111	Hungary	1.23
112	Marshall Is	1.23
113	Malawi	1.22
114	Mauritania	1.14
115	Japan	1.14
116	Guinea	1.14
117	Papua New Gu	1.13
118	N Mariana Is	1.05
119	East Timor	1.02
120	Macao	1.00
121	Nepal	0.96
122	Namibia	0.92
123	Burkina Faso	0.89
124	Guatemala	0.85
125	Mali	0.84
126	Swaziland	0.82
127	Afghanistan	0.81
128	Oman	0.75
129	Barbados	0.74
130	Albania	0.69
131	Aruba	0.68
132	Yemen	0.66
133	South Africa	0.59
134	Turks & Caicos	0.56
135	Nicaragua	0.55
136	Philippines	0.54
137	Syria	0.52
138	Virgin Is, Brit.	0.51
139	St Pierre &	0.51
140	Cayman Is	0.50
141	Falkland Is	0.50
142	Honduras	0.50
143	Eritrea	0.49
144	Anguilla	0.45
145	Micronesia	0.43
146	Jordan	0.42
147	Kuwait	0.39
148	Virgin I, US	0.39
149	Colombia	0.38
150	Qatar	0.32
151	Vanuatu	0.29
152	Switzerland	0.29
153	Gambia	0.21

154	Czechia	0.21
155	Morocco	0.18
156	Montserrat	0.17
157	Chad	0.15
158	Reunion	0.15
159	Slovakia	0.11
160	St Helena	0.08
161	W Sahara	0.08
162	Fiji	0.08
163	Estonia	0.05
164	Venezuela	0.04
165	Nigeria	-0.04
166	Bahamas	-0.07
167	Rwanda	-0.07
168	Suriname	-0.19
169	Jamaica	-0.20
170	Senegal	-0.21
171	Ivory Coast	-0.23
172	Guinea-Bissau	-0.28
173	Turkmenistan	-0.37
174	Solomon Is	-0.37
175	Bulgaria	-0.40
176	Tanzania	-0.41
177	Ethiopia	-0.42
178	Gaza Strip	-0.43
179	West Bank	-0.43
180	Zimbabwe	-0.45
181	San Tome & Principe	-0.54
182	Kenya	-0.54
183	Algeria	-0.66
184	Uganda	-0.69
185	Cuba	-0.70
186	Paraguay	-0.73
187	Congo, Rep	-0.81
188	Djibouti	-0.87
189	Gabon	-0.88
190	Comoros	-1.04
191	Croatia	-1.10
192	Benin	-1.10
193	Ghana	-1.12
194	Cameroon	-1.27
195	Central African Rep.	-1.55
196	Niger	-1.61
197	Madagascar	-1.82
198	UAE	-1.82
199	Saudi Arabia	-1.83
200	Nauru	-1.87
201	Iraq	-1.88
202	Angola	-2.01
203	Haiti	-2.07
204	Romania	-2.11
205	Mongolia	-2.12
206	Russia	-2.18
207	Macedonia	-2.22
208	Lithuania	-2.35
209	Mozambique	-2.89

210	Zambia	-2.97
211	Ecuador	-3.00
212	Bosnia	-3.41
213	Togo	-4.19
214	Latvia	-4.48
215	Belarus	-5.20
216	Somalia	-5.52
217	Liberia	-5.54
218	Sierra Leone	-5.58
219	Kazakhstan	-6.21
220	Ukraine	-7.78
221	Azerbaijan	-8.99
222	Congo, Dem R	-10.02
223	Kyrgyzstan	-11.45
224	Korea, North	-11.76
225	Kosovo	-11.85
226	Serbia	-11.85
227	Montenegro	-11.97
228	Armenia	-12.02
229	Uzbekistan	-12.13
230	Tajikistan	-13.27
231	Georgia	-13.59
232	Moldova	-16.36

Source: Calculated as (GPCPPP2000/GPCPPP1990)**(1/10)-1.

TABLE 5.20 - GDP PER CAPITA GROWTH RATES YEARS 2000-2007		
OBS	COUNTRY	GRPCRL
1	Bermuda	19.42
2	Liechtenstein	19.18
3	Qatar	18.78
4	Azerbaijan	15.98
5	Equatorial G	15.62
6	Chad	15.32
7	Virgin Is, Brit.	13.92
8	Niue	13.60
9	Macao	13.51
10	Armenia	12.84
11	Angola	10.06
12	Latvia	9.67
13	Guernsey	9.59
14	Kazakhstan	9.47
15	Jersey	9.38
16	Serbia	9.19
17	Kosovo	9.19
18	Georgia	9.17
19	Romania	9.17
20	Andorra	9.09
21	Montenegro	9.06
22	Cook Is	8.86
23	Lithuania	8.46
24	Ukraine	8.45
25	Burma	8.42

26	Belarus	8.41
27	Faeroe Is	7.66
28	Moldova	7.61
29	Sierra Leone	7.60
30	Tajikistan	7.50
31	China	7.39
32	Isle of Man	7.30
33	Fr Polynesia	7.22
34	Mongolia	7.20
35	Wallis & Futuna	7.17
36	Neth Antilles	7.13
37	Russia	7.07
38	Estonia	7.02
39	Bhutan	6.87
40	Suriname	6.87
41	Puerto Rico	6.86
42	Slovakia	6.83
43	Mayotte	6.70
44	Korea, North	6.65
45	Tuvalu	6.65
46	Trinidad/Tobago	6.50
47	Falkland Is	6.33
48	Bulgaria	6.07
49	Bosnia	6.00
50	Martinique	5.94
51	Marshall Is	5.79
52	Albania	5.54
53	Tanzania	5.53
54	Croatia	5.50
55	Czechia	5.25
56	Sudan	5.24
57	Taiwan	5.21
58	Oman	5.16
59	Uzbekistan	5.02
60	Hungary	4.97
61	Ethiopia	4.89
62	Gibraltar	4.88
63	Iran	4.86
64	Maldives	4.82
65	Zambia	4.75
66	Cambodia	4.73
67	Ecuador	4.66
68	Cayman Is	4.60
69	Greece	4.59
70	Peru	4.58
71	Poland	4.53
72	Botswana	4.42
73	Lebanon	4.36
74	India	4.35
75	Hong Kong	4.28
76	Vietnam	4.25
77	Guiana, Fr	4.20
78	South Africa	4.17
79	Turks & Caicos	4.17
80	Slovenia	4.14
81	Laos	4.14

82	Panama	4.07
83	Korea, South	4.05
84	Algeria	4.01
85	Antigua & Barbuda	3.78
86	Singapore	3.61
87	Cuba	3.53
88	Turkey	3.53
89	Tunisia	3.50
90	Thailand	3.48
91	Honduras	3.47
92	Bahamas	3.46
93	Dominican Rep	3.46
94	St Vincent	3.44
95	Ireland	3.34
96	Kyrgyzstan	3.23
97	Dominica	3.12
98	Nigeria	3.09
99	Bahrain	3.08
100	Samoa, W	3.00
101	Costa Rica	2.96
102	Luxembourg	2.87
103	Cape Verde	2.87
104	Egypt	2.82
105	Finland	2.81
106	Morocco	2.79
107	Macedonia	2.79
108	Malaysia	2.75
109	Iraq	2.71
110	Sri Lanka	2.69
111	Indonesia	2.57
112	Chile	2.51
113	Iceland	2.46
114	Bangladesh	2.30
115	Pakistan	2.29
116	Sweden	2.27
117	Argentina	2.27
118	Philippines	2.23
119	St Lucia	2.18
120	Colombia	2.17
121	Mauritius	2.15
122	Jordan	2.15
123	Mauritania	2.14
124	St Kitts & Nevis	2.14
125	Norway	2.10
126	Libya	2.07
127	UK	2.05
128	Cyprus	2.02
129	Spain	2.00
130	Namibia	1.98
131	San Tome & Principe	1.93
132	Barbados	1.92
133	Brazil	1.91
134	Saudi Arabia	1.89
135	El Salvador	1.88
136	Australia	1.85
137	Montserrat	1.83

138	Uruguay	1.83
139	New Zealand	1.81
140	Lesotho	1.77
141	Congo, Dem R	1.74
142	Cameroon	1.67
143	Belize	1.66
144	Canada	1.64
145	San Marino	1.62
146	Nicaragua	1.60
147	Bolivia	1.56
148	Reunion	1.55
149	Mali	1.55
150	Austria	1.55
151	Tokelau	1.54
152	Burkina Faso	1.54
153	Jamaica	1.52
154	Kenya	1.50
155	Mexico	1.49
156	St Helena	1.48
157	US	1.48
158	W Sahara	1.48
159	Nauru	1.44
160	Japan	1.43
161	Netherlands	1.41
162	Belgium	1.40
163	Congo, Rep	1.30
164	Denmark	1.30
165	Germany	1.28
166	Guyana	1.23
167	Guinea	1.19
168	Paraguay	1.16
169	Israel	1.14
170	Greenland	1.13
171	France	1.10
172	Switzerland	1.09
173	Tonga	1.09
174	Gambia	1.03
175	Grenada	1.01
176	N Mariana Is	0.94
177	Venezuela	0.90
178	Niger	0.87
179	Guatemala	0.83
180	Malta	0.73
181	Burundi	0.73
182	West Bank	0.67
183	Gaza Strip	0.67
184	Madagascar	0.59
185	Nepal	0.49
186	Gabon	0.49
187	Portugal	0.48
188	Yemen	0.47
189	Djibouti	0.46
190	New Caledonia	0.42
191	Brunei	0.42
192	Rwanda	0.40
193	Italy	0.39

194	Syria	0.37
195	Kiribati	0.35
196	Solomon Is	0.22
197	Turkmenistan	0.18
198	Malawi	0.09
199	Kuwait	0.04
200	Papua New Gu	0.04
201	Fiji	0.03
202	Micronesia	-0.08
203	Comoros	-0.12
204	Swaziland	-0.13
205	Anguilla	-0.15
206	Vanuatu	-0.15
207	Monaco	-0.47
208	Guinea-Bissau	-0.48
209	Seychelles	-0.49
210	Uganda	-0.56
211	Benin	-0.56
212	Togo	-0.63
213	Senegal	-0.70
214	Virgin I, US	-0.81
215	Eritrea	-0.95
216	Ivory Coast	-1.03
217	Haiti	-1.04
218	Ghana	-1.85
219	UAE	-2.06
220	Central African Rep.	-2.13
221	Palau	-2.37
222	Afghanistan	-2.51
223	East Timor	-2.62
224	Guadeloupe	-4.59
225	Aruba	-5.71
226	Somalia	-6.15
227	Mozambique	-6.41
228	Samoa, Ameri	-7.62
229	St Pierre &	-8.13
230	Guam	-8.22
231	Liberia	-10.91
232	Zimbabwe	-26.01

Source: Calculated as (GPCPPP2007/GPCPPP2000)**(1/7)-1.

CHAPTER 6. GDP GROWTH RATES

TABLE 6.1 - GDP GROWTH RATES YEARS 0001-1000		
OBS	COUNTRY	GRRL
1	Madagascar	0.53
2	Burundi	0.23
3	Zambia	0.19
4	Malawi	0.19
5	Zimbabwe	0.19
6	Mozambique	0.18
7	Swaziland	0.11
8	South Africa	0.11
9	Lesotho	0.11
10	Poland	0.10
11	Japan	0.10
12	Ireland	0.09
13	UK	0.09
14	Ghana	0.09
15	Guinea	0.08
16	Sierra Leone	0.08
17	Guinea-Bissau	0.08
18	Morocco	0.08
19	Mexico	0.07
20	Trinidad/Tobago	0.07
21	Jamaica	0.07
22	Panama	0.07
23	Costa Rica	0.07
24	Puerto Rico	0.07
25	Haiti	0.07
26	Honduras	0.07
27	Cuba	0.07
28	Guatemala	0.07
29	Ecuador	0.07
30	Colombia	0.07
31	Brazil	0.07
32	Peru	0.07
33	Chile	0.07
34	Bolivia	0.07
35	Nicaragua	0.07
36	Venezuela	0.07
37	Argentina	0.07
38	Paraguay	0.07
39	El Salvador	0.07
40	Dominican Rep	0.07
41	Uruguay	0.07
42	Latvia	0.07
43	Eritrea	0.07
44	Belarus	0.07
45	Canada	0.07
46	Denmark	0.07
47	Estonia	0.07
48	Finland	0.07
49	Lithuania	0.07

50	Moldova	0.07
51	Norway	0.07
52	Somalia	0.07
53	Sweden	0.07
54	Ukraine	0.07
55	Ethiopia	0.07
56	Russia	0.07
57	US	0.06
58	Singapore	0.06
59	Taiwan	0.06
60	Malaysia	0.06
61	Sri Lanka	0.06
62	Korea, North	0.06
63	Burma	0.06
64	Korea, South	0.06
65	Nepal	0.06
66	Indonesia	0.06
67	Afghanistan	0.06
68	Vietnam	0.06
69	Thailand	0.06
70	Cambodia	0.06
71	Mongolia	0.06
72	Philippines	0.06
73	Laos	0.06
74	Kazakhstan	0.05
75	Armenia	0.05
76	Turkmenistan	0.05
77	Uzbekistan	0.05
78	Kyrgyzstan	0.05
79	Georgia	0.05
80	Tajikistan	0.05
81	Azerbaijan	0.05
82	Hungary	0.05
83	Sudan	0.04
84	Bulgaria	0.04
85	Netherlands	0.04
86	Portugal	0.03
87	Austria	0.03
88	Botswana	0.03
89	Namibia	0.03
90	Australia	0.03
91	New Zealand	0.03
92	Belgium	0.02
93	Slovakia	0.02
94	Egypt	0.02
95	Libya	0.02
96	Tunisia	0.02
97	Czechia	0.02
98	UAE	0.02
99	Israel	0.02
100	Oman	0.02
101	Yemen	0.02
102	Saudi Arabia	0.02
103	Turkey	0.02
104	Iran	0.02
105	Syria	0.02

106	Lebanon	0.02
107	Kuwait	0.02
108	Iraq	0.02
109	Bahrain	0.02
110	Jordan	0.02
111	Qatar	0.02
112	Germany	0.02
113	France	0.02
114	Montenegro	0.02
115	Bosnia	0.02
116	Croatia	0.02
117	Macedonia	0.02
118	Slovenia	0.02
119	Serbia	0.01
120	Kosovo	0.01
121	Hong Kong	0.00
122	Albania	0.00
123	Algeria	0.00
124	Bangladesh	0.00
125	India	0.00
126	Pakistan	0.00
127	China	0.00
128	Switzerland	0.00
129	Spain	0.00
130	Romania	-0.01
131	Cyprus	-0.02
132	Greece	-0.09
133	Italy	-0.11

Source: Calculated as (GDPPPP1000/GDPPPP0001)**(1/999)-1.

TABLE 6.2 - GDP GROWTH RATES YEARS 1000-1500		
OBS	COUNTRY	GRRL
1	Finland	0.43
2	Belgium	0.40
3	Germany	0.35
4	Netherlands	0.35
5	Poland	0.34
6	Estonia	0.33
7	Italy	0.33
8	Latvia	0.32
9	Austria	0.31
10	Lithuania	0.31
11	Hungary	0.30
12	Russia	0.28
13	Romania	0.28
14	France	0.27
15	Czechia	0.27
16	UK	0.25
17	Madagascar	0.25
18	Slovakia	0.24
19	Switzerland	0.24
20	Mozambique	0.24
21	Moldova	0.24
22	Belarus	0.23

23	Armenia	0.23
24	Denmark	0.22
25	Georgia	0.22
26	Ukraine	0.22
27	Ireland	0.19
28	Azerbaijan	0.18
29	Spain	0.18
30	Japan	0.18
31	Norway	0.18
32	Slovenia	0.17
33	Sweden	0.17
34	Portugal	0.17
35	Korea, South	0.17
36	Korea, North	0.17
37	Hong Kong	0.17
38	China	0.17
39	Philippines	0.17
40	Thailand	0.17
41	Malaysia	0.17
42	Sri Lanka	0.17
43	Taiwan	0.17
44	Indonesia	0.17
45	Vietnam	0.17
46	Kazakhstan	0.16
47	Afghanistan	0.16
48	Burma	0.16
49	Singapore	0.16
50	Laos	0.15
51	Zambia	0.14
52	Burundi	0.14
53	Ethiopia	0.14
54	Botswana	0.14
55	Lesotho	0.14
56	Malawi	0.14
57	Namibia	0.14
58	Somalia	0.14
59	South Africa	0.14
60	Swaziland	0.14
61	Zimbabwe	0.14
62	Eritrea	0.14
63	Bangladesh	0.12
64	Pakistan	0.12
65	India	0.12
66	Cambodia	0.12
67	Mongolia	0.12
68	Nepal	0.12
69	Mexico	0.11
70	Croatia	0.11
71	Sierra Leone	0.09
72	Guinea-Bissau	0.09
73	Ghana	0.09
74	Guinea	0.09
75	Canada	0.09
76	US	0.09
77	Argentina	0.08
78	Chile	0.08

79	Uruguay	0.08
80	Uzbekistan	0.08
81	Serbia	0.08
82	Bulgaria	0.07
83	Paraguay	0.07
84	Cuba	0.07
85	El Salvador	0.07
86	Haiti	0.07
87	Venezuela	0.07
88	Bolivia	0.07
89	Peru	0.07
90	Brazil	0.07
91	Guatemala	0.07
92	Colombia	0.07
93	Nicaragua	0.07
94	Ecuador	0.07
95	Honduras	0.07
96	Costa Rica	0.07
97	Panama	0.07
98	Jamaica	0.07
99	Puerto Rico	0.07
100	Dominican Rep	0.07
101	Trinidad/Tobago	0.07
102	Montenegro	0.07
103	Australia	0.07
104	New Zealand	0.07
105	Turkmenistan	0.07
106	Kyrgyzstan	0.07
107	Tajikistan	0.07
108	Sudan	0.06
109	Macedonia	0.05
110	Bosnia	0.05
111	Kosovo	0.05
112	Albania	0.00
113	Libya	0.00
114	Greece	0.00
115	Jordan	-0.03
116	Syria	-0.03
117	Lebanon	-0.03
118	Bahrain	-0.03
119	Israel	-0.03
120	Kuwait	-0.03
121	Iraq	-0.03
122	Yemen	-0.03
123	Saudi Arabia	-0.03
124	Oman	-0.03
125	Iran	-0.03
126	Turkey	-0.03
127	UAE	-0.03
128	Qatar	-0.03
129	Tunisia	-0.04
130	Egypt	-0.05
131	Algeria	-0.06
132	Morocco	-0.06
133	Cyprus	-0.23

Source: Calculated as $(GDPPPP1500/GDPPPP1000)**(1/500)-1$.

TABLE 6.3 - GDP GROWTH RATES YEARS 1500-1600		
OBS	COUNTRY	GRRL
1	Netherlands	1.06
2	Taiwan	0.83
3	UK	0.76
4	Switzerland	0.60
5	Bulgaria	0.55
6	Cyprus	0.52
7	Greece	0.52
8	Czechia	0.51
9	Slovakia	0.51
10	Sweden	0.49
11	Philippines	0.48
12	Finland	0.46
13	Norway	0.46
14	Spain	0.45
15	China	0.44
16	Hong Kong	0.44
17	Germany	0.43
18	Algeria	0.41
19	Morocco	0.41
20	Austria	0.39
21	Ireland	0.38
22	France	0.36
23	Estonia	0.34
24	Slovenia	0.33
25	Belarus	0.32
26	Moldova	0.32
27	Lithuania	0.32
28	Ukraine	0.32
29	Latvia	0.32
30	Poland	0.32
31	Russia	0.32
32	Montenegro	0.30
33	Croatia	0.30
34	Serbia	0.30
35	Portugal	0.30
36	Georgia	0.28
37	Armenia	0.28
38	Mozambique	0.26
39	Denmark	0.25
40	Belgium	0.24
41	Sierra Leone	0.24
42	Guinea-Bissau	0.24
43	Ghana	0.24
44	Guinea	0.24
45	Kazakhstan	0.23
46	Uzbekistan	0.23
47	Turkmenistan	0.23
48	Egypt	0.22
49	Tunisia	0.22
50	Japan	0.22
51	Italy	0.22
52	Korea, South	0.21

53	Korea, North	0.21
54	Azerbaijan	0.21
55	Pakistan	0.21
56	India	0.21
57	Bangladesh	0.21
58	Macedonia	0.20
59	Bosnia	0.20
60	Kosovo	0.20
61	Swaziland	0.19
62	South Africa	0.19
63	Madagascar	0.17
64	Laos	0.17
65	Vietnam	0.17
66	Burma	0.17
67	Afghanistan	0.17
68	Cambodia	0.17
69	Malaysia	0.17
70	Singapore	0.17
71	Burundi	0.15
72	Lesotho	0.15
73	Nepal	0.15
74	Mongolia	0.15
75	Turkey	0.14
76	Kyrgyzstan	0.13
77	Tajikistan	0.13
78	Zambia	0.13
79	Zimbabwe	0.13
80	Thailand	0.13
81	Ethiopia	0.12
82	Eritrea	0.12
83	Hungary	0.12
84	Indonesia	0.11
85	Iran	0.11
86	Sri Lanka	0.11
87	Romania	0.10
88	Malawi	0.10
89	Sudan	0.05
90	Namibia	0.04
91	Somalia	0.04
92	Uruguay	0.00
93	Iraq	0.00
94	Albania	0.00
95	Australia	0.00
96	Bahrain	0.00
97	Botswana	0.00
98	Canada	0.00
99	Kuwait	0.00
100	Libya	0.00
101	New Zealand	0.00
102	Oman	0.00
103	Qatar	0.00
104	Saudi Arabia	0.00
105	UAE	0.00
106	Yemen	0.00
107	Lebanon	-0.03
108	Syria	-0.03

109	Jordan	-0.03
110	Israel	-0.03
111	Brazil	-0.16
112	Argentina	-0.16
113	US	-0.29
114	Chile	-0.34
115	El Salvador	-0.51
116	Nicaragua	-0.51
117	Ecuador	-0.51
118	Peru	-0.51
119	Costa Rica	-0.51
120	Guatemala	-0.51
121	Honduras	-0.51
122	Panama	-0.51
123	Colombia	-0.51
124	Venezuela	-0.51
125	Bolivia	-0.51
126	Paraguay	-0.51
127	Jamaica	-0.62
128	Trinidad/Tobago	-0.64
129	Haiti	-0.91
130	Cuba	-0.91
131	Dominican Rep	-0.91
132	Puerto Rico	-0.91
133	Mexico	-1.03

Source: Calculated as (GDPPPP1600/GDPPPP1500)**(1/100)-1.

TABLE 6.4 GDP GROWTH RATES YEARS 1600-1700		
OBS	COUNTRY	GRRL
1	Puerto Rico	1.28
2	Cuba	1.24
3	Jamaica	1.22
4	Trinidad/Tobago	1.20
5	Dominican Rep	0.92
6	Haiti	0.92
7	Mexico	0.82
8	Ireland	0.81
9	Taiwan	0.80
10	Portugal	0.70
11	Sweden	0.68
12	Netherlands	0.67
13	Uruguay	0.64
14	UK	0.58
15	Brazil	0.52
16	Argentina	0.48
17	Japan	0.47
18	Philippines	0.45
19	Albania	0.41
20	Estonia	0.40
21	Norway	0.39
22	Russia	0.39
23	Ukraine	0.39
24	Lithuania	0.39

25	Moldova	0.39
26	Latvia	0.39
27	Belarus	0.39
28	Belgium	0.38
29	Lesotho	0.36
30	South Africa	0.36
31	Swaziland	0.36
32	Switzerland	0.35
33	Romania	0.32
34	Hungary	0.30
35	Chile	0.29
36	Poland	0.28
37	Armenia	0.25
38	Georgia	0.25
39	Guinea	0.25
40	Ghana	0.25
41	Guinea-Bissau	0.25
42	Sierra Leone	0.25
43	Denmark	0.25
44	Azerbaijan	0.24
45	France	0.23
46	Madagascar	0.22
47	Uzbekistan	0.22
48	Turkmenistan	0.22
49	Kazakhstan	0.22
50	Korea, South	0.21
51	Korea, North	0.21
52	Bangladesh	0.20
53	India	0.20
54	Pakistan	0.20
55	Mozambique	0.18
56	Somalia	0.17
57	Austria	0.17
58	Finland	0.17
59	Colombia	0.17
60	Nepal	0.15
61	Mongolia	0.15
62	Tajikistan	0.15
63	Singapore	0.15
64	Malaysia	0.15
65	Laos	0.15
66	Vietnam	0.15
67	Burma	0.15
68	Afghanistan	0.15
69	Cambodia	0.15
70	Turkey	0.14
71	Burundi	0.13
72	Paraguay	0.13
73	Costa Rica	0.13
74	Panama	0.13
75	Honduras	0.13
76	Venezuela	0.13
77	Bolivia	0.13
78	Ecuador	0.13
79	Peru	0.13
80	Guatemala	0.13

81	Nicaragua	0.13
82	El Salvador	0.13
83	Slovenia	0.12
84	Kyrgyzstan	0.12
85	Indonesia	0.11
86	Iran	0.11
87	Thailand	0.11
88	Ethiopia	0.11
89	Eritrea	0.11
90	Bulgaria	0.10
91	Slovakia	0.10
92	Serbia	0.10
93	Montenegro	0.10
94	Croatia	0.10
95	Czechia	0.10
96	Greece	0.09
97	Cyprus	0.09
98	Malawi	0.09
99	Zambia	0.09
100	Zimbabwe	0.09
101	Sri Lanka	0.09
102	Germany	0.08
103	Spain	0.06
104	Sudan	0.05
105	Italy	0.02
106	Australia	0.00
107	Bahrain	0.00
108	Bosnia	0.00
109	Botswana	0.00
110	Iraq	0.00
111	Kosovo	0.00
112	Kuwait	0.00
113	Libya	0.00
114	Macedonia	0.00
115	Namibia	0.00
116	New Zealand	0.00
117	Oman	0.00
118	Qatar	0.00
119	Saudi Arabia	0.00
120	UAE	0.00
121	Yemen	0.00
122	Israel	-0.03
123	Jordan	-0.03
124	Syria	-0.03
125	Lebanon	-0.03
126	Egypt	-0.11
127	US	-0.13
128	China	-0.15
129	Hong Kong	-0.15
130	Canada	-0.15
131	Tunisia	-0.22
132	Algeria	-0.25
133	Morocco	-0.25

Source: Calculated as (GDPPPP1700/GDPPPP1600)**(1/100)-1.

TABLE 6.5 - GDP GROWTH RATES YEARS 1700-1820		
OBS	COUNTRY	GRRL
1	US	2.68
2	Canada	1.81
3	Trinidad/Tobago	1.76
4	Dominican Rep	1.48
5	Haiti	1.48
6	Cuba	1.46
7	Jamaica	1.46
8	Puerto Rico	1.46
9	Brazil	1.36
10	Ireland	1.27
11	Finland	1.07
12	UK	1.02
13	Hungary	0.97
14	Romania	0.89
15	Hong Kong	0.85
16	China	0.85
17	Russia	0.78
18	Estonia	0.78
19	Sweden	0.77
20	Belarus	0.76
21	Lithuania	0.76
22	Ukraine	0.76
23	Moldova	0.76
24	Latvia	0.76
25	Uruguay	0.74
26	Norway	0.73
27	Slovenia	0.66
28	Serbia	0.63
29	Montenegro	0.63
30	Croatia	0.63
31	Switzerland	0.59
32	Taiwan	0.59
33	Denmark	0.59
34	Argentina	0.58
35	Belgium	0.57
36	Bulgaria	0.57
37	Germany	0.56
38	Poland	0.56
39	Mexico	0.56
40	Czechia	0.54
41	Slovakia	0.54
42	Kosovo	0.53
43	Macedonia	0.53
44	Bosnia	0.53
45	Thailand	0.53
46	Greece	0.52
47	Cyprus	0.52
48	Portugal	0.52
49	France	0.50
50	Colombia	0.48
51	Guatemala	0.48
52	Philippines	0.47

53	Uzbekistan	0.44
54	Tajikistan	0.44
55	Kazakhstan	0.44
56	Turkmenistan	0.44
57	Madagascar	0.43
58	Costa Rica	0.43
59	Austria	0.42
60	Spain	0.42
61	Bolivia	0.41
62	Panama	0.41
63	Ecuador	0.39
64	Chile	0.39
65	Kyrgyzstan	0.38
66	Armenia	0.37
67	Azerbaijan	0.37
68	Georgia	0.37
69	Peru	0.37
70	South Africa	0.37
71	Lesotho	0.37
72	Swaziland	0.37
73	Albania	0.36
74	Italy	0.36
75	Algeria	0.36
76	Morocco	0.36
77	Venezuela	0.34
78	Indonesia	0.31
79	Mozambique	0.28
80	Nicaragua	0.27
81	Paraguay	0.25
82	Japan	0.25
83	El Salvador	0.22
84	Honduras	0.22
85	Burundi	0.22
86	Iran	0.21
87	Turkey	0.21
88	Cambodia	0.21
89	Afghanistan	0.21
90	Burma	0.21
91	Malaysia	0.21
92	Laos	0.21
93	Vietnam	0.21
94	Singapore	0.21
95	Mongolia	0.20
96	Nepal	0.20
97	Eritrea	0.19
98	Ethiopia	0.19
99	Pakistan	0.17
100	India	0.17
101	Bangladesh	0.17
102	Sudan	0.13
103	Lebanon	0.13
104	Jordan	0.13
105	Syria	0.13
106	Israel	0.13
107	UAE	0.12
108	Qatar	0.12

109	Kuwait	0.12
110	Yemen	0.12
111	Saudi Arabia	0.12
112	Oman	0.12
113	Bahrain	0.12
114	Guinea-Bissau	0.12
115	Sierra Leone	0.12
116	Guinea	0.12
117	Ghana	0.12
118	Korea, North	0.10
119	Korea, South	0.10
120	Iraq	0.10
121	Zimbabwe	0.10
122	Zambia	0.10
123	Malawi	0.10
124	Namibia	0.08
125	Botswana	0.08
126	Tunisia	0.07
127	Libya	0.06
128	Netherlands	0.05
129	Somalia	0.04
130	Sri Lanka	0.02
131	New Zealand	0.00
132	Egypt	-0.02
133	Australia	-0.03

Source: Calculated as (GDPPPP1820/GDPPPP1700)**(1/120)-1.

TABLE 6.6 - GDP GROWTH RATES YEARS 1820-1870		
OBS	COUNTRY	GRRL
1	Australia	7.28
2	Singapore	6.46
3	New Zealand	6.43
4	Canada	4.42
5	US	4.21
6	Hong Kong	3.97
7	Uruguay	3.78
8	Chile	3.14
9	South Africa	2.62
10	Sri Lanka	2.57
11	Argentina	2.50
12	Namibia	2.38
13	Malaysia	2.27
14	Belgium	2.24
15	Honduras	2.22
16	Swaziland	2.18
17	Venezuela	2.12
18	UK	2.05
19	Paraguay	2.04
20	Dominican Rep	2.02
21	Germany	2.00
22	Puerto Rico	1.98
23	Georgia	1.92
24	Azerbaijan	1.92

25	Armenia	1.92
26	Switzerland	1.91
27	Denmark	1.91
28	Philippines	1.84
29	Zimbabwe	1.81
30	Zambia	1.77
31	Brazil	1.77
32	Lesotho	1.74
33	Algeria	1.71
34	Netherlands	1.70
35	Norway	1.70
36	Russia	1.64
37	Cuba	1.64
38	Mozambique	1.63
39	Sweden	1.62
40	Costa Rica	1.61
41	Moldova	1.61
42	Latvia	1.61
43	Estonia	1.61
44	Belarus	1.61
45	Lithuania	1.61
46	Ukraine	1.61
47	Finland	1.58
48	Cyprus	1.56
49	Greece	1.56
50	Trinidad/Tobago	1.51
51	Ethiopia	1.49
52	Eritrea	1.49
53	Ecuador	1.47
54	Austria	1.45
55	France	1.43
56	Colombia	1.43
57	Peru	1.42
58	Malawi	1.40
59	Egypt	1.38
60	El Salvador	1.38
61	Tunisia	1.37
62	Somalia	1.36
63	Madagascar	1.36
64	Panama	1.30
65	Guatemala	1.25
66	Nicaragua	1.24
67	Italy	1.24
68	Kyrgyzstan	1.24
69	Kazakhstan	1.24
70	Turkmenistan	1.24
71	Tajikistan	1.24
72	Uzbekistan	1.23
73	Lebanon	1.23
74	Morocco	1.23
75	Czechia	1.20
76	Slovakia	1.20
77	Iraq	1.15
78	Indonesia	1.10
79	Botswana	1.09
80	Poland	1.07

81	Slovenia	1.05
82	Croatia	1.02
83	Montenegro	1.02
84	Serbia	1.02
85	Macedonia	0.95
86	Libya	0.94
87	Haiti	0.93
88	Spain	0.93
89	Israel	0.92
90	Kosovo	0.92
91	Bosnia	0.92
92	Iran	0.90
93	Laos	0.87
94	Ireland	0.87
95	Sudan	0.87
96	Vietnam	0.87
97	Syria	0.84
98	Hungary	0.83
99	Romania	0.83
100	Turkey	0.82
101	Jordan	0.81
102	Guinea-Bissau	0.80
103	Sierra Leone	0.80
104	Guinea	0.80
105	Albania	0.75
106	Bolivia	0.66
107	Portugal	0.66
108	Pakistan	0.65
109	Burundi	0.65
110	Thailand	0.62
111	Bangladesh	0.54
112	India	0.48
113	Bulgaria	0.44
114	Mexico	0.44
115	Afghanistan	0.42
116	Japan	0.40
117	Ghana	0.39
118	Burma	0.38
119	Nepal	0.38
120	Oman	0.38
121	Taiwan	0.32
122	Saudi Arabia	0.31
123	Yemen	0.27
124	Cambodia	0.18
125	Mongolia	0.15
126	Bahrain	0.09
127	Kuwait	0.09
128	Qatar	0.09
129	UAE	0.09
130	Korea, North	0.09
131	Korea, South	0.09
132	Jamaica	-0.10
133	China	-0.37

Source: Calculated as (GDPPPP1870/GDPPPP1820)**(1/50)-1.

TABLE 6.7 - GDP GROWTH RATES YEARS 1870-1880		
OBS	COUNTRY	GRRL
1	New Zealand	8.00
2	Argentina	5.80
3	Australia	4.95
4	Singapore	4.70
5	Costa Rica	4.43
6	Trinidad/Tobago	4.42
7	Hong Kong	4.32
8	US	3.98
9	Malaysia	3.96
10	Burma	3.62
11	South Africa	3.57
12	Spain	3.56
13	Colombia	3.49
14	Chile	3.38
15	Mexico	3.28
16	El Salvador	3.24
17	Panama	3.14
18	Puerto Rico	3.12
19	Poland	3.09
20	Peru	3.01
21	Bulgaria	2.96
22	Nicaragua	2.96
23	Venezuela	2.93
24	Ecuador	2.87
25	Uruguay	2.59
26	Dominican Rep	2.55
27	Slovenia	2.54
28	Croatia	2.54
29	Serbia	2.54
30	Montenegro	2.54
31	Macedonia	2.54
32	Cuba	2.52
33	Greece	2.51
34	Cyprus	2.51
35	Albania	2.42
36	Brazil	2.42
37	Guatemala	2.40
38	Namibia	2.38
39	Israel	2.33
40	Egypt	2.33
41	Vietnam	2.29
42	Japan	2.27
43	Laos	2.23
44	Paraguay	2.23
45	Switzerland	2.23
46	Bosnia	2.21
47	Bolivia	2.20
48	Canada	2.19
49	Swaziland	2.18
50	Belgium	2.16
51	Netherlands	2.15
52	Romania	2.09

53	Hungary	2.08
54	Algeria	2.07
55	Norway	2.06
56	Ukraine	2.03
57	Azerbaijan	2.03
58	Kyrgyzstan	2.03
59	Tajikistan	2.03
60	Russia	2.03
61	Latvia	2.03
62	Armenia	2.03
63	Turkmenistan	2.03
64	Lithuania	2.03
65	Moldova	2.03
66	Georgia	2.03
67	Uzbekistan	2.03
68	Estonia	2.03
69	Kazakhstan	2.03
70	Belarus	2.03
71	Austria	2.01
72	Sweden	1.99
73	Iraq	1.96
74	Tunisia	1.87
75	UK	1.86
76	Germany	1.84
77	Denmark	1.84
78	Lebanon	1.83
79	Czechia	1.81
80	Slovakia	1.81
81	Zimbabwe	1.81
82	Zambia	1.77
83	Lesotho	1.74
84	Finland	1.69
85	Syria	1.64
86	Mozambique	1.63
87	Philippines	1.60
88	Jamaica	1.58
89	Afghanistan	1.52
90	Eritrea	1.49
91	Ethiopia	1.49
92	Turkey	1.47
93	Indonesia	1.41
94	Malawi	1.40
95	Jordan	1.40
96	Iran	1.40
97	France	1.39
98	Somalia	1.36
99	Madagascar	1.36
100	Cambodia	1.30
101	Morocco	1.25
102	Thailand	1.21
103	Honduras	1.17
104	Nepal	1.14
105	Italy	1.11
106	Botswana	1.09
107	Haiti	1.02
108	Taiwan	0.97

109	Libya	0.94
110	Korea, North	0.91
111	Sudan	0.87
112	Kosovo	0.81
113	Sierra Leone	0.80
114	Guinea	0.80
115	Guinea-Bissau	0.80
116	Korea, South	0.76
117	Ghana	0.68
118	Qatar	0.66
119	Kuwait	0.66
120	Bahrain	0.66
121	UAE	0.66
122	Burundi	0.65
123	Ireland	0.60
124	Sri Lanka	0.57
125	Pakistan	0.57
126	India	0.57
127	Oman	0.54
128	Bangladesh	0.44
129	Yemen	0.44
130	Saudi Arabia	0.41
131	China	0.37
132	Portugal	0.34
133	Mongolia	0.19

Source: Calculated as (GDPPPP1880/GDPPPP1870)**(1/10)-1.

TABLE 6.8 - GDP GROWTH RATES YEARS 1880-1890		
OBS	COUNTRY	GRRL
1	Argentina	5.80
2	Singapore	4.70
3	Costa Rica	4.43
4	Trinidad/Tobago	4.42
5	Hong Kong	4.32
6	Uruguay	4.31
7	Dominican Rep	4.10
8	US	3.98
9	Malaysia	3.96
10	Australia	3.94
11	Canada	3.92
12	Burma	3.62
13	South Africa	3.57
14	Colombia	3.49
15	Chile	3.38
16	Sri Lanka	3.36
17	Mexico	3.28
18	El Salvador	3.28
19	Finland	3.28
20	Panama	3.14
21	Puerto Rico	3.12
22	Poland	3.09
23	Switzerland	3.05
24	Peru	3.01
25	Bulgaria	2.96

26	Nicaragua	2.96
27	Germany	2.93
28	Ecuador	2.87
29	Portugal	2.65
30	Venezuela	2.56
31	Macedonia	2.54
32	Bosnia	2.54
33	Slovenia	2.54
34	Serbia	2.54
35	Croatia	2.54
36	Montenegro	2.54
37	Austria	2.52
38	Cuba	2.52
39	New Zealand	2.51
40	Greece	2.51
41	Cyprus	2.51
42	Honduras	2.49
43	Japan	2.47
44	Denmark	2.46
45	Brazil	2.43
46	Albania	2.42
47	Guatemala	2.40
48	Namibia	2.38
49	Israel	2.35
50	Vietnam	2.29
51	UK	2.24
52	Laos	2.23
53	Paraguay	2.23
54	Bolivia	2.20
55	Swaziland	2.18
56	Egypt	2.18
57	Belgium	2.10
58	Romania	2.09
59	Hungary	2.08
60	Netherlands	2.04
61	Belarus	2.03
62	Tajikistan	2.03
63	Lithuania	2.03
64	Turkmenistan	2.03
65	Kazakhstan	2.03
66	Russia	2.03
67	Latvia	2.03
68	Uzbekistan	2.03
69	Armenia	2.03
70	Kyrgyzstan	2.03
71	Georgia	2.03
72	Estonia	2.03
73	Moldova	2.03
74	Azerbaijan	2.03
75	Ukraine	2.03
76	Algeria	2.02
77	Iraq	1.96
78	Tunisia	1.87
79	Lebanon	1.83
80	Slovakia	1.81
81	Czechia	1.81

82	Zimbabwe	1.81
83	Zambia	1.77
84	Lesotho	1.74
85	Sweden	1.68
86	Syria	1.64
87	Mozambique	1.63
88	Philippines	1.60
89	Jamaica	1.58
90	Norway	1.53
91	Afghanistan	1.52
92	Eritrea	1.49
93	Ethiopia	1.49
94	Turkey	1.47
95	Cambodia	1.43
96	Malawi	1.40
97	Jordan	1.40
98	Iran	1.40
99	France	1.39
100	Somalia	1.36
101	Madagascar	1.36
102	Indonesia	1.32
103	Morocco	1.25
104	Pakistan	1.25
105	India	1.25
106	Italy	1.25
107	Nepal	1.22
108	Thailand	1.21
109	Bangladesh	1.11
110	Botswana	1.09
111	Haiti	1.02
112	Taiwan	0.97
113	Libya	0.94
114	Korea, North	0.93
115	Sudan	0.87
116	Kosovo	0.81
117	Guinea	0.80
118	Sierra Leone	0.80
119	Guinea-Bissau	0.80
120	Korea, South	0.76
121	Ghana	0.68
122	UAE	0.66
123	Kuwait	0.66
124	Bahrain	0.66
125	Qatar	0.66
126	Burundi	0.65
127	Oman	0.54
128	Yemen	0.44
129	China	0.42
130	Saudi Arabia	0.41
131	Spain	0.39
132	Mongolia	0.19
133	Ireland	0.03

Source: Calculated as (GDPPPP1890/GDPPPP1880)**(1/10)-1.

TABLE 6.9 - GDP GROWTH RATES YEARS 1890-1900		
OBS	COUNTRY	GRRL
1	Argentina	5.94
2	Hong Kong	5.16
3	Dominican Rep	4.80
4	Singapore	4.71
5	Mexico	4.60
6	Costa Rica	4.43
7	Trinidad/Tobago	4.42
8	Malaysia	3.96
9	Burma	3.85
10	US	3.82
11	Sri Lanka	3.75
12	South Africa	3.57
13	Colombia	3.48
14	Germany	3.46
15	New Zealand	3.34
16	El Salvador	3.28
17	Uruguay	3.26
18	Panama	3.14
19	Puerto Rico	3.12
20	Canada	3.11
21	Finland	3.06
22	Switzerland	3.02
23	Peru	3.01
24	Chile	2.96
25	Nicaragua	2.96
26	Denmark	2.93
27	Ecuador	2.87
28	Haiti	2.78
29	Sweden	2.77
30	Austria	2.71
31	Poland	2.62
32	Venezuela	2.59
33	Japan	2.52
34	Cuba	2.52
35	Indonesia	2.50
36	Honduras	2.49
37	Cyprus	2.42
38	Greece	2.42
39	Guatemala	2.40
40	Egypt	2.39
41	Namibia	2.38
42	Albania	2.36
43	Israel	2.35
44	Bulgaria	2.30
45	Vietnam	2.29
46	Laos	2.23
47	Paraguay	2.23
48	Bolivia	2.20
49	Portugal	2.18
50	Swaziland	2.18
51	Czechia	2.17
52	Slovakia	2.17

53	Montenegro	2.12
54	Croatia	2.12
55	Serbia	2.12
56	Slovenia	2.12
57	Bosnia	2.12
58	Macedonia	2.12
59	Kyrgyzstan	2.10
60	Moldova	2.10
61	Armenia	2.10
62	Ukraine	2.10
63	Azerbaijan	2.10
64	Lithuania	2.10
65	Estonia	2.10
66	Latvia	2.10
67	Turkmenistan	2.10
68	Georgia	2.10
69	Russia	2.10
70	Uzbekistan	2.10
71	Tajikistan	2.10
72	Kazakhstan	2.10
73	Belarus	2.10
74	UK	2.09
75	Hungary	2.08
76	France	2.08
77	Taiwan	2.03
78	Algeria	2.02
79	Norway	1.99
80	Iraq	1.96
81	Romania	1.88
82	Tunisia	1.87
83	Belgium	1.84
84	Lebanon	1.83
85	Zimbabwe	1.81
86	Zambia	1.77
87	Lesotho	1.74
88	Ghana	1.73
89	Syria	1.64
90	Mozambique	1.63
91	Philippines	1.60
92	Jamaica	1.58
93	Netherlands	1.57
94	Afghanistan	1.52
95	Ethiopia	1.49
96	Eritrea	1.49
97	Turkey	1.47
98	Kosovo	1.44
99	Cambodia	1.43
100	Spain	1.41
101	Malawi	1.40
102	Jordan	1.40
103	Iran	1.40
104	Somalia	1.36
105	Madagascar	1.36
106	Italy	1.30
107	Morocco	1.25
108	Thailand	1.24

109	Botswana	1.09
110	Libya	0.94
111	Nepal	0.89
112	Korea, North	0.88
113	Sudan	0.87
114	Australia	0.81
115	Sierra Leone	0.80
116	Guinea	0.80
117	Guinea-Bissau	0.80
118	Brazil	0.79
119	Korea, South	0.76
120	Mongolia	0.69
121	Bahrain	0.66
122	Kuwait	0.66
123	UAE	0.66
124	Qatar	0.66
125	Burundi	0.65
126	China	0.61
127	Pakistan	0.58
128	Oman	0.54
129	Ireland	0.47
130	Bangladesh	0.45
131	Yemen	0.44
132	India	0.42
133	Saudi Arabia	0.41

Source: Calculated as (GDPPPP1900/GDPPPP1890)**(1/10)-1.

TABLE 6.10 - GDP GROWTH RATES YEARS 1900-1913		
OBS	COUNTRY	GRRL
1	Argentina	6.42
2	Canada	6.25
3	Philippines	5.25
4	Hong Kong	5.16
5	Uruguay	5.14
6	Cuba	4.81
7	Singapore	4.70
8	Paraguay	4.14
9	Ghana	4.14
10	New Zealand	4.01
11	Panama	3.98
12	Honduras	3.96
13	Australia	3.96
14	US	3.95
15	El Salvador	3.94
16	Colombia	3.93
17	Trinidad/Tobago	3.92
18	Malaysia	3.85
19	Italy	3.63
20	South Africa	3.57
21	Brazil	3.55
22	Costa Rica	3.55
23	Chile	3.53

24	Puerto Rico	3.41
25	Haiti	3.29
26	Venezuela	3.27
27	Nicaragua	3.27
28	Ecuador	3.25
29	Denmark	3.22
30	Turkmenistan	3.22
31	Belarus	3.22
32	Azerbaijan	3.22
33	Estonia	3.22
34	Georgia	3.22
35	Kazakhstan	3.22
36	Ukraine	3.22
37	Armenia	3.22
38	Latvia	3.22
39	Uzbekistan	3.22
40	Russia	3.22
41	Lithuania	3.22
42	Moldova	3.22
43	Tajikistan	3.22
44	Kyrgyzstan	3.22
45	Bulgaria	3.06
46	Dominican Rep	3.02
47	Germany	2.96
48	Peru	2.91
49	Finland	2.89
50	Guatemala	2.82
51	Bosnia	2.76
52	Slovenia	2.76
53	Croatia	2.76
54	Macedonia	2.76
55	Serbia	2.76
56	Montenegro	2.76
57	Indonesia	2.74
58	Netherlands	2.72
59	Norway	2.72
60	Romania	2.63
61	Mexico	2.59
62	Bolivia	2.58
63	Japan	2.49
64	Hungary	2.46
65	Austria	2.41
66	Namibia	2.38
67	Taiwan	2.36
68	Israel	2.35
69	Vietnam	2.29
70	Egypt	2.28
71	Laos	2.23
72	Burma	2.21
73	Albania	2.21
74	Sweden	2.21
75	Swaziland	2.18
76	Slovakia	2.17
77	Czechia	2.17
78	Switzerland	2.06
79	Algeria	2.00

80	Belgium	1.98
81	Cyprus	1.97
82	Greece	1.97
83	Iraq	1.96
84	Tunisia	1.87
85	Lebanon	1.83
86	Zimbabwe	1.81
87	Spain	1.77
88	Zambia	1.77
89	Lesotho	1.74
90	France	1.65
91	Syria	1.64
92	Thailand	1.64
93	Mozambique	1.63
94	Poland	1.55
95	Afghanistan	1.52
96	Kosovo	1.52
97	Jamaica	1.51
98	UK	1.51
99	Eritrea	1.49
100	Ethiopia	1.49
101	Turkey	1.47
102	Cambodia	1.43
103	Malawi	1.40
104	Jordan	1.40
105	Iran	1.40
106	Somalia	1.36
107	Madagascar	1.36
108	Sri Lanka	1.26
109	Morocco	1.25
110	Korea, South	1.24
111	Nepal	1.22
112	Bangladesh	1.13
113	Botswana	1.09
114	Pakistan	1.05
115	Mongolia	0.99
116	Libya	0.94
117	India	0.93
118	Korea, North	0.91
119	Sudan	0.87
120	Guinea-Bissau	0.80
121	Guinea	0.80
122	Sierra Leone	0.80
123	Ireland	0.79
124	China	0.78
125	Qatar	0.66
126	UAE	0.66
127	Kuwait	0.66
128	Bahrain	0.66
129	Burundi	0.65
130	Oman	0.54
131	Portugal	0.46
132	Yemen	0.44
133	Saudi Arabia	0.41

Source: Calculated as (GDPPPP1913/GDPPPP1900)**(1/13)-1.

TABLE 6.11 - GDP GROWTH RATES YEARS 1913-1920		
OBS	COUNTRY	GRRL
1	Qatar	12.18
2	Kuwait	12.02
3	UAE	10.21
4	Honduras	9.30
5	Costa Rica	7.36
6	Panama	6.53
7	Nicaragua	6.21
8	Hong Kong	5.73
9	Israel	5.59
10	Malaysia	5.11
11	Korea, North	4.94
12	Philippines	4.91
13	Taiwan	4.74
14	Peru	4.71
15	Brazil	4.66
16	Cuba	4.62
17	Korea, South	4.62
18	Bahrain	4.37
19	Singapore	4.31
20	Saudi Arabia	4.12
21	Japan	4.06
22	Paraguay	3.93
23	Dominican Rep	3.87
24	Lebanon	3.82
25	Ghana	3.62
26	El Salvador	3.57
27	Morocco	3.51
28	South Africa	3.46
29	Bolivia	3.40
30	Haiti	3.24
31	Syria	3.13
32	Greece	3.08
33	Cyprus	3.08
34	Puerto Rico	3.08
35	Trinidad/Tobago	3.00
36	Colombia	2.81
37	Iraq	2.81
38	New Zealand	2.77
39	Iran	2.66
40	Norway	2.55
41	Ecuador	2.39
42	Namibia	2.39
43	Tunisia	2.37
44	Jordan	2.22
45	Swaziland	2.18
46	Yemen	2.16
47	Jamaica	2.12
48	Netherlands	2.12
49	Guatemala	2.07
50	US	1.98
51	Algeria	1.93
52	Burma	1.83

53	Zimbabwe	1.81
54	Zambia	1.77
55	Lesotho	1.74
56	Indonesia	1.69
57	Mozambique	1.63
58	Spain	1.50
59	Eritrea	1.49
60	Ethiopia	1.49
61	Denmark	1.49
62	Venezuela	1.45
63	Malawi	1.40
64	Albania	1.37
65	Thailand	1.36
66	Somalia	1.36
67	Madagascar	1.36
68	China	1.22
69	Botswana	1.09
70	Egypt	0.97
71	Libya	0.94
72	Nepal	0.94
73	Sudan	0.87
74	Cambodia	0.83
75	Argentina	0.82
76	Sierra Leone	0.80
77	Guinea	0.80
78	Guinea-Bissau	0.80
79	Afghanistan	0.77
80	Vietnam	0.67
81	Mexico	0.67
82	Burundi	0.65
83	Pakistan	0.38
84	Australia	0.38
85	Chile	0.31
86	Switzerland	0.21
87	Bangladesh	0.19
88	Italy	0.19
89	Oman	0.17
90	Laos	0.07
91	Mongolia	-0.11
92	Portugal	-0.11
93	Poland	-0.32
94	Canada	-0.39
95	Sri Lanka	-0.50
96	India	-0.67
97	UK	-0.76
98	Sweden	-0.79
99	Uruguay	-0.86
100	Ireland	-0.91
101	Belgium	-1.11
102	Kosovo	-1.28
103	Finland	-1.41
104	Czechia	-1.44
105	Slovakia	-1.44
106	Serbia	-1.63
107	Slovenia	-1.63
108	Macedonia	-1.63

109	Montenegro	-1.63
110	Croatia	-1.63
111	Bosnia	-1.63
112	France	-1.95
113	Estonia	-2.04
114	Latvia	-2.04
115	Lithuania	-2.04
116	Hungary	-2.69
117	Germany	-4.63
118	Austria	-5.68
119	Bulgaria	-6.24
120	Georgia	-7.34
121	Moldova	-7.34
122	Romania	-7.40
123	Turkey	-8.35
124	Kyrgyzstan	-11.30
125	Tajikistan	-12.47
126	Ukraine	-12.79
127	Uzbekistan	-12.79
128	Kazakhstan	-12.79
129	Armenia	-12.79
130	Turkmenistan	-12.79
131	Russia	-12.79
132	Belarus	-12.79
133	Azerbaijan	-12.79

Source: Calculated as (GDPPPP1920/GDPPPP1913)**(1/7)-1.

TABLE 6.12 - GDP GROWTH RATES YEARS 1920-1929		
OBS	COUNTRY	GRRL
1	Venezuela	13.72
2	Qatar	12.18
3	Kuwait	12.02
4	Azerbaijan	11.88
5	Belarus	11.88
6	Russia	11.88
7	Armenia	11.88
8	Kazakhstan	11.88
9	Uzbekistan	11.88
10	Turkmenistan	11.88
11	Ukraine	11.88
12	Tajikistan	11.55
13	Kyrgyzstan	10.41
14	UAE	10.21
15	Malaysia	7.04
16	Turkey	6.78
17	Georgia	6.72
18	Uruguay	6.54
19	Slovakia	5.96
20	Czechia	5.96
21	Singapore	5.94
22	Argentina	5.69
23	Lithuania	5.63
24	Latvia	5.63

25	Estonia	5.63
26	Israel	5.59
27	Finland	5.42
28	Dominican Rep	5.24
29	Austria	5.24
30	Cuba	5.23
31	Chile	5.16
32	Hungary	5.10
33	France	4.94
34	Germany	4.92
35	Canada	4.89
36	Netherlands	4.85
37	Bulgaria	4.78
38	Switzerland	4.78
39	Honduras	4.76
40	Macedonia	4.70
41	Montenegro	4.70
42	Croatia	4.70
43	Slovenia	4.70
44	Serbia	4.70
45	Bosnia	4.70
46	Colombia	4.68
47	Guatemala	4.49
48	Nicaragua	4.38
49	Bahrain	4.37
50	Portugal	4.26
51	Saudi Arabia	4.12
52	Taiwan	4.11
53	Sweden	4.11
54	US	3.98
55	Brazil	3.95
56	Paraguay	3.91
57	Lebanon	3.82
58	Philippines	3.81
59	Hong Kong	3.69
60	Peru	3.64
61	Indonesia	3.64
62	Denmark	3.64
63	Ghana	3.62
64	Greece	3.61
65	Cyprus	3.61
66	Spain	3.60
67	Morocco	3.51
68	South Africa	3.46
69	Belgium	3.45
70	Jamaica	3.43
71	Japan	3.42
72	El Salvador	3.36
73	Puerto Rico	3.26
74	Norway	3.22
75	Sri Lanka	3.14
76	Syria	3.13
77	Australia	3.12
78	Poland	2.94
79	Burma	2.93
80	Italy	2.90

81	Haiti	2.88
82	Iraq	2.81
83	Bolivia	2.72
84	Iran	2.66
85	UK	2.64
86	Romania	2.62
87	Moldova	2.44
88	Namibia	2.38
89	Ecuador	2.38
90	Tunisia	2.37
91	Jordan	2.22
92	Swaziland	2.18
93	Yemen	2.16
94	Algeria	2.06
95	Panama	1.97
96	Thailand	1.95
97	Korea, North	1.93
98	Zimbabwe	1.81
99	Trinidad/Tobago	1.80
100	Zambia	1.77
101	Lesotho	1.74
102	Korea, South	1.74
103	Mozambique	1.63
104	India	1.58
105	Kosovo	1.49
106	Ethiopia	1.49
107	Eritrea	1.49
108	Costa Rica	1.43
109	Malawi	1.40
110	Albania	1.36
111	Somalia	1.36
112	Madagascar	1.36
113	Pakistan	1.26
114	New Zealand	1.12
115	Botswana	1.09
116	Mexico	0.98
117	Libya	0.94
118	Nepal	0.93
119	Egypt	0.90
120	Sudan	0.87
121	Cambodia	0.83
122	Sierra Leone	0.80
123	Guinea	0.80
124	Guinea-Bissau	0.80
125	Bangladesh	0.78
126	Afghanistan	0.77
127	Vietnam	0.67
128	Burundi	0.65
129	Ireland	0.49
130	China	0.47
131	Oman	0.17
132	Laos	0.07
133	Mongolia	-0.11

Source: Calculated as (GDPPPP1929/GDPPPP1920)**(1/9)-1

TABLE 6.13 - GDP GROWTH RATES YEARS 1929-1938		
OBS	COUNTRY	GRRL
1	Qatar	12.18
2	Kuwait	12.02
3	UAE	10.21
4	Hong Kong	8.90
5	Korea, North	6.08
6	Ukraine	6.07
7	Russia	6.07
8	Uzbekistan	6.07
9	Belarus	6.07
10	Georgia	6.07
11	Kazakhstan	6.07
12	Azerbaijan	6.07
13	Turkmenistan	6.07
14	Kyrgyzstan	6.07
15	Tajikistan	6.07
16	Armenia	6.07
17	Turkey	5.68
18	Israel	5.59
19	Korea, South	5.46
20	Guatemala	5.04
21	Dominican Rep	4.68
22	Bulgaria	4.54
23	Bahrain	4.37
24	Panama	4.23
25	Lithuania	4.19
26	Estonia	4.19
27	Latvia	4.19
28	Saudi Arabia	4.12
29	Taiwan	4.10
30	Costa Rica	4.04
31	Paraguay	3.94
32	Singapore	3.91
33	Finland	3.90
34	Ecuador	3.82
35	Lebanon	3.82
36	Jamaica	3.71
37	Ghana	3.62
38	Japan	3.59
39	Morocco	3.51
40	Colombia	3.50
41	Puerto Rico	3.48
42	South Africa	3.46
43	Brazil	3.36
44	Venezuela	3.35
45	New Zealand	3.30
46	Trinidad/Tobago	3.14
47	Syria	3.13
48	Norway	3.06
49	Germany	3.01
50	Thailand	2.91
51	Haiti	2.85
52	Greece	2.84

53	Cyprus	2.84
54	Iraq	2.81
55	Bolivia	2.72
56	Iran	2.66
57	Sweden	2.58
58	Philippines	2.53
59	Peru	2.50
60	Namibia	2.38
61	Tunisia	2.37
62	Denmark	2.22
63	Jordan	2.22
64	Swaziland	2.18
65	Yemen	2.16
66	Portugal	2.16
67	Australia	2.11
68	Romania	2.10
69	Mexico	1.97
70	UK	1.90
71	Moldova	1.87
72	Zimbabwe	1.81
73	Zambia	1.77
74	Lesotho	1.74
75	Mozambique	1.63
76	Italy	1.57
77	Poland	1.56
78	Hungary	1.52
79	Algeria	1.52
80	Indonesia	1.50
81	Eritrea	1.49
82	Ethiopia	1.49
83	Egypt	1.44
84	Malawi	1.40
85	Kosovo	1.40
86	Somalia	1.36
87	Madagascar	1.36
88	Bosnia	1.33
89	Croatia	1.33
90	Montenegro	1.33
91	Slovenia	1.33
92	Serbia	1.33
93	Macedonia	1.33
94	Uruguay	1.14
95	Argentina	1.10
96	Botswana	1.09
97	Albania	1.07
98	Libya	0.94
99	Nepal	0.93
100	Pakistan	0.90
101	Sudan	0.87
102	Ireland	0.87
103	Cambodia	0.83
104	Guinea	0.80
105	Guinea-Bissau	0.80
106	Sierra Leone	0.80
107	Bangladesh	0.77
108	Afghanistan	0.77

109	Vietnam	0.67
110	Burundi	0.65
111	El Salvador	0.63
112	Chile	0.60
113	China	0.58
114	Switzerland	0.56
115	India	0.48
116	Netherlands	0.33
117	Oman	0.17
118	Laos	0.07
119	Canada	-0.03
120	Belgium	-0.04
121	Czechia	-0.04
122	Slovakia	-0.04
123	Mongolia	-0.11
124	Cuba	-0.22
125	Sri Lanka	-0.25
126	Malaysia	-0.27
127	Austria	-0.28
128	France	-0.40
129	Burma	-0.44
130	US	-0.59
131	Honduras	-1.51
132	Spain	-3.71
133	Nicaragua	-3.81

Source: Calculated as (GDPPPP1938/GDPPPP1929)**(1/9)-1.

TABLE 6.14 - GDP GROWTH RATES YEARS 1938-1950		
OBS	COUNTRY	GRRL
1	Qatar	12.18
2	Kuwait	12.02
3	UAE	10.21
4	Moldova	8.34
5	Nicaragua	7.91
6	Venezuela	7.90
7	Cuba	6.01
8	Canada	5.60
9	Israel	5.40
10	El Salvador	5.35
11	Mexico	5.29
12	US	5.12
13	Hong Kong	5.06
14	Brazil	4.98
15	Dominican Rep	4.88
16	Trinidad/Tobago	4.78
17	Ecuador	4.66
18	Singapore	4.63
19	Colombia	4.46
20	Bahrain	4.37
21	Paraguay	4.35
22	Jamaica	4.25
23	Saudi Arabia	4.12

24	Panama	4.07
25	Peru	4.07
26	Sweden	3.93
27	Switzerland	3.93
28	Lebanon	3.82
29	New Zealand	3.76
30	Honduras	3.70
31	Ghana	3.62
32	Argentina	3.61
33	Costa Rica	3.60
34	Morocco	3.51
35	Kyrgyzstan	3.49
36	South Africa	3.46
37	Australia	3.43
38	Puerto Rico	3.27
39	Uruguay	3.17
40	Syria	3.13
41	Haiti	3.10
42	Kazakhstan	3.10
43	Norway	2.85
44	Pakistan	2.82
45	Iraq	2.81
46	Iran	2.66
47	Denmark	2.61
48	Thailand	2.60
49	Armenia	2.59
50	Spain	2.52
51	Portugal	2.51
52	Malaysia	2.50
53	Chile	2.45
54	Tajikistan	2.41
55	Namibia	2.38
56	Netherlands	2.38
57	Tunisia	2.37
58	Guatemala	2.34
59	Jordan	2.22
60	Finland	2.21
61	Swaziland	2.18
62	Georgia	2.17
63	Yemen	2.16
64	Egypt	2.10
65	Uzbekistan	2.06
66	Sri Lanka	2.06
67	Libya	1.92
68	Zimbabwe	1.81
69	Bolivia	1.81
70	Zambia	1.77
71	Russia	1.72
72	Turkmenistan	1.71
73	Albania	1.68
74	Mozambique	1.63
75	Estonia	1.55
76	India	1.50
77	Latvia	1.49
78	Algeria	1.45
79	Ukraine	1.41

80	Somalia	1.36
81	Madagascar	1.36
82	France	1.35
83	UK	1.34
84	Turkey	1.31
85	Azerbaijan	1.30
86	Belgium	1.29
87	Macedonia	1.24
88	Bosnia	1.24
89	Serbia	1.24
90	Montenegro	1.24
91	Slovenia	1.24
92	Croatia	1.24
93	Italy	1.14
94	Ireland	1.13
95	Bulgaria	1.12
96	Belarus	1.06
97	Nepal	0.93
98	Sudan	0.87
99	Cambodia	0.83
100	Afghanistan	0.77
101	Lesotho	0.74
102	Vietnam	0.67
103	Bangladesh	0.64
104	Austria	0.56
105	Slovakia	0.25
106	Czechia	0.25
107	Oman	0.17
108	Lithuania	0.08
109	Laos	0.07
110	Romania	-0.04
111	Botswana	-0.05
112	Mongolia	-0.10
113	Burundi	-0.23
114	Malawi	-0.36
115	Kosovo	-0.38
116	Taiwan	-0.41
117	Hungary	-0.41
118	Japan	-0.76
119	Poland	-0.91
120	Philippines	-1.04
121	Sierra Leone	-1.20
122	China	-1.29
123	Indonesia	-1.50
124	Guinea	-1.51
125	Eritrea	-1.66
126	Ethiopia	-1.89
127	Guinea-Bissau	-1.90
128	Germany	-2.10
129	Cyprus	-2.19
130	Greece	-2.19
131	Korea, North	-3.41
132	Korea, South	-3.56
133	Burma	-3.58

Source: Calculated as (GDPPPP1950/GDPPPP1938)**(1/12)-1.

TABLE 6.15 - GDP GROWTH RATES
YEARS 1950-1960

OBS	COUNTRY	GRRL
1	W Sahara	12.07
2	Libya	11.47
3	Bahrain	10.88
4	Israel	10.80
5	Iraq	10.66
6	Saudi Arabia	10.15
7	Jamaica	9.90
8	Kosovo	9.66
9	Martinique	9.41
10	Montenegro	9.21
11	Bermuda	9.08
12	Algeria	8.86
13	Jordan	8.85
14	Guadeloupe	8.82
15	Japan	8.78
16	Serbia	8.65
17	Brunei	8.38
18	Germany	8.25
19	Zambia	8.25
20	Taiwan	8.24
21	Kazakhstan	7.53
22	Romania	7.52
23	Macedonia	7.50
24	Bosnia	7.41
25	Oman	7.32
26	UAE	7.31
27	Liberia	7.28
28	Gibraltar	7.28
29	Greenland	7.25
30	Kuwait	7.25
31	Albania	7.23
32	Barbados	7.17
33	Somalia	7.16
34	Greece	7.00
35	Qatar	6.97
36	Costa Rica	6.95
37	Mayotte	6.90
38	Cyprus	6.90
39	Suriname	6.89
40	Hong Kong	6.86
41	Andorra	6.83
42	Armenia	6.67
43	St Kitts & Nevis	6.66
44	Brazil	6.61
45	Tajikistan	6.58
46	Uzbekistan	6.57
47	Neth Antilles	6.55
48	Trinidad/Tobago	6.54
49	Austria	6.51
50	Korea, South	6.49
51	Bulgaria	6.44

52	Azerbaijan	6.44
53	Mexico	6.41
54	Turkey	6.37
55	San Marino	6.33
56	Italy	6.24
57	Turkmenistan	6.22
58	Slovakia	6.18
59	Mauritania	6.10
60	Peru	6.04
61	Moldova	5.99
62	St Lucia	5.98
63	Mongolia	5.93
64	Congo, Dem R	5.92
65	Cayman Is	5.87
66	Swaziland	5.86
67	Zimbabwe	5.84
68	Macao	5.80
69	Malta	5.72
70	Kyrgyzstan	5.71
71	Monaco	5.70
72	Philippines	5.67
73	Dominican Rep	5.66
74	Iceland	5.60
75	Turks & Caicos	5.60
76	Ecuador	5.59
77	Hungary	5.55
78	Chad	5.53
79	Niue	5.52
80	Niger	5.51
81	Croatia	5.51
82	Slovenia	5.50
83	Seychelles	5.45
84	Czechia	5.39
85	Guinea	5.36
86	Thailand	5.34
87	Singapore	5.34
88	Bahamas	5.30
89	El Salvador	5.30
90	Samoa, Ameri	5.29
91	Virgin Is, Brit.	5.28
92	St Pierre &	5.26
93	Faeroe Is	5.16
94	Iran	5.13
95	N Mariana Is	5.13
96	Switzerland	5.12
97	Venezuela	5.12
98	Fr Polynesia	5.12
99	Sudan	5.11
100	Aruba	5.08
101	Panama	5.06
102	South Africa	5.03
103	Grenada	5.02
104	Liechtenstein	5.01
105	Micronesia	5.00
106	Madagascar	5.00
107	Russia	4.99

108	Georgia	4.96
109	China	4.93
110	Anguilla	4.93
111	Korea, North	4.90
112	Ivory Coast	4.88
113	Ukraine	4.86
114	Netherlands	4.86
115	Palau	4.85
116	Togo	4.83
117	Central African Rep.	4.83
118	Nicaragua	4.83
119	Poland	4.81
120	Finland	4.81
121	Jersey	4.73
122	Cook Is	4.71
123	Cambodia	4.68
124	Spain	4.67
125	France	4.63
126	Canada	4.63
127	Papua New Gu	4.60
128	Belize	4.60
129	Comoros	4.59
130	Samoa, W	4.51
131	Vanuatu	4.45
132	Equatorial G	4.43
133	Reunion	4.39
134	Tokelau	4.36
135	Guyana	4.35
136	Puerto Rico	4.34
137	Marshall Is	4.30
138	Portugal	4.29
139	Solomon Is	4.27
140	Norway	4.25
141	Botswana	4.24
142	Cameroon	4.22
143	Sierra Leone	4.21
144	Latvia	4.20
145	Cape Verde	4.20
146	Tonga	4.19
147	Lithuania	4.15
148	Colombia	4.11
149	Antigua & Barbuda	4.10
150	Mauritius	4.05
151	Australia	4.01
152	Kiribati	4.00
153	Virgin I, US	3.99
154	St Vincent	3.97
155	Wallis & Futuna	3.97
156	Guernsey	3.91
157	Belarus	3.90
158	Honduras	3.87
159	Guatemala	3.87
160	Congo, Rep	3.86
161	Kenya	3.84
162	Luxembourg	3.72
163	Tanzania	3.71

164	Estonia	3.70
165	Laos	3.59
166	Bhutan	3.56
167	Isle of Man	3.51
168	US	3.46
169	Vietnam	3.44
170	Dominica	3.43
171	Burma	3.42
172	Tunisia	3.41
173	Gabon	3.38
174	New Caledonia	3.36
175	Namibia	3.36
176	Egypt	3.36
177	Nigeria	3.34
178	New Zealand	3.34
179	Sweden	3.33
180	Angola	3.32
181	India	3.32
182	Chile	3.29
183	Malawi	3.29
184	Indonesia	3.27
185	Guam	3.26
186	Montserrat	3.26
187	Maldives	3.21
188	Djibouti	3.21
189	Gambia	3.20
190	Fiji	3.20
191	Rwanda	3.15
192	Lesotho	3.12
193	Belgium	3.08
194	Syria	3.08
195	Denmark	3.06
196	Afghanistan	3.06
197	Ethiopia	3.03
198	Sri Lanka	2.98
199	Mali	2.98
200	Benin	2.90
201	Falkland Is	2.86
202	St Helena	2.86
203	Argentina	2.76
204	Malaysia	2.72
205	Uganda	2.68
206	Burkina Faso	2.68
207	UK	2.64
208	Pakistan	2.53
209	Nepal	2.47
210	Paraguay	2.46
211	East Timor	2.41
212	Lebanon	2.39
213	Yemen	2.38
214	Eritrea	2.25
215	Morocco	1.96
216	Cuba	1.90
217	Haiti	1.88
218	Bangladesh	1.86
219	Ireland	1.77

220	Gaza Strip	1.77
221	Guinea-Bissau	1.73
222	Uruguay	1.71
223	Tuvalu	1.56
224	Senegal	1.51
225	Ghana	1.49
226	Guiana, Fr	1.37
227	Nauru	1.17
228	San Tome & Principe	0.89
229	Bolivia	0.34
230	Mozambique	-0.06
231	West Bank	-0.12
232	Burundi	-0.44

Source: Calculated as (GDPPPP1960/GDPPPP1950)**(1/10)-1.

TABLE 6.16 - GDP GROWTH RATES YEARS 1960-1970		
OBS	COUNTRY	GRRL
1	Libya	23.56
2	Oman	21.89
3	Saudi Arabia	14.60
4	Andorra	13.76
5	Swaziland	12.60
6	Bahrain	10.94
7	Iran	10.77
8	Macao	10.51
9	Japan	10.37
10	Togo	10.29
11	UAE	10.21
12	Taiwan	10.19
13	Kuwait	9.92
14	Singapore	9.83
15	Kosovo	9.82
16	Bermuda	9.79
17	Qatar	9.47
18	Spain	9.44
19	Virgin I, US	9.40
20	Israel	9.32
21	W Sahara	9.14
22	Liberia	8.91
23	Mauritania	8.90
24	Greece	8.87
25	Hong Kong	8.87
26	Korea, North	8.69
27	Botswana	8.67
28	Martinique	8.35
29	Korea, South	8.34
30	Montenegro	8.27
31	Samoa, Ameri	7.94
32	Panama	7.94
33	Serbia	7.89
34	Djibouti	7.85
35	Guadeloupe	7.81

36	Gibraltar	7.68
37	Greenland	7.60
38	San Marino	7.32
39	Equatorial G	7.23
40	Tajikistan	7.19
41	Macedonia	7.17
42	Lebanon	7.16
43	Romania	7.13
44	Uzbekistan	7.12
45	Thailand	6.90
46	Turkmenistan	6.88
47	Costa Rica	6.86
48	Reunion	6.86
49	Kyrgyzstan	6.84
50	South Africa	6.79
51	Mexico	6.77
52	Ivory Coast	6.76
53	Mongolia	6.71
54	St Lucia	6.66
55	Albania	6.65
56	Armenia	6.62
57	Barbados	6.57
58	El Salvador	6.55
59	Azerbaijan	6.51
60	Bosnia	6.48
61	Liechtenstein	6.47
62	Brunei	6.46
63	Puerto Rico	6.44
64	Portugal	6.43
65	Neth Antilles	6.42
66	Bahamas	6.40
67	Suriname	6.36
68	Kazakhstan	6.36
69	Jordan	6.30
70	Comoros	6.16
71	Cyprus	6.07
72	Malaysia	6.03
73	Ecuador	6.02
74	Tanzania	6.00
75	Italy	6.00
76	Nicaragua	6.00
77	Jamaica	5.80
78	Zimbabwe	5.78
79	Iraq	5.76
80	Pakistan	5.72
81	Turkey	5.69
82	Brazil	5.68
83	Bulgaria	5.64
84	France	5.60
85	Turks & Caicos	5.60
86	Peru	5.56
87	Niue	5.52
88	Monaco	5.48
89	Bolivia	5.45
90	Slovenia	5.45
91	Moldova	5.44

92	Fr Polynesia	5.41
93	Nigeria	5.37
94	Canada	5.34
95	Isle of Man	5.34
96	Netherlands	5.29
97	Virgin Is, Brit.	5.28
98	St Pierre &	5.26
99	Palau	5.24
100	Kenya	5.23
101	Papua New Gu	5.23
102	Croatia	5.19
103	Cayman Is	5.19
104	St Kitts & Nevis	5.15
105	Australia	5.13
106	Cape Verde	5.13
107	Angola	5.12
108	Honduras	5.09
109	Austria	5.08
110	Switzerland	5.07
111	Eritrea	5.07
112	Malta	5.07
113	Ethiopia	5.06
114	Marshall Is	5.06
115	Dominican Rep	5.05
116	Faeroe Is	5.02
117	Belgium	5.00
118	Tunisia	4.99
119	Guernsey	4.98
120	Egypt	4.98
121	Iceland	4.97
122	Jersey	4.93
123	Anguilla	4.93
124	Lithuania	4.83
125	Sweden	4.78
126	Norway	4.77
127	Cook Is	4.71
128	Georgia	4.71
129	Solomon Is	4.69
130	Belize	4.68
131	Finland	4.66
132	Congo, Rep	4.64
133	Sierra Leone	4.63
134	Aruba	4.63
135	Micronesia	4.62
136	Latvia	4.61
137	Guam	4.59
138	Colombia	4.59
139	New Caledonia	4.56
140	Ukraine	4.55
141	Belarus	4.53
142	Vanuatu	4.53
143	Poland	4.52
144	Philippines	4.48
145	Zambia	4.41
146	Germany	4.41
147	Russia	4.39

148	Guinea	4.37
149	Hungary	4.37
150	Denmark	4.37
151	Tokelau	4.35
152	Guatemala	4.34
153	Ireland	4.32
154	Gabon	4.31
155	Morocco	4.30
156	Paraguay	4.29
157	Gambia	4.29
158	US	4.17
159	Antigua & Barbuda	4.14
160	Samoa, W	4.11
161	Namibia	4.11
162	Cameroon	4.02
163	Estonia	4.01
164	Wallis & Futuna	3.97
165	Nauru	3.96
166	Venezuela	3.96
167	Maldives	3.95
168	Madagascar	3.90
169	Luxembourg	3.90
170	N Mariana Is	3.90
171	Chile	3.89
172	Seychelles	3.82
173	Grenada	3.81
174	Argentina	3.78
175	Niger	3.77
176	Lesotho	3.74
177	San Tome & Principe	3.71
178	Mayotte	3.71
179	Tonga	3.62
180	Kiribati	3.60
181	Algeria	3.59
182	Syria	3.59
183	China	3.57
184	Slovakia	3.57
185	Guyana	3.56
186	Malawi	3.54
187	Bhutan	3.54
188	Trinidad/Tobago	3.52
189	Indonesia	3.44
190	Tuvalu	3.43
191	Laos	3.39
192	New Zealand	3.38
193	Guiana, Fr	3.37
194	Congo, Dem R	3.35
195	Dominica	3.34
196	Sri Lanka	3.31
197	Montserrat	3.26
198	India	3.25
199	Czechia	3.22
200	Yemen	3.17
201	St Vincent	3.10
202	Bangladesh	3.02
203	Fiji	2.87

204	Falkland Is	2.86
205	Senegal	2.85
206	UK	2.84
207	East Timor	2.83
208	Rwanda	2.83
209	Mali	2.71
210	Mauritius	2.68
211	Burma	2.50
212	Uganda	2.49
213	Nepal	2.24
214	Cambodia	2.20
215	Ghana	2.16
216	Benin	2.07
217	Vietnam	1.88
218	Burkina Faso	1.78
219	Cuba	1.76
220	Afghanistan	1.68
221	Central African Rep.	1.46
222	Uruguay	1.33
223	Gaza Strip	1.32
224	Sudan	1.20
225	Guinea-Bissau	1.04
226	Haiti	0.71
227	St Helena	0.27
228	Burundi	0.16
229	Chad	-0.19
230	Somalia	-0.43
231	Mozambique	-0.99
232	West Bank	-3.27

Source: Calculated as (GDPPPP1970/GDPPPP1960)**(1/10)-1.

TABLE 6.17 - GDP GROWTH RATES YEARS 1970-1980		
OBS	COUNTRY	GRRL
1	Botswana	16.32
2	UAE	16.30
3	Saudi Arabia	13.57
4	Malta	11.10
5	Macao	10.63
6	Kosovo	10.48
7	Iraq	9.85
8	Singapore	9.66
9	Seychelles	9.59
10	Korea, South	9.22
11	Montenegro	9.08
12	Hong Kong	8.96
13	Taiwan	8.70
14	Serbia	8.58
15	Bahrain	8.55
16	Algeria	8.51
17	W Sahara	8.40
18	Malaysia	8.19
19	Ecuador	8.13

20	Andorra	8.06
21	Macedonia	8.02
22	Brazil	7.83
23	Paraguay	7.58
24	Egypt	7.34
25	Cayman Is	7.30
26	Jordan	7.25
27	Maldives	7.22
28	Mexico	7.15
29	Mozambique	7.04
30	Tunisia	6.92
31	Brunei	6.91
32	Dominican Rep	6.87
33	Bosnia	6.85
34	Mongolia	6.64
35	Qatar	6.28
36	Romania	6.15
37	Slovenia	6.03
38	Virgin I, US	5.95
39	Gibraltar	5.93
40	Israel	5.89
41	Congo, Rep	5.88
42	Korea, North	5.81
43	Thailand	5.80
44	Yemen	5.80
45	Croatia	5.72
46	Malawi	5.66
47	Ivory Coast	5.66
48	Panama	5.66
49	Oman	5.63
50	Lebanon	5.62
51	Lesotho	5.61
52	Indonesia	5.52
53	Mayotte	5.50
54	Norway	5.47
55	Kuwait	5.47
56	Costa Rica	5.42
57	Greece	5.36
58	Spain	5.36
59	Cameroon	5.29
60	Isle of Man	5.23
61	Bhutan	5.22
62	Iceland	5.20
63	Philippines	5.18
64	Swaziland	5.12
65	Morocco	5.12
66	Djibouti	5.11
67	Haiti	5.04
68	Turkey	4.97
69	Ireland	4.82
70	Kenya	4.82
71	Colombia	4.80
72	Portugal	4.78
73	Trinidad/Tobago	4.70
74	Syria	4.65
75	Liechtenstein	4.57

76	Gambia	4.49
77	Japan	4.44
78	China	4.35
79	Canada	4.32
80	Nigeria	4.28
81	Mauritius	4.27
82	Honduras	4.24
83	Guinea	4.24
84	Solomon Is	4.19
85	Pakistan	4.18
86	San Marino	4.17
87	Bolivia	4.15
88	Albania	4.09
89	Guatemala	4.07
90	Gabon	4.06
91	Marshall Is	3.94
92	Austria	3.94
93	N Mariana Is	3.93
94	Belize	3.91
95	Peru	3.91
96	San Tome & Principe	3.91
97	Namibia	3.89
98	Monaco	3.87
99	Suriname	3.83
100	Cape Verde	3.83
101	Bermuda	3.81
102	Sudan	3.79
103	Poland	3.78
104	New Caledonia	3.74
105	Vanuatu	3.73
106	South Africa	3.71
107	Puerto Rico	3.69
108	Tanzania	3.69
109	Turks & Caicos	3.69
110	Italy	3.66
111	Somalia	3.63
112	Samoa, Ameri	3.58
113	Rwanda	3.58
114	Ghana	3.58
115	Tuvalu	3.54
116	Faeroe Is	3.54
117	El Salvador	3.52
118	Niue	3.51
119	Virgin Is, Brit.	3.49
120	St Pierre &	3.48
121	Uganda	3.47
122	Mali	3.40
123	Finland	3.39
124	Belgium	3.39
125	Senegal	3.39
126	Fr Polynesia	3.37
127	Laos	3.37
128	St Lucia	3.37
129	Slovakia	3.34
130	Greenland	3.32
131	Anguilla	3.28

132	France	3.26
133	Cyprus	3.24
134	Australia	3.23
135	US	3.23
136	Barbados	3.22
137	Cook Is	3.20
138	Burma	3.18
139	Guam	3.18
140	Hungary	3.17
141	Czechia	3.13
142	Jersey	3.10
143	Guiana, Fr	3.09
144	Netherlands	3.07
145	Tokelau	3.07
146	Venezuela	3.04
147	Uzbekistan	2.97
148	Germany	2.93
149	Sri Lanka	2.93
150	Wallis & Futuna	2.91
151	Armenia	2.89
152	Ethiopia	2.88
153	Azerbaijan	2.82
154	Belarus	2.82
155	Guernsey	2.79
156	Kyrgyzstan	2.75
157	St Vincent	2.75
158	Zimbabwe	2.74
159	Bulgaria	2.72
160	India	2.72
161	Antigua & Barbuda	2.71
162	Guadeloupe	2.68
163	Georgia	2.57
164	Argentina	2.57
165	Iran	2.55
166	Moldova	2.54
167	Guyana	2.51
168	Tajikistan	2.50
169	Martinique	2.47
170	Turkmenistan	2.45
171	Papua New Gu	2.44
172	Latvia	2.44
173	Kiribati	2.40
174	Micronesia	2.40
175	Bahamas	2.36
176	Cuba	2.36
177	Vietnam	2.35
178	Eritrea	2.33
179	Lithuania	2.30
180	Togo	2.27
181	Montserrat	2.26
182	Estonia	2.25
183	Ukraine	2.24
184	Aruba	2.23
185	Chile	2.20
186	Russia	2.19
187	Denmark	2.18

188	Guinea-Bissau	2.18
189	Nepal	2.12
190	Mauritania	2.12
191	Uruguay	2.07
192	New Zealand	2.06
193	Fiji	2.03
194	Sweden	2.02
195	Kazakhstan	2.01
196	Benin	1.99
197	UK	1.97
198	Libya	1.88
199	Comoros	1.88
200	Bangladesh	1.86
201	Reunion	1.82
202	Falkland Is	1.75
203	Sierra Leone	1.75
204	Palau	1.69
205	Niger	1.68
206	Gaza Strip	1.63
207	Luxembourg	1.59
208	Afghanistan	1.46
209	Switzerland	1.43
210	Burkina Faso	1.41
211	West Bank	1.41
212	St Helena	1.40
213	Samoa, W	1.10
214	Grenada	1.00
215	Nicaragua	0.97
216	Cambodia	0.81
217	Nauru	0.67
218	Zambia	0.52
219	Burundi	0.47
220	Madagascar	0.45
221	Neth Antilles	0.39
222	Tonga	0.37
223	Dominica	0.34
224	Congo, Dem R	0.25
225	East Timor	-0.03
226	Central African Rep.	-0.46
227	Jamaica	-1.08
228	Equatorial G	-1.75
229	St Kitts & Nevis	-2.77
230	Angola	-4.13
231	Liberia	-5.04
232	Chad	-6.72

Source: Calculated as (GDPPPP1980/GDPPPP1970)**(1/10)-1.

TABLE 6.18 - GDP GROWTH RATES YEARS 1980-1990		
OBS	COUNTRY	GRRL
1	Angola	11.54
2	Botswana	10.82
3	Oman	10.55

4	N Mariana Is	10.11
5	Bhutan	9.70
6	UAE	8.86
7	Korea, South	8.72
8	St Lucia	8.67
9	Maldives	8.62
10	Antigua & Barbuda	8.39
11	Gabon	8.06
12	Chad	7.78
13	Singapore	7.58
14	Cyprus	7.39
15	Brunei	6.84
16	Mayotte	6.64
17	Solomon Is	6.62
18	Taiwan	6.55
19	Thailand	6.55
20	Andorra	6.54
21	Hong Kong	6.49
22	Macao	6.31
23	Malaysia	6.22
24	Grenada	6.21
25	China	6.08
26	Luxembourg	5.97
27	Cape Verde	5.91
28	Cayman Is	5.68
29	St Vincent	5.60
30	Turkey	5.55
31	Equatorial G	5.48
32	Guiana, Fr	5.42
33	St Kitts & Nevis	5.41
34	Mongolia	5.17
35	Pakistan	5.05
36	W Sahara	5.05
37	Dominica	4.88
38	Egypt	4.61
39	Vanuatu	4.59
40	Samoa, Ameri	4.56
41	India	4.51
42	Belize	4.48
43	Vietnam	4.46
44	Mauritius	4.30
45	Malta	4.15
46	Kenya	4.14
47	Indonesia	4.04
48	Kuwait	4.04
49	Japan	3.97
50	Ghana	3.95
51	Zimbabwe	3.91
52	Gibraltar	3.76
53	Ireland	3.74
54	Marshall Is	3.72
55	Swaziland	3.66
56	Cambodia	3.61
57	Tunisia	3.56
58	Reunion	3.54
59	Burkina Faso	3.53

60	Cameroon	3.51
61	Israel	3.51
62	Nepal	3.45
63	Morocco	3.43
64	Seychelles	3.41
65	Uganda	3.40
66	Malawi	3.38
67	Australia	3.37
68	San Marino	3.36
69	Rwanda	3.35
70	Spain	3.33
71	Laos	3.32
72	Guernsey	3.30
73	Syria	3.29
74	Lesotho	3.28
75	Portugal	3.20
76	US	3.20
77	Bangladesh	3.20
78	Isle of Man	3.14
79	Monaco	3.14
80	Honduras	3.13
81	Faeroe Is	3.09
82	Congo, Rep	3.08
83	Yemen	3.08
84	Greenland	3.06
85	Colombia	3.05
86	Benin	3.01
87	Finland	2.99
88	Puerto Rico	2.98
89	Micronesia	2.98
90	Fr Polynesia	2.96
91	Liechtenstein	2.94
92	Senegal	2.90
93	Comoros	2.90
94	Jersey	2.89
95	Turks & Caicos	2.87
96	Canada	2.84
97	Paraguay	2.84
98	Jordan	2.82
99	Albania	2.80
100	Gaza Strip	2.80
101	West Bank	2.78
102	Iceland	2.77
103	Jamaica	2.75
104	Norway	2.74
105	Virgin Is, Brit.	2.74
106	Sri Lanka	2.73
107	St Pierre &	2.73
108	Niue	2.66
109	Dominican Rep	2.63
110	UK	2.59
111	Anguilla	2.58
112	East Timor	2.57
113	Guam	2.56
114	Cook Is	2.56
115	Chile	2.53

116	Tokelau	2.51
117	Bahrain	2.50
118	Wallis & Futuna	2.46
119	Guinea-Bissau	2.46
120	Costa Rica	2.46
121	Gambia	2.45
122	Austria	2.44
123	Belarus	2.43
124	Switzerland	2.36
125	France	2.36
126	Bermuda	2.33
127	Italy	2.31
128	Djibouti	2.30
129	Netherlands	2.28
130	Tonga	2.25
131	Aruba	2.24
132	Barbados	2.23
133	Namibia	2.20
134	Guinea	2.16
135	Latvia	2.15
136	Georgia	2.12
137	New Zealand	2.11
138	Sweden	2.07
139	Venezuela	2.03
140	New Caledonia	2.00
141	Ethiopia	1.93
142	Philippines	1.92
143	Denmark	1.92
144	Belgium	1.89
145	Algeria	1.86
146	Montserrat	1.84
147	Azerbaijan	1.83
148	Ecuador	1.82
149	Greece	1.79
150	Mali	1.79
151	Zambia	1.77
152	Tanzania	1.76
153	Moldova	1.74
154	Palau	1.74
155	Iran	1.74
156	Kyrgyzstan	1.72
157	Mexico	1.64
158	Martinique	1.62
159	Russia	1.61
160	Guatemala	1.59
161	Burma	1.58
162	Brazil	1.58
163	Mauritania	1.58
164	Korea, North	1.57
165	Ukraine	1.56
166	Mozambique	1.52
167	Lithuania	1.51
168	Papua New Gu	1.50
169	Estonia	1.49
170	Sierra Leone	1.49
171	Bahamas	1.47

172	Somalia	1.45
173	Germany	1.44
174	Uzbekistan	1.43
175	Kosovo	1.42
176	Virgin I, US	1.41
177	Tuvalu	1.39
178	Guadeloupe	1.36
179	Fiji	1.36
180	Ivory Coast	1.35
181	Armenia	1.30
182	Falkland Is	1.28
183	Slovakia	1.27
184	Nigeria	1.24
185	Cuba	1.15
186	South Africa	1.12
187	Kiribati	1.10
188	Congo, Dem R	1.08
189	Tajikistan	1.06
190	St Helena	1.06
191	Central African Rep.	1.03
192	Qatar	0.98
193	Nauru	0.96
194	Samoa, W	0.94
195	Eritrea	0.86
196	Sudan	0.83
197	Panama	0.83
198	Burundi	0.83
199	Czechia	0.82
200	Turkmenistan	0.73
201	Kazakhstan	0.68
202	Bolivia	0.63
203	Uruguay	0.53
204	San Tome & Principe	0.42
205	Bosnia	0.39
206	Haiti	0.35
207	Slovenia	0.01
208	Macedonia	-0.02
209	Hungary	-0.02
210	Croatia	-0.23
211	El Salvador	-0.39
212	Saudi Arabia	-0.46
213	Argentina	-0.48
214	Serbia	-0.54
215	Montenegro	-0.56
216	Poland	-0.58
217	Nicaragua	-0.72
218	Bulgaria	-0.89
219	Trinidad/Tobago	-0.95
220	Madagascar	-1.28
221	Neth Antilles	-1.48
222	Togo	-1.52
223	Peru	-1.64
224	Liberia	-1.71
225	Romania	-1.77
226	Suriname	-1.88
227	Guyana	-2.33

228	Afghanistan	-2.42
229	Niger	-3.44
230	Libya	-5.51
231	Iraq	-6.58
232	Lebanon	-11.72

Source: Calculated as (GDPPPP1990/GDPPPP1980)**(1/10)-1.

\multicolumn{3}{c}{TABLE 6.19 - GDP GROWTH RATES YEARS 1990-2000}
OBS	COUNTRY	GRRL
1	Mayotte	21.47
2	Equatorial G	20.15
3	Lebanon	15.90
4	Brunei	12.13
5	Libya	11.36
6	New Caledonia	9.88
7	Singapore	7.78
8	West Bank	7.63
9	Bahrain	7.61
10	Samoa, Ameri	7.47
11	Ireland	7.46
12	Malaysia	6.90
13	Turks & Caicos	6.61
14	Botswana	6.20
15	Taiwan	6.02
16	Anguilla	6.01
17	China	5.98
18	Afghanistan	5.91
19	Maldives	5.90
20	Korea, South	5.88
21	N Mariana Is	5.85
22	Vietnam	5.82
23	Sudan	5.81
24	Luxembourg	5.78
25	Cape Verde	5.74
26	Dominican Rep	5.74
27	Gaza Strip	5.64
28	El Salvador	5.55
29	Guiana, Fr	5.36
30	Virgin Is, Brit.	5.35
31	Belize	5.31
32	Malta	5.25
33	Iran	5.24
34	Seychelles	5.23
35	Israel	5.13
36	Costa Rica	5.12
37	Chile	5.00
38	Bhutan	4.96
39	Palau	4.93
40	Cayman Is	4.92
41	Laos	4.80
42	Cyprus	4.74
43	Panama	4.72
44	India	4.63

45	Tunisia	4.50
46	Burundi	4.50
47	Cambodia	4.46
48	St Kitts & Nevis	4.45
49	Aruba	4.45
50	Jordan	4.40
51	Eritrea	4.33
52	Guinea	4.29
53	Peru	4.20
54	Yemen	4.17
55	Falkland Is	4.03
56	Burkina Faso	4.01
57	Fr Polynesia	3.99
58	Mauritania	3.99
59	Burma	3.93
60	Gambia	3.93
61	Mauritius	3.92
62	UAE	3.90
63	Norway	3.89
64	Pakistan	3.88
65	Poland	3.86
66	Bolivia	3.86
67	Guam	3.84
68	Turkey	3.84
69	Papua New Gu	3.84
70	Namibia	3.81
71	Andorra	3.78
72	Sri Lanka	3.77
73	Thailand	3.74
74	Grenada	3.71
75	W Sahara	3.69
76	Hong Kong	3.69
77	Lesotho	3.68
78	Kiribati	3.68
79	Egypt	3.62
80	Argentina	3.60
81	San Marino	3.58
82	Mexico	3.55
83	Nepal	3.46
84	Bangladesh	3.46
85	Oman	3.46
86	Australia	3.45
87	Chad	3.44
88	Niue	3.44
89	Honduras	3.36
90	Bermuda	3.30
91	Trinidad/Tobago	3.29
92	Cook Is	3.29
93	St Lucia	3.23
94	US	3.20
95	Indonesia	3.19
96	Malawi	3.19
97	Antigua & Barbuda	3.16
98	Qatar	3.16
99	Syria	3.16
100	Guyana	3.13

101	Puerto Rico	3.07
102	Macao	3.07
103	Netherlands	3.06
104	Mali	3.05
105	Guadeloupe	3.03
106	Spain	3.02
107	Guatemala	3.01
108	Portugal	2.97
109	Greece	2.95
110	Marshall Is	2.93
111	Isle of Man	2.88
112	Swaziland	2.87
113	Brazil	2.83
114	Liechtenstein	2.77
115	Philippines	2.77
116	Vanuatu	2.76
117	Canada	2.72
118	Ivory Coast	2.69
119	Nicaragua	2.68
120	Tonga	2.67
121	St Vincent	2.61
122	Nigeria	2.60
123	Senegal	2.57
124	Iceland	2.56
125	Denmark	2.55
126	Ethiopia	2.55
127	Tanzania	2.53
128	Uganda	2.50
129	New Zealand	2.48
130	Martinique	2.48
131	Solomon Is	2.45
132	Samoa, W	2.35
133	South Africa	2.34
134	Austria	2.33
135	Monaco	2.29
136	Guinea-Bissau	2.24
137	Belgium	2.22
138	Gibraltar	2.20
139	UK	2.18
140	Finland	2.16
141	Kenya	2.15
142	Benin	2.09
143	East Timor	2.05
144	Uruguay	2.05
145	Germany	2.02
146	Reunion	2.02
147	Venezuela	2.01
148	Congo, Rep	2.00
149	Niger	1.91
150	Jersey	1.84
151	France	1.83
152	Sweden	1.81
153	Colombia	1.78
154	Turkmenistan	1.76
155	Tuvalu	1.71
156	Dominica	1.69

157	Morocco	1.69
158	Bahamas	1.67
159	Slovenia	1.66
160	Gabon	1.66
161	Guernsey	1.64
162	Italy	1.61
163	Paraguay	1.59
164	Wallis & Futuna	1.56
165	Micronesia	1.53
166	Greenland	1.51
167	Japan	1.41
168	St Pierre &	1.37
169	Ghana	1.36
170	Cameroon	1.28
171	Barbados	1.28
172	Suriname	1.27
173	Algeria	1.22
174	Neth Antilles	1.17
175	Comoros	1.15
176	Saudi Arabia	1.14
177	Madagascar	1.13
178	Faeroe Is	1.13
179	Iraq	1.13
180	Fiji	1.11
181	Rwanda	1.08
182	Hungary	1.07
183	San Tome & Principe	1.07
184	Virgin I, US	1.06
185	Zimbabwe	1.02
186	Central African Rep.	0.94
187	St Helena	0.88
188	Kuwait	0.83
189	Switzerland	0.83
190	Djibouti	0.77
191	Jamaica	0.70
192	Mozambique	0.66
193	Slovakia	0.38
194	Angola	0.20
195	Tokelau	0.17
196	Czechia	0.12
197	Albania	0.03
198	Cuba	-0.21
199	Haiti	-0.22
200	Zambia	-0.55
201	Mongolia	-0.78
202	Nauru	-0.83
203	Togo	-1.17
204	Croatia	-1.22
205	Ecuador	-1.24
206	Bulgaria	-1.29
207	Estonia	-1.29
208	Macedonia	-1.61
209	Liberia	-2.06
210	Russia	-2.26
211	Romania	-2.60
212	Lithuania	-2.89

213	Sierra Leone	-4.62
214	Bosnia	-4.66
215	Somalia	-5.05
216	Belarus	-5.37
217	Latvia	-5.75
218	Montserrat	-6.28
219	Kazakhstan	-7.12
220	Congo, Dem R	-7.37
221	Azerbaijan	-8.24
222	Ukraine	-8.28
223	Kyrgyzstan	-10.40
224	Uzbekistan	-10.47
225	Korea, North	-10.60
226	Montenegro	-11.66
227	Kosovo	-11.76
228	Tajikistan	-11.94
229	Serbia	-12.05
230	Armenia	-13.24
231	Georgia	-14.93
232	Moldova	-16.84

Source: Calculated as (GDPPPP2000/GDPPPP1990)**(1/10)-1

TABLE 6.20 - GDP GROWTH RATES YEARS 2000-2007		
OBS	COUNTRY	GRRL
1	Qatar	24.16
2	Liechtenstein	20.33
3	Bermuda	' 19.93
4	Chad	18.80
5	Equatorial G	17.64
6	Virgin Is, Brit.	16.93
7	Macao	16.82
8	Azerbaijan	16.63
9	Angola	12.72
10	Andorra	12.64
11	Armenia	12.41
12	Sierra Leone	11.68
13	Mayotte	11.01
14	Kosovo	10.46
15	Kazakhstan	10.08
16	Guernsey	10.02
17	Cook Is	9.86
18	Jersey	9.82
19	Cayman Is	9.81
20	Burma	9.46
21	Bhutan	9.39
22	Montenegro	9.36
23	Georgia	9.03
24	Latvia	9.00
25	Tajikistan	8.85
26	Fr Polynesia	8.84
27	Romania	8.79
28	Serbia	8.66
29	Mongolia	8.55

30	Faeroe Is	8.45
31	Suriname	8.29
32	Isle of Man	8.28
33	Neth Antilles	8.21
34	Wallis & Futuna	8.17
35	Niue	8.09
36	China	7.98
37	Montserrat	7.95
38	Guiana, Fr	7.93
39	Belarus	7.92
40	Lithuania	7.90
41	Tanzania	7.90
42	Tuvalu	7.80
43	Falkland Is	7.77
44	W Sahara	7.77
45	Ukraine	7.57
46	Puerto Rico	7.46
47	Turks & Caicos	7.45
48	Ethiopia	7.43
49	Sudan	7.38
50	Korea, North	7.20
51	Marshall Is	7.08
52	Trinidad/Tobago	6.97
53	Slovakia	6.82
54	Estonia	6.66
55	Cambodia	6.62
56	Maldives	6.60
57	Martinique	6.56
58	Uzbekistan	6.55
59	Iran	6.55
60	Zambia	6.52
61	Russia	6.50
62	Oman	6.32
63	Bosnia	6.29
64	Moldova	6.25
65	India	6.12
66	Albania	6.01
67	Panama	5.95
68	Honduras	5.94
69	Ecuador	5.87
70	Laos	5.86
71	Peru	5.84
72	Antigua & Barbuda	5.81
73	Vietnam	5.74
74	Kuwait	5.74
75	Botswana	5.70
76	Bahrain	5.69
77	Taiwan	5.68
78	Lebanon	5.61
79	Algeria	5.57
80	Nigeria	5.50
81	Singapore	5.47
82	Croatia	5.45
83	Bulgaria	5.43
84	Czechia	5.30
85	Ireland	5.28

86	Jordan	5.27
87	South Africa	5.25
88	Libya	5.22
89	Dominican Rep	5.07
90	Mauritania	5.06
91	Burkina Faso	5.03
92	Costa Rica	4.98
93	Greece	4.96
94	Turkey	4.90
95	Egypt	4.89
96	Iraq	4.87
97	Congo, Dem R	4.86
98	Hong Kong	4.85
99	Cape Verde	4.81
100	Bahamas	4.78
101	Hungary	4.74
102	Gaza Strip	4.71
103	Malaysia	4.71
104	Belize	4.64
105	Korea, South	4.50
106	Tunisia	4.49
107	Niger	4.48
108	Poland	4.48
109	Saudi Arabia	4.36
110	Philippines	4.35
111	Kyrgyzstan	4.30
112	Slovenia	4.30
113	Kenya	4.30
114	Thailand	4.25
115	San Tome & Principe	4.25
116	Pakistan	4.20
117	Burundi	4.19
118	West Bank	4.15
119	Mali	4.15
120	Cyprus	4.15
121	St Kitts & Nevis	4.14
122	Gambia	4.12
123	Gibraltar	4.09
124	Cameroon	4.06
125	Yemen	3.97
126	Morocco	3.97
127	Sri Lanka	3.95
128	Iceland	3.91
129	Indonesia	3.90
130	Luxembourg	3.89
131	Spain	3.73
132	N Mariana Is	3.69
133	Congo, Rep	3.68
134	Bangladesh	3.67
135	Cuba	3.66
136	Chile	3.61
137	Bolivia	3.54
138	Madagascar	3.44
139	Namibia	3.43
140	Samoa, W	3.41
141	San Marino	3.41

142	Brazil	3.38
143	El Salvador	3.36
144	Argentina	3.28
145	St Lucia	3.26
146	Brunei	3.23
147	Colombia	3.17
148	Paraguay	3.14
149	Guinea	3.13
150	Finland	3.12
151	Australia	3.10
152	Mauritius	3.06
153	New Zealand	3.03
154	Reunion	3.01
155	Nicaragua	2.96
156	Israel	2.95
157	Rwanda	2.92
158	Macedonia	2.88
159	Guatemala	2.84
160	Dominica	2.83
161	Uganda	2.82
162	Syria	2.80
163	Norway	2.78
164	Solomon Is	2.77
165	Benin	2.75
166	Sweden	2.71
167	Lesotho	2.69
168	Canada	2.67
169	St Vincent	2.63
170	Nepal	2.57
171	UAE	2.56
172	UK	2.53
173	Djibouti	2.49
174	US	2.48
175	Mexico	2.45
176	Malawi	2.44
177	Venezuela	2.39
178	Papua New Gu	2.39
179	Vanuatu	2.35
180	Barbados	2.33
181	East Timor	2.28
182	New Caledonia	2.27
183	Togo	2.22
184	Kiribati	2.21
185	Gabon	2.21
186	Comoros	2.11
187	Austria	2.10
188	Senegal	2.07
189	St Helena	2.05
190	Jamaica	2.03
191	Grenada	1.99
192	Anguilla	1.98
193	Uruguay	1.93
194	Turkmenistan	1.91
195	Belgium	1.88
196	Switzerland	1.87
197	Netherlands	1.81

198	France	1.74
199	Nauru	1.73
200	Denmark	1.62
201	Guinea-Bissau	1.55
202	Japan	1.53
203	Tokelau	1.45
204	Malta	1.42
205	Greenland	1.39
206	Tonga	1.38
207	Afghanistan	1.32
208	Guyana	1.31
209	Germany	1.28
210	Portugal	1.02
211	Swaziland	0.96
212	Eritrea	0.75
213	Italy	0.73
214	Ivory Coast	0.71
215	Fiji	0.68
216	Haiti	0.57
217	Micronesia	0.45
218	Monaco	0.40
219	Ghana	0.27
220	Seychelles	0.08
221	Virgin I, US	-0.30
222	Central African Rep.	-0.48
223	Palau	-1.51
224	Somalia	-3.30
225	Aruba	-3.76
226	Guadeloupe	-3.84
227	Mozambique	-4.48
228	Samoa, Ameri	-6.23
229	Guam	-6.76
230	St Pierre &	-7.87
231	Liberia	-8.33
232	Zimbabwe	-25.51

Source: Calculated as (GDPPPP2007/GDPPPP2000) **(1/7)-1

APPENDIX: METHODOLOGY AND DEFINITIONS

DEFINITION OF GROSS DOMESTIC PRODUCT AT PURCHASING POWER PARITIES [1]

Typically the GDP is translated into U.S. dollars. The market foreign currency exchange rate, however, does not necessarily reflect differences in actual purchasing power in different countries. The use of purchasing power parities is designed to eliminate this distortion. Purchasing power parities indicate how many currency units are needed in one country to buy the amount of goods and services that can be purchased for a currency unit in another country.

DEFINITION OF POPULATION

Population of a country includes all residents regardless of legal status or citizenship — except for refugees not permanently settled in the country of asylum, who are generally considered part of the population of their country of origin. The values shown are midyear estimates.[1]

DEFINITION OF THE HISTORICAL DATA SINCE 1 AD

I used information about GDP Per Capita in purchasing power parities for 1950 and the latest (current) year as the basis points. I also appropriated Angus Maddison's hypothesis[2] that GDP Per Capita in purchasing power parities cannot be less than 400 dollars in 1990 prices, and utilized a logarithmic interpolation technique to slightly adjust Maddison's statistical curves for years other than basis years.

It is customary in historical comparisons of the countries of the world to use Gross Domestic Product (GDP) in purchasing power parities. If GDP in market exchange rates is used, then the historical picture becomes distorted in favor of the countries that have strong currencies in the last year of observations. In effect many less developed countries would appear too weak in the past, having GDP per capita less than the minimum level of 400 dollars in 1990 prices.

The data is given for countries within the current (latest year) boundaries.

I interpolated per capita GDP at purchasing power parities. The reason I interpolated per capita as opposed to gross data is that per capita growth rates are more invariant than the gross growth rates (the latter to some degree depend on the growth rates of the population, which vary by time and country).

To adjust for cross-country statistical abnormalities I have used logarithmic interpolation.

The reason I used logarithmic interpolation, as opposed to exponential interpolation is that exponential interpolation may often result in negative growth rates of per capita GDP, which seems unlikely. Logarithmic interpolation does not change the nature of the growth over an observed period: positive growth rates remain positive, negative remain negative. Moreover, the periods of faster growth remain periods of faster growth, the periods of slower growth remain periods of slower growth. The economic rationale for such an interpolation is that its most common use is when there is unaccounted inflation in the statistics of real growth. As a rule such infla-

---

1 Economics: The World Bank.
2 Economics: Maddison (1995), (2001), (2003), (2007).

tion is higher when economic growth is faster. So it makes sense to assume that the unaccounted deflator should be proportionally higher with higher growth rates. To achieve an interpolation with such qualities I had to assume that over the period of 1950 to the current year there existed a constant degree to which the reported national growth rates should be raised in order to achieve the observed growth rates between 1950 and the current year. I weighted growth rates of every country relative to the growth rates of the United States. Such a hypothesis produces a more believable growth curve than the one which would have been acquired if exponential interpolation were used.

The corresponding formulas for the interpolation of per capita GDP are:

$$Gyear_{corrected} = Gyear_{current} * (Gyear_{current} / Gcurrent_{current})$$
$$** (\log((Gcurrent_{current} * G - UScurrent_{1990}) / (G19501990 * G - UScurrentcurrent)) / \log(Gcurrent1990 / G19501990))$$

where

$$Gyear_{current} = Gyear_{1990} * (Gcurrent_{current} / Gcurrent_{1990})$$
$$G1950_{current} = (G19501990 / G - US19501990) * G - US1950_{current}$$
$$G - US1950_{current} = G - US19501990 * (G - UScurrent_{current} / G - UScurrent_{1990})$$
$$Gcurrent_{1990} = G2000_{1990} * (Gcurrent_{2005} / G2000_{2005})$$
$$G - UScurrent_{1990} = G - US2000_{1990} * (G - UScurrent_{2005} / G-US2000_{2005})$$

The notations are identified below:

GPCPPP	per capita GDP at purchasing power parities
$Gyear_{corrected}$	GPCPPP for a particular year after the interpolation
$Gyear_{current}$	GPCPPP for a particular year in the prices of the current year
$Gyear_{1990}$	GPCPPP for a particular year in the prices of 1990
$G1950_{1990}$	GPCPPP for the year of 1950 in the prices of 1990
$G-US1950_{1990}$	GPCPPP of the U.S. for the year of 1950 in the prices of 1990
$Gcurrent_{current}$	GPCPPP for the current year in the prices of the current year
$G-UScurrent_{current}$	GPCPPP of the U.S. for the current year in the prices of the current year
$G1950_{current}$	GPCPPP for the year of 1950 in the prices of the current year
$G-US1950_{current}$	GPCPPP of the U.S. for the year of 1950 in the prices of the current year
$Gcurrent_{1990}$	GPCPPP for the current year in the prices of 1990
$G-UScurrent_{1990}$	GPCPPP of the U.S. for the current year in the prices of 1990
$G2000_{1990}$	GPCPPP for the year of 2000 in the prices of 1990
$G-US2000_{1990}$	GPCPPP of the U.S. for the year of 2000 in the prices of 1990
$Gcurrent_{2005}$	GPCPPP for the current year in the prices of 2005
$G-UScurrent_{2005}$	GPCPPP of the U.S. for the current year in the prices of 2005
$G2000_{2005}$	GPCPPP for the year of 2000 in the prices of 2005
$G-US2000_{2005}$	GPCPPP of the U.S. for the year of 2000 in the prices of 2005

For the years prior to 1950, I used the formula:

$$Gyear_{current} = Gyear1990 * (G1950_{current} / G19501990)$$

Special care was taken for calculation of GDP of the former U.S.S.R. for the year of 1920. In order to calculate an index of GDP 1913-1920, I used partial data for two sectors of the economy: agriculture and industry. The production of grain in these years constituted (Davies(1994), p. 320):

Production of grain	
1913	79.7 million tons
1920	44.5 million tons

Gross industrial production constituted (ibid., p. 321):

Gross industrial production	
1913	8,431
1920	1,718

The share of agriculture in national income of 1913 constituted 50.7 percent. Assuming that non-agricultural sectors of the economy shrank by 1920 in the same proportion as the industrial production, I obtained the following putative index of GDP:

GDP Index	
1913	100
1920	38.354

REFERENCES

Central Intelligence Agency, *The World Factbook*, annual

Davies, R. W., Mark Harrison, S. G. Wheatcroft, Eds. (1994) *The Economic Transformation of the Soviet Union, 1913-1945*, Cambridge University Press, Cambridge

Encyclopedia Britannica, Book of the Year, annual

Maddison, Angus (1995) *Monitoring the World Economy, 1820-1992*, OECD, Paris

_____ (2001) *The World Economy: A Millennial Perspective*, OECD, Paris

_____ (2003) *The World Economy: Historical Statistics*, OECD, Paris

_____ (2007) *Contours of the World Economy, 1–2030AD*, Oxford University Press, New York

Mitchell, B.R. (2003)(1) *International Historical Statistics: Africa, Asia and Oceania, 1750-2000*, Palgrave Macmillan, London

_____ (2003)(2) *International Historical Statistics: Europe, 1750-2000*, Palgrave Macmillan, London

_____ (2003)(3) *International Historical Statistics: The Americas, 1750-2000*, Palgrave Macmillan, London

The World Bank World Development Indicators Online

7608524R00234

Made in the USA
San Bernardino, CA
10 January 2014